Re-imagining Indigenous Knowledge and Practices in 21st Century Africa:
Debunking Myths & Misconceptions for Conviviality and Sustainability

Editors
Tenson M. Muyambo
Anniegrace M. Hlatywayo
Pindai M. Sithole
Munyaradzi Mawere

Langaa Research & Publishing CIG
Mankon, Bamenda

Publisher:

Langaa RPCIG
Langaa Research & Publishing Common Initiative Group
P.O. Box 902 Mankon
Bamenda
North West Region
Cameroon
Langaagrp@gmail.com
www.langaa-rpcig.net

Distributed in and outside N. America by African Books Collective
orders@africanbookscollective.com
www.africanbookscollective.com

ISBN-10: 9956-552-29-1

ISBN-13: 978-9956-552-29-0

© Tenson M. Muyambo; Anniegrace M. Hlatywayo; Pindai M. Sithole
& Munyaradzi Mawere 2022

Editors and Contributors

About the Editors

Tenson Mabhuya Muyambo (PhD) is a lecturer at Great Zimbabwe University, School of Education and Culture. He teaches Family and Religious Studies modules in the Department of Teacher Development. His research interests are in indigenous knowledge systems, gender, religions, environment and education. He has published articles in refereed journal and book chapters in the said areas of interest. https://orcid.org/0000-0001-6765-5034

Anniegrace Mapangisana Hlatywayo (PhD) is a Zimbabwean Indigenous Knowledge Scholar. Her research focuses on Indigenous Knowledge Systems-based Approaches to sexual and reproductive healthcare; African indigenous sexual and reproductive health practices; African indigenous approaches to adolescent sexual and reproductive health (ASRH); African indigenous conceptualisation of food behaviour for pregnancy and postpartum. Dr. Hlatywayo has experience in research and publication; postgraduate training; community engagement initiatives and project management. Currently, she lectures in the Department of Religious Studies at Midlands State University, Zimbabwe.

Pindai Mangwanindichero Sithole (PhD) is an Academic Programs Coordinator and Senior Lecturer at Africa Leadership and Management Academy (ALMA), an affiliate college of the National University of Science and Technology in Zimbabwe. His research interest is in indigenous knowledge systems with a special focus on how they contribute to transformative and sustainable development. At different times since 2008, Dr. Sithole has taught at different universities in Zimbabwe which include Africa University (AU), Chinhoyi University of Technology (CUT), National University of Science and Technology (NUST) and the University of Zimbabwe (UZ) modules in research, development, governance and policy at graduate studies level. Sithole is also an evaluation expert and practitioner of various development projects and programs since 2000.

Munyaradzi Mawere (PhD) is Professor Extraordinarius of Interdisciplinary Research in the School of Interdisciplinary Research & Graduate Studies at University of South Africa (UNISA), and a Professor of African Studies and incumbent Research Chair in the Simon Muzenda School of Arts, Culture and Heritage Studies at Great Zimbabwe University (GZU) in Zimbabwe. He holds a PhD in Social Anthropology from the University of Cape Town, South Africa; three Masters Degrees namely: Master of Arts Degree in Social Anthropology (passed with Distinction); Master of Arts Degree in Philosophy; Master of Arts Degree in Development Studies (passed with University Book Prize); a BA (Hons) Degree in Philosophy, and a number of certificates across disciplines. Prof Extraord. Mawere is an author and editor of more than 290 publications, including an excess of 80 books and over 200 book chapters and peer-reviewed academic journals with internationally acclaimed publishers with a focus on Africa straddling the following areas: poverty and development, African philosophy, society and culture, democracy, human rights, politics of food production, humanitarianism and civil society organisations, indigenous knowledge systems, urban anthropology, existential anthropology, cultural philosophy, environmental anthropology, society and politics, decoloniality and African studies. Professor Mawere has also won several prestigious international honours such as the Wenner-Gren Research Fellowship and the much coveted Association of African Studies (ASA) Presidential Fellowship Award. His most recent book is entitled: *Covid-19 Manifestation, Ramifications and Future Prospects for Zimbabwe – A Multi-disciplinary Perspective (2021).* https://orcid.org/0000-0002-3684-6089

Contributors

George J. Sefa Dei [Nana Adusei Sefa Tweneboah] is Professor of Social Justice Education at OISE, University of Toronto. george.dei@utoronto.ca.

Jacob Mapara (PhD) is Professor and incumbent Director of the Institute of Lifelong Learning and Development Studies at Chinhoyi University of Technology, Zimbabwe. He additionally chairs the Centre for Indigenous Knowledge and Living Heritage which is housed in the same Institute. Dr. Mapara is very passionate about indigenous knowledge and decoloniality. He strives for the celebration of the diversity of human cultures, hence his stand against mono-culturalism, mono-lingualism and mono-epistemology. Prof Mapara is a firm believer in the co-creation of global knowledges. He has researched and written extensively in the areas of indigenous knowledge and living heritage. Mapara is a holder of a Doctor of Literature and Philosophy (DLitt et Phil) Degree in African Languages from UNISA.

Sylvia Madusise (PhD) holds a Doctoral Degree in Mathematics Education from Tshwane University of Technology in South Africa. Her research interests are on contextualisation of Mathematics Education, particularly the use of real life learners' experiences in the teaching and learning of Mathematics. Her PhD thesis was on Indigenisation and Mathematisation as entry points to Mathematics Education. Dr Madusise has published a number of articles on the interface of Culture and Mathematics Education.

Wonder Muchabaiwa (PhD) is a Sociologist and an educationist who has worked with communities on different livelihood projects. Currently, he is a lecturer in the Department of Policy Studies and Leadership at Midlands State University. He has published on circumstances of women as an underprivileged group in African societies. Dr. Muchabaiwa has also published articles on education and the curriculum, mentorship in education and gender issues in families, education and the informal sector. He has vast experience in Teacher Education and Gender Studies and has worked in teacher development for 13 years. Dr. Muchabaiwa has participated in the following consultancy work: Bridging the gender equity gap in Science at Women's University in Africa sponsored by IDRC as Co-principal Investigator; Market survey on food provisions in Masvingo, Manicaland and Matebeleland provinces in Zimbabwe sponsored by USAID.

Beatrice Okyere-Manu (PhD) is a Senior Lecturer in the School of Religion, Philosophy and Classics at the University of KwaZulu-Natal. She is the Programme Director for Applied Ethics. Her research interest is in ethics particularly the following areas: Family Ethics, Indigenous Knowledge in African Culture, African Environmental Ethics, Migration Ethics and Technology.

Stephen Nkansah Morgan (PhD) is currently a lecturer with the Department of Philosophy and Classics of the University of Ghana, where he teaches a wide range of philosophy courses at both graduate and undergraduate level. Stephen holds a PhD in Ethics Studies from the University of KwaZulu-Natal in South Africa, and a Master of Philosophy and Bachelor of Arts degrees in Philosophy both from the University of Ghana. His research interests are Environmental and Animal Ethics, Social and Political Philosophy and African philosophy broadly construed.

Joseph Kofi Antwi holds a PhD in Religious Studies from KNUST. His research interests are Indigenous Knowledge in African, Eco-theology African Traditional Religion, Currently, he serves on the Noguchi Memorial Institute for Medical Research Institutional Review Board (NMIMR-IRB). He is also a Member of African Association for Pastoral Studies and Counselling (AAPSC), and Alliance for Christian Advocacy Africa (ACAA). Antwi is also an Ordained Minister of the Gospel in the Presbyterian Church of Ghana and currently serving as the Clerk of Ga West Presbytery and District Minister of the North Kaneshie District of the Presbyterian Church of Ghana, in Accra.

Francis Machingura (PhD) is an Associate Professor of Biblical Studies and lecturer at the University of Zimbabwe. He is the former chairperson of the Languages and Arts Education Department, Faculty of Education, and currently the Acting Director of University of Zimbabwe Post-Graduate Centre. His areas of special interest are on the: Interaction of the Bible and Gender, Politics, Health, Inclusivity, Bible and Sexuality in Africa. He has published several books, articles and book chapters.
E-mail: fmachingura@yahoo.com / francismachingura@gmail.com

Godfrey Museka (PhD) is a Civics Religion and Ethics Education senior lecturer at the University of Zimbabwe. His research interests include: gender issues in African Indigenous Religion, religion and vulnerability, indigenous knowledge systems, environment and health as well as the pedagogy and adragony of civics religion and ethics.

Ernest Dube (PhD) is a senior lecturer and researcher for Development Sciences at Marondera University of Agricultural Sciences and Technology (MUAST), Zimbabwe. Dr Dube has an interest in the fields of disaster risk reduction and climate change, poverty and livelihoods, as well as food security and sustainable development. He has published extensively in his areas of interest and has done review work for more than 15 journals. He has been in the academic field for more than 8-years. Amongst Dr Dube's research offerings include 17 publications in internationally accredited journals. Dr Dube is also a consultant in disaster risk reduction and development related issues. Further to that, he has carried out several commissioned research projects to completion. Email: edube@muast.ac.zw

Albert Manyani (PhD) is a lecturer at Bindura University of Science Education (BUSE) in Zimbabwe and his research interests are climate change and disasters management particularly, in the context of indigenous knowledge systems.

Maradze Viriri (PhD) is a lecturer in the Department of Teacher Development at Great Zimbabwe University. He holds the following qualifications: PhD in Onomastics (UKZN), Masters in Languages-ChiShona (GZU), Masters in Educational Management and Policy Planning (ZOU), Grad CE (UZ) and B.A General (U.Z). .His research interests includes Onomatics, Culture, Gender issues and language in Education.

Sophia Chirongoma (PhD) is a Senior Lecturer in the Religious Studies Department at Midlands State University, Zimbabwe. She is also an Academic Associate/Research Fellow at the Research Institute for Theology and Religion (RITR) in the College of Human Sciences, University of South Africa (UNISA). Orcid ID: https://orcid.org/0000-0002-8655-7365

Silindiwe Zvingowanisei is a lecturer in the Department of Philosophy, Religion and Ethics and in the Department of Peace, Security and Society at the University of Zimbabwe. She is also a doctoral candidate at the University of KwaZulu-Natal, South Africa.

Mutale Mulenga-Kaunda holds a PhD in Gender and Religion. She is an independent researcher, with research interests lying in the intersection between African women's culture, religion and gender. She has published on issues around gender, sexualities, ecumenism and missiology, African women's career, marriage, rituals, health, wellbeing and African Pentecostalism.

Andile Mayekiso (PhD) is a Lecturer in the Department of Anthropology and Development Studies at University of Johannesburg, South Africa. His research interests are in the areas of gender and sexuality, decoloniality and parenthood, among others.

Daniel Gamira (PhD) holds a certificate in Agriculture, certificate in education, bachelor of education, masters in curriculum studies and a PhD in Environmental Education from the University of KwaZulu Natal. He has been a high school teacher and a lecturer at a teachers' college. He has been a lecturer in the Department of Teacher Development at the Great Zimbabwe University's Robert Mugabe School of Education, Zimbabwe from 2006 up to date. He lectures in Environmental Science, Science and Technology, Agriculture and Geography in addition to holding various posts of responsibilities in the university. He has lived a teaching life from 1985 up to now. His research interests are in Environment and Sustainability, Science Education, Agriculture Education and Geography Education. He has published some papers in those fields. His interests are into reading published articles on sustainable development, agriculture education, geography, science and technology. He has made huge influences on project writing at undergraduate level among many of his accomplishments.

Annastacia Mawere (nee Mbindi) is a Graduate teacher at Rupiri Secondary School, Gutu, Zimbabwe, and a holder of a Master's Degree in Religious Studies, specializing in African Indigenous Religion. She also holds a Bachelor of Arts General Degree in Religious Studies, a Bachelor of Arts (Hons) Degree in Religious Studies and a Postgraduate Diploma in Education.

Fortune Sibanda (PhD) is a Professor of Religious Studies in the Department of Philosophy and Religious Studies, Great Zimbabwe University, Masvingo, Zimbabwe. Sibanda has published book chapters and articles in referred journals. His research interests include new religious movements, African Indigenous Knowledge Systems, religion and health, human rights issues, religion and the environment, law and religion. Professor Sibanda is a member of academic associations including the American Academy of Religion (AAR), African Consortium for Law and Religion Studies (ACLARS), Association for the Study of Religion in Southern Africa (ASRSA) and African Association for the Study of Religion (AASR).

Bernard Pindukai Humbe is a PhD holder in Religion Studies from the University of Free State, South Africa. He is a lecturer in the Department of Philosophy and Religious Studies at Great Zimbabwe University, Masvingo. His areas of research interest include: African Indigenous Religious Knowledge Systems, Contemporary meaning of African Traditional Religion, AICS and Politics, Traditional Law and Social Development, Religion and Entrepreneurship, Religion and Social Transformation, and Religion and Power. Email: bhumbe@gzu.ac.zw

Moses Chundu is an accomplished Economist, Strategist, Development Practitioner and Thought Leader with broad and deep experience in the corporate and governance space. He is an academic with the University of Zimbabwe in the Department of Economics and Development. He is also the Executive Director of ALMA (Africa Leadership & Management Academy) a Campus Crusade for Christ graduate school affiliated to NUST. He consults on strategy and organizational development and is a registered Corporate Rescue Practitioner. He is passionate about developing leaders of integrity in all the domains of society and avid believer and researcher in application of indigenous knowledge systems in all these domains.

Nomatter Sande (PhD) holds a PhD in Religion and Social Transformation from the University of KwaZulu Natal (South Africa). Nomatter is an African Practical Theologian. He is a Research Fellow at the Research Institute for Theology and Religion (RITR) in the College of Human Sciences, University of South Africa (UNISA). Research interests include but not limited to theology, disability studies, missiology and gender issues. E-mail: pastornomsande@yahoo.com. ORCID: 0000-0002-4177-8391.

Praise Zinhuku is a Music Lecturer at Great Zimbabwe University. Zinhuku is also a lead vocalist for FeelAfrica, an Afro-Jazz outfit, championing African music performance. Her area of interest is indigenous musical arts performance.

Table of Contents

Preface

How do we resist the colonial appellation of the 'Indigenous' and steadfastly affirm 'African Indigenous' in conversations about cartographies of Indigeneities? Decolonial and anti-colonial praxis require that we not only challenge the imposition of colonial systems of knowing, but also, uphold Indigenous epistemologies as relational and that Indigeneity is an international category. By 'colonial appellation' I allude to Africa having to prove her claims to an Indigenous and Indigeneity. This insistence is a form of discursive policing of what constitutes Indigenous and who can claim it. African scholars must push back (see also Adefarakan, 2010). This does not mean that we liberalize Indigenous and Indigeneity such that everyone has unquestioned claims to be Indigenous to some Lands, place and time. The dominant/colonizer's claim to be Indigenous on other people's Lands need to be questioned. More, as I have repeatedly argued, Indigenous is marked by an absence of colonial or imperial imposition. Any peoples whose history is tied or connected to the colonial and imperial expansion of the Empire need to reassess any claims to Indigeneity. Unfortunately, uncritical conversations about the colonial appellation of Indigenous often set the terms for the colonizer to tell the colonized or the Indigene what 'Indigenous' is.

I deliberately chose to begin this Preface with this very pertinent question. This is not a collection of essays proving to anyone that African Indigenous Knowledge System is worthy of academic investigation. The time has long past for that. But we note that the negation, devaluation and de-legitimation of African Indigenous knowledge systems has been far-reaching. Enough intellectual energies can be spent defending African Indigenous in global spaces. Africa did not lose her Indigeneity with the advent of European colonialism. We are all implicated in here. There are African scholars who deny African Indigenous ways of knowings dismissing such knowledges as 'stories, myths, mythologies and spiritual ontologies' as if they are not worthy of serious intellectual conversations. We cannot afford to operate from a Eurocentric intellectual space that continues to impose and masquerade the particularity of Western dominant frames on our thinking and practice. And we must simply not uphold the idea of a certainty of knowledge, a hallmark of

Western science as a given. African history did not begin in 1492 and Europe is not the advent of human history. I will ask: what does it mean to talk of African Studies pre-1492 so as to accord a rightful place for African Indigenous?

The Indigenous is about past, present, future. Indigenous is about Land and its Earthly teachings as a knowledge system. Africa and African peoples have always maintained a connection to our Lands, spiritually, emotionally, culturally and politically. As learners we have a responsibility to nurture our knowledge systems. The struggle to create multicentric ways of knowing puts African scholars and African scholarship on trial. There is a long history of African scholarship that have called for not just the validation of African systems of thought and practice but to centre our knowledge systems as African peoples search for their footing in the academic landscape. Part of this history has also brought an awareness for us to be mindful of the commodification of our knowledge systems which leaves us with no 'control', meaning others define such knowledge for us. This is why Western corporate capital interests in our indigenous knowledge systems must be met with deep scepticism in terms of whose interests is at stake. Sharing our knowledge system must not end with local peoples losing control of their knowledges. Bringing an anti-colonial lens to African Indigeneity is a necessary requirement. The discursive link of the anti-coloniality and African Indigeneity also offers possibilities for us to think through new educational futurities for Africa.

This book allows space for African scholars to be witnesses and guardians of African Indigenous Knowledge Systems (AIKS). Taking a leaf from the title itself, the volume is a bold attempt to re-imagine African Indigenous Knowledge and Practices in view of the snipping labelling, and nefarious pejorations and caricatures that our AIKS have received over the years, particularly from Eurocentric scholars. The novelty of the current volume lies in its attempt to destabilise and debunk (and even dislodge) the Eurocentric myths and misrepresentations as well as correct misconceptions on and about AIKS in a manner that brings in sanity, collaborative voices together and sustainability in the field of knowledge studies. This is how the volume adds to the existing collection of books on AIKS. The book helps us in the re-centring of IKSs and offers a clear demonstration that we have diverse epistemologies that can be utilized in current troubling times as humanity searches for existential answers to complex challenges.

Within the Western academy (and its colonial appendages in Africa), the structure and relations of 'coloniality' suggest a particular colonial engagement of knowledge and power steeped in Eurocentric, patriarchal and imperialist cultural ideologies of modernity (Grosfoguel, 2011; Gwaranvanda & Ndofirepi, 2020). It is not a new development. In fact, throughout human history, the 'colonial-modernity' dialectic (Mignolo, 2007) has served to suppress the ontologies and epistemologies of African, Indigenous, racialized and colonized peoples, universalizing the "White", Western liberal subject as representative of all humanity. Such 'modernity/ coloniality' tandem has worked to negate, disavow, distort, and deny "knowledges, subjectivities, world senses, and life visions" (Mignolo and Walsh, 2018, p. 4). In particular, Western modernity has been marked by a particular 'race thinking' functioning to change rules of reason, standards of logic and rationality (e.g., White logic, authority, control & credibility).

It is imperative to subvert a dominant Euro-exclusive claim of modernity from the stage pad of African Indigeneity. We ask: what does decolonization have to do with modernity, science, history and knowledge production? Bolivian anti-colonial, Indigenist feminist theorist Silvera Cusicanqui reminds us that the "Indigenous world does not conceive history as linear (but that) the past-future is contained in the present" and hence, a project of "Indigenous modernity can emerge from the present in a spiral whose movement is a continuous feedback from the past to the future (offering) a principle of hope or anticipatory consciousness that both discerns and realizes decolonization at the same time" (Cusicanqui, 2012; pp. 96-7). The African Indigenous is not frozen in time, place and space. We must be able to articulate a grammar of African Indigenous futurity as striving and living for the future now, in the present and in the past as relevant (see also Campt, 2017).

The imperative of a critical discursive acknowledgement and validation of African Indigeneity requires that we take up our historical, ancestral, cultural and spiritual memories as heritage knowledge for decolonial and anti-colonial purposes. This includes affirming the power of African history, cultures, language and orality as very critical Indigeneity is a 'way of Being', acknowledging history, culture and ancestry as grounding a people's sense of Being, including our identities and subjectivities. The resistance and refusal to rethink Western dominant discursive frames constitutes an epistemic violence on the African Being.

To reiterate, Indigenous knowledge is fundamentally a teaching of the Land. These teachings bring physical, spiritual, social and cultural conceptions of Land to include the sky, water and seas constituting powerful literacies, ontologies and epistemologies. As many Turtle Island Indigenous scholars argue, these literacies are in effect cultural, spiritual, psychic memories and "living forces" we can learn from (Simpson, 2014; see also Tuck and Yang, 2012; Styres, 2019). In writing about Indigeneities, we must theorize Land and Earthly teachings of relationality, sharing, reciprocity, connections, mutual interdependence (e.g., building communities & relationships), social responsibility and accountability to enrich conversations about schooling and education. Such understandings help decolonize schooling in terms of promoting communities of learners and communities of schooling where colonial hierarchies and the privileging of particular bodies of knowledge can be subverted or abolished.

It is healthy this collection brings an expansive gaze on AIKS. Topics covered range from examinations of Indigenous epistemic systems, indigenous philosophies, culture and social structure, magic and rituals, religion and sexuality, folkloric productions, as well as food security and livestock management, among others. A particular strength is drawing upon the implications for research to reveal strengths of AIKS pursued through anti-colonial and decolonial discursive prisms. Such research offers important lessons to address some fog in the contemporary problems and challenges of African Indigenous development. We need to engage more with African scholars and our growing literature on African Indigenous knowledges globally. We can accomplish this centring anti-coloniality as a framework. Anti-coloniality allows us to flesh out the complexities and interstices of African history, culture, Indigeneity, spiritualism and colonization African cultural knowledges (oral culture/literatures – myths, legends, riddles, fables, folktales, songs, stories, proverbs, folkloric productions; as well as artworks, artifacts, landscapes, Indigenous pharmacology, agrobiodiversity, food systems, cropping systems, animal husbandry, teachings on soil fertility, meteorology, food storage and preservation, pest control, etc.) all reveal epistemologies of African Indigenous science and technology. We must understand the systems of thought behind Indigenous arts and crafts, folkloric productions, Indigenous philosophies such as proverbs, folktales, riddles, etc., as well as material technology and other folkloric production (see also, Ngulube, 2017). There is much to learn from Indigenous agrobiodiversity and the role in understanding and ensuring food security, sovereignty, and community resilience. Research investigations into Indigenous food systems, Indigenous crop systems and Indigenous animal husbandry, Indigenous crop farming systems and issues of sustainability in maintaining food security all point to ways African peoples have understood their physical, metaphysical and social environments (see Shava, O'Donoghue, Krasny and Zazu, 2009).

These knowledges demonstrate how the relations of body, mind, soul and spirit, as well as the nexus of society, culture and Nature constitute spheres of Indigenous knowledges. In such research investigations, we must pay special attention to gendered, ethnic and age dimensions of Indigenous farming and folkloric practices and processes, as well as traditional strategies for transferring local farming and ecological knowledge in households and between communities. These knowledges reveal the pedagogies of science and technology for Indigenous knowledge capacity building. To foster African science and development, we must explore Indigenous ways of teaching and learning science and technology and their assessments and applications in formal educational processes. These are important educative sites and sources for the contemporary learner, pointing to the power of Indigenous knowledge practices and innovations such as multi-cropping, soil fertility, meteorology, ecology and biodiversity, Indigenous pedagogy, food sovereignty, food storage and preservation, pest control, etc. (see O'Donoghue, Shava and Zazu, 2013).

The search for new global educational futurities acknowledging and validating different knowledge systems is also a question of educational justice. African Indigenous knowledges systems have something to teach us about educational justice. There are important lessons of social justice from African Indigenous knowledges that call for moving away from Westocentric conceptions of justice. There are teachings of social justice embedded within African Indigenous ontologies of 'life after death', the 'sanctity of human life', and the power of our ancestors as perpetual guardians. Justice may not be immediate and now. It is also not necessarily visited on the harmed or injured. Indigenous justice is about a cleaning of the soul, spirit and re-establishing relations with our ancestors. Justice is thus about restoration and healing. Consequently, we need Indigenous knowledges to heal ourselves from the oppressive tendencies of dominant Eurocentric knowledges and the coloniality of schooling to level-headed and just education.

References

Adefarakan, T. (2011). "(Re-)conceptualizing 'Indigenous' from Anti-Colonial and Black Feminist Theoretical Perspectives: Living and Imagining Indigeneity Differently". In Dei, G.J.S (Ed.), *Indigenous Philosophies and Critical Education: A Reader*. New York: Peter Lang, 34 – 52.

Campt, T. (2017). *Listening to images*. Duke University Press.

Cusicanqui, S. R. (2012). *Ch'ixinakax utxiwa*: A Reflection on the Practices and Discourses of Decolonization. *South Atlantic Quarterly 111* (1), 95–109. doi: 10.1215/00382876-1472612.

Grosfoguel, R. (2011). "Decolonising Post-Colonial Studies and Paradigms of Political Economy: Transmodernity, Decolonial Thinking and Global Coloniality." *Transmodernity: Journal of Peripheral Cultural Production in the Luso-Hispanic World* 1 (1): 1–36.

Gwaranvanda, E. & A. Ndofirepi (2020), Eurocentric pitfalls in the practice of African philosophy: Reflections on African Universities. UNISA Press. Volume 21, https://doi.org/10.25159/2413-3086/6678.

Mignolo, W. (2007). Delinking: The rhetoric of modernity, the logic of coloniality and the grammar of de-coloniality. *Cultural Studies, 21*(2-3), 449-514.

Mignolo, W. and C. Walsh (2018). *On Decoloniality: Concepts, Analysis and Praxis*. Durham, N.C: Duke University Press.

Ngulube, P. (2017). (ed.). *Handbook of Research on Indigenous Knowledge Systems in Developing Countries*. Hershey: IGI.

O'Donoghue, R, Shava, S. and Zazu, C. (Eds.). (2013). African heritage knowledge in the context of social innovation. United Nations University – Institute of Advanced Studies (UNU-IAS), Tokyo. LINK:

http://www.ias.unu.edu/resource_centre/UNU_Booklet_MB20
13_FINAL_Links_v12.pdf.

Tuck, E. & Yang, K.W. (2012). Decolonization is not a Metaphor. *Decolonization: Indigeneity, Education & Society* 1 (1), 1-40.

Shava, S., O'Donoghue, R., Krasny, M.E. and Zazu, C. (2009). Traditional food crops as a source of community resilience in Zimbabwe. International Journal of African Renaissance Studies – Multi-, Inter- and Transdisciplinary 4(1): 31- 48.

Simpson, L. (2014). Land as Pedagogy: Nishnaabeg intelligence in rebellious transformation. *Decolonization: Indigeneity, Education and Society. Vol. 3, No.3*, 1-25.

Styres, S. (2019). Literacies of Land: Decolonizing Narratives, Storying, and Literature. In. L. T. Smith, E. Tuck, & K. W. Yang (Eds.). *Indigenous and Decolonizing Studies in Education: Mapping the Long View* (pp, 24-37). New York: Routledge. Retrieved from https://ebookcentral-proquest-com.myaccess.library.utoronto.ca/.

George J. Sefa Dei [Nana Adusei Sefa Tweneboah]
University of Toronto

Chapter 1

Debunking Myths, Misinterpretations and Misrepresentations: An Introduction

Tenson Mabhuya Muyambo,
Anniegrace Mapangisana-Hlatywayo,
Pindai M. Sithole
Munyaradzi Mawere

Introduction

Books on indigenous knowledge especially as related to Africa are many, and on varied subjects. As such, the call for this book has not been necessitated by lack of books on indigenous knowledge in and on Africa, but by the perennial onslaughts on African indigenous knowledge and the continued need to amplify the efficacy of this once 'subjugated knowledge' (Semali & Kincheloe 1999) in peoples' survival and livelihoods as demonstrated by most chapters in this book. In fact, the call has been prompted by the reality that "academic scholarship has a duty to recognize these local cultural knowings as legitimate sources of knowledge for a number of reasons: foremost to recognize African peoples as producers and creators of knowledge" (Emeagwali &Dei 2014: ix). The argument being that Africans have not been merely consumers of knowledge (ibid) but active producers of the same knowledge they consume: they are in fact active 'prosumers' of knowledge.

The concept of Indigenous Knowledge Systems (IKSs) is not only contentious but raises several questions that this book intends to answer. These questions border around IKSs' use, efficacy, status, relevance, and applicability, among others. For a very long time, IKSs have been pejoratively misconstrued, misinterpreted, and erroneously described as backward, unscientific and pre-logical (Mawere & Kadenge, 2010; Mawere, 2014), to say the least. The long decades of misinformation, half-truths and vilification have left IKSs battered and rendered 'superstitious' (Ntuli 2002:52), pre-logical, primitive, unscientific and unworthy studying and using. To the chagrin of well-meaning and intentioned scholars, the misinformation, untruths and misconceptions-largely lumped by

1

Ntuli (2002) as 'lies' of highest order have been accepted as the *information, the truth and the knowledge* (emphasis ours). What this then meant and still means for many people is that IKSs as "locally engineered ideas, practices and beliefs" (Chapungu & Sibanda 2015:23), "experiential knowledge", "liveable knowledge" (Mazuru & Mapara 2015:9), accumulated knowledge acquired through daily observation (Ngulube 2017) are not only obsolete (Masitera & Sibanda 2018), but primitive and backward. The scheme to push IKSs to the periphery was resoundingly achieved, evident by the scorn that IKSs received and continue to receive in the Global South. This flies in the face of the stark reality that well before the advent of colonisation and its attendant problems, indigenes were not *tabula rasa* but were active participants in knowledge production through "trial and error" (Siambombe, Mutale & Muzingili 2018:47), the very same way that Western science went through.

Given the foregoing, this volume, crafted from a multi-disciplinary perspective, is a celebration of the efficacy of IKs and its attendant practices, a re-imagining of IKs and practices as an alternative knowledge that communities have been using generation after generation in the Global South. It is a re-centring and re-ignition of the fire of indigenous knowledge after decades of several attempts on it and its inferiorisation by the Global North who maligned (and continue to malign) Africans and their epistemologies, cosmologies and ontologies as inferior to theirs. This othering and supremacist attitude are greatly challenged in this volume as the contributors do not only unanimously agree that, indeed, IKs and practices have withstood the test of time, but that they are a culturally responsive episteme that has seen generations bequeathing it to one after the other. Essentially, the volume asks this question: Whose reality counts for it to be considered knowledge?

Whose Reality Counts?

Having realised that IKs and practices of the indigenes, Africans in particular, have been caricatured and invalidated, this book is making a bold statement that there is an urgent need to 'rupture the present relationship between 'valid' knowledge and 'not valid' knowledge and to introduce 'indigenous knowledge as legitimate ways of knowing that are both dynamic and continuous (Dei & Rosenberg 2000). The tendency to pontificate on others' knowledges has come to an end as indigenes are realising that reality is from within and not from without. The book affirmatively asserts that African indigenous knowledge is a product of indigenous people who are citizens of African origin, who are African not through being offspring of settlerism and colonialism but people with a long history of African ancestry and identify themselves on one way or another with rural communities (Kapoor &Shizha 2010). We audaciously submit that the Cartesian-Newtonian perspective about knowledge is not only oppressive but an act of violence on the indigenous peoples. In other words, this is epistemicide (Ndlovu-Gatsheni 2013b). Semali and Kincheloe (1999: 28) are instructive when they argue that "the denigration of indigenous knowledge cannot be separated from the oppression of indigenous peoples".

Inasmuch as Western knowledge, or rather Western Science is normatively taken as the knowledge, this book is of the view that there should be multiple readings of the world (Dei & Rosenberg 2000) depending on peoples' standpoint and context where indigenous knowledges of the indigenous peoples are taken into the equation. There is need to amplify the re-imagination of indigenous knowledge as a distinct but complimentary way of knowing. No one form of knowledge should impose itself on another for that is tantamount to violence and injustice in the production and consumption of knowledge. While other works on indigenous knowledge have argued in the same vein, this volume, being anticolonial or rather decolonial by design, takes the argument further by making the once objects (indigenous peoples) of analysis, 'speaking subjects' (Odora Hoppers 2002) with agency that warrant recognition. This change, or rather paradigm shift from object to subject (Platvoet 1996) is the application of indigenous knowledge in people's livelihoods for sustainable development. The book is a call for what the decolonialist scholar, Ndlovu-Gatsheni (2015) refers to as the democratization of knowledge, de-hegemonization of knowledge, de-Westernization of knowledge and de-Europeanization of knowledge. It sees the praxis and pragmatic side of indigenous knowledge as evidently demonstrated by the chapters herein contained.

Summary of Chapters in the Volume

The book's chapters cover thematic areas encompassing a multidisciplinary approach to empirically demonstrate the importance of African indigenous knowledge systems (AIKS) in sustainable development initiatives in Africa.

Chapter 1 by Tenson Mabhuya Muyambo, Anniegrace Mapangisana-Hlatywayo and Munyaradzi Mawere is an *introductory* chapter that contextualises the book. It acts as a precursor to the issues and debates that the volume raises. The chapter sets the tone, thrust and general argument the book is making, that AIKs particularly in Southern Africa are a lived reality for the indigenes and no amount of vilification from the West and its allies can plunder AIKs.

Jacob Mapara's chapter 2 entitled *Decolonizing Spaces of Inquiry: Indigenous Research and Engagement without the Colonial Matrix of Power'* argues that research is a highly contested space and sadly notes that to date, it has been given prominence by Western scholars who have dictated how it should be carried out. Mapara rightly points out that research is not a new or emerging phenomenon in African indigenous communities. It has immemorially been undertaken through observations and experiments prior to colonialism and its subsequent manifestations. Hence, in the bid to disentangle research from the Western epistemological gaze, Mapara argues the departure point for indigenous research is the place of the self – this entails positioning the researcher in the whole research matrix because indigenous inquiry is relational. The researcher is part of the story/inquiry as opposed to Western methodologies that treat the researcher as an outsider. Hence the importance of the need to decolonize the research space. In order to decolonize the research space, Mapara proposes a number of indigenous approaches to research. These include (i) treating the researcher and the researched as intertwined; (ii) need to interrogate colonial sites of memory and the need to come up with proper national histories that speak to the history of the nation; (iii) the need to incentivize research participants as a token of appreciation as well as partaking in their social activities as being part of the community. In indigenous communities, research participants may reciprocate by giving presents of higher value to the researcher – hence, the research process becomes relational; (iv) acknowledge the interconnectedness of things from an indigenous worldview – people, bio-physical environment and the extra-terrestrial world. In addition, the author points out the researcher should embrace myths and legend as told by participants as part of the relational approach to indigenous research. Of importance in this the chapter is the adoption of the method of storytelling as a means of data collection. The author points out that storytelling 'gives insights that are informed by local histories and traditions'.

The next chapter is chapter 3 entitled *Indigenous knowledge across the curriculum in the Global South: an epistemic and cognitive shifting process'* where Mapara argues for the inclusion of indigenous knowledge in the higher education curriculum in the Global South. The author notes epistemologies of formerly colonized nations are marginalized and the cultural diversity of humanity is not taken into account. The author poses a critical observation on how the 'world celebrates the diversity of human cultures but fails to embrace the diversity of the globe's knowledges yet the same cultures in their plurality are products of varied epistemologies'. Hence, the chapter presents an important call for an epistemic and cognitive shift and for all educational disciplines to incorporate indigenous knowledge in their curriculum. Additionally, the author posits such a shift is possible through Africans rediscovering and learning from their histories – histories that have to be debunked from the western epistemological gaze. Mapara proposes the indigenization of higher education curriculum through the legitimization of indigenous knowledge systems in higher institutions of learning.

Arguing from the same perspective, Madusise's chapter 4: *Towards the implementation of African indigenous mathematical practices into the mathematics curriculum in Southern Africa* explores the possibility of implementing indigenous mathematical practices in the mathematics curriculum and the application of school mathematics to cultural activities in southern African. Madusise highlights the embedded indigenous mathematical concepts through basket and mat weaving as well as the Tswana dance. The author argues that various mathematical concepts can be identified in different cultural activities. As such, a number of indigenous mathematical concepts have been identified in indigenous games such as *tsoro* and *nhodo*. These games involve counting as well as the concept of factors. Artifacts from indigenous basket and mat weaving can be used as teaching aids within the field of mathematics. The author strongly points out that mathematical knowledge provides the vital groundwork of the knowledge of the economy.

In the chapter 5, entitled *Challenges in implementing the competence-based curriculum in Zimbabwe: peeping through the African indigenous education philosophy lenses* Muchabaiwa interrogates the revised Competence-Based School Curriculum (CBSC) which has been warmly received by educationists and viewed as 'a robust and pragmatic education

5

blue-print amenable with Zimbabwe's 2030 development agenda'. The author investigates the challenges associated with the implementation of the CBSC and proposes the philosophy of African Indigenous Education as a conceptual framework for the new curriculum. The author identifies five philosophical foundations of African traditional education – preparationism, functionalism, perennialism, humanism and holisticism. The author argues that African traditional education lays emphasis on a practical approach in teaching content that is relevant to people's daily lives. Muchabaiwa points out that African indigenous education was functional and pragmatic – it was able to solve real life problems. Hence the author proposes the CBSC to adopt a learner-centred pedagogical approach which will inculcate specific competences to learners. In line with the pragmatic approach to education, the author recommends school development projects to focus constructing Science and Computer laboratories and workshops for technical subject that will prepare students for real life situations.

In chapter 6, entitled *The nhimbe practice as a community multi-disciplinary academy among the Shona and Ndebele people of Zimbabwe,* Sithole presents the indigenous practice of *nhimbe* as a sustainable community academy where the transfer of knowledge and skills takes place. In this chapter, Sithole argues that learning occurs in a classroom set-up and is aptly guided by a country's approved education curriculum. Hence, Sithole argues that this type of teaching trajectory fails to recognize indigenous epistemologies of knowledge and skills transfer prevalent in African communities. As such, the author presents the *nhimbe* practice which is centred on socio-cultural and communitarian imperatives that allow for knowledge and skills sharing in communities for socio-economic development. Sithole presents six categorized forms of knowledge and skills that are shared during nhimbe. These have been identified as (i) community history and socio-anthropology knowledge; (ii) livelihoods knowledge and skills; (iii) health knowledge and skills; (iv) marriage and family; (v) environmental protection; (vi) and peace-building and conflict resolution.

Okyere-Manu, Morgan and Antwi's chapter 7: *The ethical implications of religio-cultural healing practices on Ghana's environment: an ethno-medical interrogation* explores ethno-medicines and their impact on the environment. The chapter assess the ethical implications of religio-cultural (ethno-medical) healing practices among Ghanaians on the environment. The authors seek to examine the link between religio-cultural healing practices and the environment as well as deducing whether the practice of ethno-medicines contribute to ecological problems. The authors bemoan the marginalization of indigenous traditional values and beliefs towards environmental management. They advance the understanding that the African worldview underscores the interrelatedness and interconnectedness of humans and nature and therefore lobbies for a holistic environmental ethic. The authors further propose the use of taboos and norms that have immemorially guided indigenous people over the years to replant the near extinct medicinal plants, herbs and trees in a bid to protect animals as a way of preserving and conserving the environment for the benefit of current and future generations – a practice that has been disregarded by most practitioners of ethno-medicines. Okyere-Manu, Morgan and Antwi rightly point out the resolute call for ethno-medicine as witnessed during the COVID-19 pandemic. Hence the authors posit that if there are no measures in place to regulate the activities of ethno-medicine practitioners, their activities could possibly lead to environmental resource dilapidation. The authors therefore recommend for a traditional African ethic that acknowledges the interrelatedness of humanity and nature.

Similarly, chapter 8: *Coping with Climate Change-linked Environmental Tragedies: The Role of Shona Beliefs and Practices as Indigenous Knowledge Systems* by Francis Machingura and Godfrey Museka explores the role of African-Christian religio-cultural beliefs in aiding victims cope and make sense of climate change-driven catastrophes, suffering and loss. The authors focus on climate change-linked environmental tragedies experienced in Zimbabwe. They argue that religion has not been left behind in the discussions especially African Traditional Religion and Christianity which have dominated the spiritual market of Zimbabwe. The understanding by many Zimbabweans is that disasters have a lot to do with the anger of the divine or spiritual world hence the need to understand the religious climate change-linked symbolisms on beliefs and practices. For them Zimbabwe has tasted the brunt effects of climate change-linked environmental disasters through cyclone-related floods, droughts and heat waves. The disasters resulted in loss of human, floristic and faunistic life as well as extensive damage to infrastructure which has been a setback to poorly resourced government departments. The adverse effects of climate change-linked environmental disasters are not limited to this country but other countries in the region. However, these climatic changes effects have reignited the debate on indigenes and Christian beliefs and practices on climate change-linked environmental tragedies. We are convinced that such debates will be helpful for future generational discourses.

In chapter 9, entitled *Conventional traditional medicine: perceptions from practitioners,* Tenson Mabhuya Muyambo offers an appraisal of traditional healers and traditional medicine. He presents traditional health practitioners as agents for ensuring healthy communities. The chapter outlines the efficacy of traditional medicine and argues for the need to integrate the world's health epistemologies with a view to sustainably manage health-related issues in the African context. The chapter also seeks to debunk the misconceptions of the roles and responsibilities of traditional healers and the impact of colonization of traditional beliefs and practices which led to the inferiorisation of traditional healers. The chapter presents the contribution of traditional healers and traditional medicine to good health and well-being for humanity. The author concludes his chapter by arguing for medical pluralism – the need to unravel possible hindrances to integrate traditional healers and their biomedical counterparts.

Still arguing from an indigenous knowledge's agency perspective, chapter 10 entitled *Indigenous knowledge systems-based sexual and reproductive health: Ndau indigenous practice of masuwo for childbirth preparedness* by Hlatywayo outlines the indigenous conceptualization of health and well-being – in particular childbirth preparedness. The author, using a case study of the Ndau people of Zimbabwe, points out that pregnancy and childbirth are both biological and symbolical – hence they carry an intrinsic socio-cultural dimension. As such, they are informed by indigenous practices (IPs). Indigenous practices are therefore cited as a major source of survival in African indigenous communities. Hlatywayo presents the indigenous practice of *masuwo* as childbirth preparedness and cites their three main benefits: (i) use of *masuwo* as birth canal relaxants; (ii) use of *masuwo* as a health tonic during pregnancy; (iii) and use of *masuwo* for protection against unseen evil forces during pregnancy and childbirth. The chapter presents several beneficial properties of this indigenous practice inclusive of strengthening the mother's body thereby preparing it for childbirth; warding off evil spirits and *mamhepo*; treating the unborn child from common baby ailments before birth. M*asuwo* benefits also include increased pelvic joint mobility; stimulation of uterine contractions; relaxation of vaginal muscles and the facilitation of adequate stretching of the birth canal thereby safeguarding against perineal tearing as well as lessening labour pains. The chapter highlights that IPs are culturally resilient and deeply ingrained in the subconscious of African indigenous people. They contribute to better and improved sexual and reproductive healthcare; particularly for pregnant women.

Enerst Dube and Albert Manyani, in chapter 11, entitled *Indigenous knowledge systems for building-back-better flood-impacted communities in Zimbabwe* explore the potential contribution of indigenous knowledge systems in the building-back-better (BBB) of the flood-impacted rural communities in Zimbabwe. The authors note that communities in Zimbabwe have struggled to build-back-better in the aftermath of disasters despite these communities having indigenous knowledge that can be utilized at their disposal. The authors regard 'rural communities as an oasis of indigenous knowledge systems'. Hence the authors cogently argue indigenous knowledge is not effectually practiced to build-back-better communities in disaster prone areas in Zimbabwe. Dube and Manyani attribute this shortcoming to practitioners and communities ostracizing indigenous knowledge. As such, the authors propose government support as a strategy to conscientize communities on the importance of indigenous knowledge for building-back-better communities. They further propose that indigenous knowledge should be part of the school and tertiary education curriculum in order to promote its sustainability. In this chapter, the authors position indigenous knowledge as a bedrock for mitigating disasters and detecting early warning signs which in turn prompts communities for disaster preparedness. The authors further posit that indigenous knowledge is a strategy that can be contextualized to suit the local environment and situation – it stimulates local people to employ their grassroots knowledge towards disaster management.

Chapter 12, entitled *Medicinal indigenous knowledge systems and gender among the Shona people of Buhera South, Zimbabwe* authored by Viriri focuses on medicinal indigenous knowledge systems commonly used by the Shona people of Buhera South, Zimbabwe. Viriri cites the persistent ethno-botanical knowledge acquisition that has immemorially been part of the Shona people of Buhera. The author interrogates the gender dynamics related to the practice of medicinal indigenous knowledge systems in a society that is patriarchal. Research findings by the author also indicate the gendered knowledge of indigenous medicinal plants and their value with women being more knowledgeable than men. This gendered nature is attributed to the gender roles which are characteristic of the Shona society. However, due to the patriarchal nature that overlooks women's knowledge, the author advocates for shared knowledge between the men and women as a strategy for bringing innovation in the use of indigenous medicine for the benefit of the whole community of men, women and children.

Chirongoma and Zvingowanisei's chapter 13: *Indigenous cultural resources as a panacea for sexual and gender- based violence: a case study of the Ndau in Chimanimani community, Zimbabwe* explores sexual and gender-based violence (SGBV) and identifies the different types of violence prevalent in the community. These types include physical, sexual, economic and emotional violence. Using an African feminist approach, the authors identify unequal power relations, economic dependence, patriarch, religion and culture as the major drivers of SGBV. The authors posit that whilst African Traditional Religion perpetuates SGBV through a number of cultural practices, the same can be adopted as a useful resource for mitigating SGBV. Chirongoma and Zvingowanisei present the use of taboos, proverbs, idioms, songs and myths as indigenous cultural resources that can be used to mitigate SGBV. Hence the chapter seeks to deconstruct traditional stereotypes that depict African religious practices and beliefs as repressive to women.

On the same note Mulenga Kaunda, in chapter 14, entitled *Bemba Imbusa as African Indigenous Knowledge Framework for Life-Giving Marriage* presents the Bemba pre-marital teaching – *Imbusa* – as a marital agency of women. She makes an analysis of *Imbusa* as an oppressive and empowering resource for women's agency. The author points out the high regard and perception of marriage as sacred in African indigenous communities is what necessitates such pre-marital teachings. The *Imbusa* is taught using schematic or naturalistic forms of painting. Kaunda advocates for an African Feminist *Banacimbusa* – view to building a life-giving and life-affirming marriage. Hence, the need for an African feminist holistic sexual ethic.

In their chapter 15, entitled, *Sexuality and AmaXhosa women's agency: South African indigenous women's agency in sexual matters,* Mawere and Mayekiso explore whether young indigenous AmaXhosa and South African women in general enjoy the same agency in sexual matters as compared with their male counterparts.

Still grappling with the issue of sexuality and gender, Mayekiso and Mawere in their chapter 16 entitled *Ndiyindoda (I'm a man): Public secrets, harm and pain in Xhosa male circumcision* present the male circumcision practice undertaken for health and cultural significance by Xhosa men of South Africa. The authors cite that indoda yonkwenene (a real man) is one who can endure pain, which then is not only regarded as a sign of bravery but accords a social status and communal respect. The circumcision ritual is accompanied by the spilling of blood of an animal as introduction to the ancestors as well as serving as an identity marker for communal recognition. Hence, the authors argue a man who does not go through this culturally approved practice is ostracized. Mayekiso and Mawere present harm and pain as masculine identity-making traits – inability to handle pain impacts on one's future social standing.

The next chapter is chapter 17, entitled *Indigenous knowledge systems for sustainable cattle disease management in Masvingo District, Zimbabwe* where Gamira examines the use of indigenous knowledge systems to manage the outbreak of cattle diseases in Masvingo District. The author sought to examine the use of indigenous knowledge systems to manage young animals for breeding purposes as well as the management of breeding periods; to analyse common cattle diseases; to examine ethnoveterinary medicinal plants used by farmers to treat cattle diseases; as well as to identify common plant extracts used to cure cattle diseases in Zimbabwe. The chapter also outlines indigenous knowledge systems' methods that are used to wean calves, dehorn, castrate steers and well as cattle dipping using indigenous tree leaves and shrubs. Hence the chapter highlights ethnoveterinary trees used to treat common cattle diseases, thereby demonstrating the usefulness of IK across all sectors of human flourishing.

Arguing from a food security perspective, chapter 18: *Indigenous food intake: an alternative for mitigating food insecurity and refined foods related diseases,* Mawere and Mawere argue that African people have experienced dislocations, misrepresentations and castigations of their values and ways of life, inclusive of their indigenous foods and feeding habits. They sadly note that the global food production and food discourses are dominated by the global North. Hence the authors present indigenous food as an alternative for mitigating food insecurity and refined foods-related diseases. Mawere and Mawere therefore argue for the need to recognize the efficacy of indigenous foods given their nutritional value. The authors also point out the importance of food – it serves as a cultural and religious expression of any given people. Hence the need to resuscitate, advance African original intellectual legacy that challenge the onslaught of externally manipulated forces of mental and cultural dissociation aimed at obliterating the African original intellect and lore of life. The authors

11

posit that food is embedded in the cultural system – the cultivation, preparation and consumption – contribute to the formulation of people's identity claims. Food is part of human identity – its significance goes beyond nutrition. Indigenous worldview – food is used to show love, acceptance and humanity. As such the authors bemoan the abandonment of indigenous food in favour of refined foods which have been processed and stripped of their nutritional values. Hence the chapter positions indigenous food as an alternative for mitigating food insecurity in Zimbabwe and health problems associated with refined foods. Prior to colonialism and the introduction of Western foods, indigenous food used to be dominant to millions of people in Zimbabwe, particularly those in rural settings.

Sibanda and Humbe in chapter 19: *Rethinking indigenous knowledge systems in systematic problem-solving and decision-making: a case of Shona indigenous families'* explore African indigenous knowledge systems in systematic problem-solving and decision-making patterns in Shona indigenous families. The authors present pacifism, mediation, adjudication, reconciliation, negotiation and cross-examination as indigenous conflict resolution techniques. The authors posit that these techniques proffer peaceful co-existence as well as harmonious relations within families. Sibanda and Hume identify land disputes, chieftaincy, personal relationship issues, family property, honour, infidelity and witchcraft as some of the major sources of conflict in Shona indigenous families and the principles of equity and justice as embedded in African customs are espoused. Furthermore, the authors identify major problem-solvers and decision makers regarded as sacred practitioners in the form of *baba, tete,* and *muzukuru* among others. The authors also cite the use of oral art forms like folktales, songs, proverbs, riddles and idioms as part of African indigenous knowledge systems' systematic problem-solving and decision-making patterns.

Concomitantly, Moses Chundu's chapter 20: *The Role of the Institution of Sahwira in Resolving Conflicts at Household and Community Level: Case Study of Domboshava People,* investigates the role of the institution of *sahwira* in conflict management and peace-making and also whether the role is still prevalent in Zimbabwe. The study made use of a case study of Domboshava, a rural community north of Harare metro province. Key informant interviews and focus group discussions involving the traditional leaders and elders in Domboshava revealed that the practice is still alive. The study revealed that although the institution is still prevalent in

Domboshava, the functionalities have been somewhat diluted by modern day institutions in the likes of funeral parlours, churches, modern legal systems and counselling services. For a peri-urban community, the effects of urbanisation are now being felt with a good proportion of the citizens being foreign to the community, hence not having friends at the level of family *sahwira*. There is scope for the government of Zimbabwe to deliberately seek to revive this critical institution by officially recognising local community grievance redress mechanisms and mainstreaming the institution of *sahwira* in the current peace building and conflict management frameworks.

Nomatter Sande, in chapter 21, entitled *African Christian Traditions as Contemporary Sources for African Knowledge Production Systems Impacting Development in Zimbabwe,* notes that even in the postcolonial context, African nations are still bedevilled with poverty, health and socio-economic and political challenges. The author attributes these challenges to colonialism and incongruous western ideologies to empower indigenous development backing African Indigenous Knowledge. The author also explores how Zimbabwean African Christian Traditions have transformed to become contemporary African knowledge production systems developing strategic tools to deal with development problems bedevilling the country. The chapter draws attention to the notion that African Christian traditions in Zimbabwe use divine spiritual solutions to mitigate poverty; protest theology to curb corruption; divine healings and positive confessions to treat psychological stress as alternative strategies for development. Hence the chapter posits that African Christian traditions are contemporary sources for African knowledge production systems that can aid development.

In chapter 22: *Traditional Music and Knowledge Preservation in Colonial Zimbabwe: Recasting Chimurenga Songs as Liberation Heritage & Indigenous Knowledge for Emancipation,* Zinhuku and Mawere examine the role of musicians in Zimbabwe's protracted liberation struggle in the 1960s through the 1970s. The authors argue that during this time, chimurenga songs formed an imperative facet of the Zimbabwean liberation struggle, where musicians augmented the struggle for freedom through music. Liberation war songs advanced the struggle for liberty and inspired chivalrous sons and daughters who were fighting in the bush. In the chapter, authors explore how chimurenga songs can be tabled as a framework for preserving, memorialising and depicting Zimbabwean liberation war heritage. Their study unearthed that music can be a tool for preserving indigenous knowledge and liberation heritage due to its capacity to evoke memories through activating what can be termed as a 'remembering gaze' in people's minds. The chapter advances the argument that traditional songs are a symbol of national heritage and representation of people's memory as they can be employed to capture 'hard to describe' moments and feelings that occurred in the past.

In their next chapter 23: *Dissuading Cultural Atrophy: Fantasising Zimbabwean Traditional Dance as Strategy for Reconfiguring National Identity*, Mawere and Zinhuku address national identity as vital for any form of nation building as it revives dogmas of allegiance and *esprit de corps* while instigating national consciousness. For them [national] identity is a multifarious phenomenon tangled with communal, pecuniary, artistic, macro-culture, historic and geopolitical cohesions. Irrevocably, the question of [national] identity reconfiguration in postcolonial contexts where conceit has been exotically cloaked resulting in the loss of a concrete self-direction, self-esteem and identity consciousness are peremptory. The authors argue that identity encompasses critical cultural ingredients such as linguistic codes, moral values, indigenous knowledge systems, folklore, beliefs and dances, among others. Using an ethnographic approach, their chapter is an attempt to fantasise Zimbabwean traditional dance and position it as a strategy for national identity reconfiguration and restoration. *Muchongoyo* dance, which is one of the Zimbabwean traditional dances, is adopted as a case study, with a view to cast it as an analogue and basis for appreciating how the envisaged agenda can be accomplished.

References

Chapungu, L. and Sibanda, F. (2015) Effectiveness of conventional indigenous practices in climate change adaptation and mitigation in Masvingo District, Zimbabwe. In: Jacob Mapara and Michael Mazuru. (eds.) *Indigenous Knowledge in Zimbabwe: Laying Foundations for Sustainable Livelihoods*. Gloucestershire: Diaspora Publishers, 22-39.

Dei, G. J. S., Hall, B. L. and Rosenberg, D. G. (2000) *Indigenous Knowledge in Global contexts: multiple Readings of our World*. Toronto: University of Toronto Press.

Emeagwali, G. and Dei, G. J. S. (2014) (eds.). *African Indigenous Knowledge and the disciplines*. Boston: Sense Publishers.

Kapoor, D. and Shizha, E. (2010) (eds.). *Indigenous Knowledge and Learning in Asia/Pacific and Africa: Perspectives on Development, Education, and Culture.* New York: Palgrave MacMillan.

Mapara J. and Mazuru, M. (2015) Introduction-Picking up the broken thread. In Jacob Mapara and Michael Mazuru. (eds.). *Indigenous Knowledge in Zimbabwe: Laying Foundations for Sustainable Livelihoods.* Gloucestershire: Diaspora Publishers, 11-21.

Mawere, M. (2010) Possibilities for Cultivating African Indigenous Knowledge Systems (IKSs): Lessons from Selected Cases of Witchcraft in Zimbabwe, *Journal of Gender, Peace and Development,* 1 (3): 091-100.

Mawere, M. & Kadenge, M. (2010) *Zvierwa* as African Indigenous Knowledge System: Epistemological and Ethical Implications of Selected Shona Taboos, *INDILA Journal of Africa Indigenous Knowledge* 9 (1): 29-44.

Masitera, E and Sibanda, F. (2018) Grappling with power in contemporary Zimbabwe: The introduction. In Erasmus Masitera and Fortune Sibanda (eds). *Power in Contemporary Zimbabwe.* London: Routledge, 1-14.

Ndlovu-Gsatsheni, S. J. (2015) Decoloniality as the future of Africa. *History Compass,* 13(10), 485-496.

Ndlovu-Gatsheni, S. J. (2013b) *Empire, Global Coloniality and African Subjectivity.* New York & Oxford: Berghahn Books.

Ngulube, P. (2017) *Handbook of Research on Theoretical Perspectives on Indigenous Knowledge Systems in Developing Countries.* Hershey, Pennsylvania.

Ntuli, P. P. (2002) 'Indigenous knowledge systems and the African Renaissance: Laying a foundation for the creation of counter-hegemonic discourses' in Odora Hoppers, C.A (ed). *Indigenous knowledge and the integration of knowledge systems: Towards a philosophy of Articulation.* Claremont: New Africa Books, 53-66.

Odora Hoppers, C. A. (2002) (ed.). *Indigenous knowledge and Integration of knowledge systems: Toward a Philosophy of Articulation.* Claremont: New Africa books (Pty) Ltd.

Platvoet, J. G. (1996) From Object to Subject: A history of the study of religions of Africa. In Jan G. Platvoet, James L. Cox & Jacob Kehinde Olupona (eds.) *The Study of Religions in Africa: Past, Present and Prospects.* Cambridge: Roots and Branches, 105-138.

Semali, L. M. and Kincheloe, J. L. (1999) (eds.). *What is Indigenous Knowledge? Voices from the Academy.* New York: Falmer Press.

Siambombe, A, Mutale, Q, and Muzingili, T. (2018) Indigenous Knowledge Systems: A synthesis of BaTonga People's traditional knowledge on weather dynamism. *African Journal of Social Work*, 8(2), 46-54.

Chapter 2

Decolonising Spaces of Inquiry: Indigenous Research and Engagement without the Colonial Matrix of Power

Jacob Mapara

Abstract

This chapter argues that research, as any other academic endeavour, is a highly charged and contested space. It posits that research as it currently stands, is a dictated process that is given direction and life through acceptance and acknowledgement by western scholarship that has bothered not just the indigenous and formerly colonized, but has also dictated what research is and how it is supposed to be carried out. The chapter points out that research is not new to indigenous communities as they have through observations and experiments, carried out research prior to the onslaught of colonialism and its research approaches. It posits that research that is devoid of putting place as part of the research methods risks coming up with inadequate data. It further observes that while there are similarities that may exist between indigenous and western research methods, especially when looked at from a qualitative paradigm, there are also substantial differences. The chapter notes that the starting point of any indigenous research methods is the place of the self, the researcher in the whole research matrix because indigenous inquiry is relational. It argues that relationship is important especially with the person telling the research story or providing the data. This, the chapter argues, does not exclude others who may be listening in to the discussion. The chapter, informed by the author's experiences in the field, additionally advances the idea that the researcher who is supposed to be indigenous is part of the story and his/her being part of the story contributes to how data are interpreted, which is quite contrary to the western research system where the researcher is an outsider who does not belong to the group.

Keywords: Indigenous research, decolonial spaces, power

Introduction

The issue of research is one that on the surface is very innocent and academic inquiry is largely considered as neutral. It is for this reason that it is generally characterized as the methodical and orderly study and investigation of materials and sources for purposes of establishing and/or confirming facts and at times reach new conclusions. This definition makes the assumption that research *per se* is neutral. This unfortunately is very far from the truth. In fact, according to Smith, "the term 'research' is inextricably linked to European imperialism and colonialism. The word itself, 'research', is probably one of the dirtiest words in the indigenous world's vocabulary" (2012, p. 1). These words are quite revealing in that while research or inquiry is supposed to be about logical and methodical ways of the search for truth and knowledge, it has been used as a tool for the othering, especially of the indigenous who share the common tragic fate of being colonized, dispossessed and in some cases exterminated (Wolfe, 2006). As Porsanger notes, research has been used to misrepresent reality and has in the process been used as a tool for the colonization of indigenous peoples and the sequestration of their territories (Porsanger, 2004). It is through these acts of colonization that research has been used to prove that the indigenous and colonized are sub-human who fall at the lowest rungs of the evolutionary ladder. The methods of inquiry that have been developed have been to meet the needs and expectations of the Westerners who have come to perceive themselves as the only originators of genuine and original knowledge that they have imposed on the world as universal. The issue of othering and how so-called scientific research findings were applied is a pointer to how race has played a significant role in research. For instance, in the United States, many Black women were sterilized for dubious reasons such as being with a low IQ and feeble minded (Oleson, 2016), all informed by an equally spurious science of eugenics. Because of such a science, most Black women were considered as unfit to be, for instance, mothers because it was wrongly stated that they could produce children who were not better beings (English, 2016). Such research has had far reaching consequences as is realized even in the way more Blacks are incarcerated in US prisons when compared to Whites (Oleson, 2016).

The example of eugenics that is referenced above is an indicator of how research has been manipulated to meet and fertilize the bizarre science of racial superiority. This practice of using research findings to label and profile others who are not white is quite widespread and this explains why Smith (2012), describes the word *research* as a dirt one. It is also for the same dirtiness that the word research carries that it becomes imperative that the indigenous communities not just engage in epistemological issues relating to knowledge generation in general but also in matters relating to research. It is for this reason that there is need to emphasize the importance of coming up with an indigenous research paradigm that speaks to how inquiry or academic investigations should be carried out not just among indigenous communities, but also by indigenous researchers as well as those who may want to follow and adopt these ways even though they may not be indigenous. This chapter proceeds by a discussion of indigenous pathways that are essential for one to successfully carry out research with a focus on qualitative inquiry. While its thrust is on indigenous research methods, it does not in any way suggest that western ways have to be jettisoned. What is important is that the researcher picks and identifies methods from both the indigenous paradigm and western one that would lead to the accession of the best research data. These are of course informed by the decolonial theory which the next section turns to.

Theoretical framework

This chapter is grounded within the decolonial theory, also known as decoloniality, which is a theoretical framework that analyses the relationship, especially in academia and cultural spaces, between the Global North and South, perceiving the north as a purveyor and sustainer of oppressive policies and practices that marginalize the formerly colonized. Among its major proponents are the Latin American scholars such as Grosfoguel (2003; 2006; 2007), Mignolo (2007), Wynter (2003), Maldonado-Torres (2007), Castro-Gómez (2007), Walsh (2007), and Hernández (2018). In Africa, the main voices are Ndlovu-Gatsheni (2013; 2019) and Kessi, Marks and Ramugondo (2020). In North America, the decolonial movement is growing with the movement of Latin American scholars and others like Mavhunga to the continent. Mavhunga (2021), in fact calls for what he terms an epistemic dialogue, a situation where no knowledge is privileged over others. The idea of decoloniality is however not new, because it has largely existed in a narrower sense within the Africana Studies field where the major voices include Asante (1998;

19

2006). Those in this area do not necessarily call it decoloniality, but Afrocentricity, because their main focus is on promoting Africans on the continent and in the Diaspora on matters relating to their achievements in science, culture and technology, something that Mavhunga also speaks to. For the Afrocentric scholars there is need to decolonise the myths around civilization and religion especially as regards the Christian faith (Ramantswana, 2016; Mavhunga, 2021).

One of its outstanding features is that it questions western knowledge and points out that this consciousness which is universalized as the only and true knowledge, is the basis of western imperialism. The theory further argues that despite the formerly colonized's attainment of political independence, they are still very much in the grips of colonial hegemony as is reflected in the curriculum that they continue to follow, something that decolonial scholars call the colonial matrix of power or coloniality of power (Quijano, 2000; 2007), that:

> allows us to think through how the colonized were subjected not simply to a rapacious exploitation of all their resources but also to a hegemony of Eurocentric knowledge systems. It allows us to understand the constitutive relationship between the historical *a priori* of European thought and its off-shore adventures. It also allows us to think through the Anglo- and Eurocentric structure of thought and representation that continues to dominate much of the world today (Alcoff, 2007, pp. 83-84).

In the words quoted above, Alcoff sustains the idea that the formerly colonized are still under the yoke of colonialism, because they are still very much embedded in the thought systems of the former colonies and their colonial masters. This observation is critical and it thus calls for an epistemic shift or epistemic disobedience also called epistemic de-linking (Mignolo, 2007; 2010), or an epistemic break which really is "a thorough re-conceptualization and a thorough re-organization of knowledge systems" (Kumaravadivelu, 2012, p. 14). What it therefore means when analysed from a curriculum perspective is that there are some countries like Zimbabwe that still adhere to the British system, even when the British themselves have moved on. There is consequently the need to develop a new curriculum approach which is an epistemic disobedience, not just in terms of what is taught but also how research is carried out venturing into what Denzin, Lincoln and Smith (2008) call critical indigenous research methods, an important aspect of research or academic inquiry that is discussed in the segment that comes below.

Why indigenous research methods are important

Indigenous research methods are worth pursuing and developing because, "Indigenous peoples' interests, knowledge and experiences must be at the centre of research methodologies and construction of knowledge about indigenous peoples" (Lester-Irabinna Rigney, 1999, p. 119 cited in Porsanger, 2004, p. 105). They are intrinsic to the whole research activities because in most cases the focus of western researcher-scholars is on indigenous communities, minorities or others that are profiled as beings on the fringe such as drug addicts, but hardly on those of that are considered and accepted as main-stream people. The result is that the subjects of this study, especially the indigenous are subjected at times to dehumanizing experiences or are misinterpreted and thus misrepresented when data are finally analysed. Put differently:

> research becomes synonymous with power and control: power over what ideas and findings matter and from whose perspective. Research is seldom the idea of those being researched, and rarely directly benefits them (Snow et al., 2016, p. 358).

It thus becomes clear from the foregoing quotation that all inquiry that those from the West carry out is part of the colonial enterprise and the knowledge hegemony where western epistemologies are viewed, peddled and accepted as the real knowledge. These words as well underscore why indigenous research methods are necessary and have to be developed and deployed. The major problem is that the current or western research methods as they are currently tailored is that they are packaged as rules and guidelines that give direction to researchers to be 'objective' and be detached from the subjects/objects being studied (Snow, Hays, Caliwagan, et al., 2016). The research environment becomes even more detached when it is taken into consideration that the voices that are heard and listened to as well as the voices that speak are not those of the subjects/objects of the inquiry. This situation is further aggravated by the desire and compulsive situation in most African universities that pushes them to publish in journals that are owned by the same western institutions and systems. The solution lies in African and other indigenous universities publishing their own journals that speak to their people

21

and give the peripherised voices space. There is a tendency in such so-called conventional research practices to privilege Eurocentric perspectives and in the process most likely exclude "indigenous ways of knowing and equitable participation in research processes in general" (Snow, Hays, Caliwagan, et al., 2016, p. 358).

Some indigenous approaches to research

This chapter argues for the importance of the need to decolonize the research space (Datta, 2017; Zavala, 2013). The idea, however, is not to throw away all that is Western but to have the native methods of inquiry as the prime ones which could possibly be complemented by the Western ones at best or create a situation where research really becomes mixed methods in the true sense of the word, where both epistemologies inform each other and in turn research. In this section, I discuss at length ways and means that a researcher can deploy when s/he goes out on a research mission. These ways are based on my own experiences in the research field.

It is always important in indigenous research approaches to be a learner and not a condemner. The problem with Western-centric research approaches is that they have largely been based on the North's perceptions of the other who is to be understood as inferior and thus need to be decolonized (Datta, 2017). The result has been that they have failed to understand that research is not something new among indigenous communities. For example, it is common practice among the Shona of Zimbabwe and other Bantu groups in general to exchange cocks for their chicken broods so that they have the best breeds. The same is done even when it comes to beasts. The most important case is the avoidance of incestuous relationships through taboos and the warning that if relatives get married to one another all their children will be affected by *muterere* (an illness that leads to different diseases like stunted growth and even death) (Little & Malina, 2005). All these decisions that they came up with were informed by observations and it is these that made them to come to the conclusions that they reached. The indigenous communities also developed seed banks from which they had seed for the next season. They also shared different seeds for different crops. All these activities are indicators that show that research did not come to Africa with the advent of Europeans.

Africans made informed decisions after careful study of phenomena. That is the first thing that western scholars and researchers need to understand and appreciate. What they today call research and research guidelines are but methods that are meant to ensure that western approaches are universalized and accepted as the only ones that contribute to meaningful research. The situation is unfortunately made worse by the fact that scientific inquiry as is currently the practice, is not meant to inform policy makers for the benefit of the researched communities but of those who fund the inquiries, for instance those in business looking for markets or pharmaceutical companies looking for indigenous flora and fauna that they intend to exploit for their benefit (Snow, Hays, Caliwagan, et al., 2016, p. 359). It also seeks to create a formerly colonized person who can ape the former colonizer's ways of doing research, something that is also largely a result of indigenous governments of the Global South for example, those in some Africa countries that do not fund research and thus leave academics at the mercy of western institutions and funders. It is therefore essential to approach research issues when dealing with indigenous communities bearing in mind that these native societies are not being exposed to research for the first time through higher education or NGOs.

Another aspect that relates to indigenous research approaches has to do with the researcher and the researched or focus of the research being intertwined. Indigenous research does not accommodate a 'them' and 'I/us' approach that has been characterized by Lincoln (cited in Datta, 2017) as a rape approach where, "the researcher comes in, takes what he [sic] wants, and leaves when he feels like it" (Lincoln, in Datta, 2017, p. 3). In fact, it has to be borne in mind that when it comes to indigenous research methods, the researcher always has to bear in mind that there is a strong relationship that exists between the researcher and the story or object of the study. This ties in with, "how it is told and how the informants or collaborators and the researcher interpret the story" (Lambert, 2011, p. 3), and thus means that the researcher cannot be divorced from the study that s/he is undertaking. This, of course, is contrary to Western research models, whereby their conventions, the research task that one undertakes as well as the data are all separated from the researcher. This model has the effect of turning the researcher into an onlooker (Lambert, 2011) whereas in indigenous approaches, the researcher is included in the investigation process, not as onlooker or outsider. It becomes a course of action where the researcher's and the voices and stories of participants to the research process are heard unlike in the Western systems (Lambert, 2011). More importantly is also the fact that indigenous research has to reflect the reality that academic inquiry is inevitably value-based, and that it is a convergence of the researcher, participant, socio-political, and environmental values on research process and outcome as Kovach (2009) notes.

Smith (2012) also points out that those engaging in indigenous research have to reflect on who owns, designs, interprets, reports, and ultimately benefits from the research process and products. These insights are critical when indigenous research is carried out. What they make clear is the reality that the indigenous researcher, or one who chooses to carry out scientific inquiry riding on the back of indigenous research methods needs to also acknowledge the distortions that are products of colonial research. Through acknowledging colonial research distortions and lies as well as fabrications, indigenous research thus becomes a process of rewriting history. Smith asks the following questions as regards research with a need to emphasize the importance of indigenous research as a history rewriting exercise:

> Whose research is it? Who owns it? Whose interests does it serve? Who will benefit from it? Who has designed its questions and framed its scope? Who will carry it out? Who will write it up? How will its results be disseminated? (2012, p. 10).

These questions are critical because they point out to the fact that research is not neutral but is there to drive the agenda of the researcher, and not the researched. It is in light of this that she makes clear that research is not neutral. This observation has to be borne in mind when it comes to history and research as well as the history of research by outsiders among indigenous communities. Smith points out the fact that the way history, especially colonial history has been written, reflects that the powerful are the writers of what is passed down as history. She states:

> We believe that history is also about justice, that understanding history will enlighten our decisions about the future. *Wrong*. History is also about power. In fact history is mostly about power. It is the story of the powerful and how they became powerful, and then how they use their power to keep them in positions in which they can continue to dominate others. It is because of this relationship with power that we have been excluded, marginalized and 'Othered' (Smith, p. 35).

As Smith sees it, history has been weaponized to serve the interests of the powerful and these are the former colonizers. Their influence is not just embedded in the act of colonization but also through academic activities that among them include research. It is through research that indigenous people have been marginalized even from themselves. It is thus through research that indigenous people also need to rewrite history and correct colonial distortions and outright lies. It thus means that research by indigenous people, for example in Zimbabwe, also needs to interrogate colonial sites of memory and come up with proper national histories that speak to the history of the nation and not of a single political party or a given race and ethnic group.

Another contentious approach to research that is frowned upon by Western-centric scholars and researchers relates to the giving of presents to participants in given communities. This is perceived as some way of incentivizing the research participants and it is viewed as thus becoming some type of bribe to entice people to participate. Resnik (2015) acknowledges that it is common practice to offer research subjects financial incentives for their participation in a survey because it has the effect of boosting the numbers of participants. He, however, laments the fact that this also "raises ethical concerns, such as undue inducement, exploitation, and biased enrolment" (Resnik, 2015, p. 35). Zutlevics (2016, p. 137) argues both for and against the use of incentives or compensation. She brings forth the argument that compensation only has to be paid to participants in situations where there is potential of physical harm. The same writer, however, is against incentives in the absence of potential injury and asserts, "providing monetary incentives to people can backfire by overall reducing intrinsic motivation, in this instance intrinsic motivation to behave altruistically or undertake civic duties" (2016, p. 137).

Zutlevics' (2016) argument for non-incentivization is based on what she calls intrinsic motivation or inner drive. This argument is important if the people see the benefits accruing from the research coming their way. If they are for the researcher and her/his funders, it may be necessary to pay compensation especially if participants have to leave their chores to participate in surveys. Additionally, researchers also need to perceive all inquiry activities in cultural contexts. A good example of the value of culture is the case of the breaking of the kola nut among the Igbo in Nigeria's south east. It is generally males who break it although some women who have attained a certain status can also break it (Amadiume, 2015). The same is true of partaking in its consumption. If a stranger or outsider is welcome, then the kola nut can be broken. The same can be said of other communities. For instance, among the Bantu, if one brings a present to a chief or a person s/he wants to interact with, that present is not read as a bribe by the recipient, but as a form of respect. It therefore becomes important that incentives be given to participants because the Shona even say *Ukama igasva, hunozadziswa nekudya* (A relationship is half-full, it can only be filled up by sharing a meal). When carrying out research among indigenous communities in Zimbabwe, it therefore becomes important to carry presents or some money that can be given out as a token of appreciation. It does not mean that the researcher is buying the participants. In fact, some participants even after receiving the 'token' of appreciation actually give presents of a higher value to the researcher. To them what is important is the story that would have been shared. It thus means that research becomes relational.

Linked to the issue of incentives that has been discussed above, and that of sharing of the kola nut that has as well been discussed in the foregoing paragraph, it is significant to highlight that research can be successfully undertaken with the participation of indigenous people and in their communities in Zimbabwe if the researcher(s) partakes in the sharing of food and beverages with members of the target societies. Essential to note is the fact that eating or drinking together among Bantu communities is considered an important part that is reflective of the community's unity (Tuomainen, 2014). To therefore refuse to participate can be interpreted to mean refusal which in most contexts is perceived as meaning that the researcher(s) views the host and participant community as inferior. It is therefore imperative that if one has to successfully carry out research activities in an indigenous Bantu community, one also has to be prepared to share in communal meals and beverage consumption with them. That is a way of ensuring acceptance. Failure to do that may result in poor participant turn out or even provision of inadequate data.

Sharing food has other spinoffs that accrue from it. For instance, during a meal, ideas that may have been forgotten during interviews or during other discussions may come up and will add on to the corpus of already collected material. It also provides a platform where other 'hanging' and hazy points may be clarified or further explored, a practice that is almost akin to the western concept of discussing some things over for instance tea or coffee, but which only involves the powerful. What becomes clear is that if one refuses to share a meal or partake even in beverage consumption, the community members may consider her/him a misfit and as lacking *unhu/ubuntu* (qualities of being human/humanness).

One more way of decolonizing the research process in addition to sharing a meal with communities relates to overnight accommodation (Alsugair, 2018). Among the Shona, there is a proverb that says *muenzi haapedzi dura* (a visitor does not empty your granary). This proverb is anchored in the value that the Shona, like other Bantu groups, place on hospitality. It emphasizes the importance of taking care of visitors. It is also a call to researchers to be prepared to put up with research participants in the event that they are invited to take lodgings with members of a host community. Refusal to accept such hospitality that would have been extended to the researchers is like in the case of turning down an offer to share a meal perceived as meaning that the researchers feel that they cannot stoop so low that they have to put up in the accommodation of their research participants whom they may perceive as the 'others'. It is therefore important that researchers be prepared to stay in communities and not hotels or camping sites. Communities need to feel that researchers are part of the community and that the story they will be researching on belongs to all of them and the researcher has only become an avenue through which it is getting out to the wider world (Lambert, 2011). As in the case of sharing meals, it has to be noted that it is usually after public engagements that at times new and additional information comes from hosts and their neighbours. Such information may be something that the community may have later discussed on their own and felt that the researcher would benefit from it. From an indigenous research perspective, it is therefore clear that sharing in meals as well as taking up accommodation as a guest to one of the host community's families, has benefits to the entire research project.

Indigenous communities believe in the interconnectedness of things. To them, people cannot be divorced from the bio-physical environment neither can they be removed from the extra-terrestrial world. This relational observation that makes up the indigenous worldview has to be embraced and acknowledged when one is carrying out research among indigenous communities (Cooper, Ball, Boyer-Kelly et al, 2019). This partly explains why at times there is the bringing in of issues like totems as ways of establishing relationships/kinship since no one is ever considered as an outsider among the Shona. Totems are important because they give members of the participating community room and scope on how they can relate to the researchers. My experience in south eastern Zimbabwe in Chiredzi, as well as in Lupane in Matabeleland shows the value of totems. The use of totems is significant in that it gives room for the placement of the researcher on a family plane; coming in for example as a daughter or a son-in-law. One thus gets more information as a family member than as an outsider. It is therefore important when carrying out research to always go beyond institutional and/ organizational identity and identify oneself through a totem. One will then be accepted for example as a son, daughter or son-in-law. Such acceptance opens more avenues for information gathering as well as potential of more participants taking part. This has the potential of ensuring that one gets genuine data and not information that is just provided by those who would have passed by to just get some financial benefits from some incentives that may be provided by the researcher(s).

Another important aspect that is tied up with the relational approach to indigenous research methods is that of sharing common stories and heritage. Most indigenous communities share common practices and ancestry. The fact that these stories persist means that their owners are related. When a researcher comes to their area in search of data for a certain project, it is easier to access information if one has some knowledge of part of the story. This knowledge is further strengthened if the researcher speaks the same language with members of the community from which data are being sourced. If there is an outsider, for instance a European or one of European extract, the chances of getting genuine and adequate information are more diminished when compared to one of their own. This has to do with the belief and acceptance that one of their own will want to tell their story. It is therefore important that an outsider have the assistance of a highly proficient speaker of the language of the host community. The outsider should also be prepared to accept the hospitality of the host community. This should not be difficult if the researcher is genuine given the fact that the same westerners embrace Arab culture and even partake in communal meals when they are negotiating business matters (Khakhar & Rammal, 2013; Constantini, Sforna, & Zoli, 2016). To therefore refuse indigenous hospitality elsewhere is nothing short of arrogance which results in inadequate or even falsified information from informants. What in short, a relational approach to indigenous research methods really means is that the researcher has to place indigenous values and practices at the core of his/her inquiry, especially given the fact that research and its findings have to be centred around the indigenous communities, and in the case of Africa, around the African (Asante, 1998). If this does not happen, then the indigenous participants may not give adequate information that is sought after since they may consider the researcher as one who does not understand and appreciate them.

A relational approach to indigenous research also demands that the researcher embraces myths and legends that are told by informants. A careful digging into these would usually yield positive information that can feed into the research agenda. A good example of such myths includes those linked with taboos. For a long time, taboos have been perceived as coming from people who are unschooled and are barbaric as well as heathens or non-believers when it comes to the Christian faith. However, Chemhuru and Masaka comment on the value of taboos when they state:

> Among Shona people, environmental taboos have a pivotal moral role toward the ontological wellbeing of both the individual person and the environment at large. Prohibitions and restrictions through taboos on unsustainable use of certain plant species, forests, mountains, rivers, pools and nonhuman animals, among other ecological species in the ecosystem, is not a new epistemology among the Shona people, but reflects a long tradition (Chemhuru & Masaka, 2010, p. 121).

While Chemhuru and Masaka focus on what they refer to as environmental taboos, what is essential to note is that a genuine researcher should not be dismissive of certain belief systems and practices because inherent in these are real issues that are of great importance to a given society. The example of taboos shows why it becomes important that the researcher be a member of the community or another indigenous person who is not only sympathetic to the host community but one whose own belief systems and practices are in common with those of the researched group. What also becomes clear from this observation is that western systems and methods of research cannot be relied on when it comes to researching among indigenous communities. It highlights why it is important that researchers abandon the so-called immersion approach and just leave matters relating to research of and among the indigenous communities to the indigenous people themselves. Immersion can possibly yield positive results if the immersee has a positive attitude and perceives as well as accepts the host and researched community as equals and not as the insignificant Other.

When it comes to approaches that relate to indigenous research pathways, one that is tied with the relational one is that of storytelling. Storytelling as used in the context of research should not be confused with that which relates to folktales although there is a link in that both relate to people's lives although in the case of folktales there is creativity and fictional elements although they are also embedded with themes that are true to life and engage with for instance environmental matters (Mutasa, Nyota & Mapara, 2008). In the context of academic inquiry, storytelling can be defined as the aptitude that the narrator has to shape life events into knowledge and understanding in a "web of stories rather than a monological narrative" (Boje & Rosile, 2010, p. 898). What has to be borne in mind when it comes to this research method is that it has to be noted that it does not take the given narratives as true and accurate representations (or reflections) of one's life experience (Boje & Rosile, 2010, p. 898) and yet in the act of telling, the different layers manifest other strands of information that may be lost if people are only to rely on that which is recorded, or that which is perceived to come from the horse's mouth, yet the donkey may have a more compelling and genuine story. This thus becomes another persuasive method that can be used as an indigenous research method and when undertaking research especially among indigenous communities. Ober underscores the importance of storytelling when she states:

> Storytelling or 'yarning' is embedded within the processes and structure of Aboriginal society. Stories are empowering and uplifting, giving access to layers of deep cultural and historical knowledge that make up the social and cultural identity of Aboriginal people (Ober, 2017, p. 8).

Although Ober is referring to the Aboriginal society, of which she is a member, and which is also an Australian indigenous group, her words are applicable when it comes to matters relating to research in other indigenous communities. What comes clearly out of her words is that storytelling, which she also calls yarning, is part of the fabric of Aboriginal society and this means that it is through storytelling that narratives relating to communities and life histories are passed down. She further underscores the fact that stories do not only uplift and empower communities, but they are also access points to matters relating to culture and the communities' histories.

30

Ober's insights, in fact, reveal that the use and deployment of western or Euro-American research methods to explore indigenous points of view has over and over again been felt and perceived by the majority of indigenous people to be inappropriate and ineffective in gathering information and promoting discussion with the researcher and among community members. The situation is not helped given the fact that there is never feedback from the researcher, and the researcher largely and in most cases is not only an outsider, but in the majority of cases chooses to remain an outsider and does not speak their language, and neither does s/he understand and practice their culture. However, on a comparative basis, the use of an indigenous storytelling approach as a research tool helps to create catenae of indigenous worldviews, thus "shaping the approach of the research; the theoretical and conceptual frameworks; and the epistemology, methodology, and ethics" (Datta, 2017, p. 35).

I have benefitted from the value of storytelling and has observed that it gives insights that are informed by local histories and traditions. By local histories here is meant what the I would like to call histories from below because these stories give other versions of history that do not necessarily echo what is said to be official or recorded accounts. For instance, on a research visit to Malunku in Lupane, in Zimbabwe's Matabeleland North Province, I noted that the local people have their own version of history that debunks the notion of memorializing Alan Wilson and his troop. The story is not just a celebration of Lobengula's last stand against British imperialism (Kenrick, 2019). Its significance furthermore lies in the fact that it makes manifest the point that memory is not necessarily physically represented by obelisks and statues but can reside within the people and is passed down intergenerationally. In addition, through storytelling and song, the researcher and colleagues learnt that the idea that the Ndebele were predatory on the Shona as captured in the words, "on the pretext of protecting the 'Mashona' (Shona) people from the predations of the 'Matabele' (Ndebele)" (Kenrick, 2019, p. 9) was but one of the myths that were crafted to have a successful divide and rule venture in the colony because some the Bantu people practiced raiding as part of their political economy in the pre-colonial era (King, 2017). The reality is that kingdoms were rising and falling and this fact is backed by the reality that there is a Ndebele traditional song that celebrates the fact that the people who were once Mambo's have become Mzilikazi's. This song as well dispels the idea that the Ndebele defeated the Shona under Mambo because the fall of the

Rozvi State was at the hands of Nyamazana, a Swati female military leader (Mutasa, 1990). Storytelling thus becomes important as the case of the Malunku community's stories falls in tandem with Smith (2012) who proposes that indigenous research methods should as well contribute to the re-writing of history given the fact that those who write history are the wielders of political and economic power.

Storytelling as a means of data collection as observed in the Malunku community has revealed that cultural and economic dynamics are important if one has to collect the correct and appropriate data. My colleagues and I observed that stories in this community are told by female seniors and not by men. The only plausible reason that I could see as having contributed to the women being storytellers has to do with Bantu culture where women are the main teachers and tellers even of folktales. This position may have been buttressed by the colonial economy that proletarianized the colonized Ndebele and Shona through the creation of a migrant labour system that caused the males to work in towns, mines and on white owned commercial farms, as well as the unfortunate ones who were made to work under *chibharo* (forced labour) (Madimu, 2017; van Onselen, 1976).

The importance of storytelling is also realized when it is observed that there are toponyms or place names that come up in narratives. It is essential that researchers pay attention to the names that come up because in those names may be other story strands. There are names like Pupu that for example come out of the Malunku community's narrative. Further probing revealed that the name is derived from the sound of gunfire exchanges as the Ndebele forces tried to repulse the Alan Wilson patrol and they succeeded in killing all members of that troop.

One of the popular data collection methods that westerners use is focus group discussions (FGDs). It is one of the ways used in qualitative research to gather information. FGD involves the bringing together of people from similar backgrounds or related experiences to discuss a specific topic of interest to the researcher. This method ensures that there will be a guide or moderator whose purpose is to introduce discussion topics and chairs ensuring that members stick to the objective(s) of the discussion. While this method is a good one, one advantage it has is that it approximates the indigenous Shona and Nguni *dare/inkundla*. The *dare* system is generally understood to be a court or judicial system where matters are resolved (Gwaravanda, 2011). This however is a narrow understanding. Outside hearing cases and deciding on them, the system is also a platform for the discussion of general issues relating to any subject of interest such as hunting practices. It was also a space where skills like the making of bows were imparted to the interested ones. It was and still is largely a male space with women only attending when there is a trial. Each family has its own *dare*. More mature women may be invited to the *dare* if there are matters to be clarified, because this was a place where the importance of community and family as captured in *Ubuntu* was nurtured and was given room to thrive. The demise of the *dare* and the movement to urban areas as well as into the Diaspora has led to individualism with each family enclosed in very high perimeter walls (real and psychological), that are also another form of coloniality.

The importance of the *dare* lies in the fact that it is a platform where even visitors are welcome. It is as well a space that a researcher, through an intermediary can introduce his/her topic of research and have it attended to. The advantage of presenting one's research topic to the dare's 'pot' is that it is open to analysis from different angles and by people with different experiences. No matter how difficult the topic may be, the Shona believe that *iri mudare iri murwenga, ichaibva* (the one that is in the court is in the roasting pan, it will get roasted). They mean that answers and solutions to a case presented will be found. What the *dare* as a research platform demands of the researcher is that s/he stays for longer than a day because a case may spill over such a period. It also means that there is need for preparation for a research tour that will accommodate such cultural set-ups. One thing worth noting is that while the *dare* has largely been a male space, it has of late been opened up to females because communities now accept that there are females who carry out studies, and also that there are females who may have more insights into certain matters when compared to their male counterparts.

One other advantage of the *dare* is that it allows the research to tap into the so-called uneducated (labelled 'informal' schooling in the West), – both old and young who are usually left outside the scope of most western research systems unless the inquiries being undertaken are anthropological and are aimed at 'confirming' some racial stereotypes about a given group of people. They have certain experiences and knowledge that the others may not have. The good that comes from interacting with those labelled as uneducated is that in such a set-up they are at home and they are free to speak their mind because the value of their words is embedded in their own experiences and research. They also have an opportunity to point out where for instance some practices are going wrong.

Conclusion

This chapter cannot be said to be conclusive in matters relating to indigenous research methods. What it has, however, done is to point out that the world of academic inquiry is in serious need of decontamination and this can only be through decolonizing the research space through engaging with methods that are used. It has brought forward several approaches that are pertinent if one is to successfully carry out research in an indigenous community. The chapter has pointed out that it is important that a researcher be one who is prepared to learn and not one who is there to find faults with communities and their ways of life. Additionally, it highlighted the value that is obtained when one becomes part of the community and thus avoids a 'them' and 'us/I' approach. Indigenous research approaches also call upon the researcher to share findings and involve communities in data interpretation so that there is co-ownership of the findings. The chapter has also underscored the need to avoid the weaponization of research, for instance, where entities fund research as a tool to further global capital's interests and not community well-being. Such lecherous behaviour is evidenced in cases where other people's indigenous knowledge is stolen and used for commercial purposes. Besides always bearing in mind that indigenous academic inquiry is relational, it has also brought to the fore the need to incentivise research participants as well as partaking in meals and other social activities so as to be part of the community. This includes accepting offers of overnight accommodation in their homes if such offers are extended. Other highlighted aspects include the relational characteristic of research and the value of storytelling as an important cog in the whole indigenous research agenda and as a means of decolonizing the research space. The chapter, in addition, noted that some spaces like the *dare* are critical in indigenous research as is equally true when it comes to toponyms. What the chapter has, thus, come up with is the emphasis on the importance of ceremony as part of the research which in itself is anchored in the language of the host communities. This is so because through language, one has an avenue through which s/he has of engaging with the heart of the story and of the community's song and drum.

References

Alcoff, L. (2007). Mignolo's Epistemology of Coloniality, *CR: The New Centennial Review*, 7(3), 79-101.

Alsugair, N. (2018). Conflicting Negotiation Styles and Strategies: Comparing Perspectives from Saudi Arabia & USA. https://www.mediate.com/articles/alsugairn1.cfm Retrieved on 23 January 2021.

Amadiume, I. (Fall 2015). Of Kola Nuts, Taboos, Leadership, Women's Rights, and Freedom: New Challenges from Chinua Achebe's There Was a Country: A Personal History of Biafra. *Journal of West African History*, 1(2), 119-146.

Asante, M. K. (2006). Afrocentricity: Notes on a Disciplinary Position. In Asante, M. K. & Karenga, M. (Editors). *Handbook of Black studies*. Thousand Oaks, California: SAGE Publications, Inc., (pp. 152-163).

Asante, M. K. (1998). *The Afrocentric Idea*. Philadelphia: Temple University Press.

Boje, D. M. & Rosile, G. A. (2010). Storytelling. In Mills, A. J., Durepos, G., & Wiebe, E. (Eds). *Encyclopedia of case study research* (Vols. 1-0). Thousand Oaks, CA: SAGE Publications, Inc. doi: 10.4135/9781412957397 pp. 898-900.

Castro-Gómez, S. (2007). The Missing Chapter of Empire: Postmodern Reorganization of Coloniality and Post-Fordist Capitalism, *Cultural Studies*, 21(2-3), 428-48.

Chemhuru, M. & Masaka, D. 2010. Taboos as sources of Shona people's environmental ethics. *Journal of Sustainable Development in Africa*, 12(7), 121-133.

Costantini, V. Sforna, G. & Zoli, M. (2016). Interpreting Bargaining Strategies of Developing Countries in Climate Negotiations a Quantitative Approach, *Ecological Economics*, 121, 128-139.

Cooper, D., Ball, T., Boyer-Kelly, M. N., Carr-Wiggin, A., Cornelius, C., Cox, J. W., Dupont, S., Fullerton, C., & Wong, D. (2019). *When research is relational: Supporting the research practices of Indigenous studies scholars*. Ithaka S+R Report. https://sr.ithaka.org/publications/supporting-the-research-practices-of-indigenous-studies-scholars/. Retrieved on 23 January 2021.

Datta, R. (2018). Traditional storytelling: an effective Indigenous research methodology and its implications for environmental research. *AlterNative: An International Journal of Indigenous Peoples,* *14*(1), 35–44. https://doi.org/10.1177/1177180117741351.

Denzin, N. K., Lincoln, Y. S. & Smith, L. T. (2008). (Editors). *Handbook of Critical and Indigenous Methodologies.* Thousand Oaks, California: SAGE Publications Inc.

English, D. K. (June 28, 2016). Eugenics. In Gene, J. (Ed). *Oxford Bibliographies in African American Studies.* New York: Oxford University Press. http://www.oxfordbibliographies.com/.

Grosfoguel, R. (2007). The Epistemic Decolonial Turn: Beyond Political-Economy Paradigms, *Cultural Studies* 21(2-3), 211-223.

Grosfoguel, R. (2006). World-System Analysis in the Context of Transmodernity, Border Thinking and Global Coloniality, *Review* 29(2), 167-187.

Grosfoguel, R. (2003). *Colonial Subjects: Puerto Ricans in a Global/Comparative Perspective.* Berkeley: University of California Press.

Gwaravanda, E. T. (2011). Philosophical Principles in the Shona Traditional Court System. *International Journal of Peace and Development Studies.* 2(5), 148-155.

Hernández, R. (2018). *Coloniality of the U-S//Mexico border: Power, violence, and the decolonial imperative.* Tucson: The University of Arizona Press.

Kenrick, D. (2019). *Decolonisation, Identity and Nation in Rhodesia, 1964–1979: A Race Against Time.* London: Palgrave-MacMillan.

Khakhar, P. & Rammal, H. G. (2013). Culture and business networks: International business negotiations with Arab managers, *International Business Review*, 22(3), 578-590.

King, R., (2017). Cattle, raiding and disorder in southern African history, *Africa* 87(3), 607-630.

Kovach, M. (2009). *Indigenous methodologies: Characteristics, conversations, and contexts.* Toronto: University of Toronto Press.

Kumaravadivelu, B. (2012). Individual Identity, Cultural Globalization, and Teaching English as an International Language: The Case for an Epistemic Break. In L. Alsagoff, W. Renandya, G. Hu, & S. L. Mckay (Editors). *Teaching English as an international language: Principles and practices* (pp. 9-27). New York: Routledge.

Lambert, L. (2011). The Eberhard Wenzel Oration: Two eyed seeing: Indigenous research methodologies. In *20th National Australian Health Promotion Association Conference*, 10-13 April 2011,

Cairns, Queensland, Australia. (Australian Health Promotion Association: Cairns, Queensland, Australia).

Little, B., & Malina, R. (2005). Inbreeding Avoidance in an Isolated Indigenous Zapotec Community in the Valley of Oaxaca, Southern Mexico. *Human Biology, 77*(3), 305-316. Retrieved January 25, 2021, from http://www.jstor.org/stable/41466328.

Lincoln, Y. S. (1995). Emerging criteria for quality in qualitative and interpretive inquiry. *Qualitative Inquiry* 1(3), 275-289.

Madimu, T. (2017). Farmers, miners and the state in colonial Zimbabwe (Southern Rhodesia), c. 1895–1961. PhD thesis, University of Stellenbosch.

Maldonado-Torres, N. (2007). On the Coloniality of Being, *Cultural Studies*, 21(2-3), 240-270, DOI: 10.1080/09502380601162548 Retrieved on 26 February 2021.

Mavhunga, C. C. (2021). The Global South Cosmologies & Epistemologies Initiative. Paper presented in a virtual talk hosted by Yale University's Environmental Humanities Unit, 26 February, 2021.

Mignolo, W. D. (2010). Epistemic Disobedience, Independent Thought and Decolonial Freedom. *Theory, Culture & Society*, *26*(7–8), 159-181. https://doi.org/10.1177/0263276409349275 Retrieved on 26 February 2021.

Mignolo, W. D. (2007). Introduction, *Cultural Studies*, 21(2-3), 155-167, DOI: 10.1080/09502380601162498 Retrieved on 26 February 2021.

Mutasa, D. E., Nyota, S., & Mapara, J. (2008). Ngano: Teaching Environmental Education Using the Shona Folktale. *The Journal of Pan-African Studies*, 2(3), 33-54.

Mutasa, N. M. (1990). *Misodzi, Dikita neRopa*. Gweru: Mambo Press.

Ober, R. (2017). Kapati Time: Storytelling as a Data Collection Method in Indigenous Research. *Learning Communities: Decolonising Research Practices*. Special Issue, Number 22, 8-15.

Ndlovu-Gatsheni, S. J. (2019). Provisional Notes on Decolonizing Research Methodology and Undoing Its Dirty History. *Journal of Developing Societies*, 35(4), 481-492. doi.org/10.1177/0169796X19880417 Retrieved on 26 February 2021.

Ndlovu-Gatsheni, S. J. (2013). The Entrapment of Africa within the Global Colonial Matrices of Power: Eurocentrism, Coloniality, and Deimperialization in the Twenty-first Century. *Journal of*

Developing Societies, 29(4), 331-353.
https://doi.org/10.1177/0169796X13503195 Retrieved on 26
February 2021.

Oleson, J. C. (2016). The New Eugenics: Black Hyper-Incarceration
and Human Abatement. *Social Sciences*, 5(4):66.
https://doi.org/10.3390/socsci5040066 Retrieved on 23 January
2021.

Porsanger, J. (2004). An essay about indigenous methodology.
Nordlit, 15, 105–120.

Quijano, A. (2007). Coloniality and Modernity/Rationality, *Cultural
Studies*, 21(2-3), 168-178, DOI: 10.1080/09502380601164353
Retrieved on 26 February 2021.

Quijano, A. (2000). Coloniality of Power and Eurocentrism in Latin
America. *International Sociology*, 15(2), 215-232.
https://doi.org/10.1177/0268580900015002005.

Resnik D. B. (2015). Bioethical Issues in Providing Financial
Incentives to Research Participants. *Medicolegal and bioethics*, 5, 35-
41. https://doi.org/10.2147/MB.S70416 Retrieved on 26
February 2021.

Rigney, L. I. (1999). Internationalization of an Indigenous
Anticolonial Cultural Critique of Research Methodologies: A
Guide to Indigenist Research Methodology and Its Principles.
Wicazo SA Review, 14(2), 109-121. doi: 10.2307/1409555
Retrieved on 23 January 2021.

Smith, L. T. (2012). *Decolonizing Methodologies: Research and Indigenous
Peoples*. London and New York: Zed Books.

Snow, K. C., Hays, D. G., Caliwagan, G., Ford Jnr, D. J., Mariotti,
D., Mwendwa, J. W. & Scott, W. E. (2016) Guiding principles
for indigenous research practices. *Action Research*, 14(4) 357–375.

Tuomainen, H. (2014). Eating alone or together? Commensality
among Ghanaians in London, *Anthropology of food*
http://journals.openedition.org/aof/7718; DOI:
https://doi.org/10.4000/aof.7718 Retrieved on 23 January 2021.

van Onselen, C. (1976). *Chibaro: African mine labour in Southern
Rhodesia, 1900-1933*. London: Pluto Press.

Walsh, C. (2007). Shifting the Geopolitics of Critical Knowledge,
Cultural Studies, 21(2-3), 224-239, DOI:
10.1080/09502380601162530 Retrieved on 26 February 2021.

Wolfe, P. (2006). Settler colonialism and the elimination of the
native, *Journal of Genocide Research*, 8(4), 387-409, DOI:
10.1080/14623520601056240 Retrieved on 23 January 2021.

Wynter, S. (2003). Unsettling the Coloniality of Being / Power / Truth / Freedom: Towards the Human, After Man, Its Overrepresentation – An Argument,' *CR: The New Centennial Review* 3 (3), 257-337.

Zavala, M. (2013). What do we mean by decolonizing research strategies? Lessons from decolonizing, indigenous research projects in New Zealand and Latin America. *Decolonization: Indigeneity, Education & Society*, 2(1), 55-71.

Zutlevics, T. L. (2016). Could providing financial incentives to research participants be ultimately self-defeating? *Research Ethics*, 12(3) 137-148.

Chapter 3

Indigenous Knowledge Across the Curriculum in the Global South: An Epistemic and Cognitive Shifting Process

Jacob Mapara

Abstract

This chapter, partly informed by the author's experiences, argues for the inclusion of indigenous knowledge in the higher education curriculum in institutions of the Global South. It points out that despite robust debates on it, it has hardly been made part of the curricula in most institutions of the Global South; remaining more of a borderline case. The chapter further asserts that there is lip-service to the cultural diversity of humanity because as relates to knowledge generation and dissemination, the epistemologies of the formerly colonized are peripherized; in most cases not even accepted and acknowledged. One would ask why the world celebrates the diversity of human cultures but fails to embrace the diversity of the globe's knowledges yet the same cultures in their plurality are products of varied epistemologies. The chapter is therefore a call to all across the disciplines to embrace an epistemic and cognitive or thought shift by accepting that IK is important to curriculum development. It consequently has to be included through curriculum review as part of the academic diet of both instructors and learners. It further asserts that a cognitive shift is possible if there is a deliberate policy to empower faculty and students to appreciate the value of IK that is overshadowed by the epistemic lancer of the Global North that was bequeathed to the former colonies and has up to this day been retained and promoted as the only and real universal knowledge. The chapter concludes that an epistemic and thought shift is only possible if IK itself is made part of the research agenda as well as one of the research methods and methodologies.

Keywords: epistemic shift, epistemic disobedience, cognitive shifting, indigenous knowledge

Introduction

We live in a world shrouded in hypocrisy. There is reference to the need to celebrate the diversity of humanity's cultures, but when it comes to knowledge generation and dissemination, the epistemologies of the formerly colonized are always peripherized and in most cases not even accepted and acknowledged (Hammersmith, 2007; Mawere 2012; Angelsupport, 2016). One would ask: Why does the world even bother to celebrate the diversity of human cultures but fails to embrace the diversity of the world's knowledges yet the same cultures in their plurality are products of an assortment of epistemologies? Even though it is also true that colonialism has always been part of human history, the reality is that its effects vary from mild to extreme. For instance, the country that was at one time the globe's biggest imperial and colonial power, Britain was at one time itself a Roman colony. One of the world's biggest colonial powers in terms of cultural and political hegemony is the United States of America, which itself is a former British colony. Through the colonial enterprise, what the United States and other countries in the West (the Euro-American axis) have done is to embark on an epistemological dismemberment of indigenous ways of being and knowing by way of ignoring and demonizing other epistemologies which they have stealthily harvested and repackaged as their own (Kumar, 2019; Mukuka, 2010; Barsh, 2001). What is also worth noting as regards colonialism is that there are two types of colonialism that I will term benevolent and virulent or malevolent. The benevolent type of colonialism is like that which Britain itself was subjected to as part of the Roman Empire when it was occupied by Rome from 43 CE to 410 BCE (Salway, 2015). While the Romans as in all colonial cases were outsiders, they were not as brutal as the colonialists who were to, later on, occupy Africa and some parts of Asia and the Pacific later, neither were they as vicious as the European colonists in the Americas who went on to decimate local and indigenous communities. With the benefit of hindsight, it can be observed that the European colonization of other lands was never for purposes of trade but effective occupation and dispossession coupled with genocide where possible. It is this type of malevolent colonialism that was visited upon Africa, among other continents.

Colonialism, as practised in Africa, resulted in genocide as witnessed in the Belgian Congo also known as Leopold's Congo (Hochschild, 1999; Nzongola-Ntalaja, 2002; Reybrouck, 2014) and in

Namibia (then German South-West Africa) where the Germans committed the first genocide of the twentieth century (Baer, 2017). This genocide was a result of the othering of the colonized as non-humans or at best as sub-humans who needed the light of Christianity and Western education to catch up with their European brothers and sisters who perceived themselves as superior and more advanced, a cancer that has persisted to this day as the policing of Afro-Americans in the United States reveals (Hattery & Smith, 2018). Even though colonialism is said to have ended with the attainment of political independence, colonialism and Christianity have continued to shape and give direction to the lives of the formerly colonized. Informed by decoloniality, this chapter thus argues that while physical colonialism has ended, a new and more virulent type of colonialism (neo-colonialism) persists and it has led to the death of most indigenous communities not in the physical sense but spiritually and culturally in a form of genocide that Merhag (2006) calls identicide because of physical and intellectual relocations (Merhag, 2001). Identicide is the premeditated and intentional as well as planned and well-executed, systematic and targeted annihilation of the spaces, symbols, objects related to material culture, comprising of ideas, values and aesthetics, and other cultural property, both tangible and intangible that is accepted and held to represent the identity of a people. This is done with the deliberate aim to erase and obliterate their cultural presence and narrative. It is also carried out to demoralize a particular population; assimilate it into a different cultural/political verity, or to entirely purge an area of those people (Merhag, 2001; 2003; 2006). In light of Merhag's observations, it can be noted that deliberate epistemic violence was meted out and continues to be inflicted on the formerly colonized of the Global South and the result is an epistemicide where the knowledges of the latter are considered as non-knowledge and that of the Global North is embraced as the real knowledge and the only one that is to be acknowledged as universal/global. This Euro-American epistemological hegemony smacks of arrogance and racism because the reality is that Africa, besides other formerly colonized communities, has "local cultural knowings as legitimate sources of knowledge" and it is thus imperative to acknowledge and "recognize African peoples as producers and creators of knowledge" (Emeagwali & Sefa Dei, 2014, p. ix). It is this deliberate refrain from recognizing indigenous knowledges that has caused the brutal purging and exclusion of IK from all curricula, where at best it has

43

been embraced as pseudoscience (De Beer & Van Wyk, 2019; Shizha, 2014).

Through an epistemic and cognitive shift, the formerly colonized people right the deficient ways through which the West had defined them through a deliberate act of seeking self-determination. This very act of seeking self-determination becomes an imperative that allows them to "discover and recover their IK and sense of self, mourn the pain inflicted upon them by colonisation, etc" (Le Grange, 2019, p. 29; Mudaly, 2018). Such an act of recovery and redress through the inclusion of IK in the curriculum is important because it is in addition a restoration of the indigenous people's lost dignities (Mawere, 2012; Balfour, 2019).

In the context of this chapter, indigenous communities have to develop their local epistemologies and raise them to a level that is equal if not better to that of the West and also being guided by these knowledge forms at all levels of education, but more specifically in higher education and training where there is need for different epistemologies to engage, with African ones being made more visible (Abidogun, 2020), and thus most examples will be drawn from Zimbabwe. The higher education curriculum can for that reason benefit if the indigenous communities are allowed through engagement for an inclusive curriculum to rediscover and recover from the effects of colonialism by being given space to reclaim their culture and identity (Mudaly, 2018; Shizha, 2014; Mawere, 2012). They should also be given room to grieve over their unrelenting oppression that is perpetuated through the university curriculum. An epistemic shift is therefore attainable if they are allowed to dream and re-imagine an alternative university curriculum that is impregnated with their IK (Mudaly, 2018). Worth noting, however, is the fact that there is a need for commitment towards raising awareness on ensuring that voices of these marginalized people are not muted by the powerful such as academics and politicians; but should practically take bold and concrete steps that will be reflective of the value of their IKs (Mudaly, 2018).

Given the fact that indigenous epistemologies are grounded in indigenous knowledge (IK), it is important to first of all discuss what IK is as well as its value as both theory and practice. The chapter then goes on to discuss how as theory and practice IK informs epistemic and cognitive shifts and how these alterations can be effected through the proffering of some examples, in selected curriculum areas.

What is IK?

The word indigenous knowledge designates a structured and well thought out body of knowledge that is a cherished acquisition of a local or indigenous community of a given region that is brought about by a building up or accrual of skills and practices. These come from informal experiments and close appreciation of the surroundings in a given culture. Although the expression 'indigenous' is considered by some as a controversial one (Smith, 2012), it is used in this context to refer to the original residents of a given geographical area and who in a historical sense have not come from elsewhere. Within the framework of global politics, all people who have moved to other continents from somewhere else cannot be called indigenous. For example, those of European and Arab extract cannot be said to be indigenous to Africa, even though we now have Arabs being the dominant ones in most of North Africa and being members of the African Union. The Arabs conquered North Africa which was populated by the Amazigh among other indigenous communities from as late as around 700 AD (Arauna et al, 2017; El Aissati, 2005; Ilahiane, 2006) and embarked on among other atrocities, slavery, a practice that has persisted to this day (Dudley, 2008; ILO, 2017). On the other hand, the so-called modern and Western knowledge is awareness and understanding that is largely generated in laboratories through formalized ways of education and research although it is also tempered with racial perceptions, especially on matters relating to racial superiority through singularly regarding Western knowledge as the only genuine one.

Indigenous knowledge is significant when it comes to engagements with decoloniality and the decolonization of the curriculum. It percolates into decolonial theories as much as it feeds the practice of decolonizing the higher education curriculum. As part of the decolonial theory, it highlights the fact that knowledge is not generated from one area or a product of one race but underscores the fact that there are many knowledges and these need to be tapped into for the benefit of humanity.

IK in reality consequently becomes a general principle or body of principles that can be used to explain epistemologies of the Global South that have sustained communities for long (Gumbo, 2015) and accordingly qualify to be incorporated into theoretical frameworks as illuminators that make inclusion into curriculum matters clearer. IK is as well important in that it helps shed some light on how an

45

epistemic shift can be attained in the higher education sector when it comes to the utilization and implementation of IK as part of academic practice across the disciplines (De Beer, 2019; Sefa Dei, 2014; Shizha, 2014; Mudaly, 2018).

IK can be applied to curriculum design and implementation including areas such as methods and methodologies in instruction and research (Smith & Webber, 2019; Johnson & Nelson-Barber, 2019). The adoption and use of IK in curriculum design and even amelioration is of course only possible if there is a deliberate cognitive shifting on the part of the curriculum planners and designers and to a lesser extent on the part of the consumers, especially parents and guardians of learners (De Beer, 2019; Mawere, 2012).

Cognitive shifting

The significance and meaning of critical and reflective thinking is anchored on cognitive shifting which is the psychological and intellectual process of wilfully redirecting one's concentration from one fixation and obsession to a different one that an individual considers of great value to him/her. On the contrary, if this course of action occurred instinctively, then it is referred to as task switching. Cognitive shifting and task switching are both forms of cognitive flexibility (Cools, 2015) and both are critical when it comes to responding to curriculum issues that are discussed in this chapter. Cognitive shifting or thought shifting can also be called a mind shift which is a change of focus and insight. It has the potential to help those who undergo it to develop new insights that can be groundbreaking and that can impact not just perceptions but also the way people do things and act in given circumstances, especially in an environment where internationalization is taking root in universities and may result in the mere whitewashing of the curriculum (Du Preez, 2018; Le Grange, Du Preez, Ramrathan & Blignaut, 2020). A good example of a mind shift is the epistemic shift that Freire (1972) underwent when he developed his thoughts on education and praxis. Successful cognitive shifting is essential if the higher education curriculum is to be effectively decolonized, deconstructed and reconstructed. Linked to the idea and significance of cognitive shifting is that of an epistemic shift (Emeagwali & Shizha, 2016).

Epistemic shift

Ndlovu-Gatsheni (2013) laments the fact that Africa, despite her being the cradle of humankind is still entrapped in the "global matrices of power underpinned by Eurocentrism and coloniality" (p. 332). He further posits that notwithstanding the reality that Africans have initiated some of the most protracted and heroic anti-slavery and anti-colonial struggles, the tragedy has always been that in most cases these resistance movements have been underpinned by terminology that was shaped and given direction by the pervasive logic of modernity and coloniality that effectively turned these struggles into emancipatory and reformist forces rather than revolutionary and anti-systemic movements. The result was and has been that decolonization as a people's revolutionary project died. Ndlovu-Gatsheni is thus calling for the decolonization struggle to be picked up by the formerly colonized, and he sees the higher education curriculum as one of the spaces where engagement with colonialism has to take place, and this can be possible through an epistemic shift or disobedience.

The idea of an epistemic shift is informed by Aníbal Quijano's (2000) notion of the "colonial matrix of power" and the contestation of Santiago Castro-Gómez's (2005) unilateral knowledge production. The underlying conception is that the formerly colonized world is still in the grip of colonial hegemony which is perpetuated through Western educational models that have placed Western knowledge on the world platform and have promoted it as universal which in reality is not the case, largely so when there are unintended (to the colonized) consequences of the alienation of the self from relatives and practices as noted by Ezeanya-Esiobu (2019). What thence comes out is that through the inherited colonial education systems, colonialism has been placed in a self-sustaining mode that is further fed into by scholarships and exchange programmes that are funded by Western institutions and governments. Mignolo (2009) also comments on the non-neutrality of Western education positing on its biases towards the Global North as the bastion of knowledge. He points out that there was once a time when scholars assumed that knowledge is neutral and is untainted by the geopolitical configurations of the world. This, however, is a fallacy in a world where people are racially ranked and profiled with the regions where they come from also racially configured (Hattery & Smith, 2018). This observation speaks to the need for an epistemic shift. This necessity for an epistemic shift and delinking from the colonial matrix of power is amplified when Noda (2020, 2007, p. 1) observes "Western intellectual colonisation plays a deciding role in the development of the discipline, which is reflected not only on what is considered proper knowledge, but also in what is published". These words underscore the grip that Western hegemony has in gate-keeping as well as in promoting and entrenching Western epistemology. It is worth noting that Western intellectual colonization decides on what is acceptable and not acceptable in a world that is supposed to embrace globalization. It therefore turns out that globalization is nothing other than the westernization of the world through a different name. What it, thus, means is that there is a need for the formerly colonized to shift and not necessarily move away from western epistemologies but develop new ones that are informed by indigenous knowledge and also the best that comes out of the West. This is because Western epistemology has not been friendly to the formerly colonized. The need to treat Western epistemologies with suspicion is affirmed by the Shona proverb, "*Chabva kumwe bata nemushonga* (That which has been brought from elsewhere has to be sanitized first before it is handled) (Mapara & Mpofu-Hamadziripi, 2014, p. 172).

Situated within the discourse of decoloniality, epistemic shift proposes delinking through what Mignolo (2007) also calls "epistemic disobedience" whose aim is of course to contest the colonial matrix of power. The core thrust that this argument presents is that epistemic disobedience or defiance is important because it as is highlighted by Noda (2020), interrogates the hegemony of the West over knowledge production and the labelling of Western epistemic values as universal. The idea behind epistemic disobedience which is a more militant version of epistemic shift is to, however, not to delegitimize the Western knowledge forms that are grounded in the Judaeo-Christian heritage coupled with Latin and Greek traditions, but to question why they should be accepted and peddled as the only forms of knowledge that matter and as the only ones on which humanity can develop and prosper (Mignolo, 2007).

As can be realized in the foregoing paragraph, the call for an epistemic shift/disobedience is anchored as Mignolo notes, on the need to move away from Euro-centred thoughts, that are "ingrained in Greek and Latin categories of thoughts and the experiences and subjectivities formed from that foundation, both theological and secular" (Mignolo, 2007. p. 12). The problem of depending on a

Eurocentric epistemology is that thinkers are largely bound to evolve around the thoughts of the canonized scholars of Western thought and philosophy like Freud and Lacan such that scholars like Mignolo who may have radical views:

> won't be able to transgress the limits of Marxism, the limits of Freudism and Lacanism, the limits of Foucauldianism; or the limits of the Frankfurt School, including such a superb thinker grounded in Jewish history and German language like Walter Benjamin (Mignolo, 2007, p. 12).

In the words above, Mignolo is emphasizing the need for embracing knowledge and thinking that come from other traditions and calls upon the world to remove the cloak of Euro-centrism and embrace a truly universal one, where even thoughts and epistemologies from the Global South become part and parcel of the ingredients that contribute to what may genuinely become universal knowledge. In fact, through echoing Mignolo (2010) and Quijano (2000), some African scholars like Ezeanya-Esiobu (2019) argue for the indigenization of the curriculum.

An epistemic shift or disobedience does not, therefore, entail jettisoning all Western knowledge. It is just a negotiation for all knowledge forms to be accepted as knowledge that can empower communities and can inform innovation, creativity and development. It is in light of this that Mignolo pleads to be understood as one who is "affirming the co-existence of de-colonial thinking" (p. 12) which should thus not mean that he is in any way "delegitimizing European critical thoughts or post-colonial thoughts grounded in Lacan, Foucault and Derrida." Mignolo with reference to Lacan, Foucault and Derrida buttresses his argument on the need for epistemic disobedience by declaring:

> I have the impression that intellectuals of post-modern and Marxist bent take as an offence when the above-mentioned author, and other similar, are not revered as believers do with sacred texts. *This is precisely why I am arguing here for the de-colonial option as epistemic disobedience* (Mignolo, 2007, p. 12).

The fact that he has the last words italicized speaks to the importance that he is placing on the need for us to take the best out of both epistemologies. The idea is not to be hypnotized by only one form of knowledge but to critically analyse each and come up with the best options that can inform institutional curriculum development. This, as a result, calls not only for an epistemic shift or disobedience but also for cognitive shifting especially on the part of responsible authorities and academics in institutions of higher learning. They naturally have to bear in mind the diversity that colours our varied heritages. They should not be forced to only depend on Western informed epistemologies that are a product of one heritage, but should also look at what can be retrieved or salvaged from the heritages of the formerly colonized who through western education and Christianity have almost been spiritually and intellectually been exterminated from the face of the earth in a systematic but deliberate identicide (Merhag, 2001; 2003; 2006).

IK in and across the disciplines

Our major problem is that when guns for the liberation war fell silent we celebrated victories which in reality have turned out to be pyrrhic. After investing so much of our youths, we went ahead and entrenched ourselves in the education system of the former colonizer and even expanded it. The result of such an education is that we have a lot of people who are devoid of *ubuntu*, a people that are but the walking dead. We are physically alive but spiritually and morally dead. We act to the stimulus of Western capitalism and its cannibalistic culture and perceive and accept such a culture as progressive and civilized.

A successful epistemic shift is only possible if we learn from our histories. We first have to interrogate who the writers of our history are (Smith, 2012). In addition, through rediscovering our history, we need to rediscover ourselves as well. Most, if not all see our history as having come into being with the advent of colonialism. This sad reality was also peddled by white racist scholars like Trevor-Roper who asserted that there was no African history other than the history of the presence of the white man in Africa. He even declared that Africa was not part of the world and had nothing to exhibit (Trevor-Roper, 1964; Poulsen, 1981). Trevor-Roper's racist rants are not new because effectively what Europe has written about Africa has been about her being backward and as a geographical space that Europe discovered and brought to life. Most of what European historians, adventurers-cum-anthropologists and missionaries have written about Africa is negative. For instance, most European writers tend to present Tshaka, the founder of the Zulu nation in South Africa as

50

a brutal savage, which is not true (Wylie, 2006). Interestingly western scholars present marauding warlords like Alexander the Great in positive light despite the carnage they caused (Bowden, 2014; Freeman, 2011). Surprisingly, the same writers present the likes of ruthless and brutal European warlords such as Hitler and Rhodes, among others, as gallantry, fearless and visionary.

The problem with the current education curriculum is that it is driven and further improved on by people who have taken bucketfuls from a poisoned mega chalice. This education has caused us not to embrace histories of our own like Tshaka as discussed above, and even accept that he was a savage. Very few among most people in Africa have ever questioned what the so-called Great Alexander did (Rodney, 2011). He is presented to most Africans as great and that descriptor sticks. The same is true of one of the most brutal people in the history of the Caribbeans, Christopher Columbus who is labelled as a thief, mass-murderer and slave trader (Tinker & Freeland, 2008). What the history that is taught in our schools today, just like any other discipline, does is to place Europe at the centre of the global knowledge production machine (Akena, 2012).

What the argument that Mignolo (2012) and others like Ndlovu-Gatsheni (2014), Castro-Gomez (2005), Quijano (2000), Noda (2020), Shizha (2014), De Beer (2019) and Ezeanya-Esiobu (2019) present boils down to is the bringing on board of other epistemologies, which are effectively and largely indigenous ones. It is also a generally accepted fact that most, if not all epistemologies of the formerly colonized are found in their indigenous knowledges, whether they are the First Nations in North America, Latin America or the Occident. The same is true when it comes to the formerly colonized of the African continent. The first step towards a successful epistemic shift is cognitive shifting and this is only possible through intrinsic motivation and self-determination. One has to have it in him or her to accept that an epistemic shift on curriculum matters is possible by learning from even the history of the former colonial powers themselves. A look at Western systems of education shows that despite the similarities that exist between them, they are in some ways different in the way they are modelled and implemented. They are also each informed by the philosophies that are on the firmament of their cultures. This is what Africa needs to do. She needs to develop curricula that are informed by African values especially the philosophy of *ubuntu* and the umbrella practices that are enshrined in IK. However, these values can become

51

entrenched if we know what a curriculum is, as well as its importance in the teaching-learning engagements as well as in the broader scope of world epistemologies. It is important to point out here that the idea is not to completely jettison what Africa has inherited from the West, but that we should embellish what is already there with indigenous knowledge (Samuel, 2017). This embellishment is what is also discussed in this chapter. As efforts are made to decolonize the curriculum, members need to bear in mind that:

> Decoloniality, without a doubt, is also contextual, relational, practice-based, and lived. In addition, it is intellectually, spiritually, emotionally, and existentially entangled and interwoven. The concern of this part I then is with the ongoing processes and practices, pedagogies and paths, projects and propositions that build, cultivate, enable, and engender decoloniality, this understood as a praxis – as a walking, asking, reflecting, analyzing, theorizing, and auctioning – in continuous movement, contention, relation, and formation (Walsh, 2018, p. 19).

These words are important because they emphasize and draw attention to the actuality that higher education and education in general as well as the knowledge that is imparted through them is not neutral. What the above words also underscore is the idea that as higher education faculty members in the Global South prepare their curriculum and teaching material, they have to be alive to the fact that they operate in an environment where the "hierarchical structures of race, gender, heteropatriarchy, and class" (Walsh, 2018, p. 17) are entrenched. These persistently control among other issues people's lives as well as determining what constitutes knowledge, spirituality, and thought and ultimately determine even how knowledge, as regards these, is constructed and imparted.

Politics of the curriculum and effects on society

While in dictionaries, the term *curriculum* is habitually defined as the courses offered by a school or college; it is worth noting that it is infrequently used in such a general sense in schools and colleges. When used by education practitioners, the word curriculum refers to the lessons and academic content that is taught in a school or a particular course or program. To educators, the term 'curriculum' usually refers to the knowledge and skills that students are expected to learn in most cases in a given timeframe, which today is now measured in hours (hence credit hours). The curriculum thus includes the learning principles/values or learning objectives that the learners are expected to meet. It also includes the units and lessons that teachers teach; the assignments and projects given to students; the books, materials, videos, presentations, and readings used in a course. In the end, a curriculum should provide room for tests, assessments, and other methods that are accepted as appropriate that are used to evaluate student learning (https://www.edglossary.org/curriculum/). While these words are critical, they fall short in that they do not state the politics that come into play in matters relating to what goes into a curriculum and why this is so. It, therefore, means that no curriculum is innocent. Every learning program is a product that is shaped by the interests of its developers, not the consumers of the intended learning. What is sad is also the reality that most scholars whose texts are given in reading lists in most universities in Africa are not only the main drivers of Western cultural elements but are also largely European and male whose agenda is the domination of the world, especially sub-Saharan Africa.

A curriculum has to be understood as a product of politics (Levin, 2007). In the case of the former colonized, their curriculum is about the power and hegemony of the Global North. Since politics is about power, it is safe to conclude that a curriculum is what the powerful design for those without power to learn. This reality about politics as the exercise of power by those who wield it makes Tinder's words quite apt when she describes a political system as "a set of arrangements by which some people dominate others" (1991, p. 162). The sad reality that is carried in these words is replicated in African universities where the knowledge that is taught, assessed and approved is not that which is empowering but that which makes institutions of higher education of the Global South to be producers of labour for capitalist enterprises that are dotted across the globe. It is an education that does not empower, as it leads to what is generally called a brain drain (Falola, 2020). What is also very bad about the curriculum that is implemented is that it does not acknowledge indigenous knowledge; neither does it acknowledge indigenous peoples' achievement through, for instance, the appropriation of indigenous knowledge for areas like the sciences (De Beer, 2019; Le Grange, 2019). The effect of the non-acknowledgement of IK has uprooted the formerly colonized from their base and as a result they ape the West, but the West itself does not embrace them. This is very clear if cases of White police officers shooting and killing African

Americans in the United States and other western countries are anything to go by. Closer home is the case of xenophobia in South Africa. All victims of this Black-on-black violence are fellow Africans. The South African case is a manifestation of how the Black person has been educated to hate him/herself (Crush, 2020). The results are not just about people who do not embrace their knowledge systems but also of people who have come to hate themselves such that they even bleach their skins to get closer to being white. For an effective epistemic shift as well as cognitive shifting's success there is need to revisit the curricula that are offered in our tertiary institutions and incorporate indigenous knowledge and values so that the products who come out of such institutions are Africans not just in colour but also in thought and focus. It is therefore important that IK be taught across the curriculum. This, of course, does not mean throwing away what the West has bequeathed to us. There is a need to pick the good that is in the western-inspired curricula. This has to be combined with what comes from IK.

Indigenizing the higher education curriculum: some examples

The indigenization of the higher education curriculum is only possible if there is a willingness and a deliberate epistemic and cognitive shift on the part of the curriculum planners as well as implementers. This in actuality is what is proposed by Mbah, Johnson and Chipindi (2021) when they state that there is need for engaged universities that play important roles that relate to regional realities through the legitimation of indigenous knowledge systems, and their institutionalization. They further state that the inclusion of indigenous knowledge is essential for sustainable development utilizing a context and culture propelled contrivance. There, of course, has to be political will and a willingness to take a lead through the engagement of key stakeholders. This is possible if the key stakeholders feel that they are part of the shift and not outsiders. This has the effect of creating a sense of ownership of the curriculum. Other stakeholders like industries and other business and commerce actors need to be also brought on board.

In light of what is presented in the foregoing paragraph, what African universities such as those in Zimbabwe, as well as those of other countries in the Global South that are in the same predicament with African countries need to come up with curricula that place value on the subjugated as well as marginalized knowledge of the formerly colonized. The curricula should therefore place value on indigenous knowledge "not only for the culture that produced it but also for people from different cultures" (Kincheloe & Steinberg, 2008, p. 149). The advantage of being all-embracing lies in the fact that the relevance of what is taught and studied is material that most students, if not all can easily relate to. For Africa, there is a need to also learn from what has been appropriated from her as well as what global capitalism has in addition stolen from other cultures and made it global, but from a different axis. More importantly, however, is the need to include IK into the current university curricula and some studies have proven that this is possible (Pedzisai & Tsvere, 2019).

It is important to look at the value of indigenous ways of imparting knowledge like folktales and storytelling in some, if not all disciplines that are offered by institutions of higher education and training. For example, what is the value of the appropriated African folktales in *The Lion King* to the corporate world in terms of boardroom politics and management? What about to political scientists as regards building consensus and democracy? Naturally, such stories have a bearing to those whose critical thinking skills are well developed. Today we live in a world where some query the value of the humanities in a world that is said to be highly technologized. Those who query the value of humanities or IK fail to realize that technology is more than ICT whose focus is largely on communication. If our stories, religions, myths and legends were not important, one would ask why the US's NASA would name one of the largest craters on the dwarf planet Ceres Chaminuka. Chaminuka was the spirit that possessed one Pasipamire before what is today Zimbabwe was colonized by the British South Africa Company that Queen Victoria had granted a charter to occupy the land north of the Limpopo. He is one of the major supra-territorial and supra-tribal spirits of Zimbabwe (Auret, 2007; Chivaura, 2009). While to some this may appear to be just a naming case, the reality is that the western world and its curricula demonizes the formerly colonized's religions and spiritual leanings, and later misappropriate them (Kumar, 2019; Nayak, 2019). In the paragraphs that follow below, the chapter discusses examples of disciplines offered in Zimbabwean universities that can be indigenized; in other words, that can easily have indigenous knowledge elements incorporated as part of the curriculum.

The foregoing paragraph makes manifest the reality about what indigenous knowledge can contribute to in terms of global knowledges as well as belief systems as embodied in legends from other regions, and not just from the Global North. Maybe one important question to ask when it comes to programmes of study is: What can a logistics company learn from Indigenous weather forecasting knowledge whether at management or driver level? (Pedzisai & Tsvere, 2019). Outside the issue of myths, legends and the study of celestial bodies and other forms that are in outer space, it can be realized that indigenous ways of life can contribute to other areas such as logistics. Research by Pedzisai and Tsvere (2019) has, for instance, shown the value of indigenous knowledge when it comes to academic disciplines like Supply Chain Management. The duo point out that there is a lot, for instance, that a logistics company can learn from indigenous weather forecasting knowledge. They argue that it is important for employees, especially drivers to be aware of indigenous ways of weather forecasting that are informed by the flora and fauna of their areas of operation. They point out that this knowledge will minimize their chances of, for instance, getting stuck on slippery and muddy roads in some of the areas they would have gone to make deliveries.

With the focus still on Supply Chain Management and the value of indigenizing the existing curricula in universities and other higher education institutions, we realize that it pays to incorporate matters relating to relationships as is realized when it comes to the logistical landscape that relates to most rural businesses, especially as observed in Zimbabwe. What was noted in a study by Mapara and Saidi (2019) was that relationships play a significant role in the supply chain system for most rural businesspersons. Community relationships glued together by *ubuntu* and anchored on practices such as recognition of the value of totems (*mitupo*) place people on a relationship plane that makes some, for example, sons, daughters or even nephew/nieces (*vazukuru/abazukulu*). In such roles, it is relationships that are valued more than money and one who may have space in his vehicle, especially a truck can carry the supplies for a relative who runs a rural business just for money for a 'drink'. This does not mean that businesses do not need the money, but costs for transporting goods, for instance, from a faraway place are minimized and in some cases eliminated. Naturally, it is also essential for curriculum planners to look not just at who brings materials but also at consumers in terms of the use of either cash or other means like labour supply or barter for goods (Mapara & Saidi, 2019).

Echoing the suggestion of Pedzisai and Tsvere (2019) as well as Mapara and Saidi (2019), though with a focus on STEM subjects and in the South African context, Mudaly (2018, p. 52), states:

> To address the epistemic violence that the colonial education canon inflicts on students, I sought a new orientation to teaching and learning. This was achieved by re-appropriating IK and requesting support from an IK expert to teach part of the module.

These words are important because they underscore the veracity that lies in the values of indigenous knowledges in the creation and development of appropriate higher education curricula as part of the decolonial movement.

Another discipline that can benefit a lot from a deliberate cognitive and epistemic shift when it comes to the indigenization of the curriculum is Agriculture (Ponge, 2013). IK can contribute in the areas such as land use, seed identification and preservation as well as crop harvesting and post-harvest technology, especially in the context of improving livelihoods and food security in communities (Kuyu & Bereka, 2020; Masarirambi, Mavuso, Songwe, Nkambule & Mhazo, 2010). For indigenous communities, land use patterns are dictated by knowledge of local ecology and cultural systems such as belief systems. One way in which the Shona managed and prevented stream bank cultivation was the conversion of stream banks into burial grounds for still borne children as well as those who died before they were three or four years old. To promote this practice, a taboo which stated that if such children were not interred on stream banks, the mother's womb would become dry was used as the propellant. What the proscription meant was that the woman who would have lost her child would never give birth again if her child was buried on ground that was designated as for adults or children from five and above. The effect of this interdiction was that no one wanted to cultivate areas that were not just designated as burial ground for the very young and still-borne but also because of the fear that all stream banks are living burial areas.

The curricula should also promote teaching and research on the importance of indigenous farmers identifying and developing their seeds instead of buying hybrid ones, in the process promoting seed sovereignty, a situation where farmers are not dependent on multinational companies like Monsanto (Petersen, 2014). Although hybrid seeds are said to give better yields, in most economies of former colonies, most farmers cannot afford to always buy seeds for each cropping season because of financial incapacitation (Ezeanya-Esiobu, 2019). The other disadvantage of relying on hybrid and GMO seeds is that they are less nutritious and less tasty. This means that while they may be filling, they are not necessarily good for consumers' health.

Some elements that are indigenous and that have to be included in developing a curriculum that contributes to sustainable livelihoods and food security include those that focus on the value of the cooperative principle. In Zimbabwe, this can be found in activities like work parties (*humwe/majangano*) where people come together and work on a particular person's fields (Payn, 2012; Siambombe, Mutale & Muzingili, 2018). This is repeated as they move on to the next person's and so on. The cooperative principle also works when it comes to the type of seed to grow as well as when to plant so that people can share the burden of pests and not have one farmer becoming a victim. In addition, the same principle can be extended to working on practices like *zunde ramambo* (the chief's field) where community members either go and work on a given day in a field that is said to be the chief's but in reality is a grain reserve that is kept under the traditional leader's custody for the benefit of widows and orphans. Today, some have modified this method and now allow members to make contributions from their harvests instead of going to that specific field. Emphasis should be placed on the value of such practices to food security and sustainable livelihoods.

Several other indigenous practices can be brought on board to indigenize the higher education curriculum especially in Agriculture and Sustainable Livelihoods programmes. One of such practices is agroforestry which involves the planned and intentional maintenance and planting of trees in a given area for purposes of developing a microclimate that contributes to the protection of crops against weather extremes and also helps in reducing poverty (Nair & Garrity, 2012). By blending agricultural and forestry methods, this helps to control among other elements temperature and sunlight exposure (Liu, Yao, Wang & Liu, 2019; Rosati, Borek & Canali, 2020). The same practice helps to make available a variety of products such as food, firewood and medicine. It also contributes to the improvement of soil quality, reducing erosion, and storing carbon (Perroni, 2017).

Another important indigenous practice that contributes to food security worth incorporating into the higher education curriculum is that of crop rotation which has been in use for millennia and is still in use today in many African communities. Through this technique, farmers grow diverse crops on the same piece of land so that no plot has the same produce planted in consecutive seasons (Hamed, Fouda & Emara, 2019). Crop rotation contributes to the preservation of the productive capability of the soil (Woźniak, 2019). It also contributes to pest and disease control which increases the chances of reduction in the use of chemical herbicides and pesticides (Woźniak, 2019).

Other indigenous methods that have been marginalized but are significant in their contribution to food security, and have to be included as part of the higher education Agriculture curriculum are mixed cropping and polyculture. Also known as intercropping, mixed cropping is when farmers sow more than two crops at the same time on the same piece of land (Perroni, 2017). Through planting multiple crops, farmers make the most of land use at the same time reducing the risks associated with single crop failure. Intercropping also creates biodiversity, which attracts a variety of beneficial and predatory insects that reduce pests and increase soil organic matter, decontaminate the soil (Perroni, 2017). They, in addition, suppress weed growth while some of the weeds are harvested as vegetables that can be used later after being dried when the wet season is over (Altieri, 1995). Polyculture is related to intercropping but the two are not the same. It is a system that involves growing several plants of different varieties in the same area, often in a manner that emulates nature (Dewar, 2007). There is an advantage in increasing plant biodiversity because polyculture as a practice promotes diet diversity in local communities and also makes them more adaptable to climate inconsistency and severe weather occurrences (Dewar, 2007; Perroni, 2017). Like mixed cropping, it contributes to more resilience to pests and diseases. Polyculture additionally contributes to better soil quality, less soil erosion, and more stable yields when compared to monoculture systems that are a product of Euro-American agricultural practices.

In the areas of Agriculture, Environmental Engineering and Food Science Technology, there is a lot that the curriculum can benefit when it comes to the incorporation of IK. One widespread practice that indigenous communities in Zimbabwe follow is to collect organic waste that is scattered around the homestead to create composites. This organic waste includes cow dung that is not dropped in cattle pens as well as dead leaves of certain trees that quickly decompose. The manure that comes from such composites is used in the rainy season to feed crops. It is interesting to observe that this practice appears widespread because according to Ajibade

(2007) organic wastes from food, farmland, animal faeces, dead plants and animals is put in a container with some water, then stirred and left for some time to decompose and later used as manure.

What is as well important to take note of is the fact that in pre-colonial Africa, and specifically Zimbabwe, iron was an important commodity that was used even in marriage as a form of currency. Another important mineral was copper (known in Shona as *mhangura*). When axes and hoes got worn out they were never thrown away but were re-forged as new smaller hoes and battles axes. Some were re-fashioned into knives and razor blades, a practice that was not peculiar to the Bantu of Zimbabwe, but something that is still being done by the Veps in the Russian Federation as well as some communities in Kano, northern Nigeria (Siragusa & Arzyutov, 2020; Ajibade, 2007). In some instances, they were remade into arrows and spear weights. Like copper, it was turned into bangles that were commonly referred to as *ndarira* that were worn on ankles or as amulets. In the area of food science, the conversion of leftovers like *sadza* into *mahewu* is meant to minimize loss. It is also part of indigenous green skills that contribute to a less polluted and dirty environment.

Another area that needs serious attention is that relating to legal education. There are areas that from an indigenous perspective point to the western models of legal dispensation as vindictive and not rehabilitative. There is for instance the issue of restorative justice and restitution (Mekonnen, 2010). While the indigenous legal frame allows for restitution and rehabilitation of the offender, the western system requires that the complainant goes to the courts for restitution even after a case has been tried. This makes it clear that the system then is some form of penal approach that focuses on the state as a collective and not at the wronged part.

Conclusion

This chapter has, through examples, shown the feasibility of an epistemic and cognitive shift in higher education. It has argued a case for the inclusion of indigenous knowledge into the higher education curriculum and has further pointed out that the peripherization of indigenous knowledge has led to the self-sustaining character of colonialism which has denigrated other knowledge forms. The chapter has gone on to further argue that by embracing the same western education that has alienated them, the indigenous communities contribute not just to the dismemberment of their knowledge but also their dislocation and death as specific groups of people. Through highlighting the importance of cognitive shifting, the chapter has argued that an epistemic shift is only possible if there is a deliberate shift in the way the curriculum is constructed and implemented. Additionally, the chapter has given examples of disciplines where IK can be incorporated so that matters relating to this form of knowledge are brought to life in the lecture room as well as in research. The areas that it has focused as examples are Agriculture, Environmental Engineering, legal education and Sustainable Development and Livelihoods.

References

Abidogun, J. (2020). Introduction: African Education's Multiple Systems. In Abidogun, J. M. & Falola, T. (Eds), *The Palgrave Handbook of African Education and Indigenous Knowledge*, (pp. xvii-xxi). Gewerbestrasse 11, 6330 Cham, Switzerland: Springer International Publishing/Palgrave Macmillan.

Akena, F. A. (2012). Critical Analysis of the Production of Western Knowledge and Its Implications for Indigenous Knowledge and Decolonization. *Journal of Black Studies, 43*(6), 599-619. https://doi.org/10.1177/0021934712440448.

Ajibade, L. T. (October, 2007). Indigenous Knowledge System of waste management in Nigeria. *Indian Journal of Traditional Knowledge* 6(4), 642-647.

Altieri, M. A. (1995). *Agroecology: The Science of Sustainable Agriculture*. 2nd Edition. London: IT Publications.

Angelsupport, (May 20, 2016). Highest Hypocrite. *Global Exchange*. Retrieved April 19, 2021, from https://www.cwis.org/2016/05/highest-hypocrite/

Arauna, L. R., Mendoza-Revilla. J., Mas-Sandoval, A., *et al.* (2017). Recent historical migrations have shaped the gene pool of Arabs and Berbers in North Africa. *Molecular Biology and Evolution* 34 (2), 318-329.

Baer, E. (2017). *The Genocidal Gaze: From German Southwest Africa to the Third Reich*. Detroit: Wayne State University Press.

Balfour, R. J. (2019). Foreword. In J. De Beer (ed.), *The decolonisation of the curriculum project: The affordances of indigenous knowledge for self-directed learning* (NWU Self-directed Learning Series Volume 2), (pp. xxxvii-xxxix). Cape Town: AOSIS. https://doi.org/10.4102/aosis.2019.BK133.00.

Barsh, R. (2001). Who Steals Indigenous Knowledge? Proceedings of the Annual Meeting of the *American Society of International Law*, 95, 153-161. Retrieved April 21, 2021, from http://www.jstor.org/stable/25659474.

Bowden, H. (2014). *Alexander the Great: A Very Short Introduction*. Oxford: Oxford University Press.

Castro-Gómez, S. (2005) La hybris del punto cero: Ciencia, raza e ilustración en la Nueva Granada (1750–1816) *[The Hubris of Zero Point: Science, Race, and Illustration in the New Granada (1750–1816)]*. Bogota: Pontifica Universidad Javeriana.

Chivaura, V. (2009). Chaminuka. In M. K. Asante & A. Mazama (Eds.), *Encyclopedia of African religion* (pp. 157-158). Thousand Oaks, CA: SAGE Publications, Inc. doi: 10.4135/9781412964623.n107.

Cools, R. (2015). Neuropsychopharmacology of Cognitive Flexibility. In Toga, A. W. (Editor).

Brain Mapping: An Encyclopedic Reference, Volume 3 (pp. 349-353). Cape Town: Academic Press. https://doi.org/10.1016/B978-0-12-397025-1.00253-0.

Crush, J. (2020). *Deadly Denial: Xenophobia Governance and the Global Compact for Migration in South Africa - SAMP Migration Policy Series No. 82*. Waterloo, Ontario, Canada: Southern African Migration Programme (SAMP).

De Beer, J. & Van Wyk, B. E. (2019). Arguing for the inclusion of indigenous knowledge in the STEM curriculum: Possibilities and challenges. In J. De Beer (ed.), *The decolonisation of the curriculum project: The affordances of indigenous knowledge for self-directed learning* (NWU Self-directed Learning Series Volume 2), (pp. 117-142). Cape Town: AOSIS. https://doi.org/10.4102/aosis.2019.BK133.05.

De Beer, J. (2019). Glocalisation: The role of indigenous knowledge in the global village. In J. De Beer (ed.), *The decolonisation of the curriculum project: The affordances of indigenous knowledge for self-directed learning* (NWU Self-directed Learning Series Volume 2), (pp. 1-23). Cape Town: AOSIS https://doi.org/10.4102/aosis.2019.BK133.01.

De War, J. A. (2007). *Perennial Polyculture Farming: Seeds of Another Agricultural Revolution?* Santa Monica, CA: Rand Corporation.

Diana Auret (1982) The Mhondoro spirits of supratribal significance in the culture of the Shona, African Studies, 41:2, 173-187, DOI: 10.1080/00020188208707585.

Du Preez, P. (2018). On decolonisation and internationalisation of university curricula: What can we learn from Rosi Braidotti? *Journal of Education,* Number 74, 19-31. doi: http://dx.doi.org/10.17159/2520-9868/i74a02.

Dudley, S. (2008). Human Trafficking in the Middle East and North Africa Region. *Human Rights & Human Welfare.* www.du.edu/korbel/hrhw/researchdigest/trafficking/MiddleEast.pdf.

El Aissati, A. (2005). A socio-historical perspective on the Amazigh (Berber) cultural movement in North Africa. *Afrika Focus* 18(1-2), 58-72.

Emeagwali, G. & Sefa Dei, G. J. (2014). Introduction. In Emeagwali, G. & Sefa Dei, G. J. (Eds). *African Indigenous Knowledge and the Disciplines,* (pp. ix-xiii) Rotterdam, Boston, Taipei: Sense Publishers.

Emeagwali, G. & Shizha, E. (Eds.). (2016). African Indigenous Knowledge and the Sciences. Leiden, The Netherlands: Brill/Sense. doi: https://doi.org/10.1007/978-94-6300-515-9.

Ezeanya-Esiobu, C. (2019). *Indigenous Knowledge and Education in Africa.* Singapore: Springer Open.

Falola, T. (2020). Introduction to Africa's Educational Wealth. In: Abidogun, J. M. & Falola, T. (Eds), *The Palgrave Handbook of African Education and Indigenous Knowledge,* (pp. 3-38). Gewerbestrasse 11, 6330 Cham, Switzerland: Springer International Publishing/Palgrave Macmillan.

Freeman, P. (2011). *Alexander the Great.* New York, NY: Simon & Schuster.

Freire, P. (1972). *Pedagogy of the Oppressed.* Harmondsworth: Penguin.

Gumbo, M. T. (2015). Indigenous technology in technology education curricula and teaching. In P. J. Williams, A. Jones, & C. Buntting (Eds.),*The future of technology education* (pp. 57–76). Dordrecht: Springer.

Hamed, L. M. M., Fouda, S. & Emara, E. I.R. (2019). Conserving Soil Fertility and Sustaining Crop Performance via Soil Tillage Systems and Crop Rotation. *Alexandria Science Exchange Journal,* 40(2), 256-262.

Hammersmith, J. A. (2009). *Converging indigenous and western knowledge systems: implications for tertiary education.* Doctoral thesis, University of South Africa.

Hattery, A. J. & Smith, E. (2018). *Policing Black Bodies: How Black Lives Are Surveilled and How to Work for Change.* Lanham, Boulder, New York & London Rowman & Littlefield.

Hochschild, A. (1999). *King Leopold's Ghost: A Story of Greed, Terror, and Heroism in Colonial Africa.* Boston, MA: Houghton Mifflin.

Ilahiane, H. (2006). *Historical Dictionary of the Berbers (Imazighen).* Lanham, Maryland, Toronto & Oxford: The Scarecrow Press, Inc.

International Labour Organization (ILO) (2017). *Regional brief for the Arab States: 2017 Global Estimates of Modern Slavery and Child Labour.* Geneva: ILO.

Kinchloe, J. L., & Steinberg, S. R. (2008). Indigenous Knowledges in education complexities, dangers, and profound benefits. In N. K. Denzin, Y. S. Lincoln & L. T. Smith (Eds.*), Handbook of critical and Indigenous methodologies* (pp. 135-156). Los Angeles: SAGE Publications.

Kumar, D. R. (2019). United States Patents, Biopiracy, and Cultural Imperialism: The Theft of India's Traditional Knowledge, *Inquiries Journal,* http://www.inquiriesjournal.com/articles/1769/united-states-patents-biopiracy-and-cultural-imperialism-the-theft-of-indias-traditional-knowledge#header4page1.

Kuyu, C. G. & Bereka, T. Y. (2020). Review on contribution of indigenous food preparation and preservation techniques to attainment of food security in Ethiopian. *Food Science & Nutrition* 27;8 (1), 3-15. doi: 10.1002/fsn3.1274.

Le Grange, L. (2019). Different voices on decolonising of the curriculum. In J. De Beer (ed.), *The decolonisation of the curriculum project: The affordances of indigenous knowledge for self-directed learning* (NWU Self-directed Learning Series Volume 2), (pp. 25-47). Cape Town: AOSIS. https://doi.org/10.4102/aosis.2019.BK133.02.

Le Grange, L., Du Preez, P., Ramrathan, L. & Blignaut, S., (2020). Decolonising the university curriculum or decolonial washing? A multiple case study. *Journal of Education,* Number 80, 25-48.

Levin, B. (2007). Curriculum Policy and the Politics of what should be learned in Schools. In Connelly, M., He, M. & Fillion, J.

(Eds). *The Sage Handbook of Curriculum and Instruction* (pp. 7-24). Newbury Park: Sage Publications, Inc.

Liu, W., Yao, S., Wang, J., & Liu, M. (2019). Trends and Features of Agroforestry Research Based on Bibliometric Analysis. *Sustainability*, *11*(12), 3473. MDPI AG. Retrieved from http://dx.doi.org/10.3390/su11123473.

Mapara, J. & Saidi, E. (2019). Indigenous knowledge as a cog in the rural business logistical catenae. Paper presented at the 1st International Sustainable Strategic Supply Chain Management Research Conference, Chinhoyi University of Technology, 17-18 December, 2019.

Mapara, J. & Mpofu-Hamadziripi, N. (2014). Language, Indigenous Knowledge and Survival Strategies. In Mararike, C.G. (Editor). *Land: An Empowerment Asset for Africa – The Human Factor Perspective* (pp. 166-181). Harare: UZ Publications.

Masarirambi, M. T., Mavuso. V., Songwe V. D., Nkambule, T. P. & Mhazo, N. (2010). Indigenous post-harvest handling and processing of traditional vegetables in Swaziland: A review. *African Journal of Agricultural Research* 5(24), 3333-3341.

Mawere, M. (2012). *The Struggle of African Indigenous Knowledge Systems In An Age of Globalisation – A Case for Children's Traditional Games in South-eastern Zimbabwe*, Langaa RPCIG Publishers: Cameroon.

Mawere, M. (2013). *Lyrics of Reason and Experience*, Langaa RPCIG Publishers: Cameroon.

Mbah, M., Johnson, A. T. & Chipindi, F. M. (2021). Institutionalizing the intangible through research and engagement: Indigenous knowledge and higher education for sustainable development in Zambia, *International Journal of Educational Development*, Volume 82, https://doi.org/10.1016/j.ijedudev.2021.102355.

Mekonnen, D. (2010). Indigenous legal tradition as a supplement to African transitional justice initiatives. *African Journal on Conflict Resolution* 10(3), 101-122.

Meharg, S. J. (2001). Identicide and cultural cannibalism: Warfare's appetite for symbolic place. *Peace Research* 33(2) 89-98.

Meharg, S. J. (2003). Post-war reconstruction: humanitarian aid or profit-driven activity? *Peace Research* 35(1), 65-74.

Meharg, S. J. (2006). *Identicide: Precursor to Genocide. Working Paper* 5. Centre for Security and Defense Studies. Ottawa: Norman Paterson School of International Affairs, Carleton University.

Mignolo, W. D. (2012). *Local Histories/Global Designs: Coloniality, Subaltern Knowledges, and Border Thinking*. Princeton: Princeton University Press.

Mignolo, W. D. (2009). Epistemic Disobedience, Independent Thought and Decolonial Freedom. *Theory, Culture & Society, 26*(7–8), 159-181 https://doi.org/10.1177/0263276409349275

Mignolo, W. D. (2007). Introduction: Coloniality of power and de-colonial thinking *Cultural Studies, 21*(2-3), 155-167, DOI: 10.1080/09502380601162498.

Mudaly, R. (2018). Towards decolonising a module in the pre-service science teacher education curriculum: The role of indigenous knowledge systems in creating spaces for transforming the curriculum. *Journal of Education*, Number 74, 47-66, doi: http://dx.doi.org/10.17159/2520-9868/i74a04.

Mukuka, G. S. (2010). Indigenous Knowledge Systems and Intellectual Property Laws in South Africa. Doctoral thesis, University of Johannesburg.

Nair, P. K. R. & Garrity D. (2012). Agroforestry Research and Development: The Way Forward. In Nair, P. K. R. & Garrity D. (Editors). *Agroforestry - The Future of Global Land Use* (pp. 515-531), Dordrecht: Springer Science+Business Media DOI 10.1007/978-94-007-4676-3.

Nayak, M. (April 30, 2019). The Misappropriation of Traditional Knowledge. *The Denver Journal of International Law & Policy*. Retrieved 24 March from https://djilp.org/the-misappropriation-of-traditional-knowledge/

Ndlovu-Gatsheni, S. (2014). Global Coloniality and the Challenges of Creating African Futures. *The Strategic Review for Southern Africa, 36*(2), 181-202.

Ndlovu-Gatsheni, S. J. (2013). The Entrapment of Africa within the Global Colonial Matrices of Power: Eurocentrism, Coloniality, and Deimperialization in the Twenty-first Century. *Journal of Developing Societies, 29*(4), 331–353. https://doi.org/10.1177/0169796X13503195

Nelson-Barber, S. & Johnson, Z. (2019). Introduction to Case Studies Section. In McKinley, E. A. & Smith L. T. (Eds), *Handbook of Indigenous Education*, (pp. 1105-1111). Singapore: Springer Nature.

Noda, O. (2020). Epistemic hegemony: the Western straitjacket and post-colonial scars in academic publishing. *Revista Brasileira de*

Política Internacional, 63(1), e007. Epub July 27, 2020. https://doi.org/10.1590/0034-7329202000107

Nzongola-Ntalaja, G. (2002). *The Congo from Leopold to Kabila: A People's History.* London: Zed Books.

Payn, V. (2012) "'Ilima', 'Izithebe' and the 'Green Revolution': a Complex Agro-Ecological Approach to Understanding Agriculture in Pondoland and What This Means for Sustainability through the Creation of 'Living Landscapes'." *SUNScholar*, Stellenbosch: Stellenbosch University, scholar.sun.ac.za/handle/10019.1/20228.

Pedzisai, C. & Tsvere, M., (2019). Promotion of Sustainable Livelihoods through Indigenous Weather Forecasting Methods. Paper presented at the 1st International Sustainable Strategic Supply Chain Management Research Conference, Chinhoyi University of Technology, 17-18 December, 2019.

Perroni, E. (2017). Five Indigenous Farming Practices Enhancing Food Security. Foodtank: The Think Tank for Food. https://foodtank.com/news/2017/08/celebrating-international-day-of-the-worlds-indigenous-peoples/

Petersen, M. E. (2014). Seed Sovereignty: How can organic agriculture contribute to the development and protection of the seed? – A case study of Nepal. Retrieved April 19, 2021, from https://orgprints.org/id/eprint/27631/7/27631.pdf

Ponge, A. (2013). *Integrating Indigenous Knowledge for Food Security: Perspectives from the Millennium Village Project at Bar-Sauri in Nyanza Province in Kenya.* Nairobi & London: Institute of Policy Analysis and Research and Institute of Education, University of London.

Poulsen, S. (1981). African history: from a European to an African point of view, *Kunapipi*, 3(1), 75-80.

Quijano, A. (2000). Coloniality of Power and Eurocentrism in Latin America. *International Sociology, 15*(2), 215–232. https://doi.org/10.1177/0268580900015002005.

Rodney, W. (2011). *How Europe Underdeveloped Africa.* Baltimore, MD: Black Classic Press.

Rosati, A., Borek, R. & Canali, S. (2020). Agroforestry and organic agriculture. *Agroforestry Systems* https://doi.org/10.1007/s10457-020-00559-6.

Salway, P. (2015). *Roman Britain: A Very Short Introduction.* Oxford: Oxford University Press.

Samuel, M. A. (2017). Book Review: *Africanising the Curriculum: Indigenous Perspectives and Theories* by Vuyisile Msila and Mishack T.

Gumbo (Editors), *Educational Research for Social Change* (ERSC) 6(1), 87-92.

Shizha, E. (2014). The Indigenous Knowledge Systems and the Curriculum. In Emeagwali, G. & Sefa Dei, G. J. (Eds). *African Indigenous Knowledge and the Disciplines*, (pp. 113-129). Rotterdam, Boston, Taipei: Sense Publishers.

Siambombe, A., Mutale, Q. & Muzingili, T. (2018). Indigenous Knowledge Systems: A Synthesis of BaTonga People's Traditional Knowledge on Weather Dynamism. *African Journal of Social Work*, 8(2), 46-54.

Siragusa, L. & Arzyutov, D. (2020). Nothing goes to waste: sustainable practices of re-use among indigenous groups in the Russian North. *Current Opinion in Environmental Sustainability* 43, 41-48.

Smith, G. H. & Webber, M. (2019). Transforming Research and Indigenous Education Struggle. In McKinley, E. A. & Smith L. T. (Eds), *Handbook of Indigenous Education*, (pp. 813-822). Singapore: Springer Nature.

Smith, L. T. (2012). *Decolonizing Methodologies: Research and Indigenous Peoples*. London: Zed Books.

Tinder, G. (1991). *The Political Meaning of Christianity: The Prophetic Stance, an Interpretation*. San Francisco: HarperCollins.

Tinker, G. E. & Freeland, M. (2008). *Thief, Slave Trader, Murderer: Christopher Columbus and Caribbean Population Decline*. Minneapolis, MN: University of Minnesota Press.

Trevor-Roper, H. (1964). *Rise of Christian Europe*. London: Thames and Hudson

Van Reybrouck, D. (2014). *Congo: The Epic History of a People*. (Translated from the Dutch by Sam Garrett). London: Fourth Estate.

Walsh, C. E. (2018). The Decolonial For - Resurgences, Shifts, and Movements. In Mignolo, W. & Walsh, C. (Eds). *On Decoloniality* (pp. 15-32). New York: Duke University Press.

Woźniak, A. (2019). Effect of Crop Rotation and Cereal Monoculture on the Yield and Quality of Winter Wheat Grain and on Crop Infestation with Weeds and Soil Properties. *International Journal of Plant Production* 13, 177–182. https://doi.org/10.1007/s42106-019-00044-w.

Wylie, D. (2006). *Myth of Iron: Shaka in History*. Scottsville: University of KwaZulu Natal Press.

Chapter 4

Towards the Implementation of African Indigenous Mathematical Practices into the Mathematics Curriculum in Southern Africa

Sylvia Madusise

Abstract

The chapter explores the possibility of implementing indigenous mathematical practices in the Mathematics curriculum and the application of school Mathematics to cultural activities in Southern Africa. The research relies on Ladson-Billings' culturally relevant pedagogy theory and Yosso's community cultural wealth theory. The value of culture in relation to mathematics learning processes is focussed on using the theories. The analysis is based on two empirical ethnographic studies carried out in Southern Africa, and in particular Zimbabwe and South Africa. The indigenous practices investigated in this empirical research are described as, respectively, basket and mat weaving and the Tshwana dances. The people involved are the Karanga people of Masvingo Province in Zimbabwe and the Tshwana people of North West Province in South Africa. In Zimbabwe, three basket and mat weavers based at Great Zimbabwe Monuments were interviewed and observed whilst weaving their mats and baskets. Finished artifacts were also analysed documenting the embedded mathematical concepts. Several mathematical concepts were derived and an argument of how the implementation of the derived concepts in the Mathematics curriculum may enhance mathematics understanding is presented. It is also argued that the application of the derived concepts to indigenous basket and mat weaving may enhance production of up-market artifacts for sale. In South Africa, learners who participated in cultural activities at a cultural village in the North West Province demonstrated a Tswana dance to a Grade 9 Mathematics class. The dance was mathematised and the embedded mathematical concepts were used to introduce number patterns leading to sequences. It is argued that innovative learners could apply the learnt Mathematics in designing more dancing styles and attract more paying spectators thereby, economically empowering learners. Based on the analyses and explorations, the chapter aims to enhance the understanding of the implementation of indigenous mathematical activities in the Mathematics curriculum and the

69

application of mathematical concepts to indigenous practices for sustainable development.

Keywords: Indigenous Knowledge Systems, Ethnomathematics, Culturally-Relevant Pedagogy, Mathematisation, Sustainable Development.

Introduction

Research on indigenous mathematical practices has shown that various mathematical concepts can be identified in different cultural activities. A number of mathematical concepts have been identified in indigenous games. Masiiwa (2001), in his study of the game of *nhodo*, claims that the playing of *nhodo* involves counting and the concept of factors. *Nhodo* can be used to teach counting in phases that is one, two, three, and so on. In phase two, one learns to count in multiples of two that is two, four, six, and so on. In general, in phase n, one learns to count in multiples of n that is n, $2n$, $3n$... and so on. He claims that the game of *nhodo* provides the test of finding factors of a given number. Masiiwa (2004), in another study, also analysed how the game of *tsoro* is played extracting some high powered mathematical concepts. Using the exponential number 2^n, Masiiwa (ibid) discovers that *chihwangu* - thus winning in one turn occurs for: 2^n holes per row and $2^n - 1$ pebbles in each hole. The concept of modulo arithmetic is used in order to prove the above assertion. The proof of the assertion can provide a challenging classroom activity at Tertiary level, argues Masiiwa.

The *Tchadji* game is similar to *tsoro* game analysed by Masiiwa (2004). *Tchadji* is usually played on wooden boards, which have four rows of eight holes each (4x8 board), carved into them. It is played with a predetermined number of identical counters (usually seeds) placed in the holes. The playing of *Tchadji* involves simple and complex moves in the process of spreading seeds in the holes. The goal is to immobilize or annihilate the other player(s) by the capture of the majority of seeds (Walker, 1990). In Mozambique, the *Tchadji* game was used to teach probability in mathematics classrooms. Through mathematisation, some questions on probability were constructed and used as classroom activities. The findings showed that the implementation of indigenous mathematical practices improved the learners' performance. Mosimege (2004) and Ismael (2004) presented ethnomathematical studies on indigenous games conducted in South Africa and Mozambique, respectively. A variety of mathematical concepts such as different types of symmetries, geometrical shapes, counting, and ratio and proportion were derived. The incorporation of indigenous games in the mathematics classrooms provides learners with the opportunities to relate their experiences outside the mathematics classrooms to mathematics concepts and processes. The findings suggest that the use of games impacted positively on students' motivation and attitudes towards mathematics.

Chirenda (1993) worked with pre-service teachers on a project to examine the possibility of using local tradition artifacts to introduce mathematical concepts. Trajectory patterns of straw strips in artifacts such as hats, baskets and mats were analysed and the students' creation of geometrical shapes heightened their confidence. They began to feel that the mathematics they learn at school also comes from their lives and societies (ibid). Chirenda further claims that such activities and examples dispel the myth that mathematics has exclusively European roots. Thus, supporting Yosso's (2005) community cultural wealth theory which says that all groups of people have cultural wealth (knowledge included) that has value. Instead of viewing one set of norms/or knowledge as legitimate or superior, Yosso's theory calls for systems and institutions to treat all cultural wealth as legitimate.

Research evidence from anthropological and cross-cultural studies has emerged which not only supports the idea that from different cultural histories have come what can be described as different mathematics. One can cite the work of Zaslavsky (1973), who has shown in her book *Africa Counts*, the range of mathematical ideas existing in indigenous African cultures. There is ethnomathematics as an emancipatory movement, which is an opposition to any claim to the superiority of Western mathematics (Zaslavsky, 1973). A number of researchers in South Africa (Nkopodi and Mosimege, 2009; Moloi 2015; Nxumalo and Mncube, 2019) explored the role of indigenous materials and activities in the teaching and learning of Mathematics. Nkopodi and Mosimege (2009) explored the incorporation of the indigenous game of *Morabaraba* in the learning of Mathematics. Moloi (2015) examined the use of indigenous games in teaching problem-solving in Mathematics in rural learning ecologies. Nxumalo and Mncube (2019) argued that the use of indigenous games and knowledge can decolonise the school curriculum. Similarly, Mawere (2012) explores the agency of children's traditional games in South-Eastern

Zimbabwe in the cognitive development of children. Mosimege's (2020) study on the use of indigenous games in the teaching and learning of Mathematics explores the games of *Morabaraba* and *Malepa*. His analysis shows that the games engage learners into enjoyable classroom activities. The games also create potential avenues for connecting Mathematics and culture, that is, connections between the classroom environment and cultural activities outside the classroom.

The studies cited above highlight some of the benefits likely to be secured from the incorporation of indigenous mathematical practices in the formal Mathematics curriculum. However, the reverse is also true. This chapter also presents an argument that school Mathematics can be applied to indigenous practices and enhance production of up-market indigenous artifacts for sale. It advances that students taught in a system where indigenous practices are implemented into the Mathematics curriculum are doubly advantaged; their understanding is enhanced and they can also apply the learnt concepts to indigenous practices for their financial benefit. Thus, students taught in a system where indigenous practices are implemented are economically empowered for sustainable development.

Education for Sustainable Development and Global Citizenship

In this 21st Century, global developments bring with them an increased demand for education that goes beyond teaching knowledge and skills just to find a job (UNESCO, 2018). Students now need new perspectives to be able to understand the rapidly changing world they live in. A different kind of pedagogical approach is required to educate students as global citizens for sustainable development. According to Tilbury (2011) students should learn a topic in an interdisciplinary way, from an economic, social and environmental perspective. Such an education should empower learners to take informed decisions and responsibility for economic viability and environmental integrity for the present and future generations. The creativity, ideals and courage of the youth and the knowledge of the indigenous people are essential to achieve sustainable development. There is high demand for nations to recognise and support the identity, culture and activities of indigenous people. Eradicating poverty and reducing disparities in living standards in different parts of the world are essential to achieve sustainable development. According to Shizha (2013) school knowledge has to express the social desires and socio-cultural needs for socio-economic development.

Mathematics as a Tool for Sustainable Development

The term "development" can be understood as advancement of knowledge. It can also be viewed as the systematic use of scientific and technical knowledge to meet specific objectives or requirements. We live in a time of extraordinary and accelerating change that is a new phase of development which demands the need to use Mathematics in everyday life and in the workplace. Knowing mathematics can be personally satisfying and empowering. The underpinnings of everyday life are increasingly mathematical and technological. Just as a certain level of Mathematics is needed for economic empowerment, so too is the level of mathematical thinking and problem solving needed at the workplace. Business and industry depend on the knowledge of Mathematics. Roger Bacon (1214-1294), an English Franciscan friar, philosopher, scientist and scholar of the 13th century, once posited that neglect of Mathematics works injury to all knowledge since he who is ignorant of it cannot know the other sciences or the things of the world (cited in Fatima, 2012). It can be argued that the main aim of education is to help the learners earn their living and make them self-independent. To achieve this aim, Mathematics is considered as the most important subject than any other. It helps to prepare students for technical and any other vocations where Mathematics is applied. For example, Engineering, Architecture, Accountancy, Banking, Business, Carpentry, Tailoring, Surveying, office work and even Agriculture require the knowledge of Mathematics. Mathematical knowledge provides the vital underpinning of the knowledge of economy. It is essential in the physical sciences, technology, business, financial service and many areas of ICT. Mathematics forms the basis of most scientific and industrial research and development. Increasingly many complex systems and structures in the modern world can be understood using Mathematics. Much of the design and control of high technology systems depend on mathematical inputs and outputs. Economics of any country is developed by establishment of industries. The applied Mathematics like Computational Science, applied analysis, differential equations, data analysis and discrete Mathematics etc. are essential in industrial field. In particular, Mathematics has contributed to technology for thousands of years and still continues to do so. It finds useful applications in the construction of roads, buildings, stadiums, airports, dams, and bridges, among others. It is also applied in Mechanical Engineering, Electrical Engineering, and Civil Engineering. The "functional" aspect of Mathematics stems from its importance as the language of Sciences, Technology and Engineering, and its role in their development. Most of the demands stem directly from the need for mathematical and statistical modelling of phenomena. Such modelling is basic to all engineering, plays a vital role in all physical sciences and contributes significantly to the biological sciences, medicines, psychology, economics and commerce. Mathematics is being successfully used in this 21st century in the development of science and technology leading to sustainable economic development.

Having analysed how mathematics generally serves as a pre-requisite for sustainable development, it is crucial to analyse how best Mathematics should be taught to improve understanding. The chapter suggests that the implementation of indigenous mathematical practices into the Mathematics curriculum may enhance understanding and helps to economically empower learners.

Theoretical Framework

Irrespective of different views on cultural activities being mathematical and the use of ethnomathematics as a teaching tool, the importance of taking into consideration what the learner knows in teaching is well documented (Ausubel, 1968; Rosa & Orey, 2009; Mosimege & Ismael, 2004; Mawere, 2013). The framework used in this study draws ideas from Ladson-Billings' culturally relevant pedagogy theory and Yosso's community cultural wealth theory.

Yosso (2002; 2005) argues that community cultural wealth focuses on and learns from the array of cultural knowledge, skills, abilities and contacts possessed by socially marginalised groups that often go unrecognised and unacknowledged. Community cultural wealth offers a more expanded view of thinking about the resources and knowledge that students from socially marginalised groups bring to the classroom. Yosso (2005, p.75) defines culture as the "behaviours and values that are learned, shared, and exhibited by a group of people". Yosso (ibid) explains how culture can serve as a resource for students from socially disadvantaged groups. Thus, it is part of their funds of knowledge. School knowledge should align itself with learners' experiences that are characterised by their socio-cultural worldviews (Shizha, 2013).

Ladson- Billings (1994) asserts that culturally relevant teaching is designed not only to fit the school culture to the students' culture but also to use students' cultures as the basis for helping students understand themselves and conceptualise knowledge. Culturally relevant pedagogy is a teaching style that validates and incorporates learners' cultural background, ethnic history, and current societal interests into teachers' daily instruction. For example, culturally relevant pedagogy has been defined as a means to use students' cultures to bridge school achievement (Boutte & Hill, 2006), to validate students' life experiences by utilizing their cultures and histories as teaching resources (Boyle-Baise, 2005), and to recognize students' home cultures, promote collaboration among peers, and connect home life with school experiences (Neuman,1999). It would appear the proponents of this theory generally contend that culturally responsive teaching acknowledges the legitimacy of the cultural heritages of different ethnic groups as legacies that affect students' dispositions, attitudes and approaches to learning. Studies based on the concept of cultural differences make an assumption that students coming from culturally diverse backgrounds will achieve academic excellence if classroom instruction is conducted in a manner responsive to the students' home culture (de Beer, 2010). It will therefore be meaningful for learners to be taught in a way which links mathematics concepts with the mathematics encountered in everyday experiences. Banks (1991), Gay (2000) and Ladson-Billings (1994) in their studies of culturally relevant environments, reiterate that academic achievement of students who come from culturally and linguistically diverse backgrounds improve if schools and teachers ensure that classroom instruction is conducted in a manner that is relevant to their home community cultures.

Most studies which motivate the incorporation of ethnomathematics as a teaching tool in the mathematics classrooms argue that ethnomathematical approaches to Mathematics curriculum are intended to make Mathematics more relevant and meaningful for learners promoting the overall quality of their Mathematics learning. Little is known or established about the reverse process that is using school Mathematics to economically empower the learners for sustainable development, and hence the relevance of this chapter. This chapter focuses on using cultural

75

contexts to access school Mathematics. It also uses school Mathematics to deepen understanding of cultural activities, largely based on the position that the Mathematics content learnt in schools should be transferrable to learners' daily lives. That is a two-way process. This view considers Mathematics as relevant and practical. Mathematics has a utilitarian value and can be applied to many aspects of everyday life. For example, mathematical knowledge maybe applied in the production of cultural artifacts for sale. Thus, economically empowering the society. From this orientation, teachers play a crucial role; they must apprentice learners into ways of investigating Mathematics, and to be 'exemplars' and 'conveyors' of school mathematical knowledge (Graven & Venkat, 2007). Teachers must teach lessons in ways that will enable learners to recognise and make sense of these mathematical connections (Mhlolo, Venkat, & Schäfer, 2012). Learners' ability to make connections in Mathematics itself is crucial for conceptual understanding (Antony & Walshaw, 2009) as well as for application outside the discipline. The proposed learner-centred pedagogy empowers students to participate in social activities in their organisations, communities and personal lives. Thus, supporting education for sustainable development.

Methodology

The studies from which this chapter emerges needed hermeneutic methods seen as involving dialogue with participants as sources of information. The researcher then relied on qualitative data using a case study approach or style of inquiry in search of understanding the extent to which indigenous mathematical practices could be used as a vehicle to access academic mathematics, then use the acquired school mathematics to participate in cultural activities for economic empowerment. The first study linked the indigenous mathematical practices used by basket and mat weavers to the academic mathematical knowledge. The second study linked mathematical knowledge being taught in a school (close to a cultural village) to the knowledge and activities of the cultural village itself, interrogating connections between mathematics and indigenous knowledge systems. Apart from enabling learners to access and understand school mathematics, I also hoped both studies would equip learners with personal agency over the creation and validation of .knowledge (epistemological empowerment). Where applicable, I also hoped to equip the learners with the agentic power and ability to apply their school mathematical knowledge in coming up with indigenous artifacts for sale and in participating in cultural activities for a fee (economic empowerment). This, I argue, has a bearing on the teaching and learning of mathematics where mathematical connections enable the recognition and application of school mathematics to contexts outside school - the links between mathematics and other disciplines or the real world (Blum et.al, 2007).

Samples and sampling procedures

The first study sample composed of three indigenous basket and mat weavers who were purposively chosen in order to gain more from their exceptional expertise. In selecting the weavers, the researcher was guided by the Marketing Director at Great Zimbabwe Monuments. The Director introduced the researcher to the three weavers whom he described as the best weavers among the cohort of weavers who were participants at the Monuments' cultural village. They supplied artifacts for sale at the Monuments and they also supplied artifacts for international market.

The second study sample consisted of three mathematics teachers from one middle rural school in the North West Province of South Africa and their Grade 9 learners (218 learners in all), cultural dancers (these included some of the 218 learners). Lesedi Cultural Village was identified as the research site and Mathematics teachers who teach at a school very close to the selected cultural village were invited to participate. A cultural village was selected with the belief that it is where the community's indigenous knowledge is preserved. It was further considered that activities at a cultural village could assist teachers and learners in understanding condensed cultural ways of living. A school close to the cultural village was chosen with an assumption that its members (including learners) could be quite familiar with the indigenous activities taking place at the cultural village.

Data collection procedure

In the first study, weavers were interviewed and observed whilst weaving. Mathematical concepts embedded in basket and mat weaving activities were explored through direct observation and relatively unstructured interviews in a natural field setting. The collected data was in form of words and pictures. Some artifacts were photographed. The artifacts were mathematised to determine the mathematical concepts used in the weaving processes. A discussion on the mathematics curriculum level where the embedded concepts can be incorporated was carried out. It was checked whether or not mathematical knowledge can enhance production of up-market artifacts for sale. Weavers were interviewed to determine the availability of market for their wares.

In the second study, the researcher visited the cultural village several times to familiarise herself with the activities at the cultural village. Videos of the cultural activities were recorded and analysed by the researcher and the three mathematics teachers who were participating in the research. Embedded mathematical ideas were extracted from the activities. School mathematical knowledge was used to interpret the activities. From the extracted mathematical ideas, a lesson on number patterns and sequences was co-planned by the researcher and the teachers. The planned lesson was implemented in Grade 9 classes. Learners who participated in cultural dances performed at the cultural village were asked to demonstrate a cultural dance during a mathematics lesson. The modelling of the dance was used to introduce number patterns and sequences.

A learners' journal entry was designed to allow learners to describe the lessons where culturally-based activities were carried out. The major concern was to determine what learners foregrounded in their lesson descriptions. In the classroom environment, learning something new or different and then reflecting on what that means may reflect an important learning outcome. For this chapter, the researcher basically checked for statements suggesting the use of cultural contexts to access academic mathematics and the use of mathematics to understand cultural activities.

Learners were asked to complete a questionnaire after the lesson. Focus group interviews were also carried out with the learners. This was aimed at understanding the impact which the pedagogy used in the lesson had on learners. This enabled the researcher to explore learners' views about the use of cultural contexts in mathematics education. In the questionnaire, learners were asked to state what they liked about the way they learnt the topics taught in the culturally-based lessons.

In both studies, the researcher basically checked for statements suggesting the use of indigenous mathematical practises to access academic mathematics and the use of school mathematics to understand cultural activities. The possibility of realising some income through participating in the involved cultural activities was also checked.

Findings and Discussions

Mathematical concepts embedded in mat weaving

Fig 1: Mat: Picture photographed by the researcher at the cultural village at Great Zimbabwe Monuments; Source: Author.

Fig 1 illustrates the starting point when making mats. A pole is graduated into equally spaced grooves. The grooves are smoothened. When asked how the weaver maintains the space between the grooves equal, the mat weaver said he lays a stick from the preceding groove to mark the position of the next groove. The stick of the same length is used throughout the graduation process. There is an element of measurement being applied.

The weaving string is wound on stones on both ends. The stones are hanged freely on the pole allowing the string to pass through the smoothened grooves. When asked why he has to make sure that the grooves are smooth, the weaver said he does so to prevent the string from breaking. However, mathematically the hanging stones illustrate motion of connected particles. The grooves act as pulleys. The smooth pulley allows the tension of the weaving string to be the same throughout the hanging length. Since the string is inelastic it does not alter its length under tension, therefore the acceleration of the particles attached to it will have the same magnitude. The motion of the system can be analysed, considering the forces acting on each

79

particle separately. The force in each string is equivalent to **T-mg** where **T** is the tension in the string, **m** is the mass of the stone and **g** represents the pull of gravity. When making mats the hanging stones on each side are criss-crossed each time a strand of reeds (*nhokwe* in Shona) is added.

Mechanics concepts involving motion of connected bodies taught at 'A' Level can be introduced using videos showing the weaving process described above. Forces in the weaving strings can also be calculated. The idea of forces being in equilibrium can be illustrated from the weaving process. Besides helping students to understand the involved mathematics, students can also understand the weaving process applying the involved mathematics concepts. Innovative students may engage in indigenous mat weaving to produce artifacts for sale. Thus, economically empowering themselves.

Figure 2: Door mats

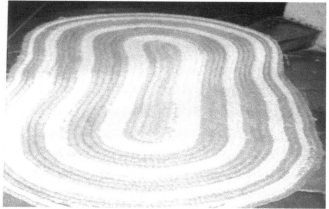

Source: Picture taken by the researcher; Source: Author.

Two different coloured strands are sewn alternately until the mat is complete. The period for the mat decoration is 2; brown rows and white rows. One brown row and one white row leads to a constant sequence 1 that is the sequence (1, 1, 1, 1...) whose terms are all equal to 1. The **n**th term is also 1. The sum of the first **n** terms of the series (1+1+1+1+...) and can be calculated by simply multiplying **n** by the constant term in the series.

Through considering the number of times the pattern repeats itself say after every 4 brown rows and 4 white rows, the concept of modular arithmetic can be derived. Some mats are made with different number of rows for each colour.

Sometimes the weaver may decide to maintain an equal number of rows per each colour. For example, two brown rows and three white rows or vice versa until the mat is complete. This leads to a periodic sequence (2, 3, 2, 3 ...) which is divergent. The terms of this sequence form a repeating pattern. Thus, pairs of brown rows and sets of three white rows. The number of times the periodical pattern repeats is determined by the desired size of the mat. For this sequence if the first term is **u,** then the **n**[th] term can be described as;

$U_n = u$ when n is odd

$u+1$ when n is even

The mathematisation of finished mats can be used as a vehicle to access some sequence concepts. The idea of constant and divergent sequences may be introduced through the analysis of the weaving process. Innovative learners can use the knowledge of sequences to come up with different mat designs. Such learners may engage in mat weaving and come up with some export quality mats for sale using indigenous materials. They may earn a living through mat weaving. Thus, leading to sustainable development.

Figure 3: *Fruit bowl*

Source: Picture taken by the researcher
Row 1: Top row with smaller toothed squares
Row 2: Bottom row with bigger toothed squares

Fig 3 illustrates some of the decorations which the basket weavers make on their baskets. On the photograph there are rows of toothed squares. Each toothed square is made up of two contrasting colours. Thus, black-and-blue or red-and-white.

Row 1: Let each tooth represent a unit square

All the toothed squares have got an equal number of unit squares; each boundary line has either four black or four white teeth on each side making the toothed squares almost congruent. The spaces between the toothed squares are almost equal. When observed whilst making the designs the weaver used her thump and the pointer finger to estimate distance from the preceding square to the next. Relating to the positions of the toothed squares in the same row, there is evidence of a movement in a straight line. Suppose the patterns are transferred to the Cartesian plane, the movement will be parallel to the horizontal axis, the x-axis. It can now be thought of as a translation whose translation vector TV = $\begin{smallmatrix} x \\ 0 \end{smallmatrix}$ where x represents that finger- estimated distance. The y-coordinate is represented by zero because the corresponding unit squares from the consecutive toothed squares are in the same horizontal line, so there is no upward or downward movement.

Row 2: The toothed squares in this row are larger than those in row 1. Each boundary side has five unit squares. The toothed squares in row 1 are similar to those in row 2. Using transformations, the squares in the second row can be thought of as an enlargement of the toothed squares in the first row. From the given analysis, the fruit bowl can be used as teaching media when teaching transformations to illustrate translation and enlargement. Also, transformation knowledge can be used to come up with different fruit bowl designs.

Figure 4: A Sugar basin and a fruit bowl

Source: Picture taken by the researcher

The patterns on Fig 4 artifacts are periodical, the same pattern is repeated in each design. The fruit bow is symmetrical with three lines

82

of symmetry. The leaf-like pattern produced depicts similarity of shapes. The red triangles produced on the basin lid design are equal in size; mathematically they can be referred to as being congruent. There is a lot of turning involved when producing the patterns in both artifacts. Thus, involving a lot of angle estimation. The basin is spherical in shape.

Besides enabling learners to understand the mathematical concepts of congruency, similarity of shapes and lines of symmetry through using the artifacts as teaching media, the involved mathematical knowledge can be applied in coming up with a variety of designs for sugar basins and fruit bowls. After completing school, learners may engage themselves in weaving projects, producing artifacts for sale.

Income Generation and Poverty Alleviation through Basket and Mat Weaving

The three weavers whose artifacts were analysed were interviewed to check on the market availability for their artifacts. Responses from the weavers indicate that the market facility is very rich since Great Zimbabwe Monuments is an attractive tourist centre. Most of the products they displayed at the monuments were bought by both local and international tourists. The international customers bought using foreign currency. The sale of indigenous baskets and mats brought the much-needed foreign currency to the country. All the three weavers indicated that business was very lucrative during festive holidays and they sometimes ran out of the products. This then suggests that learners can earn a living through basket and mat weaving after school. Mathematical knowledge may be used to produce up-market artifacts. My experience in the study revealed that learners need to be apprenticed into ways of investigating mathematics and to be 'conveyors' of school mathematical knowledge for sustainable development.

Mathematising a traditional Tswana dance

The picture below shows some learners who were participants (dancers) at the cultural village demonstrating a Tswana dance during a Grade 9 mathematics lesson. Other learners were asked to extract the mathematical ideas being used in the dance. On the other hand, this controlled the learners on what to observe, making the

83

introduction strongly framed. The inquisitive facial expressions of the learners sent a message that everyone was eager to mathematise the dance as hinted by the teacher. The main objective of the lesson was to show that cultural activities can be a vehicle for learning mathematics. The other objective of the lesson was, based on cultural consciousness, to discover the mathematics which learners' forefathers were using in their cultural dances leading to an awareness of some mathematical concepts which evolved in learners' local cultures. The cultural dance was then used as an authentic context to which learners were familiar. This helped to illustrate the connection between cultural activities and mathematics, thus blurring the boundary between indigenous mathematical knowledge and academic mathematics.

Figure 5: Demonstration of a Tswana dance. Picture taken by the researcher.

The mathematical demand of the context

Through question and answer, counting was discovered as the Mathematics which the dancers were using. It was discussed that for the dancers to be able to do the same thing at the same time, they were counting the same number of footsteps before changing direction. This was confirmed by one of the dancers. When counting was identified as the Mathematics being used by the dancers, it did not sound as deep Mathematics to other learners. Some learners were wondering why they needed to learn such elementary Mathematics in Grade 9. This was signalled by a comment from the back of the classroom.

Chorus shout: Ah ... a!

Little did they know that the traditional dance was used to capture their attention or modification of reality to enable some smooth entry into the challenging mathematics. After reaching an agreement on the number of observed steps per dancer, a table was drawn on the chalkboard showing the number of dancers in one row and their total number of steps in another row. A number pattern was observed involving the number of dancers and the number of foot-steps (see the illustration below). The second row shows the total number of steps made by all the dancers if each dancer is making five steps before changing direction.

Number of dancers	1	2	3	4	- - - -	n
Number of foot-steps	5	10	15	20	- - - -	nx5

The second row was used to introduce a sequence. Through deductive reasoning the rule connecting the terms of the sequence was generalised. The inductive reasoning engaged the learners in mathematical thinking. Learners managed to explain their understanding of a sequence leading to its definition. Given the periodic nature of the cultural dance – going forward, backward and sideways, the implied mathematics involved is periodic in motion since the steps were repeated over time. This led to another sequence - a constant sequence: 5, 5, 5, 5 ...whose n^{th} term is 5. Learners concluded that their forefathers were using mathematics in coming up with dancing styles.

Learner: The conclusion we can draw is that the Tswana dancers were doing Mathematics

which can lead us to number patterns.

Teacher: So, in the history of Mathematics, we can proudly say the Tswana people were

capable of developing number patterns which we can use in class for the learning

purpose. (Learners quietly followed the teacher's explanation with an 'Aha'

expression showing on their faces).

To accommodate other local cultures the teacher probed further on the existence of number patterns in other local cultures.

Class teacher: Where else can we see patterns in our local cultures?

Learner: In the Venda clothing.

Learner: In the Ndebele paintings and beadings.

During class discussions, some learners reiterated that they could use their knowledge of number patterns to design different dancing styles. Besides enabling learners to access Mathematics through the dance, school mathematics was used to understand the dance deeper through linking the dancing style to a number pattern.

This discovery, according to Ladson-Billings (1995) possibly led to a positive cultural identity. Ladson-Billings (ibid) defined culturally – relevant instruction as a pedagogy that can empower learners intellectually, socially, emotionally and politically by using cultural referents to impart knowledge skills and attitude.

Analysis of the group work tasks

In the class discussion on finding the next terms of the sequence formed using the dance, there was a heated debate on the possible values which the general term 'n' could take in a real dancing situation. Realistic considerations were to be recruited. By recruiting realistic considerations in engaging big values of the general term 'n' in the context – the Tswana dance, learners were critically and mathematically thinking. This triggered a debate on possible values which 'n' could take in the context.

Learner D: But mum does 'n' represent any number?

Teacher: That's a very good question. What do others think?

Learner B: I think 'n' can stand for any value.

Learner E: Hmm, I do not think it can stand for any number.

Learner F: 'n' cannot be 100 because they will be too many dancers dancing at the

same time.

Teacher: Let's find out from the dancers. Is the number of dancers limited per dance?

Dancer: Yes if we are too many we are put in groups. Sometimes we can be

up to 12 but not more than twelve. People watching the game should be able

to follow and enjoy it.

Teacher: Can 'n' be zero?

Chorus answer: No! No! No!

The learner who argued that 'n' could stand for any value might have been thinking of the function of a variable in a normal mathematical situation. Making 'n'= 0 meant no dancer, therefore no dance and making 'n' say 100 meant there were going to be too many dancers dancing at the same time. This, according to one of the dancers would hinder the spectators from reading or following the dance. In this case, the choice of 'n' as having a limiting value was drawn from the familiarity of the context. This suggests that a certain dose of the authentic context was relied upon to make sense of the situation. By attending to the learners' realistic considerations, the teacher indirectly communicated the significance of the contexts for engagement in mathematical thinking. However, in a general series the possibility of 'n' being equal to zero and 'n' being infinite for an infinite series was explained, 'n' could stand for any number. The conclusion drawn was that learners were really engaged in the lesson. This gave currency to their cultures

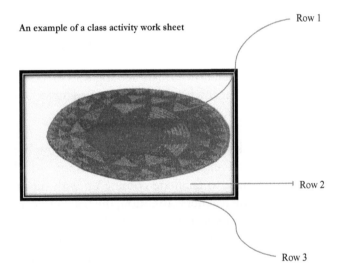

An example of a class activity work sheet

Row 1

Row 2

Row 3

The above picture is a basket from the Zulu culture.
(a) Count the number of black triangles row 1.
(b) Count the number of black triangles in row 2.
(c) Count the number of black triangles in row 3.
(d) Write down the number pattern formed using the number of triangles from
Row 1: row 2: row 3

Rows	1 2 3 4 - - - - n
Number of triangles	

To the number pattern formed determine the next three terms of the sequence.

(e) Explain the rule that generates the terms of the sequence.

(f) Find the expression for the nth term.

Although the teacher tried to make the mathematics intentions clear in all the aspects in the worksheet questions, access to mathematical problems remained difficult to some learners. The majority of learners found question (g) rather challenging. The preceding part (f) which demanded inductive reasoning was well done. The relationship between the term and its position in the sequence was not visible to many learners. Comments like the ones below were echoed:

Learner: Ha…a… it is difficult to start from the row position to the number of triangles.

Learner: We are failing to see how … (something said in Tswana) … how the number of rows meet with the number of triangles in the row.

The rule needed some knowledge of exponents. Although the learners had just completed exponents, the application of that knowledge was not immediate to facilitate coming up with the rule. As more groups called for the teachers' attention, the teacher decided to conduct a whole class discussion on the task. The rule was then deduced in class through class discussions leading to the nth term $= 2^{n-1} \times 10$. The question demanded deep approaches to learning (Biggs, 1999), whereby learners were expected to make numerous links to already known concepts (knowledge of exponents). This, according to Biggs (ibid) leads to construction of new knowledge and long term retention of those ideas and relevant facts. This deep approach to learning was rather new to the learners in this class as they were used to the surface approach to learning.

While educators cannot influence the orientations to learning that learners bring to their studies, they are able to manipulate the learning context, providing a *window of opportunity* to influence the approach that the learners adopt, and therefore the quality of learning (English, et al., 2004). After recognising the needs of the learning task, the teacher had to encourage learners to engage the most appropriate approach with the end goal being to have all learners engage in meaningful, deep approaches to learning and enhance their abilities to continue to do as well as possible.

All in all, the teacher rationalised the lesson on the premise that learners would be able to note the relevance of culturally-based activities for Mathematics learning. She paid attention to realistic considerations raised by learners in engaging some of the activities in solving mathematical tasks. She then transformed the real authentic contexts into imaginary contexts that learners were to engage, in order to make 'n', the general term take any value. This imagination assisted the learners in finding the required 'n' values. However, by doing this what the teacher implied was, what was most important was to be able to use the derived rule to find any missing term in the sequence. At the end, learners understood that the challenging task required them to produce a mathematical model (through mathematising the involved cultural activities) for finding the nth term that is any term in the sequence irrespective of the depicted realistic situations.

Other concepts to be taught using the cultural dance

During this study, it was observed that the cultural dance context can be used to teach and learn Mathematics even at Tertiary Level. For instance, by recruiting realistic considerations raised by learners, one can start thinking about **bounded sequences**. Although mathematically the produced sequences may be thought of as being infinite, according to the dancers, for the spectators to appreciate the beauty of the dance the number of dancers should be limited. This leads to an upper bound. Such sequences are usually introduced at higher levels, say at University. Having a possible maximum number of dancers dancing at the same time meant the produced sequence was *bounded above*. Suppose the produced sequence is referred to as u_n = 5; 10; 15; 20; -; - ; then u_n is said to be *bounded above* if there is a number M such that $u_n \leq M$ *for all n*. M is therefore representing the upper term (upper bound) in the sequence to be calculated using the maximum expected number of dancers to be in the game. This can easily be understood using the argument that the number of dancers should have a limiting value for the audience to be able to read the dance. The same argument can be presented when introducing the concept of being *bounded below* where this time it is the minimum number of dancers expected in the dance which is used to calculate say m the lowest term (lower bound) of the sequence. We can now say the sequence u_n is *bounded below* if there is a number m such that $m \leq u_n$ *for all n*. Since there should be a minimum number of dancers for the dance to be performed and a maximum number of dancers to have a sensible dance, the so formed sequence can be said to be both bounded above and bounded below therefore bounded.

On the other hand, acquisition of mathematical knowledge can assist in the understanding of the cultural activities. For example, knowledge of bounded sequences can be used to understand the idea of limiting the number of dancers. Since the idea of a limit pervades almost all work in calculus and analysis, the dancing context used in the study can be used in a number of mathematics teaching and learning contexts. It can then be argued that mathematisation of the cultural dance presented in the study can be used as an entry point to mathematics education.

Learners' perspectives on the connection between school mathematical knowledge and cultural activities

At the end of the lesson, learners were asked to complete journals reflecting on the lessons learnt. The majority of learners described the lesson in terms of both the Mathematics content and the context engaged.

Learner 1, for example, revealed thus: I have learnt Mathematics with the Setswana dance.

Learner 2 revealed thus: I have learnt that dancing uses number patterns.

The above statements indicate that learners were able to pull-out mathematical knowledge from a culturally–based activity, a dance. Learners positioned cultural activities as providing a smooth entry into the Mathematics. The context was used to tease out the indigenous mathematical knowledge. Some learners gave expressions like:

Learner 3: I now know how to dance and how to draw a number pattern from a dance. I

understood mathematics from that dance. I now understand how mathematics

and traditional dances work.

Learners also evaluated their knowledge of school mathematics as enabling them to understand cultural activities even much better. This is illuminated in some of the learners' remarks below: (All the underlining was done by the author to add emphasis)

Learner 4: I feel good because I have learnt how mathematics can be used to change the

rhythm of the dance. I now understand the Tswana dance better than before. I can

even design my own dancing styles using my knowledge of number patterns.

Learner 5: I now know how to dance and how to draw a number pattern from a dance. I

understood mathematical concepts from that dance. I understand how mathematics

and traditional dance work.

Learner 6: I got interested because when we go to the cultural village we can learn more about

number patterns. Mathematics has very important applications outside class which can help you to understand the subject and the activities.

Learner 7: I think much has changed because I used to see cultural activities as activities

just ended at the village but now…now I can use the activities to understand the

mathematics we learn at school, to simplify my work and also use mathematics to

understand these activities.

Learner 8: When I go to the cultural village I will focus on finding the mathematics they

will be using. I think I will spend more time trying to find that Mathematics.

According to Learner 4, mathematical knowledge helped him or her to read the dance and learn more about the traditional dance. He/she was even thinking of designing some dancing styles out of the knowledge acquired. Learners with such thinking can even start dancing clubs which may be performed at cultural villages and other entertaining functions for a fee. Thus, being economically empowered. Learner 4's comment also illustrates the agency of mathematics: "mathematics can be used to change the rhythm of a dance". This suggests that the more mathematics one knows the more dancing styles one can come up with. Learner 5's comment (I now know how to dance) in the excerpt indicates competence and confidence gained as a result of participation in the culturally relevant lesson. Learners such as Learner 7, who access mathematics through authentic cultural contexts, become doubly advantaged in that they gain access to both mathematics and practical aspects of the recruited context itself. This indicates how culture can serve as a resource for students from socially disadvantaged groups. Thus, it is part of their funds of knowledge.

The learners (for example, Learner 7 and Learner 8) seem to be suggesting that the lesson activities developed in them a skill to read the world mathematically, which they thought they would use when they visit the cultural village in future. Learners valued and appreciated the gained knowledge which they revealed would enable them to understand and experience cultural activities from a mathematical point of view. Their participation in the lesson equipped them with a mathematical lens which they said they were going to use to view and read the world mathematically. However, it was revealed that in order to induct learners into thinking mathematically and viewing the world through mathematical lenses, mathematics pedagogy should explore contexts/scenarios to both deepen understanding of mathematics and understanding of the contexts/scenarios involved (Stinson et al., 2012). Shizha (2013) also argued that pedagogy should be approached from diverse perspectives that allow the pedagogical process to be culturally sensitive, allowing classroom life to reflect the social and cultural contexts that relate to students 'experiences.

Conclusion

This chapter has raised suggestions on how artifacts from indigenous basket and mat weaving can be used as [teaching] aid in the teaching of Mathematics. The chapter has identified and analysed (through mathematisation) artifacts from indigenous basket and mat weaving processes. It has been submitted that the derived concepts can be used to enhance understanding of academic mathematical knowledge at various levels of the mathematics curriculum. The chapter has also raised suggestions on how the Tswana dance can be used in the teaching and learning of Mathematics. The mathematisation of the dance revealed embedded concepts which may be used in constructing and enhancing understanding of academic mathematical knowledge.

Despite using indigenous knowledge as a vehicle for accessing academic mathematics, the implementation of indigenous mathematical practices into the mainstream mathematics curriculum can lead to economic empowerment of the learners. Classroom experience should focus on the need to meet current societal needs. Learning has to be a meaningful and fulfilling experience that helps students to be useful participants in their society. It has been argued that mathematical knowledge can be applied to enhance participation in cultural and socio-economic activities where some remuneration is gained.

There is still a lot to explore on how mathematised different indigenous practices impact on the teaching and learning of academic Mathematics concepts. Further research still needs to be done on mathematising other cultural activities for academic purposes and for economic empowerment.

References

Antony, G., & Walshaw, M. (2009). Characteristics of effective teaching of mathematics: A review from the West. *Journal of Mathematics Teacher Education, 2*(2), 147-164.

Ausubel, D.P. (1996). *Educational Psychology: A cognitive view*. New York: Holt, Rinehart and Winston.

Banks, J. (1991). A curriculum for empowerment, action, and change. In Sleeter, C. E. (Ed.), Empowerment through multicultural education (pp. 125-141). Albany: SUNY Press.

Blum, W., Galbraith, P. L., Henn, H. W., & Nasir, M. (2007). Modelling and applications in mathematics education, [Online] Available: http//dx.doi.org/10.1007/978-0-387-29822-1. (June 2, 2011).

Biggs, J. (1999). *Teaching for Quality Learning at University*. Buckingham: SRHE and Open University Press.

Boutte, G. S., & Hill, E. L. (2006). African American communities: Implications for culturally relevant teaching. *New Education, 2*(4), 311-329.

Boyle-Baise, M. (2005). Preparing community-oriented teachers: Reflections from a multicultural service-learning project. *Journal of Teacher Education, 56*(5), 446-458.

Chirenda, M. (1993). Children's Mathematics activities stimulated by analysis of African elements. In C. Julie, D. Angelis & Z. Davis (Eds.), *Political Dimensions of Mathematics Education 2 (pp. 149-153).* Cape Town: Maskew Miller.

de Beer, M. (2010). Collaboration recommendation for culturally relevant teaching and development in Higher Education. Retrieved from http://www.cepd.org.za/files/pictures/SUBMISSION-COLLABORATION%20RECOMMENDATIONS%20FOR%20CULTURALLY%20RELEVANT%20TEACHING website:

English, L., Luckett, P., & Mladenovic, R. (2004). Encouraging a deep approach to learning through curriculum design. *An International Journal, 13*(4), 461-488.

Fatima, R. (2012). Role of Mathematics in the Development of Society. Available online at: http://www.ncert.nic.in/pdf_files/Final-Article-Role%20of%Mathematics%20. Accessed on 31March, 2017.

Gay, G. (2000). *Culturally Responsive Teaching: Theory, research, and practice.* New York: Teachers College Press.

Graven, M., & Venkat, H. (2007). Emerging pedagogic agendas in the teaching of Mathematical Literacy. *African Journal of Research in SMT Education, 11*(2), 67-84.

Ladson-Billings, G. (1994). *The dream keepers: Successful teaching for African-American students.* San Francisco: Jossey-Bass.

Ladson-Billings, G. (1995). Toward a Theory of Culturally Relevant Pedagogy. *American Educational Research Journal, 32*(3), 465-491.

Masiwa, T. (2001). Nhodo: An Ancient Teaching Aid. *Zimaths University of Zimbabwe, 5*(1), 2-4.

Masiwa, T. (2001). Chess, Tsoro and Powers of two. *Zimaths University of Zimbabwe, 5*(2), 11-13.

Masiwa, T. (2004). Tsoro: the quest for Chihwangu. Zimaths 8(2). Harare, UZ Mathematics Department pp 4-8.

Mawere, M. (2013). The struggle of African Indigenous Knowledge Systems in an Age of Globalisation: A case for Children's Traditional Games in South-Eastern Zimbabwe. Langaa RPCIG Publishers: Cameroon.

Mhlolo, M. K., Venkat, H., & Schäfer, M. (2012). The nature of the mathematical connections teachers make. *Pythagoras, 33*(1), Art. #22, 9 pages.

Moloi, T.J. (2015). Using indigenous games to teach problem-solving in Mathematics in rural learning ecologies. JHEA/RESA, 13(1-2), 21-32.

Mosimege, M., & Ismael, A. (2004). Ethnomathematical studies on indigenous games: Examples from Southern Africa. *Proceedings of the 10th International Congress of Mathematics Education (ICEM-10)*. Copenhagen. Roskilde University, 107-118.

Neuman, S. B. (1999). Creating continuity in early literacy: Linking home and school with a culturally responsive approach. In L. B. Gambrell, L. M. Morrows, S. B. Neuman & M. Pressley (Eds.), *Best practices in literacy instruction (pp. 258-270)*. New York: Guilford.

Nkopodi, N., & Mosimege, M. (2009). Incorporating the indigenous game of Morabaraba in the learning of Mathematics. *South African Journal of Education*, 29(3), 377-392.

Nxumalo A, S., & Mncube, D.W. (2009). Using indigenous games and knowledge to decolonise the school curriculum. *Perspectives in Education*, 36(20, 103-118.

Rosa, M., & Orey, D. C. (2010). Ethnomodelling: A Pedagogical Action for Uncovering Ethnomathematical Practices. *Journal of Mathematical Modelling and Application, 1*(3), 58-67.

Stinson, D. W., Bidwell, C. R., & Powell, G. C. (2012). Critical Pedagogy and Teaching Mathematics for Social Justice. 4(1), 76-94.

Shizha, E. (2013). Reclaiming our Indigenous Voices: The problem with Postcolonial sub- Saharan African School Curriculum. *Journal of indigenous Social Development*, 2(1), 1-18.

Tilbury, D. (2011). Education for Sustainable Development: An Expert Review of Processes and Learning. *UNESCO 2011*. Paris, France.

UNESCO (2018). Issues and trends in Education for Sustainable Development.

Walker, R. A. (1990). *Sculptured mancala game boards of Sub- Saharan Africa. Phd thesis.* Indiana University.

Yosso, T J. (2002). 'Toward a Critical Race Curriculum'. Equity& Excellence in Education, 35:2, 93 – 107.

Yosso, T J. (2005). Whose Culture has Capital? A Capital race Theory discussion of community cultural wealth. Race ethnicity and Education 8(1), 69-91.

Zaslavsky, C. (1973). *Africa Counts: Number Pattern in African Culture.* Chicago: Lawrence Hills Books.

Chapter 5

Challenges in Implementing the Competence-based Curriculum in Zimbabwe: Peeping through the African Indigenous Education Philosophy Lenses

Wonder Muchabaiwa

Abstract

The Competence-based School Curriculum (CBSC) has been described by educationists as a robust and pragmatic education blue-print amenable with Zimbabwe's 2030 development agenda. This study thus interrogates the challenges experienced by schools in their efforts to implement the CBSC and applies the philosophy of African Indigenous Education as a conceptual framework to illuminate good practices for curriculum implementation. The qualitative study utilised an explorative research design with eight schools in Bindura district in Mashonaland Central province. Eight school heads (four primary & four secondary) were purposively sampled for in-depth interviews while 32 teachers (16 primary and 16 secondary) were intentionally sampled to participate in Focus Group Discussions (FGDs). Further, 16 secondary school learners were also deliberately selected to participate in the two FGDs. Findings of the study show that while the CBSC remains a robust and pragmatic education blue-print, its implementation has been met with a myriad of challenges that include lack of competences by teachers (incompatible pedagogical approaches), unsuitable school infrastructure, too big class sizes, lack of synergies between schools and industries and the Covid-19 pandemic induced lockdowns. Against this backdrop, the study recommends that school development projects should focus on constructing Science and Computer laboratories as well as workshops for technical subjects to ensure responsive and conducive learning environments. Teachers' colleges should revisit their curricula, especially for primary schools such that primary school teachers specialise in particular subjects. There is also need for in-service training for primary and secondary school teachers to re-orient them to the expectations of the CBSC and equip them with techno-based pedagogies so as to allow a smooth transition to virtual or on-line teaching.

Keywords: Competence-based curriculum, indigenous philosophy, education, Zimbabwe

Introduction

The Zimbabwe curriculum framework promotes a competence-based approach which is realised through practical-oriented learning. This updated curriculum (2015-2022) aims to modernise the education system at all the three levels (infant, junior and secondary) in order to align it with global trends and with modern technologies (MoPSE, 2015). It is important to observe that the Ministry of Primary and Secondary Education (MoPSE)'s efforts to review the curriculum was a result of numerous factors including: the agrarian reform of the post-2000 period, developments in ICTs, the new Constitution which came into effect in 2013, as well as recommendations of the Presidential Commission of Inquiry into Education and Training (1999); commonly known as the Nziramasanga Commission (NC) (Gondo et al, 2019). The framework has taken on aboard the human capital, social, political, economic and technological transformations in the country to propel the 2030 development agenda. The curriculum shift from being content based to a competence based one which focuses on the learner's capacity to apply knowledge, skills and aptitude in an independent and practical way thus constitutes part of the trajectory for industrialisation and modernisation. When juxtaposed with the provisions of the philosophy of African Indigenous Education Systems, it can be observed that the Competence-based School Curriculum (CBSC) draws several parallels. However, this study explored challenges experienced in implementing the CBSC and argues that the philosophy of African Indigenous Education provides robust pedagogical approaches and a panacea to the challenges impeding the realisation of the objectives of the competence-based school curriculum and the 2030 development agenda.

Background

The curriculum review was necessitated by the fact there was observed a mismatch between the existing content- based curriculum and the development goals for Zimbabwe. Hence, a Presidential Commission of Inquiry into Education and Training (1999) – popularly known as the Nziramasanga Commission was set up. The report identified six major defects in the then curriculum and these were: (1) the old curriculum lacked national values to guide learners (2), it did not praise the virtues of self-reliance, entrepreneurship and business skills, (3), it offered little to develop the learners' natural talents and aptitudes (4) it did not aggressively promote the teaching of Science, Maths, Technology, Vocational and Technical subjects and indigenous languages, (5), it did not place adequate premium on Early Childhood Development and non-formal education and (6), it was examination oriented and summative in nature (Gondo et al, 2019). In other words, the findings and recommendations of the Nziramasanga Commission (1999) contributed to the crafting of the Competence-based school curriculum that is currently being implemented (2015-2022).

Competence-based learning refers to systems of instruction/ methodologies, assessment, grading, and academic reporting that are based on learners demonstrating that they have learned the knowledge, skills, attitudes and aptitudes they are expected to learn as they progress through their education (Kabombwe & Mulenga, 2019). According to UNESCO (2017), a competency-based curriculum emphasises what learners are expected to do rather than mainly focusing on what they are expected to know. It implies that learners should acquire and apply the knowledge, skills, values, and attitudes to solve problems they encounter in everyday life and across the globe. Thus, a Competence-Based Curriculum is a framework or guide for the subsequent detailed development of competencies, associated methodologies, training and assessment resources. One way of ensuring that the competences acquired in educational institutions are in line with the competences required by the working life in future is through intensified collaboration between educational institutions and companies, thus enhancing work-integrated learning (Aaltonen, 2013). She further elaborated that work-integrated learning can be characterized as dealing with more than just work placement, as it also deals with the recognition and acknowledgement of the social/situational, contextual, collaborative, implicit and tacit aspects of knowledge and skills. Thus, a competence-based curriculum will inculcate competences on how to transfer, exploit and make explicit the inferred norms and underlying patterns, skills, know-how, routines, praxis and behaviours from one place to the next and from one situation and person to the next.

While Zimbabwe can celebrate the successful crafting of a robust education blueprint, (the competence-based school curriculum), it is the implementation that has given educationists a headache. The achievement of the objectives at any level of education depends largely on effective implementation of its planned programme

(Ahmad & Lukman, 2015) and researches have shown that no matter how robust a curriculum is contrived, designed and documented, implementation remains a critical activity (Musingarabwi, 2017). By implication, most educational blueprints experience challenges at the implementation stage. In his opinion, Mkpa (2005) remarked that, it is at the implementation stage that many excellent curriculum plans and other educational policies falter. This study interrogates the challenges experienced in implementing the competence-based curriculum and suggests that educationists in Zimbabwe should take a leaf from the philosophy of African Indigenous education systems with regards to pedagogical approaches and learning environments.

Conceptual Framework: The Philosophical Underpinnings of African Indigenous Education Systems

African traditional education sometimes referred to as pre-colonial education focused on equipping young generations with knowledge and skills for survival in society (Adeyemi & Adeyinka, 2002). The pedagogical approaches were entrenched in oral traditions and practical work. The philosophical foundations of African traditional education were identified as preparationism, functionalism, perennialism, humanism and holisticism (Adeyemi and Adeyinka, 2002: 231).

African traditional education emphasised a practical approach in teaching content and was relevant to the people's daily lives (Fafunwa and Aisiku, 1982). The principle of preparationism which identified both formal and informal educational practices implied that the role of teaching and learning was to equip boys and girls with the skills appropriate to their gender in preparation for their distinctive roles in society. In other words, African traditional education was gender based. There was a very clear dichotomous gender divide in terms of occupations to be fulfilled. These were socially and culturally defined masculine and feminine responsibilities. Education was a preparation for life and this contradicts Dewey who observed that education was not a preparation for life but life itself (Tummons, 2012). This principle needs to be adopted with care because gender stereotyping of disciplines can be detrimental to development; the CBSC should be gender sensitive and give female and male learners to study subjects of their choice.

Fig 1.1: Indigenous Education Framework

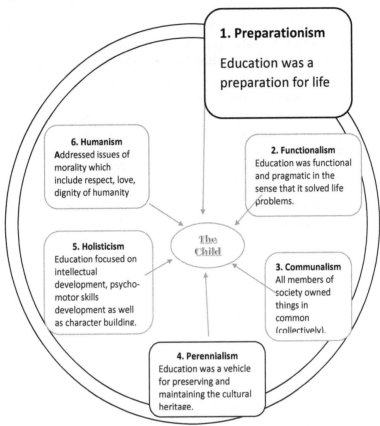

Source: *Author*

African Indigenous education was also premised in the pedagogy of functionalism and pragmatism where the guiding principles and methods of instruction were child-centred. By extension, indigenous education in pre-colonial societies in Africa was predominantly utilitarian and also a participatory kind of education in which people learned through imitation, work, oral literature and initiation ceremonies (Adeyemi & Adeyinka, 2002). Education was functional and pragmatic in the sense that it solved real life problems. Apprenticeship was the common pedagogical approach where children learned by doing the work while attached to an expert and experienced adult. In doing so, vocational skills were acquired by directly engaging in specific jobs. It becomes therefore important for the CBSC to adopt learner-centred pedagogical approaches, inculcating competences directly related to specific vocations.

Fafunwa and Aisiku (1982) also observed that the principle of communalism discouraged individualism. All members of society owned some things in common (collectively) and applied the communal spirit to life and work. Children belonged to the community and every member had a stake in the upbringing of children. Such a theme can be used in teaching the concept of teamwork. However, the concept of teamwork sounds alien if explained from the context of Eurocentric philosophy where emphasis is on the individual and simultaneously the group resulting in conflicting instructions to the learners. This calls for cooperation by all curriculum implementers to effectively execute the implementation of the CBSC.

Perennialism was another philosophical underpinning of African indigenous education which was seen as a vehicle for preserving and maintaining their cultural heritage. As the elders theorise and teach oral literature that covers fables, folktales, legends, myths, proverbs and stories, children received their socialisation and education (Tummons, 2012). Through stories children's thinking, knowledge and attitudes were extended. While in the process of storytelling, children were exposed to creative and critical thinking skills as well as the capacity to imagine and understand their world thereby synthesising, refining and redefining their experiences to open up for future possibilities (Fafunwa & Aisiku, 1982).

Education was holistic in nature as it focused on intellectual growth, psycho-motor skills development as well as character building (Adeyemi & Adeyinka, 2002). It also equipped boys and girls with skills to undertake multiple occupations. By implication, it adopted a multidisciplinary approach where a builder also learned for examples some carpentry and plumbing skills. The graduate from such an education becomes multi-skilled. Integrated learning thus becomes one of the key aspects of the CBSC.

Another potent contribution of African traditional philosophy to education is the aspect of humanism referred to as Ubuntu in Africa. It focused on character building; addressing issues of morality which include respect, love for one another, and dignity of humanity (Adeyemi & Adeyinka, 2002). Humanism is used here to refer to a philosophy that sees human needs, interests and dignity as of fundamental importance and concern. The importance of "ubuntu" shows the underlying principles of interdependence and humanism in African life to be imbued in the CBSC. Furthermore, it illuminates the communal embeddedness and connectedness of a person to other persons (Lumumba-Kasongo, 2002). It can thus be argued that the African Indigenous Education was quite comprehensive in its content, pedagogy and implementation hence the Zimbabwean competence-based curriculum can be leveraged against the provisions of the philosophy of African indigenous education.

Research Questions

The study thus sought to answer the following questions:
- What are the main challenges experienced by schools in implementing the Competence-based Curriculum?
- To what extent are the teachers trained and prepared to implement the competence-based curriculum?
- To what extent is the school infrastructure fit for the purpose and practice of the competence-based curriculum?
- What parallels can be drawn between the competence-based curriculum and the African Indigenous Education systems?
- What lessons and good practices in curriculum implementation can be learnt from the African Indigenous education systems?

Research Methodology

This study adopted the qualitative approach in order to fully understand the challenges experienced by schools in implementing the competence-based curriculum. Cohen et al (2007) describe qualitative research as involving an interpretive naturalistic approach to the world where researchers study objects in their natural settings, attempting to make sense of or interpreting phenomena in terms of the meanings people bring to them." The qualitative approach was adopted because it allows an in-depth analysis of the challenges experienced by schools in implementing the competence-based curriculum.

Purposive sampling thus allowed the researcher to identify school heads and experienced primary and secondary school teachers for both interviews and Focus Group Discussions (FGDs). Eight school heads (four primary and four secondary) as well as eight senior teachers (four primary and four secondary) were purposively sampled as participants for in-depth interviews. 32 experienced teachers (16 primary and 16 secondary) were purposively sampled for FGDs. 16

secondary school students were also selected across the forms on the basis of specific disciplines and participated in the two FGDs. Patton (2007) observes that purposive sampling allows researchers to identify information sites and it thus allowed the researcher to explore in detail challenges experienced in the implementation of the CBSC. I trained two research assistants to help with data collection.

In-depth Key Informant Interviews (KIIs)

In-depth interviews were held with heads of schools and experienced teachers in both primary and secondary schools in Bindura district with the intention of getting detailed information on the challenges experienced by both primary and secondary schools in implementing the CBSC. Focus group discussions (FGDs) were conducted with male and female teachers as well as learners at the different primary and secondary schools in Bindura district. Permission to carry out field work was sought from respective schools' authorities. The individual participants were informed about the purpose of the research and its significance and lastly anonymity and confidentiality were observed throughout the research process.

Research Findings and Discussion

Findings of the study reveal that the competence-based school curriculum draws several parallels with the provisions of the African Indigenous Education systems which emphasise the acquisition of skills relevant to specific vocations and the practical approach to learning. However, there are challenges experienced in implementing the CBSC by both primary and secondary schools which include; lack of competences by teachers (incompatible pedagogical approaches), unsuitable school infrastructure, and too big class sizes, lack of synergies between schools and industries and the Covid-19 induced lockdowns. Perceptions from participants reveal robust pedagogical approaches in African Indigenous Education with regards to skills development and knowledge transfer which could be adopted, improved and applied to implement the competence-based curriculum.

Teacher competences and the Competence-based School Curriculum

The study explores the relevance and adequacy of teacher competences with regards to the expectations of the competence-based curriculum and observed that the existing stock of teacher competences fall short. The competence-based curriculum demands that both primary and secondary school teachers acquire a new set of skills and responsive pedagogical approaches to execute their jobs efficiently and expeditiously. An interview with one secondary school science teacher reveals that:

> The competence-based curriculum requires us as teachers to use new technologies and software which we are not conversant with. All we are doing here is trial and error. The syllabuses for most science subjects emphasise research through laboratories and practicals which most of us need some in-service training. While the competence-based curriculum can be applauded as an education blueprint, it has deskilled many teachers as we continue to grapple with demands of the new curriculum.

The above sentiments point to serious skills deficit in teachers who need re-orientation through in-service training. Another teacher in the primary school shared her sentiments:

> While I appreciate the relevance of the competence-based curriculum, it has introduced too many subjects in the primary school, some of which we are not able to teach. For example, the competence-based curriculum includes Science and Technology as a subject and I specialised in teaching local languages at college. Truly speaking, I am not conversant with some of the concepts in Science and Technology. Maybe its high time primary school teachers teach specialised subjects just as is the case with secondary schools.

During focus group discussions, it emerged out quite strongly that there is a very serious problem in the primary schools where a teacher is expected to teach thirteen subjects, including those that they are not familiar with. The need for primary school teachers to specialise came out very strongly. Participants felt that primary school teachers need to be experts in specific subjects in order for them to execute the competence-based curriculum effectively There seems to be gross oversight in the primary school where a teacher who specialised in local languages is expected to teach Science and Technology, Physical Education and many other subjects. Participants felt that teachers colleges should train primary school teachers to teach

105

specific subjects and that such teachers should teach a specific subject of specialisation across the grades in the primary school.

Focus Group Discussions with secondary school learners revealed that students are sure of what is expected of them in the competence-based curriculum. They explained that they are expected to work on certain research projects, and that the teachers are not very clear on how the research projects should be carried out. This points to yet another serious teachers' skill gap with regards to research techniques appropriate for secondary learners. A follow-up interview with teachers confirms that both primary and secondary school teachers are hardly equipped to handle research issues. One senior teacher explains:

> *The competence-based curriculum emphasises discovery of knowledge through research and yet for many teachers this is area that needs in-service training. It's so sad that many teachers are not conversant with research techniques and yet they are expected to guide the learners in research projects. If one moves around the schools, it e observed that the research projects are handled differently. I think there is need for national works on conducting research such that we have a systematic procedure in conducting research y secondary school learners.*

Another teacher also explained during an interview:

> *I think there is need for in-service training or workshops to appraise teachers with requisite skills for executing the competence based curriculum. The competence based school curriculum demands that learners prepare some portfolios and many teachers have no idea on how this is supposed to be done. Further, many teachers are not conversant with techniques in continuous assessment. The challenges have stalled progress in implementing the new curriculum.*

Lack of competences in research and continuous assessment by teachers thus compromises the effective implementation of the competence-based curriculum.

While the competence-based curriculum remains a robust education blue-print in terms of its content and objectives, it is its implementation which has been met with difficulties. A robust curriculum framework should be complemented by a competent human resource base fit for deployment and practice (Kabombwe & Mulenga, 2019). Through the lenses of the philosophy of African Indigenous Education, it can be observed that the efficacy of African indigenous education revolved around the competence of an expert, an experienced mentor (Adeyemi & Adeyinka, 2002). In other words, the mentor in African Indigenous Education possessed relevant skills relevant for a specific trade or vocation, in which they initiated their youths. Possession of such skills was coupled with dynamic pedagogical approaches which hinged on learner-centred apprenticeship emphasising learning by doing as production and training were inextricably interlinked (Odora-Hoppers, 2000). It is in the same spirit that this study argues that teachers in both primary and secondary schools need reskilling such that they become experts in their respective subject areas to allow effective implementation of the competence-based school curriculum (CBSC). The competence-based curriculum requires teachers to be knowledgeable of the key principles of the curriculum and equipped with skills and desirable attitudes to teach using competency-based approaches appropriately (Mulenga & Kabombwe, 2019). The mindset of teachers needs to be refocused and they need to embrace the competence-based curriculum which emphasises competences directly linked to the expectations of vocations in industry and commerce. Lessons can be drawn from African indigenous education African which emphasised a practical approach in teaching content which was relevant to the people's daily lives (Fafunwa and Aisiku, 1982).

The prevailing situation in the primary schools is a real cause for concern where the schoolteacher is expected to teach multiple of subjects. By extension, primary school teachers cannot be jacks of all trades and masters of none. Such tendencies borders on laxity and inefficiency in the implementation of the competence-based curriculum. A situation where a teacher who specialised in teaching local languages is found teaching Science and Technology in the primary school is really regrettable. These findings corroborate findings in studies carried out by Kabombwe and Mulenga (2019) in Zambia who contend that for the competency-based approaches to be successful, teachers should be knowledgeable enough to let their learners get involved in the learning process since teachers are major players in curriculum implementation. In the same vein, Moodley (2013) further elaborate that teachers need to have expertise in their particular subjects in order for them to yield targeted products. It is against this backdrop, that this study argues that the model of primary education needs to draw lessons and good practices from the African Indigenous Education in ensuring that primary school teachers become experts in specific subject areas which they should teach across the grades. Contrary to the findings by Muneja (2015) in Tanzania who argued that most teachers did not know what a competency-based curriculum, most teachers were actually aware of what a competence-based curriculum involves. However, their problem is lack of requisite skills to efficiently execute the competence-based curriculum.

Large class sizes and pedagogical approaches

Findings of the study show that class size was another critical factor that impeded the effective implementation of the competence-based curriculum. Apparently the competence-based curriculum framework provides for learner-centred approaches including individual instruction and active participation by learners (Muneja, 2015). Such approaches are very difficult with large numbers of learners in a class. An interview with one secondary school head reveals:

> One major challenge experienced by teachers in implementing the competence-based curriculum has to do with large class sizes. Our classes are too big owing to different socio-economic factors bedevilling the country at the moment. Due to economic challenges the government has imposed a teacher recruitment freeze which has seen the teacher-student ratio rising to 1:80 instead of the normal 1:35 for secondary schools. Teachers are thus overwhelmed by such big classes and resort to pedagogical approaches that contradict the expectations of the competence-based curriculum. Individual instruction or active participation of learners becomes very difficult under such teaching and learning conditions.

On the same note, another primary school head shared her sentiments:

> With regards to class size, the situation in primary school is quite pathetic. There are classes that have 80 or even 90 learners. Learners are congested in classrooms that were initially meant for 40 learners. Under such circumstances, teachers can hardly apply learner-centred approaches or problem solving pedagogies as encouraged by the competence-based curriculum. They may resort to lecture methods which do not allow learners to demonstrate the competences learnt. Just imagine a teacher teaching 13 subjects per week in a class with 80 learners.

Another primary school teacher had this to say:

> The issue of class size has caused teacher urn-out in many. Right now, I am teaching a double class because my colleague is not feeling well and is on leave. Because of teacher recruitment freeze, the head cannot get a relief teacher. It's not possible to

108

apply learner centred approaches and teach all the subjects required by the competence curriculum. How do I assess learning progress of all these learners?

Focus Group Discussions with teachers confirmed that appropriate pedagogical approaches for implementing the competence-based curriculum tend to be compromised by large class sizes in both primary and secondary schools. Participants further revealed that the number of learners in particular classes is not commensurate with resources available, further restricting teachers to apply appropriate pedagogical approaches for implementing the competence-based curriculum. It also emerged out that while learners are expected to practice certain agricultural skills as required by the new curriculum, there is no enough land to do practicals for all learners. Class size becomes a real issue compromising the quality and quantity of written work because this has implications for the marking load.

The findings of the study show that large class sizes are a hindrance to effective implementation of the competence-based curriculum. These findings corroborate findings from a study by Tasara, Muchabaiwa and Gwirayi, (2019) which revealed that the government teacher recruitment freeze increased teacher-pupil ratios to unsustainable levels resulting in teachers being overburdened by heavy teaching and marking loads hence compromising the academic performance of learners and at the same time high teacher-pupil ratios led to teacher burn-out and low morale. It is thus argued in this study that large class sizes in both primary and secondary schools defeat the whole essence of the competence-based curriculum where learners are expected to demonstrate certain competences relevant to either commerce and industry or social services after going through a learning session. Taking a leaf from the provisions of African Indigenous education, one can realise that an expert mentor worked with very few mentees (at times even one) and direct and individual instruction allowed the transfer of skills quite easily (Fafunwa & Aisiku, 1982; Odora-Hoppers, 2000). Such pedagogical approaches allowed for effective interaction between the mentor and the mentees hence the learners were able to demonstrate the knowledge and skills learnt. These findings support the findings from a study by Kabombwe and Mulenga (2019) in Zambia where teachers argued that the competence-based approaches are time consuming to practice in relation to the content coverage hence they always opted for teacher-centred approaches regardless of the understanding of the learners. Against this backdrop, the effective implementation of the competence-based curriculum lies in reducing student-teacher ratios to the recommended ratios of 1:40 for primary schools and 1:35 for secondary schools. Such ratios will allow flexibility and scaffolding for individual learners. Unless the government revises the teacher recruitment freeze and class sizes revert to normalcy, successful implementation of the competence-based curriculum remains a myth and Zimbabwe will struggle to realise the 2030 development agenda.

Incompatible School Infrastructure and the Competence-based Curriculum

Another critical challenge impeding the effective implementing of the CBSC has to do with the school infrastructure which was found to be less compatible with the expectations of the new curriculum. The situation is further exacerbated by lack of synergies between schools and industries, and farming enterprises. One secondary school head explained in an interview:

> *The thrust of the competence-based curriculum is practically oriented and yet our school infrastructure has remained largely ideal for the previous content based curriculum which emphasised theoretical learning sessions. For example, the competence-based curriculum demands that for more than half the time, students should be in Science and Computer laboratories, workshops, and fields learning the practical skills in specific subjects. To the contrary, at this particular school we only have one Science laboratory meant for A' level students and yet all classes must have an opportunity to work in the laboratory. Implementation of the new curriculum becomes quite some challenge.*

On the same issue another secondary school head elaborated:

> *While we celebrate the crafting of a robust curriculum, relevant to demands of our economy, it is its implementation which is giving us quite some headache. As an example, for all our agricultural related subjects, we don't have enough land for practicals and experiments. Neither do we have any space for animal production. Against this backdrop, learning in Agricultural subjects remains theoretical defeating the whole essence of a competence-based curriculum.*

A head at another secondary school also explained:

> *It is given that when these schools were constructed, no one envisaged the drafting of a competence-based curriculum which demands more space for practicals and*

experiments. Many schools do not have space for further developments. What is seriously lacking now are synergies between schools and industries or farms. We need memoranda of understanding with industries and farms to allow our students to have an opportunity for practicals and experiments. Unless this issue is resolved, the implementation of the competence-based curriculum will remain a challenge.

Regarding the same issue a school head at a primary explained:

We have 60 classes here, each with an average of 65 learners and our garden for agricultural purposes measures 35m x 30m. The competence-based curriculum demands that each learner must do some practicals in Agriculture; which of course is not possible with our situation here. The ideal situation was for the school to have a farm of its own. Further, the competence-based curriculum introduced Science and Technology as a subject in the primary school and yet we don't have both Science and computer laboratories. The competence-based curriculum remains a fit for purpose education blueprint, but we seem not to have appropriate infrastructure and resources for its implementation.

Focus group discussions with primary and secondary school teachers revealed that while school infrastructure remains incompatible with the expectations of the CBSC, it is lack of provision of equipment and resources for Science and Computer laboratories that affects more the effective implementation of the new curriculum. It also emerged out that most schools including primary ones do not have functional Science and Computer laboratories and yet students are expected to undertake Science and Information and Communication Technologies (ICTs) related subjects which demand the use of these facilities. It was also revealed that there are no ready-built workshops in many secondary schools for technical subjects such as Wood Technology, Metal Work and Clothing Technology. Engagements with teachers in FGDs also revealed that the implementation of the CBSC was further compounded by the outbreak of the Covid-19 pandemic which instigated incessant lockdowns between March 2020 and February 2021. Under such circumstances, learning was expected to migrate to e-learning platforms, but because many schools lacked ICT infrastructure (both hardware and software) most schools have been closed for a full calendar year. Primary school teachers revealed that the CBSC introduced new subjects in the primary school and yet many schools failed to procure the key textbooks due to financial constraints.

These findings corroborate the findings from a study by Muneja (2010) which noted that for educationists to ensure that the curriculum is effectively implemented, infrastructural facilities, equipment, tools, and materials must be provided in adequate quantities. From an African Indigenous Education perspective, tools of the trade were a key aspect of the traditional apprenticeship model and emphasised on the appropriate environmental contexts hence certain skills were taught in certain seasons and not others (Zulu, 2006; Adeyemi & Adeyinka, 2002). The compatibility between the environment and the skills to be taught remained a cardinal requirement for different skills training sessions in African Indigenous Education systems. Similarly, the implementation of the CBSC can only be successful if the environment is right, proper and conducive.

The findings of this study also reveal a gross disjuncture between the existing school infrastructure and expectations of the CBSC making it very difficult for teachers to execute its implementation. In the same vein, findings in a study by Munikwa (2016) also reveals that the education sector in Zimbabwe has suffered the plight of inadequate instructional materials (basic structures and facilities necessary for effecting teaching). By extension, lack of critical learning facilities like Science and Computer laboratories denies full implementation of the CBSC and consequently derails Zimbabwe's efforts to achieve its 2030 development agenda as well as realising the Sustainable Development Goals. Through the lenses of the African Indigenous Education system, one would observe that learning environments were varied and situational, matching the kind of skill being taught (Zulu, 2006). This calls for educational planners to do an environmental scan and audit the existing infrastructure such that the school infrastructure transforms to conducive environments and becomes compatible with the expectations of the CBSC. Analysing the lessons and good practices of the African Indigenous Education, one would appreciate that it emphasised observation of the effects of the changing seasons on the environment including the vegetation, water levels and how these changes could affect farmers, traders, builders, hunters, fishermen and many other trades (Zulu, 2006). By implication, skills development and transfer was only possible in appropriate environmental contexts. It is against this backdrop that this study argues that effective implementation of the CBSC is only possible by taking a leaf from the philosophy of the African Indigenous

Education and provide responsive and conducive school infrastructure.

Conclusions

The CBSC remains the ideal curriculum for Zimbabwe to realise her 2030 development agenda as well as the internally instituted Sustainable Development Goals. However, the successful implementation of the CBSC hinges on the sync between teachers' competences and expectations of the CBSC supported by a compatible school infrastructure. In the effort to ameliorate challenges impeding the full implementation of the CBSC, Zimbabwe should take a leaf from the philosophy of African Indigenous Education which emphasised pragmatic teaching and learning approaches hinged on learner centred pedagogies in the context of responsive and conducive learning environments. An environment scan and audit may inform educational policies that ensure the provision of learning infrastructure (such as the Science and Computer laboratories, workshops for technical subjects as well as small scale farms for agricultural related subjects) is responsive to the expectations of the CBSC. More so, findings of the study revealed that synergies between schools and industries, and farming enterprises can accord learners an opportunity to do practicals and experiments. It has also been noted that large class sizes as a result of teacher recruitment freeze create difficult circumstances for the implementation of the CBSC as large class sizes tend to constrain available resources and compromise learner-centred pedagogical approaches. The implementation of the CBSC was further compounded by the outbreak of the Covid-19 pandemic which instigated incessant lockdowns. Since many schools were not prepared to migrate to e-learning platforms, there was no learning taking place in schools for nearly 12 months. A holistic approach to solve the problems hindering full implementation of the CBSC is thus imminent.

Recommendations

Basing on the aforementioned findings, the study makes several recommendations informed by the provisions of African Indigenous Education. It is thus important for school development projects to focus on constructing Science and Computer laboratories as well as

113

workshops for technical subjects such as Wood Technology, Building, Metal Work, Fashion Fabrics and Food and Nutrition to ensure responsive and conducive environments. Teachers' colleges should revisit their curricula, especially for primary schools such that primary school teachers specialise in particular subjects to teach in the primary school. To this end, the study recommends that deployment of primary school teachers should be on the basis specific subject areas and not grades. There is also need for in-service training for primary and secondary school teachers to re-orient them to the expectations of the CBSC and equip them with techno-based pedagogies so as to allow a smooth transition to virtual or on-line teaching. In-service training would equip teachers with research techniques which are one of the requisite skills for executing the CBSC. The government should also reconsider teacher recruitment freeze and recruit more teachers to allow the normal teacher-pupil ratio of 1:35 for secondary schools and 1:40 in primary schools. Such ratios would allow teachers to apply pedagogical approaches amenable with the expectations of the CBSC.

References

Aaltonen, K. (2013). The teacher as a Pedagogical Thinker, in Aaltonen et al (2013) eds *Practical skills, education and development – Vocational education and training in Finland,* HAAGA-HELIA University of Applied Sciences.

Adeyemi, M. A. & Adeyinka, A. A. (2002). Some key issues in African traditional education. *McGill Journal of education.* 37 (2): 223-240.

Ahmadi, A. A., & Lukman, A. A. (2015). Issues and Prospects of Effective Implementation of New Secondary School Curriculum in Nigeria. *Journal of Education and Practice,* 6(34), 29-39.

Cohen, L. Manion, L. & Morrison, K. 2007. *Research Methods in Education.* London: Routledge.

Fafunwa, A.B. & Aisiku, J.U. (1982). *Education in Africa: A Comprehensive Survey.* London: George Allen and Unwin.

Gondo, R., Maturure, K. J., Mutopa, S., Tokwe, T., Chirefu, H. & Nyevedzanayi, M. (2019). Issues Surrounding Secondary School Curriculum in Zimbabwe. *European Journal of Social Sciences Studies.* 4(2): 59-75.

Kabombwe Y.M. & Mulenga I.M. (2019). *Implementation of the competency-based curriculum by teachers of History in selected Secondary Schools in Lusaka district, Zambia.*
http://dx.doi.org/10.17159/2223-0386/2019/n22a2

Lumumba-Kasongo T. (2002). Reflections on the African Renaissance and its paradigmatic implications for deconstructing the past and reconstructing Africa. *Black Renaissance/Renaissance Noir,* 5(1): 1-16.

Mkpa, M. A. (2007). *Curriculum development.* Owerri: Totan publishers Ltd.

MoPSE (2015). *Curriculum Framework for Primary and Secondary Education* 2015-2022. Harare: GoZ.

Moodley, V 2013. In-service teacher education: Asking questions for higher order thinking. *South Africa Journal of Education,* 33(2):1-18.

Muneja, M.S. (2015). *Secondary School teachers' implementation of the competency-based curriculum in the Arusha Region, Tanzania.* MEd dissertation, University of South Africa.

Munikwa, S. (2016). *Analysis of the Current Zimbabwe's Secondary School Two Path Way Education Curriculum.*

Musingarabwi, S. (2017). Lecturers' Use of ICTs to implement the Curriculum at a Teacher Training College in Zimbabwe. *Advances in Social Sciences Research Journal,* 4(4): 1-13.

Nziramasanga, C. T. (1999). *Report of the Presidential Commission of inquiry into Education and training, Zimbabwe.* Harare: Government Printers.

Odora-Hoppers, C.A. (2000). *"African voices in education: Retrieving the past, engaging the present and shaping the future" in, African voices in education,* P Higgs, NCG Vakalisa, TV Mda & NT Assie-Lumumba (eds.). Cape Town: Juta.

Patton, M. (2007). *Qualitative Research and Evaluation Methods.* London: Sage Publications

Tummons, J. (2012) *Curriculum studies in the lifelong learning sector.* 2nd ed. Exeter: Learning Matters.

UNESCO 2017. The why, what and how of competency-based curriculum reforms: The Kenyan experience. Current and critical issues in curriculum, learning and assessment. *In Progress Reflection,* 11.

Zulu, I. M. (2006). Critical indigenous African education and knowledge. *The Journal of Pan African Studies,* 1(3), 32-49.

Chapter 6

The *Nhimbe* practice as a community multi-disciplinary academy among the Shona and Ndebele people of Zimbabwe

Pindai Mangwanindichero Sithole

Abstract

The chapter focuses on a traditional community development practice in Zimbabwe known as *nhimbe* or *ilima* among the Shona and Ndebele people respective. The main theme of the chapter is the role *nhimbe* plays in knowledge and skills transfer in rural communities. The development of the chapter is largely drawn from the earlier quasi-ethnographic *nhimbe* study by the author where qualitative data, which formed the bulk of the findings, were obtained through interviews, focus group discussions and participant observations. A small proportion of quantitative data were gathered through a semi-structured questionnaire and complemented the qualitative data. While *nhimbe* is generally understood as a socio-economic practice, the author further examined it from a perspective of an indigenous community multi-disciplinary academy. This dimension required a review of core literature which included indigenous epistemologies, Eurocentric pedagogies, transformative and sustainable community development. The chapter concludes that *nhimbe* is an indigenous community academy where community members freely share knowledge and skills. In other words, *nhimbe* provides apprenticeship of various trades to the community members. It is also noted that the knowledge and skills are sustainably passed through generations for the common good of community development.

Keywords: Nhimbe, community, academy, Shona, Ndebele, Zimbabwe

Introduction

The human pursuit for acquisition of knowledge and skills is undoubtedly nature's demand to enable humanity to adapt and survive on the planet earth through use of a multiplicity of faculties. Pertersen, Muckadell, Schaffalitzky and Hvidtfeldt (2016, p. 22)

117

emphasise this phenomenon from an angle of learning when they state that "learning is something we cannot help do because it is deeply rooted in our human genes". The authors go further to shed more light that "or it may be said that learning is something which helps us adapt to the world." Earlier, Fry, Ketteridgeand Marshall (2009) shared a comprehensive definition of learning that:

> It may involve mastering abstract principles, understanding proofs, remembering factual information, acquiring methods, techniques and approaches, recognition, reasoning, debating ideas, or developing behaviour appropriate to specific situations; it is about change. (Fry et al., 2009, p. 8).

As can be seen from the definitions above, learning takes different forms depending on the necessity, method and context. In most literature on pedagogy from the Western or Global North construct, the bias is often that learning occurs in a classroom setup guided by an approved curriculum by a regulatory education authority in a country. Furthermore, the classroom is one which is made up of well-defined group of learners and an individual called a teacher/ lecturer/tutor or instructor who delivers the teaching within a prescribed timeframe. The teacher must possess a recognised qualification in the subject matter and would have been methodically assessed on the competence and experience to transfer the knowledge and skills to the learners. Furthermore, successful learners would be given a certificate that commensurate with the level of learning completed. This trajectory of teaching and learning clearly does not recognise the indigenous epistemologies of knowledge and skills transfer in communities. This shows the damage the Western colonial knowledge discourse has done on the knowledge and learning methods of indigenous people in Zimbabwe and most African countries (Shizha, 2013; Sithole & Bondai, 2020). As will be seen later in this chapter, Western style of knowledge and skills delivery is not the only way of competence acquisition. In fact, in most African communities, some of the teaching and learning occur during traditional collective socio-economic activities in the communities like the *nhimbe/ilima* practice among the Shona and Ndebele in Zimbabwe. The classical socio-cultural theory of Vygotsky, an educational psychologist in the 1930s, is a stark recognition that knowledge and skills transfer can equally be achieved within specific geo-socio-cultural community settings. In other words, traditional community practices and rituals are socio-cultural

118

methods that are also utilised for knowledge and skills transfer among community members. One of the key tenets of Vygotsky's socio-cultural theory states that the socio-cultural methods are characteristic for providing communities with collaborative learning among people who know each other within a familiar setting for the common good (Zhou & Brown, 2017). A close examination of this notion reveals that the collaborative sharing of knowledge and skills among the communities is highly durable or sustainable. This is because of the social reproduction nature of African traditional communities whereby developing and maintaining quality relationships are social imperatives for everyone in the community. In fact, quality relationships are viewed in communities as a bedrock for facilitation of knowledge and skills transfer in the African communities (Mosia & Ngulube, 2004; Sithole, 2014). As extensively examined by Chemhuru (2017) and Sithole (2014), the Shona and Ndebele people of Zimbabwe have a unique social contract embedded in their communitarian philosophy of reciprocity which sustainably fosters social obligation among the community members to share knowledge and skills to one another. The next sections of this chapter shows that *nhimbe* practice fits in the socio-cultural theory, communitarian philosophy, collaborative learning and it is a form of social reproduction. The central theme of the socio-cultural theory is that meaningful and transformative learning and development should be aligned to the social and cultural distinctives that define the society under consideration (Zhou & Brown, 2017). As for communitarian philosophy, this generally refers to the collective action valued and practised in a given society like what is normally found among the indigenous African population (Chemhuru, 2017). Put together, when socio-cultural theory and communitarian philosophy are upheld in a community, it is highly probable that collaborative learning and development would occur for transformative change and common good of society. As will be seen later in this chapter, *nhimbe* practice is pivoted around socio-cultural and communitarian imperatives that allow for knowledge and skills sharing in the community for socio-economic development.

Generally, epistemological methods of knowledge and skills transfer in indigenous communities include storytelling (Mosia & Ngulube, 2004; Ober, 2017; Tobin & Snyman, 2008; Sithole & Bondai, 2020), music and dance (Hatfield, 2019; Nyamwaka, Ondima, Kemoni & Maangi, 2013; Sithole, 2014). In this chapter, an exploratory analysis was conducted to establish how knowledge and skills are transferred in the *nhimbe* practice among the Shona and Ndebele people of Zimbabwe.

At this juncture, it should be pointed out that the chapter is largely based on the original extensive qualitative fieldwork *nhimbe* study which was conducted by the author between 2009 and 2010 for his PhD thesis in Development Studies at the University of Witwatersrand. The study covered three communities comprising one Ndebele community (Tsholotsho, Matabeleland North Province) and two communities among the Shona people (Musikavanhu, Manicaland Province and Gambiza, Midlands Province). A quasi-ethnographic methodology was employed in the study in which interviews, focus group discussions (FGDs) and participant observations were conducted. A total of 74 community members were purposively selected and interviewed, six FGDs with community members were conducted, twelve key informants given pseudonyms K01 to K12 were interviewed. The data obtained from these three key data collection methods were complemented by the researcher's own participant observations on the *nhimbe* activities that took place in the respective communities during the study.

Brief description of *Nhimbe* practice

Nhimbe is a socio-economic community development livelihood model which has been practised by various ethnic groups in Zimbabwe since the 1800s or earlier (Muyambo, 2017; Sithole, 2014; Sithole, 2020). One of the key informants (PK02) in the Sithole (2014) *nhimbe* study described it as "…an indigenous knowledge, people who practise it have had it for a long time; they have a set of knowledge and skills which they use for development through *nhimbe* practice" (PK02, p. 144). It is a collective community development mechanism in which village members assist each other at household level to strengthen and sustain their socio-economic development initiatives. The most common development activities where *nhimbe* is applied are those which are Agriculture-based. It is also important to point out that *nhimbe* is a grassroots-based practice implemented by community members under the governance of the community traditional leadership. The way it works is that any household in the village identifies its need for which it organises a *nhimbe* to be carried out on a set date where people voluntarily provide labour and their expertise. The household that organises a *nhimbe* is known as an organiser, host or administrator and the community members who partake the *nhimbe* are *nhimbe* participants or simply participants. At a *nhimbe*, the host serves food and beverages (alcohol and non-alcoholic drinks like *maheu*) to the participants. Generally, *nhimbe* is a one-day event where the work is performed in the morning while from lunch onwards, the time is dedicated to the socialisation of various forms including ordinary conversations, feasting, cracking of jokes, music and dance. As will be elaborated later in this chapter, through these forms of socialisation, knowledge and skills sharing occur. The sharing of food is a virtue in the Ndebele and Shona culture and it is generally believed that it binds social relations as extensively discussed in Tavuyanago, Mutami and Mbenene (2010) and Sithole (2014). It should be noted that only one *nhimbe* is organised on a given day within the same village. This is done to ensure maximum attendance and optimisation of expertise from the village members on the task at hand. The community values or social lubricants that anchor the practice of *nhimbe* include helping one another, mutual trust, reciprocity, respect, peace-building and solidarity (Sithole, 2014).

To date, *nhimbe* has been analysed and understood from the perspective that it is a community development strategy to mobilise labour and expertise within the village to help households in their development needs and problems (Muyambo, 2017; Sithole, 2014). While Sithole (2014, p.262) alluded to *nhimbe* that "the practice has community apprenticeship entrenched in it" , up to now, little has been examined of it as a community academy where knowledge and skills are shared concurrently with the participants working on activities for which it is organised. In other words, the author's further reflections on the *nhimbe* research findings have provided insights that apart from it being a community socio-economic assistance practice, it is also a community multi-disciplinary academy.

Profile of *nhimbe* participants

The participants are village members in fulfilment of a social requirement that each household be represented by at least one member at an organised *nhimbe* in the village. The rationale for this social requirement is threefold: (i) attainment of maximum attendance for provision of labour required; (ii) critical mass of expertise or experience among the village members is achieved; and (iii) it becomes highly likely that the task would be successfully completed on time. It should also be pointed out that the profile of the *nhimbe* participants is quite inclusive of all working age groups of female and male village members as well as people with disabilities. In fact, social inclusion is the hallmark of the *nhimbe* practice in terms of tasks, households to help and the participants. This confirms the earlier proposition in this chapter that *nhimbe* is a manifestation of the common good at community development level. A close look at the *nhimbe* participants reveals that knowledge and skills are highly likely to pass through generations and relationships are reproduced for the continuity of the community life. This is succinctly expressed by one of the key informants in Sithole's (2014) study that "the people who practise it [*nhimbe*]...have a set of knowledge and skills which they use for [their community] development through the *nhimbe* practice" (PK02, p. 144). From this quotation, it can be seen that *nhimbe* plays a vital role on knowledge production and application for community development.

Methods of knowledge and skills transfer and strategic points during *nhimbe*

In the nhimbe research conducted by Sithole (2014), one of the key informants emphasised that "another important thing is that *nhimbe* promotes skills transfer as people share knowledge and skills on various tasks [on community development]" (PK09, p. 145). This is an affirmation that *nhimbe* is also a knowledge and skills transfer platform as buttressed by another key informant in the same study who noted that "...at a *nhimbe,* some people learn skills that would become their careers/professions in the future" (PK11, p. 145). This was further emphasised by 52 (70.3%) of the 74 study participants interviewed in the same study who expressed that *nhimbe* also benefits the communities through the sharing of knowledge and skills among the community members. The knowledge and skills shared include production and management of crops and animals of different types, harvesting techniques, food storage and preservation, marriage and family, health, fencing, woodwork, metalwork, just to mention a few as more will be given in the next section of this chapter. The 74 interviewed comprised traditional chiefs, traditional village heads, adult members of the community and young adults. They were aged between 40 and 91, the majority being in the age range of 50 to 70.

At a *nhimbe*, competences are shared through direct hands-on coaching on specific tasks of the work at hand, ordinary conversations, storytelling including folktales, cracking of jokes, music and dance. In the context of knowledge and skills sharing, the conversations would be in the form of questions and answer between the more knowledgeable, skilled or experienced individual(s) and one who wants to learn. This can be one-on-one or in a small group of individuals with the same interest to learn a particular aspect/trade. The Ndebele and Shona people use storytelling as a sustainable social technology of teaching where complex cognitive concepts and psychomotor skills are made simpler through a story that would have been crafted in an exciting and humorous manner. One scholar of African storytelling (Tuwe, 2016, p.2) highlights that sometimes "the stories are told subjectively once the theme of the story is decided". This means that even the difficult conceptual issues are simplified and made digestible through stories. As Ober (2017) and Sithole and Bondai (2020) note, storytelling creates a relaxed atmosphere, a situation which facilitates ease grasping of concepts presented through the story. Summarised below is the most compelling function of storytelling within the African socio-cultural context:

> The function of storytelling has been identified as mediating and transmitting of knowledge and information across generations, conveying information to the younger generations about the culture, worldviews, morals and expectations, norms and values (Tuwe, 2016, p. 2)

It can be seen from the quotation above that storytelling is a multipurpose social technology in the community but mainly used to convey a particular message. While cracking of jokes at a *nhimbe* is often a component of general socialisation following the completion of the work and during the feasting phase at a *nhimbe*, it is also used to teach certain aspects or necessities of life. For example, if the desire is to correct behaviour of some individuals or groups of individuals in the community, jokes are sarcastically fashioned in a way that conveys a message for behaviour change. The method of music and dance to share knowledge and skills at a *nhimbe* occurs during the feasting time after the conclusion of work. It should be noted that some of the *nhimbes* like thrashing grain, singing is imperative during the work itself. In this instance, music at feasting time will be a continuation now complemented by dance. Music and dance are key components of the Ndebele and Shona people's social life whenever they gather in celebration or in sadness. In fact, it is almost like without music and dance, the event has not yet started.

The general assumption of community music in the Ndebele and Shona culture is that everyone has the ability to create, sing and dance (Chitando, 2002; Mutero & Kaye, 2019). Obviously, the hands-on coaching occurs during the work itself while ordinary conversations are during and after the work. The cracking of jokes and singing is largely after work while the dancing to the music is after the work. The reason for minimal jokes and no dancing during the work is to avoid injuries and slowing down the pace and quality of work for the *nhimbe* was organised.

As can be seen, the concept of passing on knowledge through various socio-cultural methods or social technologies and "through generations is characteristic of indigenous knowledge system" (Sithole, 2014, p. 144). As evident in the preceding discussion, the social methods used to share knowledge and skills at a *nhimbe* during and after the work are technically varied but epistemologically complementary and reinforcing.

Some forms of knowledge and skills shared during *nhimbe*

Before the forms of knowledge and skills are discussed, it should be pointed out that *nhimbe* does not have documented curricula or model of teaching and learning. This means that the sharing of knowledge and skills is informal, as well as demand or supply driven. The fact that there is no documented curriculum and formal framework of teaching and learning, this does not mean that the knowledge and skills shared are of no value to the community or have no positive effect to one's career development. In fact, *nhimbe* provides a well-organised community-based academy in sharing of knowledge, skills and experiences free of charge and passed on through generations. Based on the studies carried out to date on the *nhimbe* practice (Muyambo, 2017, Sithole, 2020; Sithole, 2014), the knowledge and skills shared at a *nhimbe* can be grouped into six categories as discussed below.

Community history and socio-anthropology knowledge
At the *nhimbe*, the community elders or historians share the community's socio-economic, political and cultural history through impromptu or well-intended conversations on specific heritage matters. In most cases, the conversations on the community history and culture are more of reinforcement than new stories. This notion was revealed by 73 (98.6%) of the 74 study participants interviewed

in the Sithole (2014) *nhimbe* study who pointed out that *nhimbe* is a platform for people to learn and reinforce community moral values (*unhu*). The reinforcement of the community history and culture is an important curriculum to maintain community heritage, community patriotism, community values, community solidarity, desired behaviour and peace at household and community level. Music and dance combined is another popular socio-cultural method used at the *nhimbe* to convey and sustain the community's heritage as emphasised by Nyamwaka *et al.* (2013) in the quotation that follows:

> …music and dance…serve as a source of understanding the cultural history of the community. Indeed, without knowledge of a community's cultural history, the historical destiny cannot be easily comprehended. (Nyamwaka, Ondima, Kemoni & Maangi, 2013, p. 113).

The quotation above reveals that music and dance is the mirror of the community's culture and tradition. So, it can be seen that this category of knowledge sharing has an emphasis on the community structure and people's behaviour (sociology) as well as the cultural rootedness (anthropology). This social intersection and fusion of sociology and anthropology in people's socio-economic life has made this author to term it community socio-anthropology. This is to demonstrate the evident inseparability nature of these two concepts in the real life of the Ndebele and Shona people in Zimbabwe; and perhaps in other Bantu cultures in Africa and other parts of the world.

Livelihoods knowledge and skills

Knowledge and skills are shared on a variety of economic livelihoods that are contextual to the community. As found in Muyambo (2017) and Sithole (2014), most of the *nhimbe* activities are in the agriculture domain like crop and livestock production and management. In this regard, some community members actually become expert-specialists in particular crops or livestock. They are the ones who then pass on the knowledge and skills to others during a *nhimbe* of a particular crop or livestock in the community. For this reason, it is fair to call them community agricultural extension officers (cagritexo). The advantages of the cagritexos are fourfold: (i) they provide their services free of charge;(ii) they have high response rate because they live in the community; (iii) they have a better understanding of the socio-cultural context of the community; and

(iv) they are familiar with the community socio-cultural fibre and the environmental ecology.

Health knowledge and skills

Knowledge on the physical and psychological health wellbeing are shared during the *nhimbe* practice. This is aptly expressed by one of the key informants in the Sithole (2014) *nhimbe* study that "during *nhimbe* people benefit from the following: counselling, skills and knowledge sharing on health; among other things" (PK06, p. 148). On physical health, knowledge holders in the community share information on various diseases including how they are treated. The treatment mostly shared would be through use of herbs and to a less extent, spiritual intervention. The focus is often on herbs that are indigenous and are found locally for this is inexpensive and sustainable. Another point to note is that the focus on indigenous herbs helps to increase uptake and adherence because of the familiarity to community members of the trees or shrubs from which the herbs are taken. In addition, the adherence to treatment is generally high because of the testimonies from familiar people in the community who would have recovered after administration of the same treatment on them to address similar or the same illnesses. Some of the health issues shared include remedies on nursing of children at various age groups, infertility, dealing with the aged and childhood diseases.

Marriage and family

It is not unusual for community members to share knowledge and skills on marriage and family matters. This includes marital relations, dealing with barrenness, raising children, management of relationships within the nuclear and extended family setup, care and support for the elderly in the family and community and dealing with conjugal issues, to mention but a few. Often, the community elders including the religious leaders provide information and wisdom on marriage and family and this is also done in line with the socio-cultural framework of the community. For instance, the roles of parents, grandparents, uncles, aunts, nephews, cousins and friends in the family are reiterated and reinforced during the *nhimbe* activities. The main goal on sharing knowledge and skills on marriage and family is to prevent dysfunctional families, eruption of conflicts and to maintain the socio-moral compass of the community.

Environmental protection

At a *nhimbe*, community members share knowledge on the importance of environmental conservation especially indigenous fruit bearing trees and shrubs, water bodies and medicinal plants. The focus on fruit bearing and medicinal plants is quite obvious to the communities because of the necessity of food, nutrition and health wellbeing. To reinforce and instil the environmental conservation behaviour among the community members, taboos are shared too. As extensively discussed in Masaka and Chemhuru (2011) and Sithole (2020), taboos promote desired behaviour by everyone in the community for the common good of humanity, biodiversity and the environment. The quotation below from Masaka and Chemhuru is an emphasis on this point:

> ...the most important aspect of these taboos is to inculcate commendable character traits in their apprentices that would make them worthy members of society that would not only behave in a desirable way towards fellow human beings, but also relate to the environment in a manner that embodies respect for biodiversity as well as sustainable exploitation of nature's resources. Shona taboos provide prohibitions that forbid people from behaving in such manners that are a threat to the welfare and wellbeing of fellow human beings and the rest of the environment. (Masaka & Chemhuru, 2011, p. 147).

It is clear from the quotation above that taboos play a central socio-anthropological role in the Zimbabwe society; specifically moulding of desirable personal character and environmental conservation for sustenance of humanity and biodiversity. In the view of Masaka and Chemhuru, it can be seen that the Shona taboos promote a healthy co-existence of humanity and the environment. Sithole (2020, p.7) concurs with Masaka and Chemhuru on the description of taboos and their centrality in society when he reminds that "Among the Shona and the Ndebele people, ...taboos are social norms and values that discourage people from deviant behaviour, prevent conflict and promote peace in communities"). An example of a taboo is one associated with fruit trees whereby it is told that if one uses them as firewood, the smoke produced causes severe illness. The wisdom on this particular taboo is to ensure protection and sustainability of fruit trees toward achievement of food security in the community. Another one is the prohibition of community members from washing any sooty utensils at the well, stream or river and that anyone who breaches this taboo risk a mysterious disappearance in the water. The idea behind this taboo is to protect water bodies from contamination which might lead to drying up. In essence, taboos help to inculcate the anticipated disposition for the well-being of humanity and the environment. The knowledge and skills shared on environmental protection includes identification and names of plant and animal species found in the community and this is often done in indigenous languages. In addition, the overall role each element of the flora and fauna plays in the ecosystem such as medicine, food security, nutrition and agriculture are part of the knowledge shared.

Peacebuilding and conflict resolution

During *nhimbe*, sometimes people especially the community leadership, talk about the importance of peaceful co-existence between individuals, between groups of individuals, within families, between families or households and the community as a whole. Techniques and wisdom frameworks applied to resolve conflicts peacefully are often shared at a *nhimbe*. This is bound by common interest to increase the radius of peace and minimise conflicts in order to achieve transformative and sustainable community development for the common good. Wherever a conflict erupts, wisdom is also shared on how to resolve it peacefully and in a transformative manner. The recent theory of familiarity in conflict prevention and peace building by Sithole (2020, p. 7) would be probably a primary social reservoir entrenched in the *nhimbe* practice that promotes community peace building. The theory states that with high familiarity among people in a community, conflicts are likely to reduce. In this regard, *nhimbe* is an academy that provides a dense social interaction among the community members on a regular basis and this leads to high level of familiarity among the community members.

This section has illustrated that *nhimbe* fits quite well in the socio-cultural theory, communitarian philosophy of the Shona and the Ndebele people, collaborative learning and it is a form of social reproduction that internally sustains the practice in the communities. Given this understanding, it is only fair to recognise *nhimbe* as a community multi-disciplinary academy (CMDA) where knowledge and skills in various faculties of life are freely shared and reinforced.

Conclusion

In the past *nhimbe* has been analysed and understood from a socio-economic perspective with little examination of it as a schooling platform. The analysis made in this chapter has shown that the practice is also a sustainable community academy at which community members share knowledge and skills in manifestation of socio-cultural theory, communitarian philosophy and collaborative manner. Clearly, *nhimbe* is a platform that provides apprenticeship of various trades to community members in sustainable manner. It became clear that the uniqueness of it as an academy is that people learn from one another during the *nhimbe* activities without compromising the planned physical work. It also emerged that the determinants of what knowledge and skills to be shared is either need or supply driven. In other words, it has been noted that the curricula at *nhimbe* are not documented but evolving to respond to the ongoing capacity needs of individuals or groups of individuals in the community. If one lacks knowledge or certain skills required on specific tasks on the work for which a *nhimbe* has been organised, it is always an opportunity to attend that planned *nhimbe* in the community and learn from others.

The fact that *nhimbe* practice allows for knowledge and skills transfer in the community at no financial cost, it can be concluded that the practice is a socio-economic and cultural wealth for the community. It is a cultural wealth because the competences are passed on from one generation to another and the development benefits the current and future generations. It is further noted that the adaptability and resilience of the *nhimbe* practice in communities lies in its bottom-up design and implementation where the local socio-cultural contexts are inherent and enforced and this illustrates the centrality of the socio-cultural theory that anchored the chapter. The analysis presented in the chapter has clearly revealed that apart from its traditionally known socio-economic contribution to the livelihoods of communities, *nhimbe* is also a community multidisciplinary academy which functions within socio-cultural and communitarian framework.

References

Chemhuru, M. (2017). Gleaning the social contract theory from African communitarian philosophy. *South African Journal of Philosophy*, *36*(4), 505–515. https://doi.org/10.1080/02580136.2017.1359470

Chitando, E. (2002). *Singing culture: a study of gospel music in Zimbabwe* (Issue 121). http://books.google.com/books?hl=en&lr=&id=9BcnlUIXOyg C&oi=fnd&pg=PA5&dq=Singing+culture+A+Study+of+Gos pel+Music+in+Zimbabwe&ots=f0vZKPDTm8&sig=GKJjFh8 47J0dndZjFJ83bW0Qqw4

Fry, H., Ketteridge, S., & Marshall, S. (2009). Supporting student learning. In *Teaching Mathematics and its Applications* (Vol. 19, Issue 4). https://doi.org/10.1093/teamat/19.4.166

Hatfield, T. (2019). Music, musicians, and social advocacy: Environmental Conservation, Knowledge-sharing and cultivating a Culture of Wisdom in Northern Tanzania. *University of Illinois at Urbana-Champaign*.

Masaka, D., & Chemhuru, M. (2011). Moral Dimensions of Some Shona Taboos (Zviera). *Journal of Sustainable Development in Africa*, *13*(3), 132–148.

Mosia, L. N., &Ngulube, P. (2013). Managing the collective intelligence of local communities for the sustainable utilisation of estuaries in the Eastern Cape, South Africa. *South African Journal of Libraries and Information Science*, *71*(2), 175–186. https://doi.org/10.7553/71-2-624

Mutero, T., & Kaye, S. (2019). Music and Conflict Transformation in Zimbabwe. *Peace Review: A Journal of Social Justice*, *31*(3), 289–296. https://doi.org/10.1080/10402659.2019.1735164

Muyambo, T. (2017). Indigenous Knowledge Systems: A Haven for Sustainable Economic Growth in Zimbabwe. *Africology: The Journal of Pan African Studies (Online)*, *10*(3), 172–186.

Nyamwaka, E. O., Ondima, P. C., Kemoni, F., &Maangi, E. (2013). The Place of Music and Dance in the Reconstruction of African Cultural History : a Case of the Abagusii of South-Western Kenya. *Research on Humanities and Social Sciences*, *3*(10), 113–120.

Ober, R. (2017). Kapati Time: Storytelling as a Data Collection Method in Indigenous Research. *Kapati Time: Storytelling as a Data Collection Method in Indigenous Research. Learning Communities:*

International Journal of Learning in Social Contexts, *22*, 8–15. https://doi.org/10.18793/lcj2017.22.02

Petersen, E. N, de Muckadell, S, C. and Hvidtfeldt, R. (2016). What should we demand of a definition of 'learning'? *On the Definition of Learning*, 21–37. https://www.sdu.dk/-/media/files/om_sdu/institutter/ikv/forskning/forskningsprojekter/on+the+definition+of+learning/book+chapters/chapter+2.pdf?la=en.

Pertersen, E. N., Muckadell, Schaffalitzky, C., &Hvidtfeldt, R. (2016). What should we demand of a definition of 'learning'? In *On the Definition of Learning*. https://www.sdu.dk/-/media/files/om_sdu/institutter/ikv/forskning/forskningsprojekter/on+the+definition+of+learning/book+chapters/chapter+2.pdf?la=en.

Shizha, E. (2013). Licensed under Creative Commons Attribution Non-Commercial Share Alike License Reclaiming Our Indigenous Voices: The Problem with Postcolonial Sub-Saharan African School Curriculum. *Journal of Indigenous Social Development*, *2*(1), 1–18. http://www.hawaii.edu/sswork/jisdhttp://scholarspace.manoa.hawaii.edu/handle/10125/29811

Sithole, P. M. (2020). Nhimbe practice in Zimbabwe revisited: Not only a method of socio- economic assistance but also a communal mechanism for conflict prevention and peacebuilding. *African Journal on Conflict Resolution*, *2020*(2), 1–12.

Sithole, P. M., & Bonda, B. M. (2020). Taboos and Storytelling for Teaching and Learning in Zimbabwe. *International Journal of Curriculum Development and Learning Measurement*, *1*(2), 53–65. https://doi.org/10.4018/ijcdlm.2020070104

Sithole, Pindai M. 2014. Community-based development: A study of Nhimbe in Zimbabwe. Ph.D. thesis, Witwatersrand University, Johannesburg,

Tavuyanago, B., Mutami, N., and Mbenene, K. (2010) „Traditional grain Cropsin Pre-Colonial Zimbabwe: A factor for food security and Social cohesion among the Shona People". *Journal of Sustainable development in Africa*12 (6), 1-8

Tobin, P. K. J., & Snyman, R. (2008). Once upon a time in Africa: A case study of storytelling for knowledge sharing. *Aslib Proceedings: New Information Perspectives*, *60*(2), 130–142. https://doi.org/10.1108/00012530810862464

Tuwe, K. (2016). The African Oral Tradition Paradigm of Storytelling as a Methodological Framework: Employment Experiences for African communities in New Zealand. *African Studies Association of Australasia and the Pacific (AFSAAP) ,2015*(February).

Zhou, M., & Brown, D. (2017). Educational Learning Theories: 2nd Edition. In *Education Open Textbooks*. https://oer.galileo.usg.edu/education-textbooks/1

Chapter 7

The Ethical Implications of Religio-Cultural Healing Practices on Ghana's Environment: An Ethno-medical Interrogation

Beatrice Okyere-Manu
Stephen N. Morgan
Joseph Kofi Antwi

Abstract

This chapter's position is that our moral understanding of responsibility and stewardship can contribute to improving the religio-cultural healing practices (ethnomedicine) and the natural environment's well-being. This is because anthropogenic activities have contributed to environmental degradation being experienced today, resulting in various ecological problems. A number of biotic and abiotic habitats and aquatic communities are constantly threatened. Notwithstanding the awareness initiatives from various governments, environmentalists and scientists, littering, pollution, illegal mining, and deforestation are among the common practices that scholars have identified as contributing factors to the degradation of the Ghanaian natural environment. Nevertheless, an important area that has received very little attention is ethnomedicine and how the practice impacts on the environment. Against this backdrop, the current article assesses the ethical implications of Religio-Cultural (ethnomedical) healing practices among Ghanaians on the environment, and suggests practical ways to promote a moral sense of responsibility towards the sustainability of the natural environment. To do this, the chapter addresses the following questions: What is the link between religio-cultural healing practices and environmental? Does the practice of ethnomedicine contributes to ecological problems? How can ethnomedicine promote environmental sustainability?

Keywords: Religion, culture, ethnomedicine, environment, Ghana.

Introduction

The practice of ethnomedicine has been the source of healing for many people in Africa for a long time (Botha *et al.* 2001), and Ghana is no exception. From time immemorial, Ghanaians have depended on plants and in some cases, animals for medicine. An experience on a road trip from Accra to Kumasi in Ghana in 2018 informed the idea behind this chapter. The four-hour journey, saw more than ten vendors selling ethnomedicine in the form of dried backs of trees, seeds, roots, leaves and stems of different trees on the bus. At the bus stop of every big city in the course of the journey, a vendor (an ethnomedicine practitioner) would get off the bus, and another would board. Each of these ethnomedicine practitioners would use long recitals to lure people into buying their products. This drama continued unfolding until we arrived at our destination. What was particularly interesting was that each vendor had a different product that, according to them, cures various ailments from common cold, rheumatism to severe illnesses such as cancer, diabetes and high blood pressure. The products were different, but the diseases they cure seemed to be similar.

The experience was the same coming back from Kumasi but with different vendors. At one point during the return journey, some of the passengers who had had enough complained to the driver. The complaints eventually led to a conversation among the passengers on the bus. They discussed issues surrounding the trade of these ethnomedicine men, including where the vendors get the dried parts of the trees from, the safety and efficacy of the medicine they sell, deforestation and its effect on the environment, and environmental sustainability. The discussion around deforestation generated a heated debate. While some believed that the overall consequences of these emerging market are detrimental to the environment, other passengers vehemently argued that its implication on the environment is minimal as forests have the natural ability to renew itself. This latter group maintained that traditional medicine in the form of animal parts and plants have been used trustworthily since time immemorial and therefore has no means of depleting the environment. To them, this whole environmental crisis is propaganda against the business of ethnomedicine practitioners. The arguments continued till the end of the journey, albeit inconclusively. However, some of the questions and issues raised in the conversation that ensued prompted this chapter. One general observation made about the folks in the bus throughout the discussion was their general lack of accurate information on issues of environmental concerns. One older man in his late 70s, for example, was of the view that the current crisis in the environment is because the gods and ancestors have been offended and appeasing them will rectify the situation.

Against this backdrop, the chapter argues that our moral understanding of responsibility and stewardship towards the environment can contribute immensely to the natural wellbeing of the environment. This is because human activities continue to contribute to environmental degradation resulting in various ecological problems. Currently, several biotic and abiotic habitats and aquatic communities are under threat due to exploitative human activities and climate change. Notwithstanding the awareness initiatives from various governments, environmentalists and scientists, littering, pollution, illegal mining and deforestation remain the common practices that scholars have identified as contributing factors to the degradation of the African and particularly the Ghanaian natural environment. With this in mind, Segun Ogungbemi (2018:330) challenges national governments in Africa to seek a proper strategy to manage and mitigate the ecological crisis to achieve feasible environmental consciousness that takes cognizance of the causes of the environmental crisis in Africa. In the search for answers to the environmental crisis in Ghana, an important area that little studies have been done is in ethnomedicine and how it impacts the sustainability of the natural environment. As a result, the current chapter assesses the ethical implication of the religio-cultural (ethnomedical) healing practices among Ghanaians on the environment and suggests ways to promote a moral sense of responsibility towards the natural environment's sustainability.

To do this, the chapter, firstly, describes the state of the environmental crisis in Ghana. The second section explores the nature the practice of religio-cultural (ethnomedical) medicine among the Ghanaian communities. The third section addresses questions such as: what is the link between religio-cultural healing practices and Ghana's environmental crisis? How does the environmental crisis affect the practice of ethnomedicine and the wellbeing of traditional health seekers? How can the beliefs in ethnomedicine promote environmental sustainability? The final section suggests principles to promote a moral sense of stability. This is a non-empirical chapter and thus, rely entirely on critical assessment of existing literature.

Environmental problems in Ghana

Like most countries in Africa and the world as a whole, Ghana is faced with numerous environmental problems. Human beings' day to day activities toward the environment continues to be a crucial concern, particularly the degree at which harmful human activities affect the environment, and this is despite the awareness, debates and discussions by policymakers, scientists and environmentalists on the effects of the problems on current and future generations. Several scholars such as Brown *et al.* (2018:849) have noted that "in Africa, ecological problems such as increasing annual average temperatures, pollution, and the disintegration of fauna habitat are on the rise". Segun Ogungbemi (2001) has convincingly attributed the causes of environmental problems in sub-Saharan Africa to the following factors which include "ignorance and poverty, modern science and technology, and political conflict and international economics". As a result, he calls for what he terms as the 'Ethics of Nature Relatedness', which for him, is born out of traditional African beliefs and practices. For Ogungbemi, because humans are related to nature, there is the need to treat nature with respect, thereby taking just what is needed for use from the environment.

As a result of human greediness and individualism tendencies, most communities in Africa, including Ghana, have overlooked the indigenous traditional values and beliefs towards the environment. Issues to do with humans' co-existence with non-human living and non-living things and the value of taking just what one needs from the environment as hinted by Segun Ogungbemi (2001) has become less practiced. Resultantly, the physical elements of nature that support human and non-human existence such as rivers, land, and forest have been negatively impacted. In addition, Ghana is faced with the challenge of littering and pollution in all of its various forms. For example, a study by Benneh *et al.* (1994) identified pollution on a large-scale ranging from marine pollution to ambient air pollution. They warned that if serious measures are not taken to curb it, a larger scale of problems will threaten citizens' lives in Ghana and, in particular, the Greater Accra Metropolitan Area (GAMA). There is discharge of sewage into water bodies from industrial and domestic activities. Just as Nsubuga *et al.* have noted in Uganda, the use of chemicals in fishing and the rapid population growth have contributed to the lack of proper control of water bodies in the metropolitan cities (Nsubuga *et al.*, 2014).

In addition to the above, there is the problem of deforestation and illegal mining (popularly known locally as galamsey) noted as some of the major contributing factors to Ghana's environmental crisis. Mining areas in Ghana have undoubtedly suffered the most in terms of environmental degradation. As Edwin Kotey (2016) affirms in a 2010 Ghana Business News Report, "there has been incessant and blatant depletion of more than 80% of forest reserves in these mining communities, and the heavy pollution of the Birim, Ankobra, and Pra Rivers, which have been the main source of drinking water for the inhabitants over the years." All of these continue to happen unabated despite efforts of intervention put in place by various government administrations. Some of the interventions include the relaxation of the requirements of acquiring licenses to operate small scale mining (the idea was that doing so will get most illegal miners to register for proper monitoring and enforcement of the rules). There was also the provision of alternative livelihood opportunities for these illegal miners and law enforcement agents such as Police and Military crackdown of illegal miners. It is sad to report that all of these attempts seem to have failed to achieve their objectives. Several scholars (Bush 2009; Adjei *et al.* 2012; and Abdul-Gafaru Abdulai, 2017) have attributed the deplorable environmental situation to the lack of employment in the rural areas, widespread poverty, and the displacement of indigenes as a result of large-scale mining. Other contributors are said to be political leniency on the side of political actors and corruption with law enforcement officers. Therefore, not until these challenges have been attended to, illegal mining activities and its effect on the environment will continue.

Another form of environmental pollution in Ghana is noise pollution. In recent times, noise pollution has come under the spotlight, particularly in the urban areas, due to population growth and intensification of human activities. Human activities such as commercial, industrial and social events continue to increase the level of noise pollution in Ghana's cities. It must be noted that even though the Environmental Protection Agency (EPA) in Ghana has in place the expected ambient noise levels required by law in the country, the fact is that law enforcement authorities have failed to regulate noise level limits in the country (Vicky Wireko, 2013). It has been noted, for example, that in residential areas the level of noise has been set at 55 decibels (dB) during the day and 48 dB at night. Around schools and hospitals, it is set at 55 dB during the day and 50 dB at night, in commercial and industrial areas, 60-70 dB during the day and 55 -65 at night (Odoi-larbi, 2012). However, all these regulations have been overlooked including their dire effect on human well-being.

The impact of the practice of ethnomedicine on the Ghanaian environment

From time immemorial, most Africans have depended and continue to depend on plants and in some cases, animal products in treating different forms of ailments, despite the advancement of Western science and medicine. In most instances, ethnomedicine or "traditional" medicine is often regarded by indigenes as the more appropriate mode of treatment (Rukangira 2001:180). It is common knowledge that most people prefer ethnomedicine to modern Western medicine and utilize it as the first aid of remedy. Like in the introductory story, many Ghanaians prefer these forms of medicine to Western medicine, not just because they are less expensive but because traditional medicine has been trusted and used for many years for different ailments.

Ethnomedicine practices continue to be highly utilized by rural and urban populations in most African countries such as Ethiopia, Tanzania, South Africa, Zambia, Cameroon, Nigeria, and Ghana, to mention a few (Ekpere & Mshana 1997:2; Stekelenburg *et al.* 2005:78; Betti 2004:3). The local people regard most plants as valuable for food, medicine and shelter. Plants are known to form a link between communities and their surrounding environment and a source of their economic livelihood. As a result, ethnomedicinal practices have become one of the fastest growing businesses in Ghana in recent times. George Foster and Barbara Anderson (1978 in James Anquandah, 1997: 289) describes ethnomedicine as: "Comprising those beliefs and practices relating to disease which are the products of indigenous cultural development and are not explicitly derived from the conceptual framework of modern medicine". Evans-Anfom (1986:26) best captures the practice in his description of ethnomedicine as:

> a collection of individually evolved practices developed in different families over generations and transferred to a limited number of people by apprenticeship; that the practices are as varied and divergent as there are practitioners and also as different in form as there are ethnic groups in a country.

The description above suggests that the knowledge acquisition of ethnomedicine is mostly handed down from one generation to another orally. Some acquire the medicinal knowledge from their parents while others obtain it from relatives and friends. More so, for some others, they attained the knowledge by observation while undergoing treatment from traditional healers for their ailment. Others offer themselves as apprentices to understudy senior practitioners (Daniel Wodah & Alex Asase, 2012:809).

Ethnomedicine has been practiced before the advent of orthodox medicine and is trusted by most communities and thus, explains why in Ghana, despite the availability of Western medicine, many people continue to depend on indigenous medicines, which comprises of plants, herbs and parts of animals as their primary healthcare, what is commonly referred to as traditional medicine. As cited by Antwi-Baffour et al. (2014:50), statistics in Ghana reveals that traditional medicine caters for the health needs of about 75-85% of the rural people and 45-65% of urban dwellers. According to the authors, a census held in September 2010 in Ghana revealed that there were 400 people to every Traditional Medical Practitioners (TMP) compared to a ratio of 1:17,733 for orthodox medical practitioners (OMP) (Antwi-Baffour et al. 2014:50). It is not surprising that Ghana established a Centre for Scientific Research into Plant Medicine at Mampong-Akuapem in the Eastern Region of Ghana. The Centre aims to preserve, restore and standardize African Traditional Medicine and indigenous science (Kerwegi, 2001) in the country. The Centre and most of the Traditional Medical Practitioners involved in the production of herbal medicine rely solely on plants from the natural environment in the form of tree barks, decoctions, ointments and powders (Fisher, 1998:116).

The fact that the practice was handed down from one generation to another also explains why there are different categories of traditional health healers. There are spiritual healers, herbalists, technical specialists (for instance, bone-setters), and traditional birth attendants who use various forms of herbs, roots, leaves, tree bark, and animals such as birds in the preparation of curative, protective and preventive medicine for health seekers. In addition, some use wildlife species and their parts for healing and consultation with ancestors (Anyinam, 1995:322). In describing the three main categories of traditional healers in Africa, James Anquanda (1997: 289) mentioned that:

Firstly, a group of herbalists with profound knowledge of plant medicine who produce and dispense products made from herbs and other natural resources. Secondly, there is a group of herbalists willing, in addition to pure herbal practice, to engage in supernatural occult practices. A third group comprises shrine/cult priests who have herbal knowledge but operate essentially as media or agents of deities from whom they receive directions regarding disease diagnosis and cure.

The underlining responsibility of all these groups of healers is to use their herbal knowledge to bring about holistic healing and well-being to communities. Interestingly, the collection and production of ethnomedicine are done in secrecy. In some instances, the medicinal products are collected at night in the deep forest to protect the secrecy of their product and raw materials. Similarly, these products are often collected in large quantities to serve the various needs of the clients.

Arguably, the mass production of pharmaceutical and herbal products continues to endanger the environment. As noted earlier, medicinal plant products have become lucrative employment for collectors or gatherers, producers (those who prepare them) and sellers. In addition to these herbal medicines, sometimes, traditional healers may request some specific animals for sacrifices and rituals as directed by the gods or ancestors. These are to appease the gods of any sins committed by the patient or as a pre-condition for the healing.

These practices demonstrate the direct link between the natural environment and the people's religio-cultural healing practices in most communities in Ghana and the extent to which the practice is dependent on the thriving of their local natural environment for its sustenance.

The Effects of ethnomedicine on the environment

The effect of ethnomedicine on the Ghanaian environment cannot be overemphasised. As noted earlier, traditional healers and other herbal product manufacturers continue to rely heavily on animal parts and plant products for their trade or practice, thereby gradually depleting them (Ameyaw *et al.* 2016: 2) to unsustainable levels. It can be argued that the indigenous practice of ethnomedicine without a conscious effort by the practitioners to replace the plants and herbs that they use in making their medicines encourage the gradual depletion of these plants. Ultimately, the more the demand, the more frequent they take from the plants, trees and herbs. Animals whose parts are needed for some of these medicines too will eventually become endangered.

Most of these medicinal plant's habitats are mainly along riverbanks, highlands, and deep forests, however, with the continual anthropogenic activities, these areas, have been gradually destroyed. Also, places that were previously designated as sacred groves have been tainted and defaced. The African worldview that emphasizes the interrelatedness and interconnectedness of humans and nature and encourages a holistic environmental ethic—an ethic that has guided the people for many years to treat the environment with respect and dignity (De-Valera, 2012:6)—has eventually been put on the side-line. This ethic together with other traditional African ethical values such as the use of taboos and norms that have guided the people over the years to replant the near-extinct medicinal plants, herbs and trees and protect animals as a way of preserving and conserving the environment for the benefit of current and future generations have been ignored by most practitioners of ethnomedicine. The desire for quick money vis-a-vis the mass demand of ethnomedicine seems to compromise the people's sense of responsibility towards the environment.

The high demand of ethnomedicine, particularly during the period of the COVID-19 pandemic, suggests that if efforts are not made to regulate the activities of ethnomedicine practitioners, their activities could become one of the major causes of environmental resource dilapidation in the country. It is true, as mentioned by one of the bus discussants that the ethnomedicine practice has been around for a long time with minimal effect on the environment, but this was because practitioners then were not doing it for money and as such took just what they needed for a particular healing procedure. The situation is not the same today because this time around the practitioners are business-minded and motivated by profit. They tend to take more than they need from nature and nature is not afforded enough time to replenish itself. Neither are the practitioners making any effort to sustain them. Under these conditions, the fear for these local plants becoming extinct is real, and should this happen, the repercussion it will have on the people's economic life, health, and general way of life will be dire. The natural environment will also eventually suffer, and we would have succeeded in denying future generations the opportunity to also benefit from these healing plants.

Challenging the moral responsibility of ethnomedicine practitioners

The nature and effects of the practice of ethnomedicine in Ghana have been briefly examined above. From the discussion so far, it is evident that the practice improves citizens' health, well-being, and livelihoods; however, in doing so, practitioners have overlooked the impact of their practice on the environment upon which human and wildlife's existence depends. This raises several important ethical questions: should humans' health needs and their general well-being be considered morally wrong and intolerable because it affects the environment? The answer to this question is not a straightforward one. This is because, regardless of how the question is answered, a further question can be raised. It is evident that humans, as part of nature and located within the philosophy of nature-relatedness, cannot entirely avoid relying on the natural environment for their existential needs. The question then is: how far should humans go? Also, how can they determine what is enough or acceptable? These questions are critical in light of humans' survival, considering the earth's very scarce and mostly fixed resources. In other words, what is the best way to marry human survival needs with environmental sustenance? These questions bring us back to our moral responsibility towards ourselves and the entire environment.

Since the environment and all living beings have intrinsic value, there is need for human beings to care for the environment. Any form of neglect has implications for current and future generations. If ethnomedicine's practices lead to the environment's degradation, then clearly the next generation will suffer if practical measures are not taken to replace what we take from the environment. As a result, humans have a moral obligation to strategize how best to sustain the environmental resources. As we know it, the environment does not only include human beings but nature as a whole, and therefore the degradation of nature for whatever reasons should be prohibited (Sideris, 2003:148). All of these inhabitants of nature ought to be given an equal chance of survival. Marion Hourdeguin (2015:3) posits that environmental ethics does not prevent us from using environmental products to improve our lives, but it questions our actions and challenges us of our responsibilities towards the environment as caring beings. While pursuing our human needs and interests, according to Hourdeguin, we can consider our fellow human beings' well-being, other living things, and our planet as a whole. Thus, to improve ourselves and live flourishing lives, we ought to do an ethical reflection of our actions and how they impact on humans and non-humans alike as we cohabit in the natural environment.

One way to address these issues is to reflect critically on what African environmental ethicists have suggested are the attitude of traditional African people towards their natural environment and how we can effectively employ them today. Segun Ogungbemi (1997), for instance, has reminded us of the ethics of nature-relatedness, which according to him, is "an ethic that leads human beings to seek to coexist peacefully with nature and treat it with some reasonable concern for its worth, survival and sustainability" (ibid: 270). This same idea is expressed by Godfrey Tangwa (2004) as an 'eco-bio-communitarian' ethics, which for him accentuates the notion of humans' interrelatedness with all things nature. Tangwa notes that this traditional ethics towards the environment identifies a "recognition and acceptance of interdependence and peaceful coexistence between earth, plants, animals and humans (Tangwa, 2004: 389). This peaceful co-existence and the appreciation of nature's worth ought to inform humans' everyday activities, especially those that have direct consequences on the natural environment, including the activities of practitioners of ethnomedicine. Living with respect may mean not abusing the environment by depleting it off of what makes it valuable to us and "other beings" (Mawere, 2014).

How do governments and policymakers employ these ethical ideals practically and effectively? It is evident that current and future lives depend on the environment, our attitude and actions must be morally appropriate to respect the dignity and sanity of the environment. Whether we believe the environment exists for our use (anthropocentrism) and that we have no obligation to treat it with respect, or whether we believe non-human beings or nature as a whole has moral status, we cannot run away from the critical fact that a degraded natural environment leads to a devastating effect. In fact, there is an urgent need to reorient and reassess our individual responsibilities toward the environment. Traditional medicine practitioners ought to adopt the philosophy of live-and-let-live within their trade. This suggests that they do not only think about the benefits they derive from the environment but also how to give back to nature.

Governments can lead these crucial efforts by creating awareness and educational programmes for the practitioners and setting up a strong secretariat to regularize their activities. Proper scientific, environmental education for the rural folks, who mostly are involved in ethnomedicine production, can lead to positive change. There must also be the willingness on the part of governments and policymakers to deploy people to the rural areas to be on the guard and work hand in hand with the practitioners, encouraging them to observe sound environmentally sustainable methods for their trade. The education must appeal to the people's moral responsibilities regarding the environment and the need to relate respectfully with nature, as it has been their forefathers' practice.

Chiefs and elders as custodians of the rural environment also have a vital role to play in environmental sustenance. Chiefs are invested with powers to penalize their subjects who break norms and customs of the society. They are highly respected and revered by their subjects, and as such, their inclusion can be essential.

Conclusion

The chapter has shown that although ethnomedicine remains a highly practised trade in Ghana and other African countries, very little research has been done to assess how the practice impacts the natural environment. The chapter points out the various ways that the practice of ethnomedicine contribute to humans' exploitation of the natural environment, a practice that can result in the eventual depletion of some aspect of the natural environment if left unchecked. The chapter suggests the need to re-orientate our individual moral responsibilities toward the environment by resorting to traditional African philosophical and ethical approaches to the environment. To be more specific, the chapter has called for the traditional African ethics that acknowledge the interrelatedness of humans and nature alike, and based on this relationship calls for peaceful co-existence of humans with nature. It further challenges us to be circumspect with our use of the natural resources in furthering our existential needs. The chapter concludes that governments and traditional authorities should assume the leading role in educating stakeholders and providing a proper monitoring mechanism. Thus, even though the practice of ethnomedicine is vital to the economy, health and the people's way of life, there is the need to find ways to ensure the environment does not suffer unduly.

References

Abdul-Gafaru Abdulai. (2017). The Galamsey Menace in Ghana: A Political Problem Requiring Political Solutions? POLICY BRIEF No.5. http://ugbs.ug.edu.gh/ugbs-policy-briefs. (Accessed date 15 December 2020).

Adjei Samuel, N. K. Oladejo, I. A. Adetunde, (2012). The Impact and Effect of Illegal Mining (galamsey) towards the Socio-economic Development of Mining Communities: A Case Study of Kenyasi in the Brong Ahafo Region. *International Journal of Modern Social Sciences*, 2012, 1(1): 38-55.

Anyinam, C. (1995). Ecology and Ethnomedicine: Exploring Links between Current Environmental Crisis and Indigenous Medical Practices. *Social Science and Medicine* 40:322

Anquandah James. (1997). African Ethnomedicine: An Anthropological and Ethno-Archaeological Case Study in Ghana. *Africa: quarterly review of studies and documentation of the Italian-African Institute* 52:2. 289-298.

Ameyaw, Yaw. (2005). Quality and Harvesting Specifications of Some Medicinal Plant Parts Set Up by Some Herbalists in the Eastern Region of Ghana. *Ethnobotanical Leaflets.*

Betti, J. L. (2004). An ethnobotanical study of medicinal plants among the Baka pygmies in the Dja biosphere reserve, Cameroon. *African Study Monographs*, 25:1. 1-27.

Benneh, G., Songsore, J., Nabila, J.S., Amuzu, A.T., Tutu, K.A., Yangyuori, Y., and McGranahan, G. (1993). *Environmental Problems and the Urban Household in the Greater Accra Metropolitan Area (GAMA) Ghana*. Stockholm, Sweden: Stockholm Environment Institute.

Brown, T., LeMay, E., Burstein, B., Murphy, C., Woodward, P and Stoltzfus. (2018).

Chemistry: The Central Science Pearson New International Edition, London Pearson.

Bush, Ray. (2009). Soon there will be no-one left to take the corpses to the morgue: Accumulation and abjection in Ghana's mining communities. *Resources Policy*, 34. 57–63.

De-Valera Botchway and Yaw Sarkodie Agyemang. (2012). Indigenous religious environmentalism in Africa. *Religions: A Scholarly Journal*, 77. DOI: 10.5339/rels.2012.environment.6

Evans-Anfom, E. (1986). *Traditional Medicine in Ghana, Practice, Problems and Prospects*. Accra: Academy of Arts and Sciences.

Ekpere, J. A., and R. N. Mshana. (1997). *Medicinal Plants and Herbal Medicine in Africa: Policy Issues on Ownership, Access and Conservation.* Nairobi: BDCP Press.

Fisher, B. Rebort. (1998). *West African Religious Traditions: Focus on the Akan of Ghana.* New York: Orbis Books.

Hourdequin, Marion. (2015). *Environmental Ethics: from Theory to Practice.* London: Bloomsbury Publishing Pic.

Kerwegi S. A. (2001). *Traditional Skin Care Using Plant Extracts,* Kampala, Uganda.

Kotey, E. (2016). Galamsey: A curse in a mess? Available online at: http://m.myjoyonline.com/marticles/opinion/galamsey-a-curse-in-a-mess. (Accessed date 12 September 2020).

Mangena F. (2014). Environmental Policy, Management and Ethics in Zimbabwe, 2000-2008. *The Journal of Pan African Studies,* 6:10. 224-240.

Nsubuga FNW, Namutebi EN, Nsubuga-Ssenfuma M. (2014). Water resources of Uganda: an assessment and review. *Journal of Water Resource and Protection,* 6. 1297–1315. Available online at: https://doi.org/10.4236/jwarp.2014.614120. (Accessed date: 10 November 2020).

Odoi-Larbi, S.EPA sets guidelines for noisemaking. The Chronicle (16th May), 2012, The Chronicle, http://thechronicle.com.gh/?p=44464. Accessed date: 20 December 2020.

Ogungbemi, S. (2018). An African perspective on the Environmental crisis" in Pojman, Louis J.(ed) *Environmental ethics, readings in theory and application,*2nd ed Belmont. C.A Wadsworth Publishing Company.

Rukangira, E. (2001). Medicinal Plants and Traditional Medicine in Africa: Constraints and Challenges. *Sustainable Development International,* 4. 179-84.

Sideris, H. Lisa. (2003). *Environmental Ethics, Ecological theology and natural selection.* New York: Columbia University Press.

Stekelenburg J, Jager BE, Kolk PR, Westen EH, van der Kwaak A, Wolffers I. N. (2005). Health care seeking behaviour and utilisation of traditional healers in Kalabo, Zambia. *Health Policy,* 71:1. 67-81. doi: 10.1016/j.healthpol.2004.05.008. PMID: 15563994.

Van der Merwe D, Swana GE, Botha C. J. (2001). Use of ethnoveterinary medicinal plants in cattle by Setswana-speaking people in the Madikwe area of the North West Province of

South Africa. Journal of South African Veterinary Association 72, (4): 189–96.

Wireko, V. (2013). Reality Zone: Clamp down on noise making - is it too little too late? (February 20, 2013 Daily Graphic). Available online at: https://www.graphic.com.gh/features/features/reality-zone-clamp-down-on-noise-making-is-it-too-little-too-late.html Accessed date 26 November 2020).

Wodah, Daniel and Alex Asase. (2012). Ethnopharmacological use of plants by Sisala traditional healers in northwest Ghana. *Pharmaceutical Biology*, 50:7. 807-815, DOI: 10.3109/13880209.2011.633920. (Accessed date: 16 December 2020).

Chapter 8

Coping with Climate Change-linked Environmental Tragedies: The Role of Shona Beliefs and Practices as Indigenous Knowledge Systems

Francis Machingura & Godfrey Museka

Abstract

There have been debates on climate change-linked environmental tragedies experienced in Zimbabwe of late. Interestingly, religion has not been left behind in the discussions especially African Traditional Religion and Christianity which have dominated the spiritual market of Zimbabwe. The understanding by many Zimbabweans is that disasters have a lot to do with the anger of the divine or spiritual world hence the need to understand the religious climate change-linked symbolisms on beliefs and practices. Zimbabwe has tasted the brunt effects of climate change-linked environmental disasters through cyclone-related floods, droughts and heat waves. The disasters resulted in loss of human, floristic and faunistic life as well as extensive damage to infrastructure which has been a setback to poorly resourced government departments. The adverse effects of climate change-linked environmental disasters are not limited to this country but other countries in the region. However, these climatic changes effects have reignited the debate on indigenes and Christian beliefs and practices on climate change-linked environmental tragedies. We are convinced that such debates will be helpful for future generational discourses. In this chapter, we therefore explore the role of African-Christian religio-cultural beliefs in aiding victims cope and make sense of climate change-driven catastrophes, suffering and loss.

Keywords: Climate change, environment, tragedies, Shona, Beliefs, IKSs

Introduction

From the turn of the century, Zimbabwe has been experiencing unprecedented adverse effects of climate change-linked environmental disasters largely through cyclone-related floods, El Nino-related droughts and heat waves. In the year 2000 for example, the devastating cyclone Eline that swept across Zimbabwe resulted in some very arid areas in Matebeleland South, Masvingo and Manicaland receiving uncharacteristically high rainfall. Consequently, around 500 000 people were affected by the floods leaving 96 000 of them needing assistance in terms of food, shelter, health, water and sanitation, education, transport and communication (United Nations Country Team, 2000). The disaster resulted in loss of human, floristic and faunistic life as well as extensive damage to infrastructure particularly in areas such as Chipinge, Chimanimani (Manicaland province) and Muzarabani (Mashonaland Central province).

In March 2019, another devastating cyclone named Idai caused unparalleled calamity mostly in Chimanimani and Chipinge. Cyclone Idai affected 270 000 people, leaving 341 dead and hundreds missing (IFRC, 2020). A total of 17 608 households were left homeless, 12 health facilities damaged, 139 schools affected with 33 primary schools and 10 secondary schools provisionally closed leaving 9 084 pupils temporarily out of school (IFRC, 2020). In addition, 362 cattle, 514 goats and sheep as well as 17 000 chickens were lost (IFRC, 2020). In terms of infrastructure, 90% of the road network was damaged with 584 km of the roads rendered impassable (IFRC, 2020). The scars of cyclone Idai are yet to heal. The impact of these climatic tragedies has not been limited to the physical, social and demographic spheres. Religiously and psychologically, the disasters have triggered post-traumatic stress disorder (PTSD), which according to Madakasira and O'Brien (1987) is a damaging effect of experiencing disasters like floods. While the focus of this chapter is on Zimbabwe, it is important to note that the adverse effects of climate change-linked environmental disasters are not limited to this country. Other countries in the region, for example, Mozambique, Malawi, Madagascar and South Africa have been prone to climate change mishaps. These climatic changes effects have called for a relook into indigenes beliefs and practices that are ecologically friendly and helpful for future generations.

Despite vulnerability to climate change-related environmental adversities, the majority of people in prone areas have repeatedly rebutted efforts to be moved from their ancestral land. Even those that would have been displaced almost always express interest to relocate to their original homes (United Nations Country Team, 2000). This desire to remain *in situ* in spite of the potential hazards defies logic and requires interrogation. In this chapter, we therefore explore the role of beliefs in aiding victims cope and make sense of climate change-driven catastrophes, suffering and loss. The beliefs are rooted in Indigenous African religion and Christianity. The beliefs in these two dominant religious traditions are intricately interwoven, interdependent and syncretistic due to mutual engagement or interaction. Thus, in order to appreciate the role of indigenous beliefs in coping and making sense of climate change-related environmental disasters, there is need to understand African and Christian cosmologies.

The Shona Indigenous Cosmology

According to Matthews, cited in Bowie (2006), all world communities have cosmologies, meaning stories, legends, tales, proverbs, myths and theories that account for the origin and nature of the universe. These stories, myths and theories further explain ways in which peoples in diverse cultures understand the world of their experience. No culture can, therefore, be fully understood outside its context. In this regard, we contend that religion shapes and regulates the rhythm of life, that is, the lived everyday experiences. Etymologically, the term cosmology is derived from two Greek words, cosmos and logos (Kanu, 2013:533). When interpreted, cosmos and logos mean universe and science. Put together the two words mean 'science of the universe' or the study of the universe to appreciate their surroundings. According to Bourdillon (1990) and Bowie (2006) cosmology is a conception of the nature of the universe and its operations. It also depicts the place of humanity and other creatures (animate and inanimate) within the universe. Similarly, Okon (2006:4) defines cosmology as,

> The sum total of people's opinion concerning life, happiness, fears, purpose of life, death and after-life. It is the fundamental commonalities of a given culture such as folkways, language ... and social structure.

This definition resonates with the understanding of cosmology as the complex of community's beliefs and attitudes concerning the origin, nature and structure of the universe and the interaction of its beings with particular reference to humanity (Okon, 2006:4). All cosmologies, therefore serve as a compass that gives direction to human life in a specific context. To this end, we agree with Tarusarira's (2017) assertion that African cosmology gives meaning and direction to the adherents. Cosmology functions to orient the community to its universe by defining the place of human-kind in the cosmic scheme of things. Masaka and Chemhuru (2011) are therefore right in pointing out that cosmic orientation or re-orientation attends to humanity's questions that include; who are we? where do we stand in relation to the rest of creation?

In terms of structure, the indigenous Zimbabwean Shona cosmos appears to be tripartite. Shoko (2012) and Museka (2018) concur that the three-tier structure comprising the macro-cosmos, the micro-cosmos and the meso-cosmos constitute the indigenous Shona cosmos. The macro-cosmos (supernatural) is believed to be the abode of the Supreme Being (*Mwari*), ancestors (*midzimu*) and the firmament; hence it is regarded as the highest and most sacred part of the universe. In local parlances, this part of the cosmos is referred to as *kumhepo* or *nyikadzimu*. It is supernatural, spiritual, invisible and mythical. *Mwari* is believed to be the creator (*Musiki*) of the universe. *Guruuswa* and *Mwedzi* myths of creation clearly elaborate this belief and also emphasise the centrality of Mwari in the Shona cosmic view. These myths negate Cox's (2014) theory of the invention of God in indigenous Shona society by missionaries. Furthermore, the myths disavow the chance perception held by those whose worldview is materialistic and the big-bang theory of the universe. Myth, according to Eliade quoted in Allen (2002:184), is not a false story but a narration of "…how, through the deeds of Supernatural Beings, a reality came into existence, be it the whole reality, the Cosmos, or only a fragment of reality…"

For the traditional Shona people *Mwari* and *midzimu* cannot be dichotomised because in unison they form the divine council that superintend human affairs on earth. The relationship between *Mwari* and ancestors, however, seems to be hierarchical in that *Mwari* is generally considered superior to ancestors who play a complementary as well as an intermediary role. This hierarchical relationship is evident in the perception of *Mwari* as *mudzimu mukuru* (great ancestor) or *mudzimu unoyera* (the most sacred ancestor). Since *Mwari* is the great-great ancestor, *midzimu* are believed to be the messengers and mediators between *Mwari* and humanity. Ancestors are, therefore, not an end in themselves but means to an end. As such, *Mwari* is largely thought to be transcendent though actively involved in human affairs. This does not undermine the fact that ancestors are a powerful set of spiritual beings. They are indispensable functionaries in the theocratic government of *Mwari* and executive heads of various departments in the Supreme Being's monarchic and theocratic organogram.

Apart from being closely linked to the Supreme Being, ancestors constitute membership of the living community and their presence is often acknowledged and invoked when individual, family or clan life is threatened with danger. As such, Chitando (2007) contends that ancestors are authority figures that superintend moral behaviour, norms and customs and cause afflictions when these are breached. Similarly, Magesa (1997:51) argues that ancestors "are the direct watchdogs of the moral behaviour of the individual, the family, the clan and the entire society with which they are associated." These sentiments resonate with Obengo's argument that,

> The moral guardianship provided by the ancestors is seldom expounded, yet it remains the most relevant portion to the majority of modern Africans irrespective of their conversion to Christianity, Islam or any other religion (1997:48).

Belief in ancestors is quite strong among the indigenous populations. Ancestors are grouped into three categories depending on their sphere of influence, that is; family, clan/tribal and national ancestors (Gelfand, 1973). While the sphere of influence of family ancestors is limited to the family; that of the clan/tribal ancestors extends to the whole tribe; and that of the national ancestors covers the entire nation. Blessings and calamities, depending on their geographical widespread and magnitude are traced to these ancestral categories. The ancestral spirits manifest through natural phenomena, animate and inanimate objects. Relationships between and among human beings, human and natural objects is governed and regulated through taboos. Breaching taboos is regarded as a serious immoral act which causes life-threatening illnesses or events at micro and macro levels. It is important to note that for the traditional Shona people ancestral vengeance may not be necessarily targeted on the transgressor. Instead, it can be directed to the transgressor's kith and kin or the entire territory.

In contrast, the micro-cosmos (natural/human) to the Shona people represents the everyday practical, religious, technological, social and collective life of humanity. The micro-cosmos comprises human beings, animate and inanimate objects. Occupants of this cosmic sphere are, however, not isolated and insulated from the macro-cosmos. Sacred practitioners, hierophanies and other spirit emissaries bridge these two worlds particularly through divination. Residents of the macro-cosmos also break into the micro-cosmos in order to warn, punish, guide and perpetuate human life. Animate beings that include pangolin, lion, python and baboon as well as inanimate objects such as caves, mountains and rivers are some of the sacred elements of the universe. These beings and objects are believed to be permeated with the animus or spirits. Thus, all species and objects of nature are considered sentient. To this end, Olupona (2000) contends that;

> African spiritual experience is one in which the "divine" or the sacred realm interpenetrates into the daily experience of the human person so much that religion, culture, and society are imperatively interrelated (Masondo, 2011:20).

The third category for the Shona people comprises the meso-cosmos (underworld). It is a no man's land which consists of a myriad of spirits, both benevolent and malevolent. Spirits that dwell in the underworld are generally classified as nature and alien spirits. According to Bourdillon (1990), alien (*shayi*) spirits result from strangers (aliens) who died away from their homes. Such spirits are believed to be not settled because proper funerary rituals have not been performed hence they wander around restlessly. They express themselves by possessing people they are not related to. Alien spirits can confer extra-ordinary skills in hunting, healing and stealing. Typical examples of alien spirits include; *shayi reudzimba* (associated with hunting), *shayi redzviti* (associated with fighting) and *shayi rehuroyi* (associated with witchcraft). Skills conferred by these spirits can be beneficial or detrimental to the community. The African or Shona world is full of spirits. As opposed to alien spirits; nature spirits comprises people who fail to join the ancestral board, either because they lived immorally, died prematurely or died with grievances (Shoko, 2007, 2012). Their spirits wonder around the earth as nature spirits causing untold suffering to the living. Examples of nature spirits are avenging (*ngozi*), mermaid (*njuzu*), dwarf (*chidhoma*), ghost (*goritoto*) and spook (*chipoko*). These spirits are viewed as unpredictable and dangerous to health and wellbeing of the living. They can be manipulated by witches in their anti-life activities. However, some of them, for example the mermaid spirit, are believed to be ambiguous in that they simultaneously act as contented agents of blessings and discontented agents of affliction. In this regard, Sow quoted in Dyk (2001) contends that the meso-cosmos can be called "the 'structured collective imaginary' because it gives rise to all good and bad fortunes and also gives form to people's desires, fears, anxieties and hopes for success." Belief in the macro-cosmos, micro-cosmos and meso-cosmos demonstrate that the traditional Shona belief system life is cyclic in that it revolves around the obits of birth, death and re-birth. On the whole, the Shona cosmos has numinological (community's understanding of the ultimate reality), anthropological (beliefs about human condition) and soteriological (salvific beliefs) underpinnings (Cox, 2010:133).

While we are aware of the debates on whether the African and in this case indigenous Zimbabwean Shona cosmology is anthropocentric, bio-centric and eco-centric, we adopt Shoko's (2012) implicit argument that the Shona cosmos is anthropocentric. According to the anthropocentric hypothesis humanity occupies the central position in the Supreme Being's scheme of creation. This means, the indigenous Zimbabwean Shona cosmology resembles an isosceles triangle, with the Supreme Deity and ancestors at the apex, alien and nature spirits at the bottom and humanity at the centre. The triangle imagery implies that humanity is the epicentre upon which all other cosmic forces or objects converge. The idea that humanity occupies the centre of the Shona cosmos is succinctly clear in Mbiti's (1969:92) contention that "man is at the centre of existence and African people see everything else in its relation to this central position of [human] ... It is as if God exists for the sake of human." Ikenga-Metuh (1991:109) echoes similar sentiments when he posits that; "everything else in African worldview seems to get its bearing and significance from the position, meaning and end of humankind." In addition, and more aptly, Magesa points out that;

> In the moral vision of African Religion, God stands as the ultimate guardian of the moral order of the universe for the sole and ultimate purpose of benefiting humanity. Humanity, being central in the universal order, is morally bound to sustain the work of God by which humanity itself is, in turn, sustained. Humanity is the primary and most important beneficiary of God's action (1997:50).

This theory views humanity as the priest that link the universe with the Supreme Deity. The anthropocentric hypothesis further argues for the centrality of humanity in the cosmic scheme because the vital force is more intense in human beings compared to other creatures, animate or inanimate. The superiority of humanity is further evidenced by the fact that moral blameworthiness and answerability is always on the shoulders of humanity and not animate or inanimate objects. Magesa (1997) views all creation as intended to serve and enhance the life force of humanity. The whole purpose of

155

cosmic order, is to ensure that human life endures and flourishes to its full capacity. This hypothesis views the earth as a divine gift to humanity. As such, all material resources found on earth are public property that humanity must use sustainably. In view of the indigenous Zimbabwean Shona cosmological views, we explore folk theories or alternative explanations of climate change-related environmental disasters. The coming of colonialism and Christianity did not delete the indigenous peoples' attachment to their culture, beliefs and practices.

The Christian Cosmology

According to Sindima (1990), Christianity through a Middle Eastern phenomenon came to Africa as part and parcel of Western cultures and civilization. As a result, much of what goes into defining African cosmology is what outsiders have imposed on it and the condemnation of everything African as backward and irrational (Viriri and Mungwini, 2010). So, Christianity compounded the situation as well creating an identity crisis for Africans through Christianity that tried to change their traditional value systems and how Africans engaged their world views let alone their hermeneutic engagement of scriptures and their environment. The Bible itself is a conundrum of cultures. If Africans have used their cultures to engage the Bible and not other peoples' cultures, the damage to the environment would not have been dire as in the present case. The African understanding of the world is life-centred, which provides the African understanding or framework or thinking process or interpretation of the world, interaction with other persons, nature (earth itself) or the divinity. The African interaction with the environment fits so well with the Jewish portrayal of God's expectation of His children to take care of the environment as relevant stewards. The African/Shona fullness of life is measured or seen in the bondedness to nature and everything in it. The current mechanistic view of the environment characterised by exploitation, greed, suffering of other humans and animals let alone accumulation of resources/wealth is a foreign cultural imposition and non-African (Sindima, 1990). And the western mechanistic orientation or materialistic philosophy towards the world destroyed the African systems and values as well as their interaction with nature. The Shona generally view nature and persons as one where there is sacred interdepedence between creatures hence the religious universe characterised by religious significance.

Bondedness or interconnectedness implies that everything holds significance and importance. Nature for the Shona plays an important role in human life and growth. Persons and nature are interwoven by creation into one fabric of life where there is interdependence between all creatures (Sindima, 1990). Unfortunately, our environment is in a mess and needs urgent attention. Governments and organizations have poured money in the fight against environmental degradation, noise pollution, veld fires, air or water pollution, land pollution and garbage accumulation. The response by the African Christians to some extent is that of silent observers and passivity yet there has always been a nexus between Africans and the environment. Christians are so concerned about going to heaven yet it is bad to hold to a theology that encourages negative exploitation of the environment where future generations will reside. For obvious reasons, it is rare to hear preachers talking, preaching and teaching about environmental issues. As a result, Churches and African Christians have been lukewarm in addressing environmental matters due to a number of factors that include foreign theology which they hold and not informed by their local traditional theology that preserved the environment for generations. If the number of Zimbabweans believed to subscribe to Christianity is anything to go by, the environmental problems witnessed in Zimbabwe leave a lot to be desired. The gravity of environmental threats in Zimbabwe cannot but express shock, dismay and anger because the threats have increased with time.

Biblical texts are cited and evoked on environmental matters such as: Numbers 35:33-34, Genesis 2:15, Jeremiah 2:7, Genesis 1:26-28, Psalm 24:1, Ezekiel 34:18, 1 Corinthians 10:26, Proverbs 12:10, Deuteronomy 20:19, Deuteronomy 11:12, Deuteronomy 22:6, Deuteronomy 25:4, Matthew 6:26 etc. The popularly cited texts are: "the earth is the Lord's-Psalms 24:1-2; 1 Cor. 10:26 "The earth is the Lord's, and everything in it." Believers are so excited to read such biblical texts that give them such unfettered powers to the environment. Most Christians feel that entitlement to do as they will since they are God's children. On most occasions, when Christians make patronizing and royal claims over the earth, the claims have nothing to do with Christians being responsible to the environment but being domineering patrons, e.g., mercilessly cutting down trees and exterminating other species such as animals without any recourse

157

of preserving them for future generations. In many contexts, Christians are not environmental activists and at the same time environmental activists are not Christian. The attitude of Christians towards the environment has been found not surprising because of western-cultural and scientific ideologies. Yet the traditional world view took every member of the community as critical in the preservation of the environment. There is need for engagement of Christians and their traditional world views on the environment. It is humanity's responsibility to serve and keep God's creation (Ps. 19:1; Gen. 2:15).

Every African-Christian is a stakeholder in keeping our environment clean. African-Christians must read the Bible positively and relate their reading to African traditional ways when it comes to the environment. The preservation of the environment must not be left to Government, Environmental Management Authority, Council authorities, academics, media and non-governmental organisations. Bible readers and African-Christian believers tend to misinterpret Genesis 1:26-28 because of western cultural influence giving them a blank cheque in terms of how they must treat the environment as indicated below;

> [26] Then God said, "Let us make mankind in our image, in our likeness, so that they may rule over the fish in the sea and the birds in the sky, over the livestock and all the wild animals,[a] and over all the creatures that move along the ground."[27] So God created mankind in his own image, in the image of God he created them; male and female he created them. [28] God blessed them and said to them, "Be fruitful and increase in number; fill the earth and subdue it. Rule over the fish in the sea and the birds in the sky and over every living creature that moves on the ground."

Believers take "rule" and "dominion" selfishly yet the Hebrew word- רדה *râdâh, raw-daw* literally means to rule by going down and walking among the subjects as an equal (Lynn, 1967). The Hebrew verb *radah* imply that that man is to rule over the animals as his subjects, not as a dictator, but a benevolent leader (Lynn, 1967). People must show benevolence and care to our environment as one cannot talk about morality outside the environment. For John Calvin, dominion means responsible care and keeping that does not neglect, injure, abuse, degrade, dissipate, corrupt, mar, or ruin the earth. A literal reading of Genesis 2:15 put it thus: "And Jehovah God takes the man and causes him to rest in the Garden of Eden, to serve it

158

and to keep it." Serving and keeping creation, not oppressive domination, is the biblical idea of kingdom economy and this agrees with African traditional view on the environment. The concept of life centeredness amongst Africans could be a vital basis that help saves the environment when all indigenes take it as their duty to protect the whole environment as sacred and under the watchful eyes of divine. The bondedness and life-centeredness will possibly help alleviate the suffering and negative/reckless exploitation of environment. IKSs have always provided solutions and interventions in case of climate change-related environmental misfortunes.

Climate Change-Related Environmental Misfortunes: Alternative Explanations

World communities; be they literate, semi-literate or illiterate express widespread recognition of climate change (Sachdeva, 2016). Local discourses on unprecedented changing seasons, unmatched climate instability and increased droughts and floods point to a deep understanding of climate change and variability. Scientific data validate this understanding of climate change. However, explanations regarding the causes of climate change differ from culture to culture, tradition to tradition, society to society and between the scientific positivist and folk sectors. In the scientific sector, climate change-related environmental tragedies are explained in terms of geophysical and climatological theories. In contrast, folk theories (often dismissed as myth by positivists) constitute bodies of knowledge or beliefs that differ from science. We advocate for a paradigm that does not inadvertently debunk religious views because religion, as argued earlier, shapes and regulates the rhythm of life particularly in the context of adversity. In adopting this stance, we are cognisant of the scathing attacks that are often levelled against sympathetic engagement with non-scientific beliefs regarding climate change and ensuing environmental tragedies. Sympathetic engagement with emic view on climate change is viewed as giving succour to the enemies of scientific logic and comfort to charlatans exploiting the vulnerable. We maintain that populations that uphold folk theories regarding climate change-related environmental disasters are not climatically ignorant and have no reasons for maintaining folk theories. In fact, such communities/societies are better equipped to deal with their situations/contexts whenever there are challenges and opportunities.

159

As key components of the IKSs, Shona indigenous beliefs and practices are a dictionary of life for the believers. Nyaundi (2011) underscores this when he argues that African indigenous beliefs and practices provide conventions on human-nature relationships. They regulate and shape the thoughts and actions of believers. Shona indigenous beliefs and practices are an essential part of the believers' day to day life. They do not exist in isolation with the general rhythm of life. Instead, they are the source of ethics and moral values which thread through the socio-economic, political and ecological structures of various communities. Beliefs provides the believer with a view of the world in which events do not simply happen, but have meaning. In this regard, we agree with Ranger (1991) that African indigenous religious knowledge is about relationships with the dead, the living, the environment, animals, spirits, and divinities. Indigenous beliefs and practices are a kind of pedagogy and andragogy through which believers are taught and learnt that misfortunes and illness are a net result of breaches of such relationships. The knowledge places ancestral ethics at the centre of all climatic events.

The knowledge or beliefs are ingrained in experience and passed-on explanations (Nyong, Adesina and Elasha, 2007; Tanyanyiwa, 2019). As part of the IKSs, Shona indigenous beliefs and practices comprise locally generated knowledge that function as the basis for decision-making on fundamental aspects of life. Within the realm of folk theories environmental phenomena, be they beneficial or hazardous are accounted for in terms of a breach of moral codes. The indigenous Shona people largely understand and explain climate change-related environmental misfortunes in metaphysical and bio-moral terms. From an indigenous African cosmological point of view, nothing in the universe happens by chance. All calamities result from human's moral, spiritual or religious transgressions which trigger a chain reaction that angers ancestral spirits (Sachdeva, 2016). This argument resonates with Dickinson's (2014:16) contention that "bio-moral theory ascribes disease, sickness and misfortune to deviations from prescribed moral codes of behaviour." Natural disasters are, therefore, largely perceived as retributive justice from territorial or national spirits for sins of omission or commission. In some instances, environmental tragedies such as lightning, earthquakes, floods and droughts are considered manifestation of divine displeasure. While less-threatening events are often considered normal and ignored, life-limiting phenomena, for example, floods and droughts, cause a great deal of anxiety and are often attributed to metaphysical cause(s). In this regard, Gyekye (1987) argues that extraordinary events such as drought engage African minds by calling for causal explanations. Such events, he adds, "are discrete and isolated; they appear to be puzzling, bizarre, and incomprehensible; they are not considered subsumable under any immediate known law of nature" (1987:78). All intriguing, grievous or malignant events are attributed to supernatural causation. The net effect of beliefs in macro-cosmos and meso-cosmos is the understanding that every event is either a reward or punishment from the spirits.

Environmental calamities that include; droughts, floods and earthquakes are extraordinary events that indicate fault-lines or gaps in the cosmos. Occurrence of cosmic gaps points to disharmony between humanity, nature and spiritual beings. The existence of cosmic gaps is always attributed to humanity's immoral behaviour and negligence across religions and societies. Humanity suffers most when there is disharmony in the cosmos. In light of this, Magesa (1997:54) rightfully points out that "moral culpability is always on the shoulders of humanity." We find the same understanding in religious such as Judaism and Christianity. In the indigenous Zimbabwean Shona worldview, environmental tragedies points to cosmic gaps and do not mark an end of the world. Instead, they awaken humanity to supernatural displeasure. This awakening usually culminates in the performance of divination and regressive rituals. The African indigenous causal model for climate change-related environmental tragedies is deeply rooted in religious beliefs and calls for different intervention approaches to the Eurocentric Cartesian rationality climate change models which side-line religious dimensions. This includes other models that are not indigenous or foreign oriented. Thus, instead of running away, when an environmental tragedy occurs, believers ask; why did it happen to us? Who caused it? What should we do about it?

Coping with Climate Change-Induced Environmental Tragedies

In Shona indigenous religion, divination marks the first step towards coping and making sense of climate change-induced environmental disasters. Christianity and other religions failed to some extent change or influence the thinking of African Indigenes. Most of the solutions from Christianity are foreign and alien because they are western oriented. Diviners like prophets play an important role act as long as they are indigenes to the audience understudy. Thus, after consulting diviners regarding the possible cause of environmental tragedy (cosmic disharmony), an appeasement ritual in the form of a sacrifice or offering is usually performed to remedy the situation. Traditional leaders and diviners are sources of IKS. To this end, Mbiti (1991) posits that humanity creates harmony with the universe through sacrifices and offering. Thus, following the 2015-2016 devastating drought, water levels in Kariba dam drastically lowered to the point of adversely affecting electricity generation for the country. In line with the indigenous bodies of knowledge, traditional leaders performed rituals to appease the spirits and redress the calamity. Coincidentally, the country received incessant rains in the 2016-2017 seasons. More recently, communities in Chimanimani and Chipinge with support from traditional leaders from other districts and government officials performed cleansing and redressive rituals following the cyclone Idai induced environmental catastrophe that killed, maimed and displaced thousands of residents.

In December 2020 meteorologists/climatologists predicted that Zimbabwe, in particular Chimanimani district, was to experience a destructive wave of tropical storm Chalane. Whilst more than 600 residents agreed to be evacuated, the majority resisted the evacuation initiatives. Indeed, the tropical storm Chalane swept across Zimbabwe in the evening of 30 December 2020 with minor damages reported at Chimanimani hospital, Ndima primary school and a local Church (OCHA, 2020). Viewed from an emic perspective, this miraculous survival can be attributed to the rituals performed in response to the devastating effects of cyclone Idai in the previous year. Thus, in the context of environmental disasters, African rituals such as prayers and sacrifices help victims persevere and survive distress thereby providing a sense of protection from future negative events and foster a belief that future environmental misfortunes are less likely to happen. To non-believers, rituals appear ineffectual response but for the initiated they serve key functions that help victims adapt to environmental crises.

The occurrence of disasters such as cyclones signifies chaos in the universe. Through redressive ritual, believers symbolically perform the acts of the Supreme Deity that are told over and over in myths about how they brought order to the environmental chaos. This implies that ritual enactment or re-enactment breathes life into myth. In this regard, Bell in Segal (2006:402) avers that while "myth recounts these divine acts, ritual re-enacts them." Given that ritual makes creation over again, a fresh victory over forces of chaos is experienced every time the cosmogonic myth is repeated in ritual. This sense of victory transforms and renews the believers. To this end, Ray (1976:17) argues that "every African ritual is a salvation event in which human experience is re-created and renewed ..." Myth and ritual are, therefore, inseparably bound and their enactment serves to kowtow experience to normative patterns of meaning thereby controlling and renewing the shape and destiny of the universe. Rituals, sacrifices and offerings denote human attempt to resolve essential environmental problems created by their condition in the world. This means the Shona worldview has a soteriological dimension and is, therefore, salvific.

In the context of environmental tragedies, ritual eases nervousness. Thus, according to Malinowski (1948), in situations where an individual or community is faced with life-threatening events, ritual serves to alleviate anxiety. Magical rituals, he posits, are inevitable whenever human knowledge is deficient. Thus, for Malinowski as well as Segal quoted in Hinnells (2005), ritual functions to dispel feelings of helplessness before nature. In addition, Kurtz (1995) posits that ritual communicate theories regarding the origin of the problems they are designed to alleviate. In other words, they communicate a theory of evil. They mark boundaries between good and evil and identify evil forces as the source of all calamities which need to be resolved. IKS play a great role when it comes to the protection and practice of eco-justice.

Environmental tragedies cause social disorder and Shona indigenous knowledge on rituals, for example regressive, appeasement and prayer, serve to re-establish social order. Thus, Hubert (1872-1927) and Mauss (1873-1950) as well as Smith's quoted by Bell in Segal (2006) argue that as a binary process, comprising sacralisation and desacralisation, sacrifice functions to re-establish social equilibrium after it has been disturbed. While sacralisation denotes a situation whereby a profane offering is consecrated so that it acts as a means of communication and communion between the sacred and the profane worlds, desacralisation is a process which concludes the rite and serves to re-establish the necessary demarcations and everyday social order that exist between the sacred and the profane worlds. As such, ritual sacrifice is not a mere gift or bribe to the spirits but a dynamic process through which the community renews itself and re-establishes order.

163

Shona indigenous knowledge often broadcasted and diffused through beliefs and practices further provide an explanatory model and situate natural disasters within a larger divine plan. This helps to create a sense of order and continuity in the midst of a tragedy, suffering and loss. Belief in the supernatural cause of environmental disasters helps victims to heal by providing justification for the loss. Schmuck's (2000), is therefore right in asserting that religious explanations are more effective in helping victims understand why natural disasters happen in their locality and how best to survive them. The idea of attributing environmental tragedies to supernatural deity or ancestors is not unique to the Shona people Zimbabwe and other ethnic groups in Africa. After the 2004 Tsunami in South Asia, Buddhist monks provided naturalistic explanations for the disaster by relying on traditional Buddhist teaching which emphasise the importance of taking responsibility for one's actions in order to alleviate suffering (Sachdeva, 2016). Similarly, Muslim clerics explained the disaster in terms of Allah's wrath due to human sins (Muza, 2019). These explanations serve to show that for religious people environmental calamities result from a breach of moral codes or taboos. Conversely, the desire to avoid breaching environmental taboos promotes environmental stewardship. However, in their study findings among agro-pastoralists at larger Makueni district in Kenya, Sanganyado, Teta and Masiri (2017) found out that 45% of the respondents believed that droughts were part of the greater plan of the supreme deity and as humans they could not do anything to mitigate. This attitude regarding climate change and its associated environmental misfortunes, they argue is fatalistic. This interpretation cannot be generalised because many African communities conduct rainmaking rituals to mitigate the crises (Mubaya and Mafongoya, 2016).

Climate change-related environmental tragedies also cause post-traumatic stress disorder (PTSD), that is, a downstream effect of experiencing disasters such as floods and earthquakes (Madakasira and O'Brien, 1987). Given that Shona indigenous religious beliefs and practices are an oasis of indigenous knowledge which provides believers with a conviction of higher purpose in life, they can be useful in helping victims to adapt and cope with PTSD. According to Sachveda (2016) victims who perceive themselves as having a higher purpose in life and other positive religious and spiritual dimensions, for example the belief that God and/or ancestors are their partners in the crises exhibits fewer symptoms of PTSD. This explains why most victims of climate change-induced environmental tragedies almost always express interest to remain *in situ* or return to their ancestral land after temporal displacement. IKS therefore play an important role.

Conclusion

This chapter demonstrates that, as key components of IKSs, Shona indigenous beliefs and practices have the capacity to foster mitigation and adaptation to climate change-triggered environmental tragedies. This is despite similarities or coming of other cultures, religious beliefs and practices such as Christianity. The rituals performed after or in anticipation of an environmental misfortune have a role to mitigate the misfortune. In the same vein, rituals performed after the ravaging effects of climatic disaster help believers adapt, cope or adjust to the impact of the tragedy at local level. This IKS is a framework through which communities and individuals view and interpret any environmental calamity. This context-specific knowledge about how local people can cope with environmental disasters has the potential to provide important guidelines for addressing current and future life-limiting events linked to climate change. IKS therefore play an important role for every African community, the Shona people included. Other religious beliefs and practices such as Christianity which has become part of the indigenes' life. However, IKS have continued to play a resilient role against foreign beliefs, practices and cultures.

References

Allen, D. (2002). *Myth and religion in Mircea Eliade*. New York and London: Routledge.

Bell, C. 2006. Ritual. In R.A. Segal (Ed). *The Blackwell Companion to the Study of Religion*, 397-412. Malden: Blackwell Publishing.

Bourdillon, M.F.C. (1990). *Religion and Society: A Text for Africa*. Gweru: Mambo Press.

Bowie, F. (2006). *The Anthropology of Religion: An Introduction*. Malden: Blackwell Publishing.

Chitando, E. (2007). African indigenous religions in the HIV and AIDS contexts. In M.W. Dube (Ed.), *Theology in the HIV and AIDS Era series: The HIV and AIDS curriculum for the programmes and institutions in Africa*, pp.1-129. Geneva: World Council of Churches.

Cox, J.L. (1992). *Expressing the sacred: An introduction to the phenomenology of religion.* Harare: University of Zimbabwe Publications.

Cox, J. L. (2010). *An introduction to the phenomenology of religion.* New York: Continuum International Publishing.

Dickinson, D. (2014). A different kind of AIDS: Folk and lay theories in South African townships. Auckland Park: Fanele.

Gelfand, M. (1973). *The genuine Shona: Survival values on an African culture.* Gweru: Mambo Press.

Gyekye, K. 1987. *An essay on African philosophical thought: The Okon conceptual scheme.* Philadelphia: Temple University Press.

Ikenga-Metuh, E (1991). *African religions in Western conceptual schemes.* Jos: Imico.

International Federation of Red Cross and Red Crescent Societies (IFRC). (2020). Zimbabwe:

Tropical cyclone Idai final report, DREF Operation: MDRZW014- situation report. *https://reliefweb.int/report/zimbabwe/zimbabwe-tropical-cyclone-idai-final-report-dref-operation-n-mdrzw014.*

Kanu, I.A. (2013). The dimensions of African cosmology. Filosofia theoretica: *Journal of African Philosophy, Culture and Religion,* 2(2):533-555.

Kurtz, L.R. (2007). *God's in the global village: The world's religions in sociological perspective (2nd Edition).* London: Pine Forge Press.

Madakasira, S., and O'Brien, K. (1987). Acute posttraumatic stress disorders in victims of a natural disaster. *Journal of nervous and mental disease,* 175(5).

Magesa, L. (1997). *African Religion: The moral traditions of abundant life.* Nairobi: Pauline Publications Africa.

Malinowski, B. (1948). *Magic, science, and religion and other essays.* New York: Doubleday Anchor.

Masaka, D. and Chemhuru, M. (2011). Moral dimensions of some Shona taboos (Zviera). *Journal of Sustainable Development in Africa,* 13(3):132-148.

Masondo, S. (2011). The practice of African traditional religion in contemporary South Africa. In T.W. Bennett (ed.), Traditional African religions in South African law, pp19-36. Cape Town: UCT Press.

Mbiti, J.S. (1969). *African religions and philosophy.* London: Heinemann.

Mbiti, J.S. (1991). *Introduction to African religion (2nd Edition)*. London: Heinemann.

Mubaya, C.P., and Mafongoya, P. (2016). Local-level climate change adaptation decision-making and livelihoods in semi-arid areas of Zimbabwe. *Environ Dev Sustain*, 19:1-17.

Museka, G. (2018). *African traditional religio-cultural rituals in the era of HIV and AIDS: assets or liabilities?* PhD Thesis, University of Zimbabwe.

Muza, K. (2019). *Religion and ecology: climate change between Christian and Shona religious beliefs and practices*. PhD Thesis, University of Pretoria.

Nyaundi, N.M. (2011). African traditional religion in pluralistic Africa: A case of relevance, resilience and pragmatism. In T.W. Bennett (ed.), Traditional African religions in South African law, pp1-18. Cape Town: UCT Press.

Nyong, A., Adesina, F., and Osman-Elasha, O. (2007). The value of indigenous knowledge in climate change mitigation and adaptation strategies in the African Sahel. *Mitigation and adaptation strategies for global change*, 12:787-797. Doi: 10:1007/s11027-007-9099-0.

Obengo, T.J. (1997). The Role of ancestors as guardians of morality in African Traditional Religions. *Journal of Black Theology in South Africa*, 2(2):44-63.

Okon, E.E. (2006). Ekpu-Oro: Studies in Oron cosmology and cultural history. *African Journal of Religion, Culture and Society*, 1(1):2-26.

Olupona, J. K. (2000). Introduction. In J.K. Olupona (ed.), African spirituality: Forms, meanings and expressions, pp xv-xvii. New York: The Crossroad Publishing co.

Ranger, T.O. (1991). African traditional religion. In P. Clarke and S. Sutherland (eds.), The world's religions: The study of religion, traditional and new religions, pp106-110. London: Routledge.

Ray, B.C. (1976). *African Religions: Symbol, ritual and community*. Englewood Cliffs/New Jersey: Prentice Hall.

Sanganyado, E., Teta, C., and Masiri, B. (2017). Impact of African traditional worldviews on climate change adaptation. *Integrated Environmental Assessment and Management*, 14(2):189-193.

Sachdeva, S. (2016). *Religious identity, beliefs and views about climate change*. Climate Science-Oxford-Research encyclopaedias. Oxford University Press.

Schmuck, H. (2000). "An act of Allah": Religious explanations for floods in Bangladesh as survival strategy. *International journal of mass emergencies and disasters*, 18 (1):85-95.

Segal, R.A (2006). "Myth and ritual." In J.R. Hinnells (Ed). *The Routledge Companion to the Study of Religion*, 355-378. London and New York: Routledge.

Shoko, T. (2007). *Karanga indigenous religion in Zimbabwe: Health and well-being.* Aldershot and Burlington: Ashgate.

Shoko, T. (2012). Teaching African Traditional Religion at the University of Zimbabwe. In E. Chitando and B. Bayete (Eds.), *African Traditions in the Study of Religion in Africa: Emerging Trends, Indigenous Spirituality and the Interface with other World Religions*, pp53-65. Burlington: Ashgate.

Sindima, S. (1990). Community of life: Ecological theology in African perspective, in Birch, C, Eakin. W and McDaniel J.B (eds), Liberating Life: Contemporary Approaches to Ecological Theology, Oregon: Wipf and Stock.

Spear, D., Selato, J.C., Mosime, B., and Nyamwanza, A.M. (2019). Harnessing diverse knowledge and belief systems to adapt to climate change in semi-arid rural Africa. *Climate services*, 14: 31-36. Doi: 10.1016/j.cliser.2019.05.001.

Tanyanyiwa, V.I. (2019). Indigenous knowledge systems and the teaching of climate change in Zimbabwean secondary schools. *Sage open*, pp1-11. Doi: 10.1177/2158244019885149.

United Nations Country Team. (2000). Floods disaster in Zimbabwe. *http://reliefweb.int/sites/reliefweb.int/files/resources/5DEECD113DE C5728C125689E004B7F2C-zimappeal.pdf.*

United Nations Office for the Coordination of Humanitarian Affairs (OCHA). (2020). Southern Africa, flash updates No.6: tropical storm Chalane (as of 31 December 2020). *https://reliefweb.int/report/zimbabwe/southern-africa-flash-updat-no6-tropical-storm-chalane-31-december.*

Van Dyk, A. (2001).Traditional African beliefs and customs: Implications for AIDS education and prevention in Africa. *South African Journal of Psychology*, 31(2):60-66.

Chapter 9

Conventional and Traditional Medicine: Perceptions from Practitioners

Tenson Muyambo

Abstract

This chapter is an appraisal of traditional healers and traditional medicine against a barrage of criticisms that researchers and their erstwhile masters have heaped on the indigenous health custodians and their artefacts. There is a plethora of literature on traditional medicine in Zimbabwe on the efficacy of traditional medicine but little has been on the traditional healers and their clients' perceptions about traditional medicine *vis-à-vis* allopathic medicine (Mawere, Sigauke, & Chiwaura 2014). It has always been reviews on how traditional medicine was and is still being perceived without an attempt to get the voices of the traditional healers and their clients, who are increasing each passing day. To illustrate that traditional healers and their medicine are an agency in ensuring healthy communities, the chapter focuses on traditional healers of south-eastern Zimbabwe to get their own and clients' narratives rather than relying on anecdotes. The study adopted a mixed methods approach-which are ethnographic research methods, to gain an in-depth understanding of the efficacy of the trade of traditional medicine. Face-to- face interviews with key participants the traditional healers and their clients, were conducted in south-eastern Zimbabwe from May 2017-February 2018. To triangulate the research methods, observations and documentary analysis were also utilised to gather data. Using the Sankofa and Afrocentricity perspectives, I argue that the misconceptions, half-truths and misinformation about traditional healers and their medicine are as a result of the failure to go back into the past, take that which has been sustaining humanity into the present in order to chant the way forward. One of the fundamental Sustainable Development Goal 3: *Good Health and Well-Being* will remain a mirage if no efforts to learn from our past are taken. There is need to integrate the world's health epistemologies with a view to sustainably manage health-related issues in Africa. The chapter suggests an integration on an equal footing without one epistemology assuming a superior status, an integration based on complementarity and sustainability.

Keywords: Traditional healers, medicine, sustainable development goals, Sankofa, Afrocentricity, south-eastern Zimbabwe.

Introduction

One of the fundamental Sustainable Development Goal 3: *Good Health and Well-Being* will remain a mirage if no efforts to learn from our past are taken. There is need to integrate the world's health epistemologies with a view to sustainably manage health-related issues in Africa. Negative perceptions about traditional healers and medicine hit their lowest ebb during and after colonisation. Whether this has to do with the impact of colonisation on traditional beliefs and practices as well as the aftereffects of colonisation remains to be seen in this chapter. Literature abounds where traditional healers and medicine are vilified as evil (Chavunduka, 1994, Shoko, 2007, Last & Chavunduka, 1986, Kazembe, 2007, Makinde, 1988, Sindiga, Chacha &Kanun ah, 1995, Gelfand, 1964). The traditional healer is a 'rogue' and 'deceiver' who did not only prohibit the work of missionaries but "prevented many patients, who would otherwise be treated effectively with modern Western drugs and surgery, from reaching government and mission hospitals" (Chavunduka, 1994:5). As if this was not scornful enough, the early missionaries and colonial government officials unfoundedly and unjustifiably "felt that traditional healers encouraged the belief in witchcraft, which was regarded as one of the greatest hindrances and stumbling blocks in the way of Christian missionary work" (ibid). Chavunduka (1994) further states the missionaries were heavily opposed to traditional medicine as they accused it of encouraging local people to worship their ancestors instead of God, a sinful disposition.

The negative portrayal continued in post-colonial despite efforts to 'professionalise'[1] (Last and Chavunduka, 1986) the traditional medicine. The inferiorisation of the traditional healer and medicine falls in the face of the World Health Organisation's (WHO) understanding of traditional medicine as ways of protecting and restoring health that existed before the arrival of modern medicine (WHO, 1996). WHO in this instance does not insinuate that traditional medicine is anachronistic. If this definition from WHO is anything to go by one may ask: Where do the misconceptions, half-truths and misinformation associated with traditional healers and medicine come from? To answer this question, the first part of the

---

[1] For lack of a better word, I use this word 'professionalise' with pain because it presupposes that the traditional healer and medicine were and are not professional on their own and would need something else, for instance, Western medicine, to professionalise it.

170

chapter discusses how traditional healers and medicine continue to be understood in the 21st century, decades after colonisation. The second part reflects on how the traditional healers and their clients understand traditional medicine. The third part, being the last part, is a suggestion of how SDG3 can be realised when approaches of complementarity and heterogeneity are embraced in world health matters. The chapter concludes by foregrounding the need for African communities to continue preserving and practising the trade of traditional medicine whilst embracing realistic and practical adjustments with western bio-medicine for good health and well-being for all.

Theoretical Framework

This chapter draws insights from the Sankofa and the Afrocentricity perspectives as guiding theories. The Sankofa is an African word that originated from the Adinka people of the Akan of Ghana (Slater, 2019). Etymologically, the word is a combination of *san,* meaning 'to return', *ko,* meaning 'to go', and *fa,* meaning 'to fetch or to seek'. Put together *Sankofa* is translated as 'Go back and take it' or 'Go back and fetch it'. This concept is symbolised by a mythical bird whose feet is planted firmly on the ground and the head is turned backwards. When translated, the symbol means 'it is not a taboo to go back and retrieve what you have forgotten or lost' (Temple, 2010). Quarcoo (1972:17) describes the concept as:

> learn from or build on the past. Pick up the gems of the past. [It is a] constant reminder that the past is not all shameful and that the future may profitably be built on aspects of the past. Indeed, there must be movement with the times but as the forward march proceeds, the gems must be picked up from behind and carried forward on the march.

Put simply, the *Sankofa* perspective is the realisation that the past is not hordes of useless entities, but that there are essential elements people must pick up as they move forward. The past determines the present and the present defines the future. For this study, the *Sankofa* perspective implies that traditional healers and their medicine are an essential cog from the time immemorial that ensured and still ensure good health and well-being for the majority of Africans. The concept has become a form of resistance with respect to rejecting Eurocentric worldviews and insisting on the relevance of using African conceptual possibilities to define and characterise African life. Using

171

the perspective, the chapter is suggesting resistance to relying on what allopathic medicine dictates for the African people and that they should insist on their way of keeping good health and well-being informed by the 'gems' from the past. This explains why it is essential to approach traditional medicine from the traditional healers' and traditional medicine users' point of view, an approach mostly ignored by scholars of traditional medicine.

Closely related to the *Sankofa* but using a different approach to reaffirming the significance of the past, is the Afrocentric theory. Afrocentricity [Afrocentric paradigm], as a philosophical and theoretical paradigm is said to be the brainchild of Molefi Kete Asante, a Pan-Africanist scholar. Popularised in his *The Afrocentric Idea* (1987), *Afrocentricity* (1988) and *Kemet, Afrocentricity, and Knowledge* (1990), Afrocentricity "is the placing of African ideals at the centre of any analysis that involves African culture and behaviour" (Asante, 1987: 6). It is an intellectual paradigm that privileges the centricity of African people within the context of their own historical experiences (Asante, 2014). According to Zulu (1999:15), the main objective of Afrocentricity is to free the study of Africa, and people of African descent from European domination and the racist claws of European scholarship.

Put simply, Afrocentricity is about African experiences from an African perspective or point of view, thus looking at African history, philosophy, religion, among others, through an 'African spectacle'. According to Bonsu (2016:110), the paradigm has become necessary since the bulk of African experiences have been written from Eurocentric perspectives. In this chapter, Afrocentric paradigm would be used as a theoretical base for examining some misleading and racially motivated terminologies used in reference to traditional healers and medicine, since the paradigm is best used for studying Africa and its people's beliefs and practices from an African perspective. The next section is on methodology.

Methodology

This study was part of the researcher's doctoral studies. It employed participatory methods. According to Liamputtong and Ezzy (2005) participatory methods acknowledge that local communities have valuable stores of knowledge which can guide development. Acknowledging the ideals of participatory methods, Gutie´rrez *et al.* (2015) note that modern health programmes in rural

172

communities are often culturally-biased and paternalistic, lacking participation of the community in question. To avoid the omission, this study adopted a mixed research methods approach where interviews and observations were adopted to gain an in-depth understanding of (often concealed) practices and beliefs concerning traditional healers and medicine of south-eastern Zimbabwe. Ethnographic research methods, where face-to-face interviews were conducted from 2017-2018 with ten traditional healers, ten clients/patients and five nurses, two medical doctors to examine how these participants understood the trade of traditional medicine. The inclusion of five nurses and two visiting medical doctors in the local clinics was meant to get a representative opinion from allopathic medical system towards traditional healers and medicine. Investing time and effort in trust-relationships with healers and patients was crucial. To facilitate this, local research assistants served as gate-keepers. They introduced the researcher to healers and patients through purposive and snowball sampling. Understanding and trust built over time alleviated the healers' concerns that the researcher was trying to "steal" their herbal concoctions for profit, and enabled respectful and appropriate conduct. The interviews were done in the local language and were later transcribed and translated into English. Where translation was distorting and diluting the meaning, the local language was used as gotten from the participants.

Frequent non- participant observations were scheduled at healers' homesteads, from where they attended to their patients. The researcher observed traditional healers carrying out their business with their clients, listening to their conversations with clients as clients feedback on their conditions as well as observing the administering of various concoctions. Observational data provided insights into practices of healers; they confirmed the impressive efficacy of traditional medicine and served to validate information from interviews.

In addition, available references or reports on the perception of traditional healers and medicine were consulted from published scientific journals, newspapers, books, and reports. Literature was searched on international online databases such as B-Org, Google and Google scholar. Words used on these databases and by scholars were "Traditional medicine or healer", and "medicinal plants". Publications were limited to English language. Ethical considerations such as informed consent, confidentiality, privacy and anonymity were catered for. Because of the low levels of literacy (Krah, de Kruijf and Ragno, 2018), meaning the ability to read and write, verbal informed consent in local languages was obtained from all participants prior to participation. For those who could append their signature consent form in local the language were administered. The purpose of the study was fully explained, assuring participants that the information they provided was to be kept highly confidential and by using pseudonyms for the participants' privacy. Data collected was thematically analysed. Not surprisingly, the results of this research may not have universal applicability because it utilised a case study approach that focused on traditional healers and clients of south-eastern Zimbabwe. Therefore, interpretation beyond that group of individuals can only be done in a tentative manner at this time. Results of the study are presented below.

Results

Two thematic areas emerged, through which traditional healers and medicine were perceived and misperceived in 21st century Africa. First the available literature sifted through indicated that up to the time of writing this chapter, traditional healers and medicine were still characterised by ambivalence between partial acceptance and continued inferiorisation. Despite efforts made by organisations like WHO to integrate and make traditional medicine and allopathic medicine collaborate, terminology that still exists in referring to traditional healers and medicine continues to illustrate the incompatibility between the two healthcare systems. The second theme was that traditional healers and their clients/patients made no mistake about traditional medicine and were more than ready to collaborate and integrate with allopathic healthcare system on an equal footing as the sections below demonstrate.

The following section is meant to show how traditional healers and medicine are perceived in several writings. In this section I demonstrate the errors of terminology that are used in literature to describe traditional healers and their trade, descriptions that make traditional medicine and biomedicine incompatible. Hence making integration of the two systems of health provision a herculean task.

Traditional healers and medicine in 21st century Africa

Literature consulted reveal that while efforts to make traditional healers and medical staff in modern medicine collaborate and integrate their trades, suspicion and misunderstandings abound. The suspicion and misunderstandings are categorically demonstrated through the terms that are still being used in referring to traditional healers and medicine. Notably, these terms are still widely used by both African and non-African scholars and researchers. Surprising enough, some African scholars have been brainwashed by Europeans, hence they also use these racial and misleading terms whether knowingly and unknowingly in describing traditional healers and their practice. The terms, picked from literature, are discussed below.

Witch doctor

The term 'witchdoctor' or 'native doctor' (Adekson, 2003) was a racially motivated term that was used to belittle the practice of traditional healers. In a foreword, Welensky describes Gelfand's (1964) book: *Witchdoctor: Traditional Medicine Man in Rhodesia* as an attempt to remove the preconceived and erroneous fallacy that is so widely held in the outside world that the African witchdoctor is of necessity evil. The British English Dictionary defines 'witchdoctor' as a magician credited with powers of healing, divination, and protection against the magic of others found among tribal peoples. Confining a 'witchdoctor' to local people suggests that there are people who are not local. This is a fallacy because humanity by nature is tribal. Within the British we have native tribes such as the Epidii, the Caledones, and so are the Americans. Tribalism is not a monopoly of the African people alone, but others including the acclaimed non-Africans. While traditional healers heal, practise divination and protect people from being bewitched, really to describe them as witchdoctors is not only racial but bigotry. Is it proper to describe a dentist as 'teeth doctor'? If not why would it seem alright to describe a traditional healer whose *muti* prevents people from being bewitched by others as 'witchdoctor'? The term falls too far short of the office of a traditional healer and must be abandoned. Traditional healers are more than what we get from the definition.

Rogue and Deceiver

There are still other investigators and writers who have defined a traditional healer as both a 'rogue' and a 'deceiver' (Chavunduka 1994). The British English Dictionary defines 'rogue' as a dishonest and unprincipled man. It further states that a rogue is a person whose behaviour one disapproves but who is nonetheless likeable and attractive. One wonders how one disapproves one's behaviour but still likes and feels attracted to the same person. Closely related to the 'rogue' tag is the 'deceiver' namesake. The English Dictionary defines a 'deceiver' as an individual who deliberately cause someone to believe something which is not true. The colonial governments and early Christian missionaries used these terms, 'rogue and deceiver' referring to traditional healers. Their argument was that traditional healers "prevented many patients, who would otherwise be treated effectively with modern Western drugs and surgery from reaching government and mission hospitals" (Chavunduka, 1994:5). What these governments and missionaries forgot was that they came amidst a people who had their own way of looking after their health and well-being. Such deliberate omissions cannot be tolerated. It is mere bigotry. Evidently, traditional healers and medicine consultation is on the increase with WHO declaring that 80% of Africa's population rely on traditional medicine for their primary healthcare (Ritcher, 2003). Ritcher (2003) further states that in sub-Saharan Africa, the ratio of traditional healers to the population is approximately 1:500, while medical doctors have a 1:40 000 ratio to the rest of the population. It is clear that traditional healers play an influential role in the lives of African people and have the potential to serve as crucial components of a comprehensive health care strategy. The colonial governments and missionaries deliberately decided to forget that "traditional healing practices have existed in Africa long before conventional medicine" (Agbor & Naidoo, 2016:133).

Efforts to suppress traditional healers and medicine by the colonial governments and missionaries were initiated and propagated through the use of derogatory terms such 'witchdoctor', 'medicine men' and others but they did not succeed. Surely, the terms 'rogue' and 'deceiver' have no place in the 21st century healthcare provision where concerted efforts are supposed to be directed towards achieving sustainable development goal, number 3: *Good Health and Well-Being*.

Root doctor

To continue efforts meant to annihilate traditional healers and medicine, the traditional healer is derogatorily referred to as 'root doctor' (Adu-Gyamfi & Anderson, 2019). This could have arisen due to the undisputed use of tree roots by traditional healers in their trade.

Be that as it may, can we describe practitioners by the tools of trade they use? If that is acceptable, why are Western medical practitioners like medical doctors not being referred as 'drug doctors' since they use drugs in their profession? The use of the term *root doctor* is meant to discourage would be practitioners in this 21st century. But such attempts have outlived their use and are bound to fail as "the overall use of traditional and alternate medicine has increased in the last decade…" (WHO, 2013).

Bone setter

To further demonstrate the lack of appreciation of traditional healers by even 21st researchers and academics, such terms as 'bone setter' (Krah & Ragno, 2018) are still in use. Again, the use of the term could have been prompted by the generalised perception that all traditional healers use bones *(hakata)* as they diagnose their patients/clients (Shoko, 2007). This is a classic example of the misconceptions about traditional healers and medicine. Not all traditional healers cast bones *(kuringidza* in Ndau language). Some use dreams, visions and others do not use *hakata* but are specialised herbalists. To paint all traditional healers as bone-setters is unjustifiably delving in traditional medicine homogeneity yet we have traditional healers specialising on different aspects of traditional medicine. Kazembe (2010) rightfully identifies them as either herbalists or *n'anga*. Although it is possible to have them doubling these roles there are instances where herbalists exclusively deal with herbs and nothing else.

Non-evidence-based medicine

Western medicine is erroneously considered to be *evidence-based medicine* (emphasis mine) (Okello & Musisi, 2015) giving the impression that traditional medicine is non-evidence-based. As shall be demonstrated by the traditional healers themselves in the preceding sections, traditional medicine is not and has never been non-evidence-based medicine. As admitted by progressive scholars (Gelfand, 1964, Chavunduka, 1994, Shoko, 2007, WHO, 2013, Musyimi, Mutiso, Nandoya & Ndetei, 2016), traditional medicine could not have attracted such attention and interest had it be non-evidence- medicine. The argument that traditional medicine deals with the supernatural and hence cannot be placed under evidence-based-medicine is frivolous and scandalous. If anything, traditional medicine has been tried and tested through trial and error. It has withstood the test of time and this explains its resilience and tenacity. If it was not evidence-based it could have been abandoned long back.

Traditional medicine

Another problematic word that has not only been used for African medicine but its religion as well is 'traditional medicine'. The use of the word has been interpreted to mean 'primitive' and 'backward' medicine. For Bonsu (2016), the term is meant to portray African medicine as 'outmoded'. The implication is that by referring to African medicine as 'traditional', the net effect will be to dismiss it as uncouth. The meaning of the term 'traditional' is far from being what is given above. Awolalu succinctly defines traditional as:

> We need to explain the word "traditional". This word means indigenous, that which is aboriginal or foundational, handed down from generation to generation, upheld and practised by Africans today. This is a heritage from the past, but treated not as a thing of the past but as that which connects the past with the present and the present with eternity (1976:1).

For purposes of this chapter, the term 'traditional' is used and shall continue to be used as it helps us distinguish and delineate the type of medicine we are referring to. The term does not imply primitiveness or backwardness. Many scholars and researchers alike have been hoodwinked to think of traditional in the negative terms. Some have abandoned it and prefer to use 'indigenous', but Awolalu is apt.

The above captured misperceptions, untruths and misunderstandings are also witnessed in scholars and researchers' attitude to traditional healers. When HIV and AIDS epidemic emerged a lot of unfounded stories were told about traditional healers. A good example is that traditional healers are urging HIV and AIDS male patients to have sexual intercourse with virgins as a way of wadding off the virus. Such stories are peddled as a way of discouraging people from seeking assistance from traditional healers. The advent of COVID-19 pandemic has equally seen traditional medicine denied the room to be part of the solution to a world health crisis. Madagascar was castigated on social media when it mentioned traditional remedies to the pandemic. These stories may have contributed to a negative sentiment held towards all traditional healers and to all traditional healing practices (Ritcher, 2003). No efforts are being made to either prove or disapprove the claims that there are traditional medicines that can deal with the COVID-19. The dismissal of traditional medicine is attitudinal.

The depiction of traditional healers and their medicine captured above seems to suggest that traditional medicine is 'unqualified' and 'informal'. This classification leaves little room for integration. But before we make the conclusion that traditional medicine and allopathic medicine are incompatible and efforts to integrate them are in vain, as literature above shows, we need to obtain what the traditional healers and their clients have to say. Bonsu (2016) is insightful when he argues that in order to avoid bias and misrepresentation in the study of African Traditional Religion, of which traditional healers are a part (Kazembe, 2010), scholars and researchers ought to rely on primary sources, preferably, oral sources and firsthand observation of African religious practitioners. The section below does precisely so.

Traditional healers and their clients: Narratives from within

It is important to understand how the traditional healers and their clients understood themselves and their trade. Interviews held with traditional healers and traditional medicine clients (hereto referred as clients) revealed that the now called 'traditional healers' did not understand themselves by that name. They viewed themselves as health providers like doctors, physicians and counsellors from allopathic medicine. They viewed themselves as having been 'called' names by those who were against their practices. The clients referred to the traditional healers as [v]ana chiremba (medical doctors) and it was interesting to observe that signposts at their homesteads were inscribed: Doctor so and so. Vontress (2003: xi) in a foreword to *The Yoruba Traditional Healers in Nigeria* admits that his use of the name *healer* instead of doctor is to refer to lay practitioners who treat more than eighty percent of people in sub-Saharan Africa. Traditional healer is used to distinguish them from physicians, psychologists, social workers, counsellors, and other healthcare personnel trained in Western methods of healing. This implies that the distinction has no basis since both healthcare systems are common. The distinction, like indicated by the errors of terminology above, is racial and prejudiced.

Interview data showed that traditional healers and the clients were aware of traditional medicine entailed. One of the traditional healers pointed out that traditional medicine involves the use of herbs to prevent and/or cure ailments that infect humanity. The traditional

179

healer's views were confirmed by another who stated that "*uyu mushonga wemadziteteguru edu, siya usiye*" (This medicine is from our elders and ancestors. It has been there from generation to generation). One client echoed the same thinking as she indicated that traditional medicine is concoctions used from time immemorial before the coming of colonisation for the African people to cater for their primary healthcare needs. This conceptualisation of traditional medicine is confirmed by Mahomoodally (2013:2) who defines traditional medicine as "the oldest, and perhaps the most assorted, of all therapeutic systems". UNAIDS (2006:9) defines African traditional medicine as "the primary, and often the only, accessible health-care option for the vast majority of people living in sub-Saharan Africa". Adekson (2003) defines traditional healers as individuals who specialise in healing psychological, social, emotional, spiritual and holistic problems. The above understanding of traditional healers and medicine underlies the primary healthcare of the Africans and has been in use before, during and after colonisation.

The traditional healers and clients made no mistake as to the significance of their practice and that given the chance to prove themselves, they could do equally well like biomedical practitioners. This was summarised by one of the traditional healers, Sauti, who had this say:

> Our medicine is holistic. It covers the spiritual, mental and the physical person. We have many clients who come to us even after having visited the hospitals and clinics. It is only that people look down upon our work. We have been offering these services even before the coming in of hospitals and clinics.

The above submission was echoed by one of the clients, Mazveshe, who intoned:

> I went to a traditional healer soon after having been diagnosed in a hospital. I felt my illness was more spiritual than physical. When I got there, evil spells were cast out and traditional medication was administered to me. Within a week I was feeling much better and I fully recovered after a month.

It is deduced from the submissions above that traditional healers and the client interviewees straddle both the traditional and allopathic healthcare systems. In a study carried out in Eastern and Southern

Africa by Moshabela, Bukenya and Darong (2016), similar findings were obtained where both the traditional healers and the clients admitted having visited the two health systems.

On traditional healers' working relationship with allopathic medicine staff, the traditional healers indicated that they were not in competition with them. One female healer stated that she was eager to learn from them as well as they (allopathic medicine staff) had something to learn from her. The female healer interviewee's willingness to collaborate with allopathic medical staff creates possibilities for different medical systems to work collaboratively to foster a cohesive form of health pluralism. However, the medical staff (nurses), interviewed had misgivings about traditional healers and medicine. The misgivings were summarised by one nurse, Mbuya, who had this to say:

> The problem with traditional healers is that they claim to have medication for very ailment. They are not scientifically trained and leave a lot to be desired. When it comes to dosages they are found wanting. In fact, traditional medicine cannot be compared to western medicine. The staff is properly trained whereas traditional healers are not.

The two medical doctors, John and Suzzane, concurred when they said:

> Traditional medicine has no efficacy. It is based on guesswork and in most cases the prescriptions given to clients are not accurately measured. In fact, traditional medicine is unscientific and relies on hearsay. It lacks scientific research and is applied in unhygienic environments.

The above excerpts do not only demonstrate the nurse's and medical doctors' lack of knowledge on traditional healers and medicine, but demonstrates a superiority complex that 'blinds' them. They seem to be ignorant that traditional healers take years of training as apprentices (Adekson 2003; Makinde, 1988). The interviewees' attitude towards traditional healers and medicine resonates with what was found in a study done by Moshabela et al (2016) in eastern and southern Africa where HIV and AIDS patients were rebuked for seeking medical assistance from traditional healers by hospital and clinic staff. The fear by the hospital staff is a manifestation of deep-seated mistrust between the two world health systems.

However, whereas some literature's portrayal of traditional healers and medicine is monolithic and unpalatable, our data shows that traditional healers and patients view their trade as a contemporary that deals with health issues in the 21st century. The data further shows that traditional healers are willing to collaborate with allopathic medicine practitioners. Since available literature (Kazembe, 2010; Mawere, 2011; Mawere, Sigauke & Chiwaura, 2014; WHO, 2013; Krah et al. 2018) is also showing the readiness of western medicine practitioners to collaborate, the question is what is stopping the two systems of health to integrate? Evidence abounds that allopathic medicine wants to remain normative and wants to homogenise if not monopolising the health sector. It is this stark reality that calls for more investments in traditional healers and biomedical staff in order to bridge the gap between the two forms of health care. In the next section, I attempt at possibilities and opportunities the two systems of health must embrace for good health and well-being for humanity.

Complementarity and Heterogeneity: Avenues for Good Health and Well-Being

The study sought to explicate the contribution of traditional healers and medicine to good health and well-being of humanity in south-eastern Zimbabwe from the practitioners' (healers and clients) perspective, and to unravel possible hindrances to integrate traditional healers and their counterparts in bio-medicine. Admittedly, traditional healers are a significant cog in primary healthcare as evident from this study and other studies elsewhere.

The presence of Zimbabwe National Traditional Healers Association (ZINATHA) to regulate and control the practice of traditional healers is promising. But the association is not doing enough to make traditional healers and medicine more visible and recognisable. This has been very conspicuous in the era of Covid-19. While on another project, I discovered that most traditional healers had scant information about COVID-19 while their counterparts, Western medicine staff were abreast with information regarding the pandemic. The traditional healers do not engage in seminars, conferences, workshops and in-service training for them to be at par with their counterparts.

Both available literature and findings from this study indicate that there is room for complementarity for the two healthcare systems.

Indications are that for complementarity to be achieved there is a need to acknowledge, first and foremost, that the two healthcare systems are heterogeneous. This recognition, coupled with training of both staff from the two healthcare systems will make it possible for the derogatory terms to be erased and the mistrust therein removed. Observations are that there are fundamental in-roads by traditional medicine into the Zimbabwe's mainstream healthcare needs. The Zimbabwe airwaves are inundated by adverts by traditional medicine practitioners such as Herbal Centre which is opening offices in every city, town and growth point of Zimbabwe. Such opening of the health space needs to be buttressed by the right training, research and policies that ensure integration of the two healthcare systems.

The argument this chapter is making is: Now that the under-researched traditional healers' perceptions about their trade has revealed that traditional healers have no ill feelings about their counterparts, an avenue for both parties to warm towards each other is open and the onus is on the two systems to understand themselves as heterogeneous with one mission, SDG3: *Good Health and Well-being*. They must unlearn the negativity that characterised their relationship and relearn to integrate and complement each other. For this to happen, there is need for the political will and financial support to invest in more research into the two systems for both traditional and allopathic medicines to fully understand how each operates. This can be done through the government availing a budget (as it does with the so-called conventional medicine) to support the operations of traditional healers.

There is also need to train both practitioners to learn to appreciate each other. It is hoped that when more research and education are done, the problems of misconceptions, half-truths, untruths and misinformation will be resolved. I cannot put it more succinctly than Makinde (1988: xvi) who argues that "the world would be a better place to live in, if we come to know each other's way of life and thinking through proper integration".

Conclusion

In conclusion, this chapter demonstrates that it is possible to have medical pluralism provided the two 'conflicting' health systems treat each other in a complementary rather than alternative manner, and therefore not intended to replace one another. The chapter gave errors of terminology that are still in use in referring to traditional healers and medicine, and traditional healers as well as their clients' perceptions about traditional medicine. The traditional healers and clients' voices did not only enhance the study's validity and reliability, but filled in a lacuna that pervades most studies related to this one. While it is possible that there could be unscrupulous traditional healers who prey on their clients, opportunists in the advent of pandemics such as HIV and AIDS and the recent COVID-19, to paint the whole traditional medicine profession as evil is unconvincing. This chapter motivates that until and unless scholars and researchers, alike, replace the errors of terminology used to refer to traditional healers and medicine by sensitive ones that are not discriminating and stereotyping, integration may remain a mirage. Health pluralism accepts the reality that traditional medicine and biomedicine are heterogeneous hence the need to have practitioners of the two systems straddle the two health worlds as they deem necessary and that African governments need to accept this stark reality. The biggest challenge facing health pluralism intervention efforts relates to the reluctance and unwillingness of allopathic practitioners to embrace the notion of health pluralism. More research needs to be carried out to address this challenge. Training of both practitioners of the two health systems is long overdue and must be embarked to realise Sustainable Development Goal 3: *Good Health and Well-Being* thereby fostering a cohesive form of medical pluralism, which functions in the best interest of plural users of the two health-worlds.

References

Adekson, M.O. (2003). *The Yoruba Traditional Healers in Nigeria.* London: Routledge.

Adu-Gyamfi, S. and Anderson, E.A. 2019. Indigenous Medicine and Traditional Healing in Africa: a systematic synthesis of the literature. *Philosophy, Social and Human Disciplines,* vol. 1, 69-100.

Agbor, A.M. and Naidoo, S. (2016). A review of the role of African Traditional Medicine in the management of oral diseases. *African Journal of Traditional Complement Alternative Medicine,* 13(2), 133-142.

Asante, M. K. (2014). Afrocentricity: Toward a new understanding of African thought in the world. In M. K. Asante, Y. Miike, & J.

Yin (Eds.), *The global intercultural communication reader*. 2nded. New York, NY: Routledge, pp. 101-110.

Asante, M. K. (1987). *The Afrocentric idea*. Philadelphia: Temple University Press.

Asante, M. K. (1988). *Afrocentricity*. Trenton, NJ: Africa World Press.

Asante, M. K. (1990). *Kemet, Afrocentricity, and knowledge*. Trenton, NJ: Africa World Press.

Awolalu, J. O. (1976). "What is African traditional religion"? *Studies in Comparative Religion*, vol. 10 no. 2. Retrieved from: www.studiesincomparativereligion.com

Bonsu, N.O. (2016). African Traditional Religion: An Examination of Terminologies Used for Describing the Indigenous Faith of African People, Using an Afrocentric Paradigm. *Africology: The Journal of Pan African Studies*, vol.9, no.9, 108-121.

Chavunduka, G.L. 1994. *Traditional Medicine in Modern Zimbabwe*. Harare: University of Zimbabwe Publications.

Gelfand, M. (1964). *Witchdoctor: Introduction to Medicine man in Rhodesia*. London: Harvil Press.

Gutie'rrez J. M., Burnouf, T., Harrison, R. A., Calvete, J. J., Brown, N., Jensen, S. D., et al. (2015) A Call for Incorporating Social Research in the Global Struggle against Snakebite. *PLoS Negl Trop Dis* 9(9): e0003960. https://doi.org/10.1371/journal.pntd.0003960 PMID: 26379235

Kazembe, T. (2007). Traditional Medicine in Zimbabwe, +*Croix, The Rose Journal* Vol 4, 55, www.rosecroixiournal.org.

Kazembe, T. C. (2010). Traditional Medicine and Traditional Religion should be included in the School Curriculum in Zimbabwe? *Zimbabwe Journal of Education*, 22 (1): 62-86.

Krah, E., de Kruijf, J. and Ragno, L. (2018). Integrating Traditional Healers into the Health Care System: challenges and opportunities in Rural Northern Ghana. *Journal of Community Health*, 43, 157-163.

Last, M. and Chavunduka, G.L. (1986). (Eds.). *The Professionalisation of African Medicine*. Manchester: Manchester University Press.

Liamputtong P, Ezzy D. (2005). *Qualitative Research Methods*. 2nd ed. Victoria, Australia: Oxford University Press.

Mahomoodally, M.F. (2013). Traditional Medicines in Africa: An Appraisal of Tent Potent African Medicinal Plants. *Evidence-Based Complementary and Alternative Medicine Volume 2013*, Article ID 617459, 1-14. http://dx.doi.org/10.1155/2013/617459

Makinde, M. A. (1988). *African Philosophy culture and traditional medicine.* Athens: Ohio University Center for International Studies. Monograms in Inter- national Studies.

Makinde, M.A. (1988). *African Philosophy, Culture and Traditional Medicine.* Ohio: Ohio University.

Mawere, M., Sigauke, J., & Chiwaura, H. (2014). "Connoisseurs of traditional medicine: The use of traditional medicine in pregnant women health care", In: Mawere, M. & Mubaya, T. R. (Eds). *African Cultures, Memory and Space: Living the Past Presence in Zimbabwean Heritage,* Langaa RPCIG Publishers: Cameroon

Moshabela M, Bukenya D, Darong G, *et al.* (2016). Traditional healers, faith healers and medical practitioners: the contribution of medical pluralism to bottlenecks along the cascade of care for HIV/AIDS in Eastern and Southern Africa. *Sex Transm Infect.* Downloaded from http://sti.bmj.com/ 15 October, 2020.

Musyimi, C.W., Mutiso, V.N., Nandoya, E.S. and Ndetei, D.M. (2016). Forming a joint dialogue among faith healers, traditional healers and formal health workers in mental health in a Kenyan setting: towards common grounds. *Journal of Ethnobiology and Ethnomedicine,* 12 (4), 1-8.

Okello, E. and Musisi, S. (2015). The role of Traditional Healers in Mental Healthcare in Africa. In Emmanuel Kwasi Akeampong, Allan Hill and Arthur Kleinman (Eds), *The culture of Mental Illness and Psychoatric Practice in Africa.* Indiana: Indiana University Press.

Ritcher, M. (2003). Traditional Medicine and Traditional Healers in South Africa. Discussion paper prepared for the Treatment Action Campaign and AIDS Law Project.

Shoko, T. (2007). *Karanga indigenous religion in Zimbabwe: Health and Well-Being.* Aldershot: Ashgate Publishing Company.

Sindiga, I., Chacha, C.N. and Kanunah, M.P. (1995). (Eds.). *Traditional Medicine in Africa.* Nairobi: Eastern African Educational Publishers Ltd.

Slater, J. (2019). Sankofa—the Need to Turn Back to Move Forward: Addressing Reconstruction Challenges that Face Africa and South Africa Today. *Studia Historiae Ecclesiasticae,* 45 (1): 1-24.

Temple, C.N. (2010). The Emergence of Sankofa practice in the United States. A Modern History. *Journal of Black Studies,* vol.41, No.1, 127-150.

UNAIDS. (2006). Collaborating with Traditional Healers for HIV Prevention and Care in sub-Saharan Africa: suggestions or

Programme Managers and Field Workers. Geneva: WHO Library Cataloguing-in-Publication Data. (Google Scholar).

Vontress, C. E. (2003). Foreword. In Mary Olufunmilayo Adekson. *The Yoruba Traditional Healers in Nigeria.* London: Routledge, xi-xiii.

WHO. (1996). Traditional Medicine. https://apps.who.int/gb/ebwha/pdf_files/EB134/B134_24-en.pdf

WHO. (2013). *Traditional Medical Strategy 2014-2023.* Geneva: WHO.

Zulu, I. M. (1999). *Exploring the African centred paradigm: Discourse and innovation in African world community studies.* Los Angeles, California: Amen-Ra Theological Seminary Press.

Chapter 10

Indigenous Knowledge Systems-based Sexual and Reproductive health: Ndau indigenous practice of Masuwo for childbirth preparedness

Anniegrace Mapangisana-Hlatywayo

Abstract

This study is based on the premise that people live in diverse cultural and ecological settings which influence their sexual and reproductive practices. As such, pregnancy and childbirth are viewed beyond the bio-medical perspective. They are influenced by specific socio-cultural beliefs and practices. Framed within a postcolonial indigenous paradigm, the study sought to explore cultural practices adopted for childbirth preparedness by the Ndau people of Zimbabwe. Data were collected through focus groups discussions and personal interviews. Research findings reflected the indigenous practice of *masuwo* carried out during the last trimester of pregnancy. Central to *masuwo* is the use of traditional medicinal plants for precautionary and curative benefits. *Masuwo* are used as birth canal relaxants; health tonics and for protection against *mamhepo*/bad airs. The case of the Ndau women reflected their agency in managing pregnancy and childbirth using community-based knowledge systems. As such, concerted research in indigenous plant pharmacopoeia to explore the risk factors in terms of safety and toxicity is needed.

Keywords: Indigenous practices, sexual and reproductive healthcare, pregnancy, childbirth, *masuwo*, Ndau, traditional medicinal plants

Introduction

The holistic nature of indigenous conceptualization of health and wellbeing is shown by the fact that pregnancy and childbirth are both biological and symbolical. In African indigenous communities, pregnancy and childbirth are revered as they represent the reproduction of future generations and the reincarnation of ancestors. The African indigenous worldview posits that ancestors return to earth through the birth of a new child (Lionjanja 1999;

189

Oduyoye 1992). Likewise, among the Ndau of south-eastern Zimbabwe, women are expected to be fertile and to procreate in order to preserve the family lineage. Similarly, Ngomane and Mulaudzi (2010) argue that pregnancy is regarded as an accomplishment and a fulfilment of societal expectations. A pregnant woman is accorded respect, power and status within the community.

Pregnancy and childbirth have an intrinsic socio-cultural dimension. They are informed by specific indigenous practices (IPs) which include rituals, beliefs, songs and dance inherent to a particular culture (Mogawane 2014; Mothupi 2014). IPs are also referred to as folk or traditional practices (Moawed 2001). They are shaped by and embedded in a society's cultural belief system such that they become the way of life. Ngomane and Mulaudzi (2010) posit that IPs constitute the major source of survival in Africa, America, Asia and Australia. They also serve as indigenous healthcare interventions for managing pregnancy and childbirth.

IPs influence and give meaning to health seeking behaviours of pregnant women. Among the Ndau of south-eastern Zimbabwe, pregnant women adhere to the IP of *masuwo* during the last trimester of pregnancy. *Masuwo* refers to the physical and spiritual preparation of a pregnant woman for childbirth. They also serve as a measure of protection against unforeseen eventualities that might result in the malformation of the foetus and loss of the baby or the life of the mother. A key element of *masuwo* is the use of traditional medicine (TM) for managing childbirth preparedness. Hence *masuwo* are traditional medicinal plant (TMP) concoctions taken during the last trimester of pregnancy for childbirth preparedness. The IP of using TMP for preventative and therapeutic benefits is informed by religio-cultural, social and metaphysical beliefs and conceptions of illness and health. Writing from the context of Zimbabwe, Maroyi (2013) argues that TM remains one of the most affordable and easily accessible source of treatment for primary healthcare in poor and marginalized communities. He further points out that traditional plants have been historically used by local people for their medicinal properties (Maroyi 2013). Hence TM is commonly utilised for managing pregnancy and childbirth.

Whilst pregnant women are encouraged to undergo *masuwo* ritual for childbirth preparedness, Ndau traditional culture deems it necessary for every primigravida to adhere to the IP of *masuwo* for her protection and that of the unborn child from *mamhepo* and to consequently ensure a smooth birthing process. Van der Kooi and

190

Theobald (2006) also indicate that the IP of using TM in late pregnancy and labour is also practised by the Tswana of South Africa. The study carried out in the North West province reported the use of *kgaba*, a composition of different types of traditional medicine which is used during the last trimester of pregnancy (van der Kooi and Theobald 2006). *Kgaba* is used not only to treat physical problems associated with pregnancy but is believed to offer protection against harm from evil spirits. It is used to stimulate a smooth delivery and to induce labour when overdue. Abrahams et al. (2002) also reports on the adherence to indigenous healing practices during pregnancy by Xhosa speaking women of Cape Town, South Africa. These indigenous healing practices are believed to strengthen the womb against sorcery, to ease labour and to treat symptoms that Xhosa women believe cannot be treated by biomedical services (Abrahams et al. 2002).

Theoretical considerations

The study is guided by two integrative conceptual frameworks within the context of African indigenous knowledge systems (AIKS); Afrocentricity and Postcolonial African Feminism. Afrocentricity is a philosophical and theoretical paradigm founded on the works of Molefi Kete Asante. Popular among his works are the Afrocentric Idea (1987); Afrocentricity (1988); Kemet, Afrocentricity, and Knowledge (1990) among others. According to Asante (1987) Afrocentricity is "a paradigmatic intellectual perspective that privileges African agency within the context of African history and culture transcontinentally and trans-generationally" (2007:41) Asante (1991) describes Afrocentricity as a framework that views phenomena from the perspective of the African people. He explains that Afrocentricity advances African ideals by positioning them at the centre of any analysis that involves African culture and behaviour (Asante 1987). In this regard, the main tenet informing Afrocentricity is the central role that reflects the agency of African people in responding to phenomena through their own traditional and human interest. In conceptualising Afrocentricity, Karenga (1988) defines this paradigm as a framework that is embedded in the cultural image and human interests of African people. Accordingly, Karenga argues that the human interest of African people is made explicit through ensuring that a conceptual framework is "supportive of the just claims African people share with other humans" (1988:404).

Afrocentricity is characterised by an interest in psychological location, commitment to finding the African subject place, defence of African cultural elements, commitment to lexical refinement and commitment to correct the dislocations in the history of Africa (Asante 2007). It promotes the defence of African cultural values and elements. Through the Afrocentric paradigm, the study seeks to theoretically position African knowledge as an autonomous knowledge system. The Afrocentric framework is used throughout the study to bring to the fore the agency of Ndau women in producing, managing and preserving IK on pregnancy and childbirth. Adopting the Afrocentric theory for this research also supports the cultural and social proximity of the researcher in the phenomena under study as opposed to scientific distance.

The study also conceptually acknowledges the importance of looking at the conditions of African women in a postcolonial situation as a product of circumstances created by colonialism. The study also propagates that the different cultural and ecological conditions under which African women live should be taken into consideration in the analysis of postcolonial African feminism. It is on the basis of this consideration that the study focuses on the beliefs and practices of the Ndau women in managing pregnancy and childbirth as a contribution to the global pool of knowledge on postcolonial African feminism. A postcolonial theoretical approach that takes into account issues of race, ethnicity, identity and gender has been adopted for the study (McEwan 2009). Postcolonial theory describes how knowledge of the colonised people was marginalised at the expense of the coloniser's interests. It is also concerned with how knowledge is produced under specific relations between the powerful and the subjugated and it seeks to destabilise dominant discourses (McEwan 2009). Chilisa argues that a postcolonial epistemology concerns itself with the "continuous struggle by non-Western societies that suffered European colonization, indigenous peoples, and historically marginalized groups to resist suppression of their ways of knowing" (Chilisa: 12). It discharges the notion that knowledge is the only form of legitimate knowledge. Similarly, Dube (1999) notes that the term postcolonial refers to the cultural, economic and political contact of the coloniser and the colonised and the subsequent reactions emanating from this contact. The postcolonial framework seeks to subvert the legacies of colonialism.

Postcolonial African Feminism seeks to restore previously marginalised indigenous cultures on one hand, whilst on the other

192

hand, re-interprets the aspects that are harmful and oppressive to be holistic, life-giving and mutually inclusive. Dube (2002) expresses that this entails challenging repressive and damaging aspects of indigenous culture within African communities while on the other hand, working towards the restoration of those aspects of indigenous culture that are life-giving and embracing them for the empowerment of African women and whole communities. A Postcolonial African Feminist conceptual framework recognises the African woman as an active participant in all aspects of life for survival. However, to bring out the holistic agency of African women, holistic aspects of the precolonial status of African women are reassigned to enable them to take part in all crucial aspects of African life without the influence of colonial edicts which relegated them to the fringes of the social, economic and political sphere. Additionally, since it is correspondingly acknowledged that tradition comprise sites and sources of cultural disempowerment for particular groups especially women, Postcolonial African Feminism is an ideal framework for the study as lenses through which the creative agency of African women in the quest for survival is duly acknowledged in both the public and private sphere of life. Whilst these two frameworks may not fully account for every component in this study, they provide a sound philosophical foundation for understanding the research problem. The Afrocentric paradigm centres on defining phenomena from the perspective of the African people, privileges collective creation of knowledge and promotes the agency of the African women. On the other hand, through the lens of Postcolonial African Feminism, an inquisitorial perspective is employed on tradition without the total rejection of African indigenous culture. A Postcolonial African Feminist framework is also used to bring to the fore Ndau ways of knowing through an articulation of the beliefs and practices informing pregnancy and childbirth.

Methodology

A critical qualitative research approach was used to explore the attitudes, behaviour and experiences of Ndau women during pregnancy and childbirth. The critical qualitative approach sought to obtain in-depth opinions of the research participants through in-depth interviews and focus group discussions. All interviews were audio-recorded in Ndau, transcribed and translated into English.

Study Setting

This study is based on the view that indigenous knowledge is place-based because different cultural groups live in specific ecological zones. The Ndau as a cultural group in their specific ecological zone in Zimbabwe have developed their own beliefs and practices on managing pregnancy and childbirth. The Ndau are situated in the south-eastern highlands of Zimbabwe. They are a minority group consisting of about 2.5% of the total population of Zimbabwe which stands at about 13.1 million people. The Ndau people are highly spiritual, with African traditional religion (ATR) and Christianity as the dominant religious affiliations.

Access to bio-medical care is limited due to financial constraints hence the persistent adherence to IPs inclusive of the use of traditional medicinal plant remedies for managing pregnancy and childbirth as the first choice for maternal healthcare. Field research was conducted in two sub-districts of Chipinge which are Zamuchiya and Chikore Mission Station. Negotiating entry into the community for research was reliant upon that community's culture. Therefore, the official and social authority to enter the community for research was sought from the local headmen.

Participants

Indigenous knowledge in African local communities consists of specialised knowledge, shared knowledge and common knowledge. The research sample was purposively selected taking these different aspects of indigenous knowledge management into consideration. Study participants comprised thirty-one women between the ages of eighteen and eighty-five. This represented women of child-bearing age; women who had a recent experience of the phenomena under study; traditional birth attendants (TBAs); and elderly women known as *masungukati*/community sages conversant with Ndau indigenous beliefs and practices on pregnancy and childbirth. A snowballing technique, which was informed by the gradual accumulation of a sample through contacts and references was used to complement the purposive technique in constructing the research sample (Durrheim and Painter 2006). Informed consent was obtained prior to data collection and participants were assured of their anonymity, confidentiality and the right to withdraw at any given time.

194

Data Analysis

Data were analysed using thematic and comparative analysis. Main themes informing the study were generated. The data from the different sources was compared and contrasted in continuity until no new themes emerged. The process of data analysis involved coding (breaking up the data analytical relevant themes); elaboration of the coded data and interpreting the data.

Results

The data reflected an exceptional adherence to the IP of *masuwo* by Ndau pregnant women. The predominant philosophy behind the common IP of *masuwo* is due to its holistic preventative and therapeutic benefits during pregnancy and childbirth. *Masuwo*, in the form of TM, are taken during the last trimester of pregnancy and are prescribed by the mother-in-law or the eldest paternal aunt within the husband's lineage.

Masuwo comprises ingestible and non-ingestible traditional medicinal plant concoctions. The ingestible *masuwo* concoctions consist of the leaves, roots or bark of traditional medicinal plants which are boiled or soaked in water and are taken orally two or three times a day. The non-ingestible, mostly in the form of a thick paste, are massaged on the vaginal/and or birth canal. Three main benefits of *masuwo* were derived from the data: (i) use of *masuwo* as birth canal relaxants, (ii) use of *masuwo* as a health tonic, (iii) and use of *masuwo* for protection against unseen evil forces.

Masuwo as birth canal relaxants

Masuwo are used to ease childbirth. They are perceived to be effective birth canal relaxants which serves to ensure a quick, easy and uncomplicated delivery. Among the Ndau, virginal birth is considered a rite of passage hence the use of *masuwo* to ensure a natural as opposed to a caesarean birth. Whilst *masuwo* are used for most pregnancies, they are considered a must for a primigravida. This was explained by one of the study participants:

According to Ndau indigenous culture, it was unheard of for a primigravida to deliver without having taken *mushonga wemasuwo*/birth canal relaxants. Now because of modernity, they say it does not matter you can just give birth without taking *mushonga wemasuwo*. The resultant is a medically extended birth canal. Yet culturally it did not mean that you could not give birth if you did not take *masuwo* but it

195

was solely done to ensure the pregnant woman did not suffer from prolonged labour, perineal tearing or had her birth canal extended during delivery.

As such, *masuwo* are commonly used to minimise perineal tearing during childbirth. Research participants described perineal tearing as undesirable as it presented health challenges and unwelcome effects on sexual relations after childbirth. Similarly, Goodburn, Gazi and Chowdhury (1995) argues that whilst perineal tears are common during pregnancy, small tears are not considered a serious challenge. However, it is the large tears that are regarded as problematic as they present the risk of being septic resulting in complications that might lead to loss of life (Goodburn et al. 1995).

Use of *masuwo* as a health tonic

Masuwo are taken by pregnant women as a health tonic to ensure good foetal development and to improve the general well-being of the pregnant woman. The health tonic is used to shield both the pregnant woman and the foetus from common illnesses (Kudzionera 2015). Certain *masuwo* concoctions are used to prevent stillbirths and spontaneous abortions and to tone the uterus and the birth canal in preparation for childbirth. Other *masuwo* health tonics are used to treat the fontanelle of the foetus before birth. Most new-borns are believed to suffer from *chipande/chirwere chenhova* (illness associated with the fontanelle) which, if left untreated, can be fatal for a new-born baby (Chomusaida 2015).

Use of *masuwo* for protection against evil spiritual forces

The period of pregnancy and childbirth is considered delicate and susceptible to attacks from evil spirits. Hence the need to protect the mother and the unborn child from evil forces that might lead to miscarriages and birth defects. This practice is equally cited by Ngomane and Mulaudzi (2010) whose research participants indicated the need to physically and spiritually preserve pregnancy using herbs. As such, pregnancy is strengthened in order to prevent malformation of the foetus and possible miscarriages as well as protecting the pregnant woman from evil spirits that may be contracted through contact with other pregnant women (Choguya 2014; Ngomane and Mulaudzi 2010). Equally among the Ndau, a pregnant woman is advised, if possible, to shy away from public gatherings or from being in contact with other pregnant women in order to avoid *kuhakira mweya yetsvina* – being contaminated with evil spirits.

196

Common ingestible indigenous medicines for *masuwo*

The most common ingestible medicine for *masuwo* among the Ndau is the *demamhandwe*[2]. This plant was mentioned by all of the research participants within the different ecological zones as the most effective and efficient traditional medicinal plant remedy for *masuwo*. *Demamhandwe* is a wild plant that grows throughout the year although it is at its peak during the rainy season. The plant has rhizomes resembling white potatoes. These rhizomes are boiled with water and the concoction is consumed three times a day. The plant concoction is also mixed with *mahewu* (a traditional drink made from ground sorghum and mealie-meal porridge) as a therapeutic meal.

The *demamhandwe* is the most commonly used traditional medicinal plant remedy by Ndau women and no side effects have been reported. This was confirmed by one of the participants:

> Common among the Ndau is the *demamhandwe*, I have never heard of any side effects or complaints arising from the use of this type of medicine for *masuwo*. During all my pregnancies, I took the *demamhandwe*. My first child weighed about 3.8kg at birth and I did not have any stitches added and the birth was smooth, this followed with all my subsequent pregnancies.

The second most common *masuwo* is made from the leaves of hymenocardia mollis pax. The leaves of the hymenocardia mollis pax are soaked in hot water which is then cooled and drunk three times a day (Maposa 2015). Other *masuwo* medicinal concoctions are prepared using either the leaves or roots of the *intsia quangensis* and k*igelia pinnata* (Kudzionera 2015; Mhlanga 2015).

Elephant dung is also used as a birth canal relaxant though not very popular among the Ndau. The elephant dung is soaked in warm water which is then cooled and is drunk two to three times a day. One of the research participants explained:

When I requested for *masuwo* medicines from my mother-in-law, she gave me elephant dung and instructed me to soak it in water and then to take the concoction three times a day to avoid perineal tearing during birth. The mixture from the elephant dung is tasteless. Unfortunately, my birth canal was extended when I gave birth. My mother-in-law told me that I have bad blood which failed to absorb the medicines I was taking. However, when I gave birth for the

---

[2] At the time of submission for publication of this chapter, the ethnobotanical name for this plant had not been established.

197

second time, my blood accepted the medicines and my birth canal was not extended (Mapungwana 2016).

Soil from a burrowing mole was also cited as an effective birth canal relaxant. The soil is mixed with water and the concoction is drunk three times a day. The participants mentioned that if a pregnant woman drank the concoction made from the soil burrowed by a mole, the speed taken by the mole when burrowing through the soil is the speed that is adopted by the contractions during labour resulting in a quick delivery. Mureyi, Maonera and Maponga (2012) have also cited the practice of using elephant dung and soil from a burrowing mole to widen the birth canal and to avoid perineal tearing as common among some pregnant women in Harare, Zimbabwe.

Non-ingestible *masuwo* medicinal concoctions

Apart from the ingestible *masuwo*, there are other types that are massaged on the vaginal opening to relax the vaginal muscles and to enlarge the birth canal. The commonly used massaging medicine is made with the fruit of the a*belmoschus esculentus* plant. The plant has different varieties and is also an edible vegetable that is rich in mucin content which is believed to loosen the mucosa of the vagina thereby enabling an easy delivery (Mutambirwa 1985). The fruit of the a*belmoschus esculentus* is crushed into a thick paste that is soaked in water. The resultant slimy mixture is massaged on the vaginal opening using a clenched fist. This procedure is repeated twice daily until the clenched fist can easily fit through the vaginal opening. The use of a*belmoschus esculentus* plant is preferred for its safety as it does not exhibit any known toxic effects. One of the participants thus explained:

We encourage the use of a*belmoschus esculentus* for *masuwo*. These days some of the traditional medicinal plant concoctions taken orally through drinking are being discouraged. Some people tend to overdose and this can cause harm to the baby resulting in a negative attitude towards traditional medicines which are then labelled harmful. Other people get these traditional medicines from unreliable sources in the form of hawkers and bogus traditional healers who are after money. It is these people who tarnish our traditional herbs. So, it's better for pregnant women far away from home to use the a*belmoschus esculentus* as it is safe and has no side effects (Mbuya Mutape 2014).

The a*belmoschus esculentus* is also a healthy vegetable used as part of the dietary requirements for pregnant women. Mureyi et al. (2012) indicate that the *abelmoschus esculentus* plant is cooked and taken orally in the third trimester for both nutrition and widening the birth canal.

The bark string from the a*nnona senegalensis* tree are also used for *masuwo*. A round ball made of the bark string is inserted in the vagina during the day and taken out at night. The size of the ball is increased with the widening of the canal and the procedure is stopped when a ball equivalent to the size of a clenched fist can pass through the vaginal opening (Simango 2015). Whilst the participants cited this particular method, they were quick to point out that it is now discouraged due to fears of its unknown toxicity which might lead to cervical cancers and associated gynaecological ailments.

Benefits of *masuwo* during pregnancy and childbirth

The IP of *masuwo* is adopted for its holistic preventative and therapeutic beneficial properties during pregnancy and childbirth. During pregnancy, *masuwo* are believed to strengthen the mother's body thereby preparing it for childbirth; ward off evil spirits and *mamhepo*; and treat the unborn child from common baby ailments before birth. During childbirth, *masuwo* are believed to offer increased pelvic joint mobility; stimulation of uterine contractions; relaxation of vaginal muscles; facilitation of adequate stretching of the birth canal thereby safeguarding against perineal tearing; protection against a caesarean birth; and the lessening of associated labour pains.

Beliefs and practices associated with *masuwo*

Whilst the IP of *masuwo* is a common practice, it is equally informed by certain beliefs and practices that are precautionary measures to ensure their efficacy. When a pregnant woman assumes the observance of *masuwo* during the last trimester of pregnancy, she is expected to abstain from sexual intercourse until after childbirth. Sexual intercourse is believed to interfere with *masuwo* thereby cause inefficiency. Similarly, other studies indicate pregnant women are advised against sexual intercourse during *masuwo* as it is believed to counter the effects of the birth canal relaxant (Maimbolwa, Yamba, Diwan and Ransjo-Arvidson 2003; Mutambirwa 1995). The practice of sexual abstinence in late pregnancy is supported by a study carried out by Ngomane and Mulaudzi (2010) where research participants indicated that pregnant women are encouraged to abstain from intercourse in order to protect the unborn child from harmful influences. In this regard, the sperm is believed to contaminate the foetus.

Whilst sexual abstinence during the last trimester of pregnancy is a common IP, this practice is also encouraged from a Western biomedical perspective (Larsen, Msane and Monkhe 1983). Sexual abstinence is believed to be beneficial as it reduces the incidence of bacterial infections of foetal membranes and its associated complications which include, but not limited to, premature rupture of membranes; increased incidence of *abruptio placentae*; premature labour and perinatal mortality (Larsen, Msane and Monkhe 1983). Even though IPs do not have to be validated through western perspectives, this biomedical viewpoint fortifies the importance of the wisdom behind certain IPs. Secondly, *masuwo* concoctions are stored in a private place that is only accessible to the pregnant woman. The privacy observance serves as a measure of protection against people with evil intentions who may temper with the concoctions.

Discussion

The conventional public healthcare system dominated by western ways of knowing and value systems tends to conceptualize reproductive healthcare as a mere biological issue. As indicated by the case of the Ndau, indigenous healthcare models, have a holistic approach to health and well-being. They encompasses the physical, socio-cultural, religious and metaphysical perceptions of health and well-being. Central to indigenous healthcare are indigenous practices inclusive of the use of specific traditional medicinal plants, rituals, beliefs, songs, dance, and other cultural values and practices.

Among the Ndau, pregnancy embodies a highly constructed socio-cultural worldview with dictates, through IPs, which have to be observed by pregnant women. At the core of IPs informing pregnancy and childbirth is the use of traditional medicinal plants. Research shows that in Africa, the use of traditional medicinal plants and healing practices are well established for both their preventative and therapeutic benefits in the management of pregnancy and childbirth (Abdillahi and Van Staden 2013; Attah and O'Brien 2012; Gruber and O'Brien 2011; Maroyi 2013; Maimbolwa et al. 2003; Mureyi et al. Mutambirwa 1995; Towns and Andel 2016). This is guided by specific community-based religio-cultural, social and metaphysical beliefs and conceptions of illness and health (Abdillahi and Van Staden 2013; Kamatenisi-Mugisha and Oryem-Origa 2007; Malan and Neuba 2011; Steenkamp 2003).

Traditional medicinal plant (TMP) remedies during pregnancy and childbirth are often used to tone the uterus muscle, induce labour, for the removal of retained placenta, to improve the safety of the delivery process, to avoid perineal tearing and to prevent postpartum bleeding (Attah et al. 2012; Gruber and O'Brien 2011; Mureyi et al. 2012). Djah and Neuba (2011) argue that some of the plants traditionally used during pregnancy and childbirth contain some essential nutrients and other beneficial components. The study by Djah and Neuba (2011) found out that some of the traditional medicinal plants used by pregnant women had antinociceptive, anti-inflammatory, antibacterial activities and powerful antioxidants with chemo-preventative potential (Djah and Neuba 2011).

The prescription of TMP is the domain of family elders and local traditional health practitioners. The knowledge and the correct use of TMPs has been acquired and improved over many generations (Attah and O'Brien 2012). As such, this has resulted in experiential modification of medicinal plant remedies for safety and efficacy (de Boer 2009). Among the Ndau, TMP knowledge is held by family elders and is passed down from one generation to the other. Each family has distinct medicinal plants and accompanying rituals for managing pregnancy and birth.

Most ethnic groups in Zimbabwe observe the *masungiro* ritual whereby the pregnant woman is sent back to her maternal home in her last trimester of pregnancy for *masuwo* (Chinyoka and Ganga 2017). In this case, it is the mother or the aunties who administer *masuwo* according to the family's cultural beliefs. The *masungiro* ritual is not observed by the Ndau and pregnant women are expected to give birth in their husband's families. The beliefs and practices for pregnancy and birth are observed according to the husband's family beliefs.

Whilst the bulk of the *masuwo* traditional medicinal plants are orally administered as liquid concoctions, elsewhere in Cote d'Ivoire among the Anyi-Ndenye women, the common administration procedures of medicinal plants during pregnancy are the anal route using enema bag (65.6%); oral route consumed like a 'therapeutic meal (28.7%) or drink (5.7%) (Malan and Neuba 2011).

Apart from the oral *demamhandwe* concoctions, the majority of the participants including TBAs, revealed they were moving away from both prescribing and taking oral traditional medicinal concoctions as a safety precaution against unknown toxic effects which may cause harm to both mother and child. Instead, massaging herbs were regarded as a safer alternative of widening the birth canal in preparation for childbirth. This shifting behaviour in the method of use of TMPs is equally cited by Mogaware, Mothiba and Malema (2015) who pointed out the reduction of prescribed indigenous oral medicine that is used to hasten labour due to their potential toxicity.

IPs are culturally resilient and are deeply ingrained in the subconscious of African indigenous people irrespective of their educational and professional eminence and governing ethics. One of the participants explained that upon admission in hospital for delivery, the attending midwife inquired of her - *"makanasira ere nzira yemwana?"* literally translated as 'did you prepare the baby's path?' The participant expounded that whilst pregnant women were discouraged from using TMP remedies for *masuwo* by the resident gynaecologist at the hospital, the elderly nurses and midwives did not condone the use of *masuwo* concoctions in the monitored waiting shelters and in the labour wards. Instead, they advised the pregnant women to be discreet in the presence of biomedical practitioners. Although the Ndau pregnant women observed the *masuwo* IP, most deliveries were done in local clinics and/or hospitals.

The use of TMP during the last trimester of pregnancy is also common among South African women and is used for inducing labour, expelling a retained placenta and to prevent postpartum haemorrhage (Kaido, Veale, Havlik and Rama 1997). Xhosa women are reported to take a decoction of the roots of *Agapanthus africanus* orally or per rectum during the last two months of pregnancy to ease childbirth (Kaido et al. 1997). The herbal decoctions used in pregnancy and childbirth are known as *isihlambezo, imbelikisane* or *inembe. Isihlambezo* is taken orally by both Zulu and Xhosa women to ensure healthy foetal growth and to enable the delivery of the placenta (Kaido et al. 1997; Maputle, Mothiba and Maliwichi 2015).

Participant's narratives also reflected the multi-cultural behavioural approach of Ndau women in managing pregnancy and birth as evidenced by the utilisation of both bio-medical and indigenous healthcare systems. In the African context, all aspects of health, health care and health seeking behaviours are influenced by cultural beliefs and norms (Amzat and Razum 2018). Hence holistic health outcomes cannot be achieved without incorporating the discourse of culture in healthcare intervention strategies. Embedded in the cultural discourse are indigenous beliefs, practices, values and norms which give essence to a particular group of people (Amzat and Razum 2018). Similarly, Sadomba and Zinyemba (2014) argue that indigenous healthcare systems evolved out of and as part of local cultures. As such, they are deeply entrenched in the norms, beliefs and philosophies of life (Sadomba and Zinyemba 2014). Hence indigenous healthcare practitioners espouse this worldview in their practices whereby treatment caters for the spiritual, physical and psychological aspects. Familial relations are also taken into consideration. Therefore, among the Ndau, elderly female in-laws are tasked with guiding the family's *makoti*/daughters-in-law through pregnancy and childbirth. The support of in-laws in caring for and preserving the pregnancy of the *makoti* is equally cited as common in the South African context by Ngomane and Mulaudzi (2012).

In order to reduce maternal mortality and to promote safer birthing experiences, there is need to promote cultural-sensitive healthcare models. Graham (1999) calls for a partnership paradigm for improved healthcare. The partnership paradigm is defined as a mutual cooperation of biomedical and indigenous systems and it is positioned as an alternative to the dominant top-down culturally inappropriate mainstream healthcare models (Graham 1999).

Recommendations

Despite the persistent use of TMP for the management of pregnancy and childbirth, limited scientific evaluation to test their safety and toxicity has been done. In order to attain improved maternal healthcare standards for local communities, there is need to develop a cohesive and integrative approach to healthcare that is culturally sensitive, allows for ease of access and is cost-efficient and effective. There is therefore need to investigate, document, and analyse traditional knowledge of medicinal plants and their associated knowledge drivers for improved maternal healthcare. There is need for the full recognition of the character of TM and the significant role of traditional health practitioners that has always been misconstrued.

Conclusion

Framed within a postcolonial indigenous paradigm, the study explored the IPs adopted for childbirth preparedness by the Ndau of south-eastern Zimbabwe. The study brought to the fore, knowledge that was previously marginalised – knowledge that serves as the backbone of the survival strategies of women in African indigenous communities. This knowledge is embedded in their ways of life even though it is not overt due to its suppression and stigmatisation in the contemporary era where modernity and Christianity take precedence over indigenous ways of life. Therefore, drawing from the research results, it is evident that neither modernity with its highly technological advancements nor the medicalization of reproductive healthcare and childbirth has forestalled the use of IPs that inform pregnancy and childbirth. Additionally, the persistent use of traditional medicinal plants for managing pregnancy and childbirth is indicative of their potency. This may lead to new discoveries in the development of medicinal remedies for managing pregnancy and childbirth.

Author's contributions

This chapter is based on the author's PhD research work with the University of KwaZulu-Natal. The research work was supervised by Professor Sarojini Nadar and Professor Hassan Kaya as supervisor and co-supervisor, respectively.

Acknowledgements

Financial support was provided by the National Research Foundation (NRF). The author also expresses sincere gratitude to all participants, who are the indigenous knowledge holders, for sharing their knowledge and experiences. Special thanks are also extended to Professor Hassan Kaya, under whose mentorship the chapter was written.

References

Abdillahi, H. S. and Van Staden. J. (2013). "Application of Medicinal Plants in Maternal Healthcare and Infertility: A South African Perspective". Planta Med 79: 591–599.

Abrahams, N and Jewkes, R. (2001). "Health care-seeking practices of pregnant women and the role of the midwife in Cape Town, South Africa." *Journal of Midwifery and Women's Health* 46(4): 240-247.

Asante, M. K. (2007). *An Afrocentric Manifesto*. U. K: Polity Press.

Asante, M. K. (1991). The Afrocentric Idea in Education. *Journal of Negro Education* 60(2): 170-180.

Asante, M. K. (1987). *The Afrocentric Idea.* Philadelphia: Temple University Press.

Attah, A. F., O'Brien, M., Koehbach, J., Sonibare M. A., Moody, J. O., Smith, T. J. and Gruber C. W. (2012). "Uterine contractility of plants used to facilitate childbirth in Nigerian ethnomedicine." *Journal of Ethnopharmacology* 143: 377-382.

de Boer, H.J., (2009). African plants as antipathogen agents: efficacy and clinical evidence. In: Watson, R., Preedy, V. (Eds.), *Botanical medicine in clinical practice.* CABI, UK, pp. 3–12.

Chilisa, B. (2012). *Indigenous Research Methodologies.* Los Angeles: SAGE Publications Ltd.

Choguya, N. Z. (2014). "Traditional Birth Attendants and Policy Ambivalence in Zimbabwe." *Journal of Anthropology*, Article ID 750240, 9 pages, http://dx.doi.org/10.1155/2014/750240. Accessed on: 21 August 2018.

Djah F. M. and Neuba, D. F. R. (2011). "Traditional practices and medicinal plant use during pregnancy by Anyi-Ndenye women (Eastern Cote d'Ivoire)." *African Journal of Reproductive Health* 15(1): 85-93.

Dube, M. W. (2002). Postcoloniality, feminist spaces and religion. In Postcolonialism, feminism and religious discourse, eds. Donaldson, L. E. and Pui-lan, K. New York; London: Routledge.

Dube, M. W. (1999). Searching for the lost needle: Double colonisation and postcolonial African Feminism. *Studies in World Christianity* 5(2):215

Goodburn, E. A., Gazi, R. and Chowdhury, M. (1995). "Beliefs and practices regarding delivery and postpartum maternal morbidity in rural Bangladesh." *Studies in Family Planning* 26(1): 22-32.

Graham, S. (1999). *"Traditional Birth Attendants in Karamoja."* PhD diss., South Bank University, Uganda.

Gruber, C. W. and O'Brien, M. (2011). "Uterotonic plants and their bioactive constituents." *Planta Medica* 77: 207-220.

Kaido, T. L., Veale, D. J. H., Havlik, I. and Rama, D. B. K. (1997). "Preliminary screening of plants used in South Africa as traditional herbal remedies during pregnancy and labour." *Journal of Ethnopharmacology* 55: 185-191.

Kamatenesi-Mugisha, M, and Oryem-Origa, H. (2007). "Medicinal plants used to induce labour during childbirth in western Uganda." *Journal of Ethnopharmacology* 109: 1-9.

Karenga, M. (1988). Black Studies and the Problematic of Paradigm: The Philosophical Dimension. *Journal of Black Studies* 18(4): 404

Larsen, J. V., Msane, C. L., and Monkhe, M. C. (1983). "The Zulu traditional birth attendant: an evaluation of her attitudes and techniques and their implications for health education." *South African Medical Journal* 63: 543-545.

Lionjanja, R. (1999). *"The cultural beliefs and practices amongst urban antenatal Botswana women."* Masters diss, University of Witwatersrand, South Africa.

Maimbolwa, M. C., Yamba, B., Diwan, V. and Ransjo-Arvidson, A. B. (2003). "Childbirth practices and beliefs in Zambia." *Journal of Advanced Nursing* 43(3): 263–274

Maputle, S. M., Mothiba, T. M. and Maliwichi, L. (2015). "Traditional Medicine and Pregnancy Management: Perceptions of Traditional Health Practitioners in Capricorn District, Limpopo Province." *Ethno Med*, 9(1): 67-75.

Maroyi, A. (2013). "Traditional use of medicinal plants in south-central Zimbabwe: review and perspectives." *Journal of Ethnobiology and Ethnomedicine* 9(31). http://www.ethnobiomed.com/content/9/1/31. Accessed on: 13 September 2018.

McEwan, C. (2009). *Postcolonialism and Development.* London and New York: Routledge.

Mothupi, M. C. (2014). "Use of herbal medicine during pregnancy among women with access to public healthcare in Nairobi, Kenya: A cross-sectional survey." *BMC Complement Altern Med* 14: 432.

Mogawane, M. A. (2014). *"Indigenous practices of pregnant women at the Dikolong Hospital of the Greater Tubatse Municipality in the Limpopo province."* Masters' diss., University of Limpopo. South Africa.

Mogawane, M. A., Mothiba, T. M. and Malema, R. N. (2015). "Indigenous practices of pregnant women of Dilokong hospital in Limpopo province, South Africa." *Curationis* 38(2): Art. #1553, 8 pages.

Mureyi, D. D., Monera, T. G. and Maponga, C. C. (2012). "Prevalence and patterns of prenatal use of traditional medicine among women at selected Harare clinics: a cross-sectional study." *BMC Complementary and Alternative Medicine* 12, 164.

http://www.biomedcentral.com/1472-6882/12/164. Accessed 19 September 2018.

Mutambirwa, Jane. (1985). "Pregnancy, childbirth, mother and childcare among the indigenous people of Zimbabwe." *Int. J. Gynaecol. Obstet* 23: 275-285.

Nelms, L.W. and Gorski, J. (2006). "The role of African traditional healers in women's health." J. *Transcult Nurs* 12(2): 184-9.

Ngomane, S. and Mulaudzi, F. M. (2012). "Indigenous beliefs and practices that influence the delayed attendance of antenatal clinics by women in the Bohlabelo district in Limpopo, South Africa." *Midwifery* 28: 30-38.

Oduyoye, A.M. (1992). Women and Ritual in Africa. In Oduyoye, M.A and Kanyoro, M. R. (eds.): *"The Will to Arise: Women, Tradition, and the Church in Africa."* Pietermaritzburg: Cluster Publications

Sadomba, W. Z. and Zinyemba, I. (2014). "Socio-cultural foundations of caregiver institutions: Lineage and community networks in Zimbabwe's health care system." *Asian Journal of Humanity, Art, Literature* 1(3): 169-185.

van der Kooi, R. and Theobald, S. (2006). "Traditional medicine in late pregnancy and labour: perceptions of *kgaba* remedies amongst the Tswana in South Africa." *Afr. J. Trad. CAM* 3(1): 11 – 22.

Schedule of Interviews

Participant Name	Place of Interview	Date of Interview
Mbuya Chomusaida	Mariya Village, Chipinge	09 April 2011
Mbuya Kudzionera	Chinaa Village, Chipinge	09 May 2015
Mbuya Maposa	Shekwa Village, Chipinge	10 March 2015
Mbuya Mhlanga	Zamuchiya Village, Chipinge	16 October 2014

Chapter 11

Indigenous Knowledge Systems for Building-back-better Flood-Impacted Communities in Zimbabwe

Enerst Dube & Albert Manyani

Abstract

This chapter discusses the potential contribution of indigenous knowledge systems in the building-back-better of the flood-impacted rural communities in Zimbabwe. Most parts of Zimbabwe, especially in rural areas, have been experiencing devastating flood disasters, resulting mainly from tropical cyclones – Cyclone Eline in 2000, Cyclone Dineo in 2017 and Cyclone Idai in 2019. The impacted communities have often found it difficult to build-back-better in the aftermath of the disasters, despite them having indigenous knowledge at their disposal. This study is guided by the following objectives: to assess the nature of losses caused by floods in the rural communities of Zimbabwe; to evaluate the role of indigenous knowledge systems in disaster risk reduction; and, to examine the potential contribution of indigenous knowledge as a strategy to build-back-better disaster-impacted communities. The study was based on literature analysis involving 52 publications on indigenous knowledge, the Sendai Framework for Disaster Risk Reduction (SFDRR) and on the build-back-better concept. The findings of the study were that flood disasters impacted human lives, infrastructure, shelter and important livelihoods of the communities. The communities most impacted were those located near water basins such as rivers and dams, and those located in low-lying land. Further, the study found that indigenous knowledge was not effectively practised to build-back-better communities in disaster risky areas in Zimbabwe. Practitioners and some communities have been shunning the knowledge. However, the study found that indigenous knowledge plays an important role in disaster risk reduction as it resonates with the SFDRR to achieve the goal of building-back-better communities in disaster recovery, reconstruction and rehabilitation. The study recommends government support, so that acceptance of indigenous knowledge by practitioners and communities is increased. Further, indigenous knowledge should be part of the school and tertiary education curriculum for it to be sustainable.

Keywords: Build-back-better; Community; Disaster; Flooding; Indigenous knowledge

Introduction

When disasters from natural hazards strike, it has been found that communities, especially those located in rural areas, suffer massive losses in terms of human lives, infrastructure, livelihoods and environmental degradation. What has been more evident is that rural communities tend to suffer most from disasters emanating from natural hazards than communities that are located in urban areas. Communities have suffered from different types of disasters from natural hazards such as earthquakes, droughts, tsunamis, cyclones and floods. However, scholars have found that floods have been dominating in natural hazard damage globally (Kolen and van Gelder 2018; Muhonda et al. 2014). As such, rural people have faced many challenges in an endeavour to build-back-better their communities following disaster impact. This has been happening despite that fact that rural communities are an oasis of indigenous knowledge systems. Dube and Munsaka (2018) assert that local people have a wealth of experience and understanding of their local environment. Therefore, the building-back-better of communities through indigenous knowledge systems makes them to effectively recover from disaster impact, at the same time making communities to be resilient to future hazards. The build-back-better concept following disasters came to prominence in 2004, following the severe impact of the devastating Indian Ocean Tsunami (Fernandez and Ahmed 2019; Khasalamwa 2009; Mannakkara, and Wilkinson 2012). Hence, this study argues that rural communities can leverage on their indigenous knowledge systems to fully recover from disaster impact – hence, building-back-better.

Different schools of thought have been expressed by scholars and practitioners, as to what constitutes indigenous knowledge. However, what could be easily understood about indigenous knowledge is that it is grounded in the local culture that informs people's interpretation of the world around them (Sillitoe, 2017). It is "peasants knowledge, traditional environmental knowledge and folk knowledge" (Tharakan, 2015) of the local communities. This, therefore, suggests that indigenous knowledge can play a crucial role in disaster risk reduction at the local level since it can be contextualised to the local environment and situations. Indigenous knowledge has also been regarded as a body or system of skills, know-how, information and practices developed by specific communities in response to stressors in particular geographic localities (Ayaa and Waswa, 2016). In this case, it can be viewed as a system of skills, knowledge, information and practices developed by local communities living with flood risk and vulnerability in Zimbabwe's rural communities. Nyamwanza (2014) opines that this knowledge supports the use of local resources that are available for communities, to assist the communities to cope with the impacts of extreme weather events. This type of knowledge has local or traditional origins and has for a long period guided human interactions with their environment. This suggests that indigenous knowledge should be used as a sustainable strategy for solving community problems, especially for dealing with hazards and disasters. The knowledge may not be effective and successful, if used as a once-off and passing strategy. In Zimbabwean communities living with flood vulnerability and risk, this knowledge can be preserved so that it can be relied upon to deal with future hazards and disasters.

In Zimbabwe, rural communities have experienced disaster losses caused by flooding. Such impact has been experienced in many districts including Tsholotsho (Dube, Mtapuri and Matunhu 2018; Dube and Mhembwe 2019), Muzarabani (Mudavanhu 2014), Masvingo, Chimanimani and Chipinge (Chanza et al. 2010). This is despite the fact that many rural communities, and communities in rural Zimbabwe, have indigenous knowledge systems that apply to disaster risk reduction. Such indigenous or local knowledge can be used to deal with many flood hazards and disasters occurring around the country. Adger et al. (2011) argue that despite the important role that indigenous knowledge can play in reducing the risk and vulnerability of disasters, the knowledge has not been highly considered in disaster policy and science. The same scenario has been happening in Zimbabwe, where the role of indigenous knowledge has been less considered in civil protection policy and legislation. For instance, the Civil Protection Act of 1989, Chapter 10:01 does not make provisions for the use of indigenous knowledge in disaster situations. However, rural populations in Zimbabwe have the potential to effectively build-back-better communities if their indigenous knowledge is put into practice. Where possible, such knowledge can be blended with scientific disaster knowledge to achieve the goals of disaster risk reduction are achieved (Mallapaty 2012).For instance, the Indian Ocean Tsunami was credited with sparking interest in the indigenous knowledge and its integration with scientific knowledge for disaster risk reduction (Mallpaty 2012). Thus, this study argues that indigenous knowledge of rural people can also play a vital role in building-back-better rural communities in Zimbabwe in the aftermath of disasters, especially those disasters influenced by flooding. As such the study aims to prove that the local people can play a crucial role in disaster risk reduction by contributing their grassroots knowledge. The objectives of this study are to assess the nature of losses caused by floods in the rural communities of Zimbabwe; to evaluate the role of indigenous knowledge systems in disaster risk reduction; and, to examine the potential of indigenous knowledge as a strategy to build-back-better disaster-impacted communities.

The study is organised into sections to provide a logical argument about the role of indigenous knowledge in disaster risk reduction. Besides, the sections provide a logical flow to the discussion, making the study easy to follow. The study is divided into the main headings as follows: Introduction, Theoretical framework, Materials and Methods, Findings and Discussion, Conclusion, and References.

Theoretical framework: Sendai Framework for Disaster Risk Reduction

This study revolves around the dictates of the Sendai Framework for Disaster Risk Reduction (SFDRR) 2015 – 2030. The SFDRR was adopted during a United Nations Third World Conference on Disaster Risk Reduction in Sendai, Japan in March 2015, to succeed the Hyogo Framework for Action (HFA) (Kelman and Glantz 2015). It emphasises effective disaster risk reduction at national and local levels, and with a strong institutional basis for implementation (UNISDR 2015; Maly and Suppasri 2020). This framework focuses on four priority areas for disaster risk reduction: (1) Understanding disaster risk; (2) strengthening disaster risk governance to manage disaster risk; (3) Investing in disaster risk reduction for resilience, and (4) enhancing disaster preparedness for effective response and to "build-back-better" in disaster recovery, rehabilitation and reconstruction. All the four priority areas of the SFDRR are relevant for recovery processes since there is a need for communities in Zimbabwe to have the relevant knowledge to understand the nature of the disaster risks they face. The SFDRR also advocates for the use of indigenous people's knowledge and practices to complement scientific knowledge in disaster risk assessment (UNISDR 2015; Dube and Munsaka 2018). Besides, indigenous people have important capacities, in terms of strengths, skills and resources for effective and proper governance of disasters. In line with Priority 3, communities should invest in their disaster risk reduction processes and activities for capacity building. Huge investment in disaster risk reduction programmes results in huge benefits in the future. Priority 4 is more relevant to the study, as it is about enhancing disaster preparedness to ensure effective response and recovery – resultantly building-back-better.

What is evident from the SFDRR is that the first three priority areas of the framework support Priority 4, in which the SFDRR encourages nations and local communities to pursue the goal of 'enhancing disaster preparedness for effective response and to "build-back-better" in recovery, rehabilitation, and reconstruction' (UNISDR 2015; UNISDR 2017). United Nations Office for Disaster Risk Reduction (UNDRR) (2017) defines build-back-better as "the use of disaster recovery, rehabilitation and reconstruction phases after a disaster to increase the resilience of nations and communities through integrating disaster risk reduction measures into the restoration of physical infrastructure and social systems, and to revitalise livelihoods, economies and the environment". Hence, this study takes a bias towards priority 4, whose achievement can result in the effective restoration of disaster-impacted communities in Zimbabwe's flood-prone areas. Dube (2020:1) argues that build-back-better is "... a post-disaster recovery process that offers communities, stronger infrastructure, better houses, better livelihoods, and better systems and services, at times in surpluses, compared to what was lost in a disaster event". In the context of this study, rural communities impacted by flood disasters in Zimbabwe can be guided by SFDRR to restore their infrastructure, shelter, livelihoods, systems and services in an improved manner, through using indigenous knowledge of the local people. The understanding is that rural communities possess untapped indigenous knowledge that has always been shunned by governments and disaster practitioners. The SFDRR encourages investing in disaster risk for resilience by the government and stakeholders (UNISDR 2015). Hence, building-back-better of the rural communities following a devastating disaster event ensures that rural communities are better positioned to deal with future hazards and their vulnerabilities (Dube, 2020). Therefore, communities in Tsholotsho, Muzarabani, Masvingo, Chimanimani and Chipinge can take advantage of their indigenous knowledge systems to rebuild their infrastructure, livelihoods and systems in a better and more sustainable way.

However, numerous challenges have been encountered by nations and communities in their endeavour to operationalise the SFDRR, and to build-back-better societies. According to Mavhura (2020), the SFDRR is yet to be fully embraced at the local level. Hence, flood-impacted communities in Zimbabwe may find it a challenge to build-back-better through pursuing the goals of the framework. Like in every disaster risk reduction programme, the implementation of the SFDRR requires the support of various stakeholders. Such support is anticipated to be mainly in the form of resources – financial, human and material. Hence, without proper support from the government and stakeholders, it might be a challenge to build-back-better communities in Zimbabwe, even if the dictates of the SFDRR are followed. The section that follows discusses the materials and methods that informed the study.

Materials and Methods

The study is based on literature analysis about the contribution of indigenous knowledge in disaster risk reduction, and the potential of such knowledge to help in building-back-better rural communities. The study considered literature from 52 publications to provide the argument. The literature was chosen from the authors who have published about indigenous knowledge in disaster risk reduction. Further, literature about the Sendai Framework for Disaster Risk Reduction and the build-back-better was considered. The SFDRR is the theoretical framework guiding the study - the framework encourages nations and local communities to build-back-better using indigenous knowledge systems (UNISDR 2015). Amongst such publications chosen 36 were written by international authors, whilst 16 were written by Zimbabwean authors. These publications provided the context of the discussion of the flood hazards and indigenous knowledge systems in Zimbabwe. The study considered literature from authors who have written about the role of indigenous knowledge to manage hazards and disasters in Zimbabwe.

Findings and discussion

The discussion is based on the relevant literature on indigenous knowledge of disaster risk reduction. Furthermore, the discussion is also influenced by the literature on the build-back-better concept. Such literature was considered to show the influence of indigenous knowledge on effective disaster recovery through building-back-better. The research findings are discussed in line with the objectives of the study, which are to assess the nature of losses caused by floods in the rural communities of Zimbabwe; to evaluate the role of indigenous knowledge systems in disaster risk reduction; and, to examine the potential of indigenous knowledge as a strategy to build-back-better disaster-impacted communities. Therefore, the following subheadings are adopted to give direction to the discussion: flood impact in the rural communities of Zimbabwe; indigenous knowledge systems in disaster risk reduction; the potential of IKS to support the building-back-better of communities.

Nature of losses resulting from floods impact in the rural communities of Zimbabwe

Rural communities in Zimbabwe have been experiencing severe floods impact for a long time now. Most of the flooding events in Zimbabwe have been exacerbated by tropical cyclones that have been hitting the country since 2000. For instance, in 2000, 2017 and 2019, tropical cyclones, Cyclone Eline, Cyclone Dineo and Cyclone Idai resulted in severe destruction, loss of life, and environmental losses in Southern Africa, including Zimbabwe (Hartfield, Blunden and Arndt 2018; Moses and Ramotonto 2018; Mavhura 2020). Available evidence shows that the flood disasters have impacted rural communities in Zimbabwe, destroying human shelter, damage to roads, school buildings, bridges, dams, infrastructure and disruption to community livelihoods (Dube, Mtapuri and Matunhu 2018). Mhlanga et al. (2018) note that in Zimbabwe alone, Cyclone Eline and Cyclone Dineo affected approximately 2.7 million and 20,600 people, respectively. Also, other studies have revealed that there was a severe impact of floods on the infrastructure of communities located in flood-prone areas. The impacted infrastructure was either constructed from weak material or it was because of its location in dangerous and risky areas (Mavhura 2019; Mudavanhu 2016; Dube 2017). This is against the SFDRR's encouragement to build-back-better communities, especially using local knowledge and resources. Pérez-Fructuoso (2007), states that the destruction of houses and infrastructure by disasters is usually accompanied by deaths, injuries, loss of livelihoods and the stagnation or reversal of local economies.

Apart from destroying the infrastructure, flood in Zimbabwe has also caused disharmony through disrupting the daily functioning of the communities. For instance, the 2014 flooding of the Tokwe-Mukorsi River in Masvingo Province displaced more than 29,000 smallholder farmers (Mavhura 2020). Recently in 2019, Cyclone Idai devastated Africa and left approximately 2.6 million people homeless, in addition to more than 500 deaths and over a billion dollars in economic damages (African Risk Capacity 2019). Hence, the devastating impact of floods in Zimbabwe, resulting mainly from cyclones, calls for the effective building-back-better of the communities. This study argues that the build-back-better exercise can succeed through leveraging the indigenous knowledge of the local communities such predicting heavy rains by studying clouds, and constructing temporary wooden bridges (Dube and Munsaka 2018). Community livelihoods have not been spared by flood disasters in Zimbabwe's rural areas. Dube (2017) and Mavhura (2020) note that community livelihoods that include crops, water sources and banana plantations have also been affected. If indigenous knowledge was effectively practised in all the places affected by floods in Zimbabwe, disaster losses could have been minimal.

Following flood disasters, stakeholders and the local people in disaster-impacted areas in Zimbabwe have often tried to build to recover from the impact using mostly scientific measures, ignoring the potential of indigenous knowledge. Chanza et al, (2020) note that Cyclone Idai in Zimbabwe exposed deficiencies in the country's disaster management system. This study argues that some of the deficiencies are related to the non-consideration of indigenous knowledge as part of measures to help communities recover from flood disasters.

Again, the deficiencies in the disaster management systems of the country do not support Priority 2 of the SFDRR, which calls for the strengthening of disaster risk governance. The motivation to use local knowledge is even more evident in the United Nations SFDRR, which calls for the use of indigenous knowledge in reducing disaster risk (UNIDR 2015). However, if indigenous knowledge of the communities is correctly applied as part of the disaster risk reduction measures in Zimbabwe, the local people have the potential to build-back-better their communities. Advocates of the use of indigenous knowledge in disaster risk reduction often contest that such indigenous knowledge can function effectively in saving human lives and property from disasters impact (Hiwasaki, Luna and Syamsidik 2014; Dube and Munsaka 2018). As such, the use of indigenous knowledge systems is in line with the SFDRR (UNISDR 2015). Many communities living with flood vulnerability in Zimbabwe are those that located along rivers and low-lying areas, such as communities in Tsholotsho district (Dube 2018), those that are in flood plains, such as communities in Muzarabani. Of late, flood disasters have also revealed the vulnerability of the communities living in mountainous areas of Chimanimani and Chipinge districts. For instance, according to Chanza et al. (2020), Rusitu Valley in Chimanimani is one of the low-lying areas where Cyclone Idai left a trail of destruction and severe damage. Local solutions should be available for communities living in low-lying areas so that they are saved from flooding.

The role of indigenous knowledge systems in disaster risk reduction

Indigenous knowledge systems play a vital role in disaster risk reduction and as such knowledge has been visible in some communities in Southern Africa, including Zimbabwe. According to Shaw et al. (2008) local people possess knowledge and capacities date back to centuries. Such capacity and knowledge used over time and proved to be sustainable, empowering and effective in managing both hazards and disasters (Shaw et al. 2008). For instance, Domfeh (2007) observes that local people in Swaziland use indigenous knowledge to predict floods by studying the height between birds' nests and river surfaces. When the nests are low, chances of flooding are none and when high in the tree tops the likelihood of flooding would be high. If this knowledge used in Swaziland can be adopted in other areas living with flood hazards, communities will be better.

In Zimbabwe, people in Tsholotsho district have also relied on nature as part of their indigenous knowledge systems. Dube and Munsaka (2018) contend that people in Tsholotsho can predict flooding through dark clouds and animal behaviour during rainy seasons. They use this as part of the early warning systems to signal the start of the rainy season or onset of heavy rains. This knowledge is in line with SFDRR Priority 1, which is about understanding disaster risk. Such warnings show that people living with flood hazards in Tsholotsho understand their risk; hence they can take appropriate action as part of disaster preparedness. The knowledge about early warning systems is part of the SFDRR's build-back-better approach, since the knowledge's continued existence and use may almost guarantee the safety of the communities through the provision of relevant information. As part of disaster response and recovery, the Tsholotsho people practice land zoning and relocation of livestock to higher ground (Dube and Munsaka 2018). This is enough evidence to suggest that indigenous knowledge is vital in all major phases of disaster risk reduction – mitigation, preparedness, response and recovery. Identification of permanent livestock relocation places to move the livestock during times of flooding is another build-back-better strategy, which involves land-use planning. The Tsholotsho scenario resonates with build-back-better systems in the flood-prone areas in Bangladesh. In Bangladesh, local communities relied on indigenous knowledge systems to build their shelter on raised land to prevent water from reaching them (Clark et al. 2008; Paul and Routray 2010).

However, it is important to note that indigenous knowledge provides both structural and non-structural measures of recovering from flood disasters in Zimbabwe. According to Mavhura et al. (2013), the Chadereka community of Muzarabani in Zimbabwe uses structural measures such as the construction of barriers around houses. This strategy ensures that the housing structures are not in contact with floodwater. The same community also constructs kitchens and storerooms on a raised platform so that food, drinking water, fuel and other valuables do not get into contact with floodwaters (Mavhura et al. 2013). This strategy resonates with SFDRR's main focus to reduce disaster risk and create resilient communities. If this kind of knowledge practised in Zimbabwe and somewhere outside, is transferred to other communities experiencing the same disaster problem, such communities would be resilient, safer and be able to withstand future hazards.

The potential of indigenous knowledge in building-back-better communities

Based on the discussion presented in subsection 3.2, the study argues that indigenous knowledge has a great potential to build-back-better communities in Zimbabwe. Dekens (2007) argues that the prominence of indigenous knowledge and practices for disaster risk reduction has increased since the 1970s. This shows that indigenous knowledge systems have stood the test of time. Hence, the knowledge, if seriously considered, has the potential to assist in the building-back-better of many communities. Lack of the build-back-better considerations in disaster recovery processes of flood-impacted areas in Zimbabwe does not address future risks and vulnerabilities. Instead, such actions simply restore the communities to pre-disaster state, characterised by high levels of vulnerability and disaster risk (Kennedy et al. 2008; Mannakkara, and Wilkinson 2014). For example, the simple restoration of systems following the 2005 Kashmir Earthquake in Pakistan resulted in the loss of life and the destruction of the structures rebuilt on the same earthquake zone, using the same weak building materials (Halvorson and Hamilton 2010). The rebuilding of infrastructure using weak materials suggests the low-risk perception by the Kashmir community, which perpetuates the vulnerabilities of communities. Such action does not support endeavours towards building-back-better disaster-impacted communities.

Although indigenous knowledge has the potential to improve disaster risk reduction, and to build-back-better disaster-impacted communities, its limitations cannot be overlooked. Dekens (2007) observes that indigenous knowledge has faced complicated barriers such as politics, lack of funding, and environmental barriers. Also, practitioners with the duty to serve disaster-impacted communities usually do not trust the efficiency and effectiveness of indigenous knowledge systems (Dube and Munsaka 2018). The lack of trust by disaster practitioners stems from the view that regards indigenous knowledge as backward, outdated and without documentation (Banda 2008; Herbert 2000). Naidoo (2007) also observes that the acceptance of indigenous knowledge of communities by disaster managers has not always been easy; hence the knowledge use has not been sustainable. The mistrust of indigenous knowledge by practitioners has, therefore, affected its implementation within many communities as a strategy for managing hazards and disasters. Studies have shown that even though some communities such as Tsholotsho and Muzarabani, have used this knowledge to build-back-better after disaster impact, practitioners are still sceptical about its contribution and value (Dube and Munsaka 2018; Mavhura, Maniema, Collins, Manatsa 2013). Hence, acceptance and sustainable use of the knowledge by the practitioners and communities can help strengthen the knowledge contribution in building-back-better of communities in Zimbabwe. This study argues that indigenous knowledge can be sustainable if there is government support on its use and preservation, and if the knowledge is made to be part of the education curriculum in schools, colleges and universities.

Indigenous knowledge systems intersect with SFDRR to build-back-better

Indigenous knowledge systems are part of the SFDRR (UNISDR 2015). When the role of indigenous knowledge and implementation is seriously considered, indigenous knowledge can support the focus of the SFDRR. Hence, in Zimbabwe, indigenous knowledge systems of communities intersect well with the SFDRR to achieve the framework's goal to build-back-better disaster-impacted communities. Without leveraging local knowledge of the communities, disaster risk reduction activities, especially disaster recovery which demands building-back-better, may not be a success. Therefore, there is a need to simultaneously consider indigenous knowledge and Priority 4 of the SFDRR, so that community can fully recover. Indigenous knowledge supports the SFDRR endeavours because the use of local knowledge and resources ensures the full participation of the local communities. Mwaura (2008) notes that indigenous knowledge is an empowerment tool for members of the community to take leading roles in disaster risk reduction activities. This ensures that local communities are part of the build-back-better programmes. Whilst embracing indigenous knowledge ensures high participation of the local communities, the SFDRR ensures that the build-back-better efforts are meant to prevent the re-creation or exacerbation of pre-disaster conditions (Mulligan et al. 2012; Rempel 2010). Besides, the build-back-better concepts emerged specifically as a response to the need to improve recovery practices and to build safer communities (Clinton 2006; Lyons 2009). Hence, the two concepts of indigenous knowledge systems and the SFDRR's build-back-better, when harmonised, can be an effective disaster risk reduction strategy.

Conclusion

Valuable conclusions can be drawn from the discussion on the role of indigenous knowledge systems in building-back-better disaster-impacted communities. First, the study concludes that flood disasters in Zimbabwe have been frequent, causing loss of life, destruction of infrastructure and property, and affecting important community livelihoods. Communities affected by the flood are those that are located in flood-prone areas such as riverbanks and other water basins, low-lying areas. Further, the study concluded that indigenous knowledge of the local communities has been applied in some communities in Zimbabwe to deal with flood disasters. Hence, knowledge has an important role to play in the building back better of the communities as it can contribute to the establishment of safer and resilient communities. However, despite its potential value in disaster risk reduction and acceptance by the rural communities, indigenous knowledge has been shunned by the practitioners. However, the knowledge intersects and resonates well with the SFDRR. The use of indigenous knowledge systems supports the SFDRR's endeavours to "build-back-better" communities during the recovery, rehabilitation and reconstruction. The study calls for government support in the use of the indigenous knowledge systems so that the knowledge use becomes sustainable. Also, practitioners should seriously consider using the indigenous knowledge of communities, alongside modern scientific knowledge. Besides, knowledge acceptance can be increased if the knowledge is to be part of the curriculums in schools and tertiary education institutions.

References

Adger, W.N., Barnett, J., Chapin, F.S., III & Ellemor, H. (2011). This must be the place: Underrepresentation of identity and meaning in climate change decision-making, *Global Environmental Politics* 11(2), 1–25. https://doi.org/10.1162/GLEP_a_00051.

African Risk Capacity. (2019). Update on tropical Cyclone Idai in Southern Africa. ARC river flood model (AFM-R). Johannesburg. Retrieved from www.africanriskcapacity.org.

Ayaa, D.D., Waswa, F. (2016). Role of indigenous knowledge systems in the conservation of the bio-physical environment among the Teso community in Busia County-Kenya. *Afr. J. Environ. Sci. Technol.* 10 (12), 467–475. https://doi.org/10.5897/AJEST2016.2182.

Chanza, N., Siyongwana, P.Q., Williams-Bruinders, L. *et al.* (2020). Closing the Gaps in Disaster Management and Response: Drawing on Local Experiences with Cyclone Idai in Chimanimani, Zimbabwe. *International Journal of Disaster Risk Science,* 11, 655–666. https://doi.org/10.1007/s13753-020-00290-x

Chianese, F. (2016). *The traditional knowledge advantage: Indigenous peoples' knowledge in climate change adaptation and mitigation strategies,*

International Fund for Agricultural Development (IFAD), Rome.

Clark, P., Lees, F., Greaney, M., Greene, G. and Riebe, D. (2008). Resilience in exercise and diet: factors predicting "getting back on track" in a community-dwelling older adult population, *Gerontol.* 48, 585–586.

Clinton, W.J. (2006). Lessons Learned from Tsunami Recovery: Key Propositions for Building Back Better, Office of the UN Secretary-General's Special Envoy for Tsunami Recovery, New York, USA.

Dekens, J. (2007). *Local knowledge for disaster preparedness: A Literature review*, International Centre for Integrated Mountain Development (ICIMOD), Kathmandu.

Dube, E. (2017). Towards Enhanced Disaster Risk Management Interventions for Flood Hazards and Disasters in Tsholotsho District, Zimbabwe, Unpublished PhD thesis, Midlands State University (MSU), Gweru.

Dube, E. (2020). The build-back-better concept as a disaster risk reduction strategy for positive reconstruction and sustainable development in Zimbabwe: A literature study, *International Journal of Disaster Risk Reduction,* 43(101401), doi: https://doi.org/10.1016/j.ijdrr.2019.101401.

Dube, E., Mtapuri, O. and Matunhu, J. (2018). Managing flood disasters on the built environment in the rural communities of Zimbabwe: lessons learned, *Jamba: J. Disaster Risk Studies* 10(1), a542, https://doi.org/10.4102/jamba. v10i1.542.

Dube, E. & Munsaka, E. (2018). The contribution of indigenous knowledge to disaster risk reduction activities in Zimbabwe: A big call to practitioners, *Jamba: Journal of Disaster Risk Studies* 10(1), a493. https:// doi.org/10.4102/Jamba. v10i1.493

Domfeh, K.A. (2007). Indigenous knowledge systems and the need for policy and institutional reforms: Tribes and tribals, indigenous knowledge systems and sustainable development, *Relevance for Africa* 1(5), 41–52.

Fabiyi, O.O. & Oloukoi, J. (2013). Indigenous knowledge system and local adaptation strategies to flooding in coastal rural communities of Nigeria, *Journal of Indigenous Social Development* 2(1), 1–19.

Fernandez, G., Ahmed, I. (2019). "Build-back-better" approach to disaster recovery: research trends since 2006, *Prog. Disaster Sci.* 1 (100003), https://doi.org/ 10.1016/j.pdisas.

Hartfield, G., Blunden, J., & Arndt, D.S. (2018). A look at 2017: Takeaway points from the state of the climate supplement. *American Meteorological Society*, 1950, 1527–1540. https://doi.org/10.1175/BAMS-D-18-0173.1.

Halvorson, S.J. and Hamilton, J.P. (2010). In the aftermath of the Qa'yamat: the Kashmir earthquake disaster in northern Pakistan, Disasters 34 (1) (2010) 184–204.

Hiwasaki, L., Luna, E. & Syamsidik, S.R., 2014, *Local and indigenous knowledge for community resilience: Hydro-meteorological disaster risk reduction and climate change adaptation in coastal and small island communities*, UNESCO, Jakarta.

Lyons, L. (2009). Building-Back-Better: The Large-Scale Impact of Small-Scale Approaches to Reconstruction, *World Development*, 37: 385-398.

Kelman, I. and Glantz, M.H. (2015). Analysing the Sendai framework for disaster risk reduction. *International Journal of Disaster Risk Science*, 6, 105–106. https://doi.org/10.1007/s13753-015-0056-3.

Kelman, I., Mercer, J. & Gaillard, J.C., 2012, Indigenous knowledge and disaster risk reduction, *Geography* 97(1), 12–21.

Kennedy, J., Ashmore, J., Babister, E., Kelman, I. (2008). The Meaning of 'Build Back Better': Evidence From Post-Tsunami Aceh and Sri Lanka, *Journal of Contingencies & Crisis Management*, 16: 24-36.

Khasalamwa, S. (2009). Is 'build-back-better' a response to vulnerability? Analysis of the post-tsunami humanitarian interventions in Sri Lanka, *Nor. J. Geogr.* 63 (1):73–88.

Kolen, B. and van Gelder, P. H. A. J. M. (2018). Risk-based decision-making for evacuation in case of imminent threat of flooding. *Water*, 10, 1–15. https://doi.org/10.3390/w10101429.

Maly, E. and Suppasri, A. (2020). The Sendai framework for disaster risk reduction at five: Lessons from the 2011 great east Japan Earthquake and Tsunami. *International Journal of Disaster Risk Science*, 11, 167–178. https://doi.org/10.1007/s13753-020-00268-9.

Mannakkara, S. and Wilkinson, S. (2012). Build-back-better Principles for Land-Use Planning, The University of Auckland, Auckland.

Mannakkara, S. and Wilkinson, S. (2014). Reconceptualising 'building back better' to improve post-disaster recovery. *Int J*

Manag Proj Bus, 7(2–3): 327–41. https://doi.org/10. 1108/IJMPB-10-2013-0054.

Mavhura, E., Maniema, S.B., Collins, E. and Manatsa, D. (2013). Indigenous knowledge, coping strategies and resilience to floods in Muzarabani, Zimbabwe. *International Journal of Disaster Risk Reduction*, 5(2013): 38 – 48.

Mavhura, E. (2019). Systems analysis of vulnerability to hydrometeorological threats: an exploratory study of vulnerability drivers in northern Zimbabwe, *Int. J. Disaster Risk Sci.* 10:204–219, https://doi.org/10.1007/s13753-019-0217-x.

Mavhura, E. (2020). Learning from the tropical cyclones that ravaged Zimbabwe: policy implications for effective disaster preparedness. *Natural Hazards* **104,** 2261–2275. https://doi.org/10.1007/s11069-020-04271-7.

Mavhura, E., Manyangadze, T., Mudavanhu, C. & Pedzisai, E. (2020). An assessment of riparian communities' preparedness to flood risk: the case of Mbire community in Zimbabwe, *GeoJournal.* https://doi.org/10.1007/s10708-020-10329-7.(0123456789

Melchias, G. (2001). *Biodiversity and conservation*, Science Publishers, Enfield.

Mhlanga, C., Muzingili, T., & Mpambela, M. (2019). Natural disasters in Zimbabwe: The primer for social work intervention. *African Journal of Social Work*, 9(1), 46–54.

Moses, O., and Ramotonto, S. (2018). Assessing forecasting models on prediction of the tropical cyclone Dineo and the associated rainfall over Botswana. *Weather and Climate Extremes*, 21, 102–109.

Mudavanhu C. (2014). The impact of flood disasters on child education in Muzarabani District, Zimbabwe, *Jàmbá: Journal of Disaster Risk Studies* 6(1), Art. #138, 8 pages. http://dx.doi.org/10.4102/jamba.v6i1.138.

Mudavanhu, C. (2016). Reframing Children's Participation in Flood Risk Management: the Case of Chadereka Ward, Muzarabani District, Zimbabwe, PhD thesis, Bindura University Science of Education, Bindura.

Muhonda, P., Mabiza, C., Makurira, H., Kujinga, K., Nhapi, I., Goldin, J., & Mashauri, D. A. (2014). Analysis of institutional mechanisms that support community response to impacts of floods in the middle-Zambezi river basin, Zimbabwe. *Physics and*

Chemistry of the Earth, 76–78,64–
71. https://doi.org/10.1016/j.pce.2014.11.013.

Mulligan, M., Ahmed, I., Shaw, J., Mercer, D. and Nadarajah, Y. (2012). Lessons for long-term social recovery following the 2004 tsunami: community, livelihoods, tourism and housing, *Environmental Hazards* 11(1): 38–51, https://doi.org/10.1080/17477891.2011.635186.

Mwaura, P., 2008, *Indigenous knowledge in disaster management in Africa*, United Nations Environment Programme, Nairobi.

Nyamwanza, A.M. (2014). 'Bridging policy and practice for livelihood resilience in rural Africa, lessons from Mid-Zambezi Valley, Zimbabwe', *Journal of Rural Community Development* 9(4), 23–33.

Paul, S.K. and Routray, J.K. (2010). Flood proneness and coping strategies: the experiences of two villages in Bangladesh, *Disasters* 34 (2010): 489–508.

Pérez-Fructuoso, M.J. (2007). Economic damages and the impact of natural or anthropic disasters: Main features of an evaluation framework. *Risk Manag*, 98: 22–42.

Rempel, H. (2010). The challenge of spending tsunami assistance well, *J. Asia Pac. Econ.* 15 (2): 106–127, https://doi.org/10.1080/13547861003700463.

Shaw, R., Takeuchi, Y., Uy, N. & Sharma, A. (2008). *Indigenous knowledge: Disaster risk reduction policy note*, European Union/ISDR, Kyoto.

Sillitoe, P. (2017). Indigenous knowledge and natural resources management: an introduction featuring wildlife. In: Sillitoe, P. (Ed.), *Indigenous Knowledge: Enhancing its Contribution to Natural Resources Management*. CAB International, pp. 1–14.

Tharakan, J. (2015). Indigenous knowledge systems – a rich appropriate technology resource. *Afr. J. Sci. Technol. Innov. Dev.* 7 (1), 52–57. ttps://doi.org/10.1080/20421338.2014.987987.

UNDRR (2017). Terminology on Disaster Risk Reduction: Basic Definitions on Disaster Risk Reduction to Promote a Common Understanding on the Subject for Use by the Public, Authorities and Practitioners, UNDRR.

UNISDR (2015). Sendai Framework for Disaster Risk Reduction 2015–2030. http://www. wcdrr.org/preparatory/post2015.

UNISDR (2017). Build-back-better in Recovery, Rehabilitation, and Reconstruction: in Support of the Sendai Framework for Disaster Risk Reduction 2015 – 2030, UNISDR.

Chapter 12

Medicinal Indigenous Knowledge Systems and Gender among the Shona People of Buhera South, Zimbabwe

Maradze Viriri

Abstract

This chapter focuses on medicinal indigenous knowledge systems (IKSs) common among Shona men and women in Buhera South, Zimbabwe. The chapter looks at the nature of these belief systems which are common in the area and how they relate to gender dynamics in a society which is typically patriarchal in nature and come up with reasons for the prevailing scenario. Benefits of these IKSs among the selected society are also sought together with the challenges paused by the phenomenon. The study is informed by Afrocentricity and the Gender theory. It employs the qualitative paradigm and uses interviews with ten elderly people; both men and women from Buhera South, to solicit information. Findings of this study show that medicinal IKS in Buhera South are gender specific and not neutral and universal. There are therapeutic knowledge systems which are peculiar to men and others to women. Based on these findings, the chapter argues for ways to make gendered therapeutic knowledge neutral and universal so that it benefits every member of the society for development. The study, thus, calls for the two genders to share this indigenous knowledge for the benefit of everyone in the society.

Keywords: Indigenous knowledge systems, medicine, gender, Afrocentricity

Introduction

Health matters are central to humanity. For the African people, and the Shona included, the wellness of any people depends on the community's health and wellbeing and as such medicinal indigenous knowledge system (also known as ethnobotanical knowledge) is at the life blood of the people of Buhera South. The selective value of ethno-botanical knowledge acquisition has been considerable throughout history. From time immemorial, the Shona people of

227

Buhera South relied on hunting and gathering for their livelihood, they were increasingly proficient in cognitively organizing and efficiently exploiting their wild material resources and medicine. Chavhunduka (1994) says that the identification and utilization of medicinal knowledge in most rural communities in Zimbabwe is done by both men and women at varying degrees.

Traditional knowledge associated with medicinal herbs is a highly gendered activity in most communities. According to the UNDP Report (2007), in many cultures women and men have different knowledge of medicinal plants and this is linked to the division of labour in these cultures. The Report goes on to mention that in many rural-based and indigenous communities, women play key roles in delivery of informal health care alternatives based on medicinal plants. This is corroborated by Nguemo (2015) who postulates that most rural dwellers in developing countries have no proper access to conventional medicine but rely on informal healthcare alternatives. The high cost of imported medication in Africa has become prohibitive to many people thereby necessitating the continued use of traditional medicine by local communities. Rankoana (2012) has it that 80% of people in developing countries still rely on traditional medicine for their primary healthcare needs. The role of both men and women within the Indigenous knowledge systems as custodians of particular types of knowledge is particularly important. However, this knowledge varies across gender divide. In Buhera South of Zimbabwe, the variation in the use of herbs between men and women is attributed to the patriarchal nature of the society. Men usually operate in environments different to that of women and as such their knowledge of medicinal herbs is different to that of women. There is division of labour between men and women in Buhera South and this automatically means that men and women usually work in different spaces. UNDP (2007) has it that in many regions women and men perform different, complimentary roles in cultivating, harvesting and using medicinal plants, however quantitative and qualitative data describing women's specific roles in collecting, growing or marketing medicinal herbs are difficult to obtain. Recent studies seem to suggest that in most countries there are well-defined gender roles in biodiversity management and these vary across cultures.

The passage of time has also influenced the culture of the people of Buhera South. The gender roles have since changed due to a number of factors. Many of the material and spiritual relations with the plant kingdom which the people of Buhera South had since time immemorial still persist in Buhera South. The major pressing threat to the knowledge and existence of medical plants in Buhera South is culture change due to seductive influence of globalization. The need for firewood as a source of energy has also witnessed a massive destruction of the forests in Buhera South resulting in some of the herbs going extinct. The cognitive link with nature sustained by traditional healers and their oral traditions may well be at greater risk of extinction than the floras (Cox, 2000).Western missionaries and other religious zealots continue to school rural converts to abandon the use of medicinal plant recipes, arguing that the occult powers of magical and medicinal plants are thinly veiled manifestations of paganism (Voeks 1997). This has resulted in many residents in Buhera South resorting to modern medicine in hospitals and clinics. However, the cost of Western medicine still remains a prohibitive factor to many and as a result traditional herbs still have a wider appeal in Buhera South. The culture of depending on medicinal plants for medication will continue in Buhera South since the area is drought -prone hence the residents will not afford the costs associated with modern medicine. The only problem is that the use of traditional herbal medicine in Buhera South is likely to face a natural death in the future since there is little or no interest among the present generation to assimilate and pass on the medicinal plant legacy of the previous generations to future generations.

Background to the study

The people of Buhera South face Challenges in accessing health care due to their geographical location. The bad state of roads to access Murambinda General Hospital and Birchenough Bridge General Hospital makes it very difficult for the residents to access health care. The local clinics at Mutiusinazita, Muzokomba and Chabata usually have limited drugs to service the community. One other limiting factor is that these clinics charge a fee for one to get a service of which a majority of the residents cannot afford. As a result of such factors, most Buhera South residents resort to medicinal herbs for their treatment and that of their animals as well. The other factor is that the area is drought prone and as a result some of the people of Buhera South cannot afford the costs associated with modern medicine. These medicinal knowledge systems manifest themselves through different dimensions. Among these are

229

agriculture, medicine, security, botany, zoology, craft skills and linguistics. Indigenous knowledge systems are rooted to a particular set of experiences, and generated by people living in those places. Thus, the people of Buhera South have their own knowledge on medicinal herbs which they use to cure themselves and their animals respectively. The community cherishes this knowledge so much that they speak highly about it. Hlatshwayo (2017) argues that the continued use of traditional medicine can be explained by its accessibility, adaptability acceptability and affordability. Shonhai (2016) says that the other reason that renders traditional medicine to be on high demand is its holistic approach to diseases or sickness. Rural communities believe much in the use of these medicinal herbs due to their location and culture. Buhera South community being one of these rural communities is no exception, it depends very much on these medicinal herbs for health care. Both men and women have knowledge about the use of the herbs found within their surroundings. The community, being patriarchal in its set up assigns roles to men and women in almost every facet of their lives resulting in even the medicinal herbs information being gendered as well.

Theoretical framework

This study on the medicinal Indigenous Knowledge Systems peculiar to men and women in Buhera South is guided by the Afrocentric theory propounded by Molefi Kate Asante. According to Asante, Afrocentric theory is 'a paradigmatic intellectual perspective that privileges African agency within the context of African history and culture trans-continentally and trans-generally.' Asante (2015) acknowledges that the Afrocentric theory advocates Africans to uphold that which is African which is found in their culture. Tembo (2012) says that the Afrocentric theory emphasizes the 'centrality of African people and phenomenon' while paying particular attention to the self-definition of Africans and everything that is African, the belief system included. This theory is a framework that views phenomena from the perspective of the African people. Afrocentric theory celebrates that which is African, advocating for African values especially those values which define us as a people. Furusa (2002) regards Afrocentric theory as, 'part of the African worldview and philosophy of life' as it describes the production of African views with regard to the way they view life. It stresses the commemoration of African culture and heritage.

230

One of the advocates of this theory, Asante (2015) suggests that Africans should disencumber themselves from viewing the world through Western spectacles but rather they must use African lenses to identify problems and use African solutions to solve these problems. In line with this view is this study which looks at how people of Buhera South use local herbs to cure various ailments. The tenets of this theory resonate well with the thrust of this study which seeks to interrogate the medicinal herbs peculiar to men and women in Buhera South. Medicinal indigenous knowledge is one of the values which the people of Buhera South cherish so much. In propounding this theory, Asante (2015) emphasized putting of African perspectives at the centre stage in all issues pertaining their lives, cultural, social, political and economic. Indigenous Knowledge systems fall under the belief system of the people of Buhera South. Belief systems constitute the culture of people in Buhera South. Medicinal herbs which fall under indigenous knowledge systems are part and parcel of the culture of the people of Buhera South. The Afrocentric framework is used in this study to bring to the fore the agency of the Shona people in Buhera South in treating various ailments using local herbs.

Methodology

The research design was purely qualitative; as the study sought to understand the medicinal herbs peculiar to men and women in Buhera South hence, use of qualitative research design paved way for men and women to make sense of their experiences and the world in which they lived (Holloway 1997). It facilitated the analysis of the social practices and relationships that took place in the identification and use of traditional medicinal herbs from the participants' points of view and this enabled an understanding of the phenomenon of gender in the use of traditional medicinal herbs in Buhera South in their natural context in greater depth (Denzin and Lincolin 2008). Qualitative research design also resonates well with the Afrocentric theory which guides this research as both emphasize on the importance of social context and wholeness, that allow individuals to be studied not cut off from interactions and relationships with other people (Fine and Gordon , 1989). This facilitated an in-depth mapping of different herbs that men and women in Buhera South know. Qualitative research also brings to surface voices which are often silenced (Frisby, Maguire and Reid 2009) thus enabling even women who have long been subordinated and marginalized from knowledge construction and public spheres to express their knowledge on herbs freely in this study. Phenomenological qualitative research design was specifically used as the intent was to understand the traditional medicinal herbs peculiar to men and women in Buhera South.

Purposive and judgmental sampling was used to identify the primary participants for the study. The sample was selected based on the judgement of the researcher targeting men and women who were 65 years and above of age. This age group was selected as the researcher considered them old enough to know the traditional medicinal herbs. Interviews were contacted with a total of 10 participants (5 males and 5 females).Consent was sought from the participants right from the start. The participants accepted to participate in the research after the researcher explained to them that the research was purely academic and their contributions were therefore going to be used for academic purpose only. Data was collected between October and November 2020. In –depth unstructured interviews were used to collect data. Unstructured interviews were found to be suitable for the study because they are receptive to unexpected information from the participants, thereby giving both men and women the freedom and opportunity to articulate their subjective experiences (Cohen et al, 2007). This type of an interview also enabled participants to voice their experiences, unconstrained by the researcher, thus decreasing the power differences that may exist between the researcher and the participants. Unstructured interviews also ensured that participants are not objectified or placed in a passive role but rather they will be played an active part during the interview session. The researcher had to abide by the Covid protocols to avoid risking his life and that of the participants. Thus, the researcher made sure all the participants were putting on face masks during the interview sessions and maintaining the required social distance during the interviews.

Results and Discussion

Findings revealed that there are various medicinal herbs which are peculiar to men and women in Buhera South. Information was sought through face to face interviews with elderly people who were presumed to be custodians of medicinal indigenous knowledge systems. In Buhera South, gendered division of labour among the subsistence communities predominate the community set up. Thus, men are often engaged in livestock herding, hunting and fishing. These activities often take them relatively to undisturbed habitants distant from their settlements thereby exposing them to herbs which can be used for treatment of a wide range of diseases. Their knowledge on herbs was so vast. Women on the other hand were said to be involved in managing local resources, such as home gardens and other disturbed habitants relatively nearer their home and as such their knowledge on herbs is also influenced by the environment which they usually patrol and as such women displayed knowledge on herbs which differed to that of their male counterparts. Hlatshwayo (2017) posits that people give names to and learn about the properties of plants that are highly visible, familiar and accessible to them. Differences in areas of operations by men and women attributed to variations in their knowledge on herbs as was evidenced by this study. This study established that medicinal herbs knowledge in Buhera South is gendered.

The table below shows the medicinal herbs commonly used by women in Buhera South:

Name of herb and part of the tree used	Name of diseases cured by the herb
Mupfura (barks and roots)	Safeguards infants against yellow fever
Ruzangaruvire (roots)	Treats stomach aches
Rupupu (leaves)	Treats Chipande and Chipembwe
Chinharara (roots and leaves)	Treats diarrhoea, measles and prevents Polio
Chibhamubhamu (roots)	Treats Measles and whooping cough (Chipembwe)

Source: Compiled by the author, 2021

From the research women displayed detailed knowledge about medicinal herbs which treat various ailments which usually affect infants. These ailments include measles, yellow fever, stomach ache, whooping cough, diarrhoea, polio and excessive dehydration. Various trees were mentioned as sources of medicines for curing these diseases. Mupfura [Amarula] barks was said to be used to cure yellow fever on infants. One interviewee said, "Mwana achangozvarwa anofanira kugezeswa mumvura inenge yakaiswa makwande emupfura kudzivirira chirwere cheyellow fever." (An infant needs to be bathed using water which is mixed to Mupfura

233

barks to safeguard the infant from yellow fever). Ruzangaruvire (A plant which looks like a sweet potato plant) is said to be a remedy to all stomachaches which usually affect infants. Rupupu leaves were said to be the remedy to Chipande and Chipembwe. Fernandez (1994) argues that women are very active in medicinal Indigenous Knowledge system. Muyambo (2019) in his research about Bota reshupa demonstrated the centrality and agency of the Ndau women in matters of health, identity as well as their culture and situation. Muyambo (2015) defines *bota reshupa* as a herbal porridge which is prepared by using a concoction of traditional herbs soaked in water. The watery substance, which is kept in a calabash, is then mixed with millet or rapoko to prepare the porridge. Muyambo established that Ndau women just like other Shona women in Buhera South are the masters of indigenous herbal medicine especially herbs which treat infants. The Ndau women are known to be the masters and custodians of the Shupa. The research by Muyambo (2019) also noted that although the Ndau women were the custodians of the Shupa practice, the real owners of the culture are the Ndau men. One woman interviewee said that her husband usually collects the herbs for her and she will then prepare the concoction. Bogossi et al (2000) says that elderly women in Brazil achieve considerable community prestige as a result of their healing abilities. Women in Buhera South, especially the older women represent the primary healthcare providers for the family and the community, a situation that prevails in many other regions in the developing world (Nyawa and Voeks, 2001). The results of the present study largely mirror how medicinal indigenous knowledge systems are gendered in Buhera South. This research established that Buhera South women are major agency in primary health care. In contrast to popular beliefs in most societies were women play second fiddle to their male counterparts, Buhera women are very active when it comes to matters of healthcare through their detailed knowledge about medicinal herbs especially those that treat diseases which affect infants. Kanjere, Thaba and Teffo (2011:246) believe that women especially rural women are negatively affected by prejudices because most men in such areas claim to be staunch custodians of culture.

From the interviews, it was evident that Buhera South women are very active when it comes to the use of herbs in treating various ailments which affect infants and expecting mothers. Swai (2010) concurs with this idea when he argues that women occupy a special place in the improvement and promotion of health care services, mainly because they participate in and manage many health care activities that affect the health of their families. Thus, Buhera South women are health care workers not by formal training but by the experience in dealing with herbs which treat infants and expecting mothers within their society. World Bank (2006:2) has it that elderly women have "considerable knowledge and experience related to all aspects of maternal and child development, and that they have a strong commitment to promoting the well-being of children and their families. Heferran (2008:1) argues that although rural women are often presented as silent, absent and under-appreciated, they probably represent the world's most powerful untapped natural resource, and they are key to world stability and understanding. From the interviews carried out, it came out that most of the herbs which are known by Buhera women are for infants and pregnant women. From the interviews it was evident that women in Buhera South managed pregnancy and childbirth using their own community-based knowledge systems.

The most common herbal medicine taken by pregnant women was *mudzingamakore* which is also called *demamhandwe* in Ndau. One interviewee said, *"Vakadzi vakazvitakura vanokurudzirwa kunwa mudzingamakore kuti pakuzvara vasaita dambudziko sezvo muti uyu unokudza nzira inobuda nemwana"* (Woman who are pregnant are encouraged to take mubhubhunu so that they don't face complications when giving birth because this herb widens the birth canal).This plant was mentioned by all participants as the most effective indigenous remedy for pregnant women. Its roots which are in form of bulbs are boiled in water and the concoction is consumed three times a day by an expecting mother. This will help the expecting mother to have a smooth delivery of the baby. Elephant dung is another herb which was mentioned by two of the participants as one of the herbs taken by expecting mothers. It is used as a birth and canal relaxant. The elephant dung is soaked in warm water and is drunk two to three times a day. It has the same effect with that of mubhubhunu. From the interviews it also came out that pregnant women are usually encouraged to take okra now and again. One woman participant said, *"Derere* (okra) *rinoita kuti pakubereka mwana abude nyore"* (Okra makes it easy during giving birth).Okra is eaten and it has to be crushed and soaked in water and when the water will be used to rub on the opening of the vagina. It is believed that it will help to widen the birth canal. The women get these herbs from their local bushes and gardens. Chavhunduka (1998) says that most traditional herbs are obtained from either tree bark, roots or leaves. This was also confirmed by some of the interviewees when they were explaining how to prepare concoctions for some of the diseases.

The table below shows herbs commonly used by men in Buhera South.

Name of herb and part of tree used	Type of diseases cured by the herb
Muzeze (leaves)	Treats toothache
Murumanyama (bucks and roots)	Treats sexual transmitted diseases
Murovamhuru (leaves)	Treats backache
Murovan'ombe (leaves and roots)	Treats whooping cough, measles and diphtheria
Guniti (barks)	Treats mental illness
Mushangura (roots)	Snake bites

Source: Compiled by the author, 2021

From the interviews men on the other hand showed that they do have knowledge on medicinal herbs which treat a wide spectrum of diseases for all age groups unlike women who specialized more on herbs for infants and expecting mothers. During the interview sessions it was evident that men displayed vast knowledge about medicinal herbs which treat a wide range of infections. Buhera South community believes so much in the existence of witchcraft and as a result most men claim to have knowledge on herbs which they say will safeguard their families against witches and also herbs to safeguard their property from thieves. One elderly male interviewee had this to say, *"Ini muti wandinonyanya kuziva ndewe kudzivirira mhuri yangu kumhepo dzinounzwa nevaroyi uye kudzivirira zvipfuwo zvangu kubva kumbavha."* (The only herbs which I am well versed with are those which protect my family from the bad spirits brought about by witches and those which protect my animals from thieves). From the interviews Guniti bark was cited by most of the interviewees as a major herb which they use to drive away evil spirits bought about by witches and enemies. The interviewee said that he was not prepared to divulge the herbs which he uses to protect his animals from thieves.

Muramanyama tree was cited as a major herb which they use to treat sexually transmitted diseases. On the use of Murumanyama tree one interviewee has this to say, *"Uyu muti unobatsira kurapa zvirwere zvizhinji zvepabonde zvakanyanya."* (This herb helps to treat sexually transmitted diseases).Most Buhera South men are polygamous and as such chances of people contracting sexually transmitted diseases is high. It is from this background that most of the interviewees claimed to have knowledge about herbs which treat sexually transmitted diseases. Most of these interviewees mentioned *Murovamhuru* herb used to treat backache. They claim that since most of them are polygamous, they must have strong backs to sexually satisfy their many wives in bed. Momsen (2004) says that because men and women often travel and toil in different spaces, their familiarity with nature is bound to vary. This was evidenced during the research as there were herbs known by men and not known by women and vice versa.

Most of the interviewees revealed that in most of the instances they will have to mix more than one herb to come up with a particular concoction to treat a particular illness. Chirisembu (2009) holds the view that most indigenous trees in African communities are agency for primary health care needs for the communities, owing to the vast use of the trees' roots bark and leaves. Okello, Nyunja, Netondo and Onyango (2010) confirm this when they state that the Sabaots in the Kapsiro division of Mt. Elegon in Kenya use medicinal plants to treat cold by chewing Tagetesminuta leaves. Malaria is treated by boiling and drinking Artemisia afra leaves and ulcers are treated by boiling and drinking the root of Heteromorpha. What is worth noting is that different herbs serve the same purpose in different settings like the case of Buhera South. This difference show how localized medicinal herbs are but also that they are varied (Odora Hoppers). Chinsembu (2009) noted that the function of a particular herb vary from place to place when he studied the local communities in Namibia, he discovered that what a particular herb cured in one community could differ in another community. The same scenario was noted in Buhera South during the interviews when a particular herb's use varied with gender. For instance, women said that Murumanyama is used to treat stomach aches in infants but men said it is used to treat sexual transmitted diseases.

One male interviewee said, *"Mishonga yemiposo tinoitora nyikamukanza chaiko".* (We get herbs to cure people who have been bewitched faraway places." Another male interviewee hinted that he gets most of his herbs as far as Chipinge. Logan and Dixon in Voeks (2007) seem to agree with the male interviewee when they say that men often get herbs from relatively undisturbed nature, a plant kingdom under the influence of mostly natural ecological processes.

Of the ten participants, all showed that they know about the medicinal value of some herbs. However, women demonstrated

237

knowledge of a wide variety of herbs and the diseases which can be cured using these herbs. Forty percent (40%) of the interviewed men said they only knew a limited number of these herbs. The results show that both men's and women's knowledge of medicinal properties of the local flora grows during their lifetimes. It is also evident from the results that women accumulate this knowledge of nature more rapidly throughout their lives than men. Thus, in old age, women know much more about the medicinal properties of plant than do their male counterparts.

All the five women, that is (100%) participants presented deeper knowledge on plant medicine and they even went to mention the various ailments cured by these herbs. Their knowledge centred much on diseases which normally affect infants. On the side of livestock, they showed knowledge on herbs which treat poultry. Men for example made it clear that they knew very little about herbs which are used to cure diseases which normally attack infants. This was surprising because the men were of the same age range with their female participants. The male participants also demonstrated that the herbal knowledge which the male participants exhibited was purely folkloric because as the researcher noted, they personally some of them displayed shallow knowledge compared to the female participants.

Two elderly women participants provided valuable information on the use of medicinal herbs in the Shona society in Buhera South. They said, "*Mukadzi woga woga muChiShona anotarisirwa kuziva midzi yekurapa vacheche sezvo mwana achigona kumurwarira ari oga pamba*". (Every woman in the Shona society is expected to know herbs which cure diseases which usually affect infants because a baby can fall sick when the woman is alone at home). Begossi et al (2002) report that women know a greater number of medicinal species than men, although men show an overall higher diversity and heterogeneity of plant citations. On the other hand, male participants indicated that knowledge on herbs is usually a preserve of the old males in their society. Heckler (2002) has it that men and women in indigenous Venezuelan communities maintain similar levels of ethnobotanical knowledge. This Venezualan study seems to concur with the Buhera South situation were both men and women are experts in medicinal herbs. Chavhunduka (1994) points out that before Zimbabwe became a colony traditional healers enjoyed tremendous prestige in their society. He goes on to say that traditional healers were specialists in their own right and ensured the traditional societies' wellbeing. Both

238

men and women in Buhera South helped in making sure the community was well catered for when it comes to health matters. This research though points to sharp ethnobotanical unconformities between women and men and this is attributed to the patriarchal nature of the society which still believe in the division of labour between genders. This research established that women seem to know more of medicinal herbs regardless of their age. The research established that women at childbearing age will have an idea of herbs which cure infants and those for fowls. However, it was found out that this knowledge increased as they grow older. The gendered knowledge gap grows over the years, to the point that middle aged to elderly women constitute cognitive repositories of traditional ethnomedical knowledge. Coe and Anderson in Voeks (2007) reported that Garifuna women in Nicaragua are much more knowledgeable about medicinal species than men. Luoga et al (2000) in Voeks (2007) also found out that women in eastern Tanzania know more about herbaceous plants, whereas men are more knowledgeable about trees.

This research established that women and men quite clearly exhibit differing knowledge of their local herbs. Women in Buhera South are significantly more proficient than men in identifying, naming and describing the medicinal properties of plant species which treat infant ailments in their locality. When it comes to medicinal indigenous knowledge, women tend to know much about medicinal herbs which treat pregnant women and infants. With regard to medicinal indigenous knowledge about animals women are seen to be well versed with poultry. On the other hand, men were seen to be experts in medicinal indigenous knowledge about herbs witch treats ailments associated witchcraft, snake bites and sexually transmitted diseases. With regard to animals men showed vast knowledge about cattle, goats, sheep and donkeys. This is in synch with the World Bank Report (2007) which notes that due to gender differentiation and specialization, the traditional medicinal knowledge and skills held by women often differ from those held by men, affecting patterns of access, use and control, while resulting in different perceptions and priorities for the innovation and use of indigenous knowledge. Rahman Khan (2003) says that such a scenario impacts the way in which indigenous knowledge is disseminated, documented and passed on to future generations. Thus, there is gender division of plant knowledge in Buhera South. The gendered knowledge gap grows over the years, to the point that

239

middle-aged to elderly women constitute cognitive repositories of traditional ethnomedical knowledge. On the other hand, elderly men are also experts in medicinal herbs which treat illness associated with witchcraft, sexually transmitted diseases and other illnesses which usually affect men. What is disturbing to note is that despite the importance of traditional medicine to the people of Buhera South research into traditional medicine remains minimal in Zimbabwe. There is reluctance on the part of the government to openly recognize the importance of this type of medicine in the healthcare of most Zimbabweans especially those who stay in rural areas like Buhera South. With the high rate at which the forests in Zimbabwe are being destroyed to pave way for agricultural land and residential stands there is a high probability that most of the herbs will go extinct. Muyambo (2019) observes that what is even more threatening to this vital indigenous knowledge in traditional practices, especially medicines is that it is dying out along with their holders. As the old generations who are the custodians of the knowledge on herbs which can treat various ailments are dying, they are dying without passing this precious knowledge to the current generations. It may also be that the current generation is not willing to take this knowledge as such the knowledge is fast disappearing. Such a scenario is an irretrievable loss as the traditional practices in the use of traditional medicine hold solutions to the problems that are plaguing most Zimbabweans.

Conclusion

The medicinal indigenous knowledge system in Buhera South is gendered due to the gender roles which characterize the Shona society. Results of this research largely mirror the gender division of medicinal herbs knowledge in Buhera South. The source of this gendered ethnobotanical division can be attributed to the fact that men and women operate in quite different spaces resulting in them being exposed to herbs which might be far-fetched to the other gender group. This is attributed very much to the culture of the people of Buhera South. Buhera South community is patriarchal in its set up hence men and women operate in different spheres in their day to day operations. Such a scenario means that men and women will always have different experiences with regard to medicinal. The Study found out that men and women in Buhera South have vast knowledge about medicinal herbs though this knowledge vary across the gender divide. This study found it necessary that this knowledge be shared between men and women. The role of women within the indigenous knowledge systems particularly in the medicinal herbs section as custodians of a particular of important information with regard to various herbs is very important. This special position of women in Buhera South is inadequately provided for. If this knowledge can be shared between the two genders so that it will benefit the society at large. In the past women's knowledge has been overlooked due to the patriarchal nature of the Shona society set up in Buhera South. Sharing of this precious information will bring innovation in the use of these herbs thereby benefiting the community of Buhera South. This study has argued that the vast knowledge on herbs from men and women be integrated for the benefit of the entire society.

References

Asante, M.K. (2015) *The History of Africa: The Quest for Eternal Harmony.* New York: Routledge Publishers.

Bagossi A, Hanazaki N, Tmashiro J Y (2002) *Medicines plants in the Atlantic forest: Knowledge, Use, and Conservation.* Human Ecology 30, 281-99.

Begossi A, Hanazaki N, Peroni N (2000) *Knowledge and use of biodiversity in Brazilian hot spots.* Environment, Development and Sustainability2, 177-93.

Chavhunduka, G.K. (1994) *Traditional Medicine in Modern Zimbabwe.* Harare: University of Zimbabwe Publications.

Chinsembu, K.C. (2009) Model and experiences of initiating collaboration with traditional healers in validation of ethnomedicine for HIV/AIDS in Namibia. *Journal of Ethnobiology and Ethnomedicine,*5 (30), 5-30.

Cohen, L., Manion, L, and Morrison , K. (2007) *Research Methods in Education.* 6th Ed. New York. Routledge.

Denzin, N.K. and Lincoln, Y.S. (2008) *Collecting and Interpreting Qualitative Materials,* Los Angeles. Sage Publications.

Frisby, W., Maguire, P. and Reid. C. (2009) *The 'F' Word has everything to do with it: How Feminist Theories Action Research.* Action Research. 7. (1) :13-19.

Halloway, I (1997) *Basic Concepts for Qualitative Research.* Oxford, Blackwell Science.

Heckler S (2002) Traditional ethnobotanical knowledge loss and gender among the Piaroa. In Stepp J. Wyndham F, Zarger R (eds) *Ethnobiology and Biocultural Diversity Proceedings of the seventh International Congress of Ethnobiology,* 532-4. University of Georgia Press, Athens.

Hlatshwayo, A.M. (2017) '*Indigenous Knowledge, beliefs and practices on pregnancy and childbirth among the Ndau people of Zimbabwe:*' Unpublished PhD thesis, University of KwaZulu Natal, Pietermaritzburg, South Africa.

Howard P (2003) Women and the plant world: An exploration. In Howard PL (ed) *Women and Plants: Gender Relations in Biodiversity Management and Conversation,* 1-48, Zed, London.

Kainer KA and Duryea M (1992) *Tapping Women's Knowledge: Plant resource use in extractive reserves.* Brazil. Economic Botany 46, 408-25.

Letherby G. (2003) *Feminist Research in Theory and Practice.* Philadelphia, Open University Press.

Mohamed- Katerere, J. (1996) *Gender and Indigenous systems and Sustainable Development.* The Zimbabwe Law Review Vol. 13 20-27. Harare: faculty of Law (UZ).

Momsen J (2004) *Gender and Development.* Routledge, London.

Muyambo T (2018) Indigenous Knowledge Systems of the Ndau people of Manicaland Province in Zimbabwe: A case study of Bota Reshupa; *Unpublished PhD thesis.* University of KwaZulu Natal.

Odora Hopper, C.A (2002) Indigenous Knowledge and the Integration of knowledge systems in Odora Hoppers, C.A. (ed).*Indigenous Knowledge and the integration of knowledge systems: Towards a philosophy of articulation.* Claremont: New African Books.

Pfeiffer. J. (2002) Gendered Interpretations of bio-cultural diversity in eastern Indonesia: Ethnoecology in the transition zone. In Lansdowne H, Dearden P, Neilson W (eds) *Communities in Southeast Asia: Challenges and Responses,* 43-63. University of Victoria Press, Victoria.

Shonhai, V. F. (2016) '*Analysing South African Indigenous Knowledge Policy and its alignment to government's attempts to promote Indigenous vegetables*', Unpublished PhD thesis, Durban, University of KwaZulu Natal.

Stepp JR (2004) *The role of weeds as sources of phameticals.* Journal of Ethnopharmecology 163-6.

Tembo. C. (2012) *Post Independence Shona Poetry: The Quest and Struggle for Total Liberation.* UNISA. Unpublished PhD Thesis.

Voeks R A (2007) *Are women reservoirs of traditional plant knowledge? Gender, Ethnobotany and Globalization in northeast Brazil.* Journal of Tropical Geography 28, 7-20, National University of Singapore and Blackwell Publishing Asia Pvt Ltd.

Voeks R A, Nyawa S (2001) *Healing Flora of the Brunei Dusan.* Borneo Research Bulletin 32, 178-95.

Voeks, R A, Sercombe P. (2000) *The scope of hunter- gatherer ethnomedicine* social science and medicine50, 1-12.

Voeks J R (1997) *Sacred leaves of Condemble: African Magic, Medicine and Religion in Brazil,* University of Texas Press. Austin.

World Bank. (2006). 'Grandmothers promote maternal and child health: the role of indigenous knowledge systems' managers'. No. 89. February: 1-4.

Chapter 13

Indigenous Cultural Resources as a Panacea for Sexual and Gender Based Violence: A Case Study of the Ndau in Chimanimani Community, Zimbabwe

Sophia Chirongoma & Silindiwe Zvingowanisei

Abstract

This chapter deliberates on the issue of Sexual and Gender Based Violence (SGBV) among the Ndau of Chimanimani rural community in Zimbabwe. It identifies various forms of violence that are prevalent in this community which include physical, sexual, economic and emotional. The chapter singles out unequal power relations, economic dependence, patriarchy, religion and culture as the major causes of SGBV. Such is achieved through the use of the African feminist approach which analyses power relations between men and women. The phenomenological approach which prioritizes the practitioner's point of view is also key to this study. In terms of data collection, the research extensively relies on interviews. The study posits that although African Traditional Religion (ATR) legitimizes several harmful cultural practices which perpetuate SGBV, there are several positive indigenous cultural values which if appropriately adhered to; can become useful resources for eradicating SGBV in this community. This includes the use of taboos, proverbs, idioms, songs and myths that protect women from SGBV. The argument proffered here is that not everything about indigenous culture is negative and harmful. In that light, employing positive and progressive indigenous resources can make great strides in mitigating the prevalence of SGBV. The chapter concludes by asserting that utilizing African tools to solve African problems arising in an African context can result in a gender-violence free society. This conclusion is also informed by the fact that indigenous cultural resources can be embraced easily since they are not far removed from the people as they are part and parcel of their day to day lives.

Keywords: African feminist Approach, Chimanimani rural community, Indigenous Cultural Resources, Sexual and Gender Based Violence, Zimbabwe

Introduction

Sexual and gender-based violence (SGBV) has persisted in Zimbabwe in-spite of the numerous measures that have been put in place to curb it through conducting some campaigns and adopting several international, regional and national legislations and policies. This includes Zimbabwe's adoption of the Universal Declaration of Human Rights; the Convention on the Elimination of All Forms of Discrimination against Women (CEDAW); the African Charter on Human and People's Rights; the African Agenda 2063; Zimbabwe's 2013 Constitution as well as the emphasis on gender equality and women empowerment enshrined in the UN 2030 Agenda which was adopted by the government of Zimbabwe. Women comprise the bulk of victims of SGBV in Chimanimani district whilst most of the perpetrators are men. This is mainly influenced by the community's patriarchal culture. Men claim to have been licensed by some patriarchal norms and values to perpetuate SGBV targeted against women and girls. It is against this background that this chapter seeks to investigate the problem and how it can be addressed. The chapter proposes the use of the Ndau culture in Chimanimani community as a resource for addressing sexual and gender-based violence given the low acceptance of the laws and policies that were put in place to address the problem. The authors are also cognisant of the fact that religion is regarded as a major factor that promotes SGBV against women, given the patriarchal nature of almost all religions (Mapuranga 2010). Hence, the chapter interrogates some beliefs and practices found in religions which act as drivers of SGBV.

The Shona people constitute the majority of the Zimbabwean community. There are many ethnic tribes among the Shona which include the Ndau, Karanga, Zezuru, Manyika and Korekore *inter-alia*. In this chapter, we make reference to the Ndau, specifically the Ndau of Chimanimani rural community. Chimanimani is located in Manicaland province in Eastern Zimbabwe. It is to the South-East of the provincial capital city, Mutare. The community is a male dominated patrilineal society. Being in the male dominated spaces, women suffer oppression at the hands of men. As is the case in most patriarchal societies, some men take advantage of their dominance and authority to abuse women. Abuse is caused by a plethora of factors which include unequal power relations, economic dependence and patriarchy among others. The power of religion should not be underestimated. It has the capacity to command, manipulate as well as to destroy. The Shona traditional religion of the Ndau in Chimanimani has responded to the challenge of SGBV in a number of ways. This is the task of this chapter. The chapter also contends that though Shona traditional religion has had negative effects in light of SBGV, the same religion has positive resources that can curb the prevalence of SGBV. We therefore argue that making use of its indigenous cultural resources could be helpful in fighting against SGBV.

In Zimbabwe, the problem of SGBV has and continues to be addressed by implementing laws, conducting workshops, seminars and the like. These have proved to be ineffective in eradicating the challenge. Religion is one of the root causes of SGBV, yet solutions offered to end the problem do not consider religious insights. Given how religion is one of the drivers of SBGV, there is need to investigate how religion can be used to address the problem which it causes (SGBV). The chapter argues that Acts such as the Domestic Violence Act [Chapter 5:16] have not yielded the desired results as evidenced by the alarming and unprecedented increase in cases of SGBV. In spite of these efforts, the problem remains unaddressed. Thus, there is need to explore other ways of dealing with SGBV. There is need for indigenous solutions to address SGBV within the diverse Shona indigenous society such as Chimanimani community. ATR has and continues to be viewed negatively. In concurrence with other African feminist scholars such as Phiri and Nadar (2006) who proffer that African culture contains numerous life-giving cultural practices and values that can be gleaned in order to alleviate certain oppressions, our chapter seeks to investigate the positive elements within the Ndau culture that can be used to curb SGBV. The chapter is significant in that it aims at identifying locally available indigenous resources which can be used to curtail the problem of SGBV which is rampant in Chimanimani rural community. As such, the chapter examines possibilities of tapping into some African indigenous cultural traditions and practices as vital resources for curbing SBGV. Scholars such as Chitando (2015) and Mapuranga (2013) have researched on the causes of gender based violence and how African religion promotes violence against women. In fighting SGBV, scholars such as Katembo (2015) proposed the use of public campaigns, workshops and seminars as ways of addressing SGBV. This chapter however, takes the discourse further by proposing different indigenous solutions in a bid to fight against SGBV. Focusing on the positive and life-enhancing traditions, the chapter investigates how the Ndau traditional beliefs and practices can be harnessed and utilised positively to fight SGBV. This is in sync with other African feminist scholars who have also been discussing possible ways of engaging African culture to glean positive values (see Oduyoye 1995; Mananzan and Oduyoye 1996; Dube 2002 and Njoroge 2006).

Pursuing the same thrust with the foregoing discussions started by fellow African feminist scholars, our chapter also aims at deconstructing traditional stereotypes that deem African religious beliefs and practices as always harmful and oppressive to women. Whilst acknowledging that some elements of abuse can be encountered in ATR, our focus herein is to foreground the fact that ATR is not always bad news for women.

The chapter is divided into three parts. The first part analyses the major causes of SGBV. The second part discusses how Shona traditional religion promotes GBV. Focusing on the Ndau people of Chimanimani community, it analyses indigenous cultural resources such as myths, proverbs, idioms and taboos of the Shona as well as other beliefs and practices that promote GBV. Contrary to the second part, the third part investigates those beliefs, practices, values and norms of the Ndau people of Chimanimani that challenge SGBV. The major thrust of this chapter is to demonstrate how ATR can be used as a panacea for curbing SGBV regardless of how it has been abused to perpetuate the same.

Methodology and Theoretical Framework

Steeped in the African feminist approach, with a special focus on the work done by African feminist theologians, the chapter beams a spotlight on the Ndau indigenous cultural resources. It proposes how some of the positive values can be tapped into towards solving the problem of SGBV. As noted by Mohanty (1991: 333-334) "African feminism lives through narratives of women who have chosen to call themselves African feminists." The African feminist conceptual framework places African women at the centre stage of proactively transforming all sectors of life, not only for their benefit but for the benefit of all (Oduyoye 1994; Dube 2002). Since this is a case study of the Ndau people in Chimanimani rural community, the discussion draws insights from the interviews conducted with twenty-five women and ten men in Chimanimani community. The age groups interviewed ranged between 18 and 65 years. In light of the fact that women constitute the bulk of those who are on the receiving end of SGBV, in our study sample, we deliberately selected more females than male study participants so as to provide a platform for women to vocalise their experiences. This resonates with the African proverb which goes, "Until the lion learns to talk, the hunter will always tell the story." It also echoes the views restated by African women theologians who contend that "[we] have come to realize that as long as men and foreign researchers remain the authorities on culture, rituals, and religion, African women will continue to be spoken of as if they were dead" (Oduyoye and Kanyoro 1992:1).

In adopting the African feminist approach, we resonate with Desiree Lewis (2008: 77-79) who defines African feminists as a group of African women scholars "who share intellectual commitment to critique traditional gender norms and imperialism. [An] important part of this is also a shared focus to create continental identity that is moulded by the historical relations of subordination." In the same light, our use of the African feminist approach avers with Arnfred (2001:2) who propounds for this theory against the background that "the ways of thinking and analysing in western feminism may have been done in ways and from vantage points that are biased and uninformed about women's real experiences in Africa." The same point is reiterated in a report produced at a historical conference convened by the third African feminist forum in 2010. The delegates at this conference concluded that:

> [The] African feminist theory has also been influenced by the socio-economic realities of the African continent and its historical marginalization and exclusion. This theory therefore recognizes the influence of factors such as race, colonialism, imperialism, religion, ethnicity, culture, class and globalization on African women's experiences. It follows that it considers the multiple and intersecting layers of marginalization that African women face (Nkutu 2010: 8).

Our discussion in this chapter finds resonance with the above excerpt because we are paying particular attention to how the religio-cultural values of the Ndau women have shaped their experiences of SGBV. As such, we propose that the different layers of marginalization experienced by the Ndau women in Chimanimani can be effectively addressed by utilizing the positive and life-affirming values within their culture to interrogate their vulnerability to SGBV.

Causes of gender based violence

There are a number of elements that cause sexual and gender based violence. Although both men and women experience gender based violence, arguably, the latter suffer more. This status-quo is a result of four main factors, that is, unequal power relations that exist between men and women, teachings in religions and culture, patriarchal ideologies and gender based economic inequalities. Most causes of gender based violence are therefore embedded in these factors.

a) Unequal power relations

According to Jewkes (2002), violence is a product of inequality. Whenever there are power imbalances, oppression is bound to occur. Those with more power take advantage of their power to oppress or abuse the powerless party. The oppression that comes with unequal power relations can also be witnessed between men and women. Sexual and gender based violence is rooted in unequal power relations between men and women. The reality is that violence against women and girls is a result of the inherent power disparities between males and females. Because of these unequal power dynamics, women have been placed in a subordinate position, with men dominating them. Such power inequalities make women vulnerable to abuse and gender based violence.

Unequal power relations is one of the main tenets of patriarchy. It is from such unequal power relations that men subjugate and abuse women. Men thus take advantage of such patriarchal privilege to oppress women. Katembo (2015) notes that patriarchy causes gender based violence because of the myopic perspective that men are natural leaders of social units hence, they ought to control and dominate. This was also revealed in an interview with Chamwapiwa (pseudonym)[3], a middle aged woman from Chimanimani. She shared the following:

A common example of physical violence is wife battering which is usually inflicted if the husband feels the need to 'discipline' his wife. Most cases of violence have to do with men saying that women disrespect them by failing to recognise their positions as heads of the families. The wife can also be battered if the husband feels that she

---

[3] In order to safeguard the study participants' confidentiality, all the interviewees cited in this chapter are identified with pseudonyms

is not a good cook. One can also be physically abused if the husband suspects that his wife is having an affair.

Violence thus, becomes a sign of power. It must be noted that such authority and power stems from patriarchal socialisation that the man is the dominant figure in the home.

Another fecund ground for SGBV is on the marital bed. The power differences hinder especially married women from having a say on how and when sex is done. Even if they know or suspect that their husband has been unfaithful, they cannot propose for or insist on safer sex. Culturally, women have no right over their sexual life. It is men who control their sexuality. Some women are raped in matrimony because men claim to have authority over their wives' bodies. Despite being oppressed, sometimes women endure in these types of marriages because of the socialisation they receive. In a Shona traditional setup, being married comes with status. It gives one dignity. Unmarried women (who would have passed a marriageable age of 20 or 25 years) and single mothers are stereotyped as women of loose morals. It is such stereotyping that makes most women to endure violence in their marriages. Another problem is to do with how the family members may put the blame on the woman in cases of violence. Katembo thus observes that,

In the Zimbabwean environment, a woman suffers double violence from the husband and from family members when she tries to escape. They are commonly blamed for the violence they receive and there is a strong family and social pressure for women to remain in relationships no matter how abusive (Katembo 2015:30).

It is even more heart-wrenching to note that patriarchy co-opts those it oppresses such that women end up subtly endorsing certain acts of SGBV. For instance, when a woman is oppressed, her paternal aunt (tete) who is the adviser in the Shona traditional set up can sometimes blame the victim by accusing her of certain actions/inaction as the cause of the abuse. Such is the power of patriarchy to make those it oppresses identify with it. The paternal aunt thus, becomes an agent of patriarchy who sometimes sides with patriarchal ideas that oppress women. There is therefore need to do away with the culture that justifies male violence. With the conviction that unequal power relations that patriarchy creates cause SGBV, there is need to transform the mind-set of men to regard women as equal beings, thus, doing away with the culture of violence. Equally important is the need for empowering women to develop a firm

251

sense of self-worth and affirmation so that they will be able to stand in solidarity to resist SGBV.

b) Religion

The portrayal of women tends to vary from religion to religion, given the differences in beliefs and practices across religions. However, there has been a thread of sameness across almost all religions of the world. Religions in terms of gender relations, are mostly characterised by male dominance and female subordination, which are some of the major tenets of patriarchy. This male dominance is a prime obstacle for women's advancement and development. This therefore tallies with Skinner and Ruether's assertion that religions are deeply entrenched in sexism and do not view women as equal to men (Skinner and Ruether, 2006). Similarly, Mbiti (1990) and Oduyoye (1995) reiterate the fact that the dichotomy between religion and the secular is blurred in African communities. The power of religion should therefore not be overlooked as religion has the power to control how people ought to behave. Because of its scared nature, whatever is proffered by religion is treated with reverence. Due to the patriarchal background, most religious beliefs, practices, norms and values are androcentric. This elevates men into a dominant position whilst pushing women to a lower pedestal, consequently exposing women to the vulnerability of suffering oppression at the hands of men.

African traditional religion which is the core religion under investigation, reinforces SGBV. Although it does not have written sacred texts, its beliefs and practices that circulate orally have elements of male dominance and they tend to endorse SGBV. There is a plethora of beliefs in Shona traditional religion that are oppressive to women, for instance, *kugara nhaka* (wife inheritance) (Wangulu 2011). This religious practice promotes sexual violence given that some women are inherited against their will. Apart from being oppressive, they pose as a challenge in the era of HIV and AIDS. A myriad of other beliefs and practices that portray how religion is a cause of SGBV will be detailed in the ensuing section. Suffice to note at this point is the fact that religion with its patriarchal assumptions is a cause of sexual and gender based violence. Besides, male religious leaders sometimes take advantage of patriarchal authority to abuse women.

c) Culture

Culture is regarded as a heritage which is passed on from generation to generation. It is viewed as a way of life that shapes human behaviour and action (Smith 2001). From these definitions of culture, one can appreciate how culture is related to religion. It is difficult to separate religion and culture given how the two are intertwined. Religious traits are in a people's culture and cultural traits can also be found in a people's religion. It therefore becomes difficult to separate African Traditional Religion from the African culture (Mbiti 1990). In this chapter, African culture and African religion are regarded as a single entity.

Just like religion, culture is another factor which provides a launch pad for incidences of SGBV in Zimbabwe. Galtung (1990) as quoted by Katembo posits that, "culture preaches, teaches, admonishes, edges on and dulls us into seeing exploitation and repression as normal and natural or not seeing it at all" (Katembo 2015:32). Culture governs how individuals ought to behave and because of the patriarchal nature of the Shona culture, it works towards subjugating women and often times, culture justifies women's oppression. There are a number of Shona cultural practices that work towards female oppression, thereby causing SGBV. These include *kuripa ngozi* (appeasing avenging spirits), *kugara nhaka* (wife inheritance), *chigadzamapfihwa* (sororate marriage) *inter-alia*. Apart from sexual violence, Shona cultural beliefs also promote physical violence against women. With reference to wife battering, Katembo further postulates that African culture accepts violence against women as a form of correctional measure that men can do without hesitation (Katembo 2015). Such a belief promotes a culture of violence in men. Another devastating element of culture is how it teaches women to endure male violence. Gender based violence is thus normalised as men's behaviour. This shows that instead of using its power to challenge SGBV, culture is used in promoting and reinforcing violence against women. There is therefore need to address the harmful culture that promotes gender based violence by socialising young boys and men to embrace positive and transformative masculinities so that they will not inflict violence towards their female counterparts. Despite being used to cause, promote and perpetuate violence, if interpreted well, culture can work as a mechanism that curbs sexual and gender based violence. Culture has been used to satisfy patriarchal selfish needs, thereby oppressing women. There is therefore, need to harness the good elements in culture that promote a gender-violent free environment.

d) Lack of economic independence

Economic dependence is another factor that can be blamed as a cause of gender based violence. Some men take advantage of how women economically depend on them to abuse them. In general, the dependency syndrome promotes inequality. It could be between nations or between people. From a dependency theorist perspective, men being the core, create reasons for women to depend on them. Women who do not have access to resources as well as capital depend on men in the household as breadwinners. As dependency is socially constructed to benefit those who are at the centre, dependency was socially constructed to benefit patriarchy (men). It is against this background of being dependent on men that women face violence. Just as colonisers destroyed and weakened all forms of power which existed in colonies as the aim was to create a vulnerable people who could easily accept aid, some men deprive women access to anything that has the potential to empower them to the point of escaping from the cycle of being dependent on men (Matsa 2012). Hence, some Shona men are not happy to be in a relationship with a woman who can sustain herself through business, education and other income generating avenues.

Although some women who are economically independent face oppression, cases of abuse and violence are usually rampant among economically dependent women. Because of such dependence, they continue to live with violent partners as these men provide for their livelihoods. It is this dependency syndrome that makes women vulnerable to physical, sexual as well as emotional abuse. Some men take advantage of their economic muscle over women to control and oppress them. In a bid to curb and reduce cases of violence, there is need for women to be proactive so as to be self-reliant.

The foregoing section has explored the general causes of gender based violence within African traditional communities, Chimanimani rural district to be particular. It has shown that no one factor can be singled out as the cause of sexual and gender based violence; but a combination of various factors. There is therefore need to develop a culture of non-violence in men in a bid to curb SGBV. The next section examines the Ndau people's indigenous beliefs, practices and norms that promote sexual and gender based violence so as to gain

254

insights on how best the same culture can work as a tool for fighting against the same.

It can therefore be concluded that some cultural practices and beliefs have devastating effects on women in the context of SGBV. Though culture is changing, cases of wife inheritance, *chigadzamapfihwa*, *kuzvarira*, wife battering, *chiramu* (sanctioned teasing) and *kuripa ngozi* (appeasing the avenging spirits) are still practiced. The extent is however not as rampant as before. Patriarchy stands out as the major vehicle which is used to perpetuate women's oppression. Patriarchy has proved to be too stubborn to be easily mitigated against. Be that as it may, it must be appreciated that despite this, the Ndau culture is not always abusive to women. Culture is not always bad news to women. The next section therefore, explores the positive elements of the Ndau culture and it analyses how the use of these positive elements could help in redressing the prevalence of SGBV.

Fighting from within: Ndau culture and SGBV

The preceding section examined the Ndau cultural beliefs and practices which pose a challenge in the context of SGBV. It demonstrated that although some of the harmful practices are being abandoned with changes in culture and some legal provisions, patriarchy has proved to be too powerful to be challenged. This section, therefore, explores the positive factors that can be used to fight against SGBV. A cultural approach shall be appropriated, hence the section looks into the Ndau beliefs and practices, norms and values that give women a special status in the society.

Positive Status of the Ndau women

Although the previous section deliberated on the harmful cultural practices that translate to violence against women, it is also important to acknowledge that the Ndau culture is not always bad news to women. Women occupy a special status in the Ndau worldview. They are respected as mothers, sisters and wives. Such special status of women can be derived in proverbs, myths, idioms, metaphors, similes as well as taboos and avoidances of the Shona people. According to Bourdillon (1987), there is a common misconception that women had little or no status in traditional African societies. However, such is not the case, women are respected and revered in the African society. The same point was reiterated by one of the study participants, Mbuya Chidoko who said, *"Kana dai arume achishungurudza vakadzi, chianhu chedu pachiNdau chinokoshesa akadzi."* (Although men abuse women, our Ndau culture respects women) (Mbuya Chidoko, interview: 2019).

Shona Proverbs fighting sexual and gender-based violence

Proverbs are a fountain of knowledge. As such Africans, in this case the Ndau of Chimanimani use proverbs to address life situations. Given the oral form of the Shona tradition, proverbs work as manual guides that govern people. Taringa (2014:396) opines that, "Proverbs form part of traditional Shona philosophy and they are still part of Shona curriculum which educates the nation on the virtues and vices of society." Below are some of the proverbs that portray the special status of women in a Shona cultural set up.

●*Musha mukadzi* which literally means the woman is the pillar of the home is one Shona proverb that shows their special status in a Shona setup. Bourdillon noted that women have more influence in the homestead (Bourdillon, 1987). For Taringa (2014), the understanding of the proverb *musha mukadzi* is that a home cannot be whole without a woman or a wife. Such understanding gives women a special status in the society. This proverb is quite similar to *Mukadzi mutsigo wemusha* which means that the woman is regarded as the support base of the village/homestead (Gelfald 1973). As such, proverbs can act as tools to challenge SGBV. An affirmation of women's invaluable role by men can lead to a respectful and gender violent free society. As one of the male study participants, Sekuru Purasi aptly put it,

●*Munhu wemukadzi akakosha pamuzi. Kuti muzi umire, mukadzi. Kuti pamuzi panangisike, mukadzi. Kutamika kwemunhu wemukadzi, musha unoparara. Saka adoko anofanira kufundiswa aziye kukosha kwemunhu wemukadzi.* (A woman is an important figure in the home. For a home to be a good home, it is because of a woman. The absence of a woman in the home brings disorder. For that reason, men, especially the young ones ought to be taught to appreciate the importance of women).

The above remarks from an elderly Ndau man clearly gives insights of how the Ndau culture is highly appreciative and respectful of women.

256

Apart from the above analysed proverbs, there are other proverbs that demonstrate women's worthiness. They include the following:

- *Kusina mai hakuendwi* (A place where the mother is absent is a no go area). This is because mothers are renowned for providing love, care and warmth to the family. One cannot therefore go to a place where one's mother is absent as the above services will not be guaranteed.

- *Nherera inoguta musi wafa mai wayo* (The orphan's last full meal is upon the mother's death). This emanated from the fact that mothers are regarded as nurturers of children. Since it is the mothers who are usually in charge of feeding their families, it therefore follows that the day she dies is the last day the orphan will eat to the full. Thereafter, the orphan's access to food cannot be guaranteed.

- *Nhamo inhamo hayo, mai haaroodzwi* (No matter how poor one is, one cannot give a mother in marriage). This proverb is premised on the backdrop that mothers are sources of life since they are the ones who give birth to children. This is why in Shona culture the Earth/land is personified as a woman because it is also a source of life (nature). The land/Earth is therefore, sometimes referred to as Mother Earth. For this reason, just as the land cannot be sold in Shona culture so one cannot give away their mother, no matter how poor one is.

It is against this backdrop that women gain respect and dignity in society. If men appreciate such cultural status attached to women, they will refrain from physically, sexually, economically and emotionally abusing caregivers, providers, nurturers, sources of life and pillars of the home among many other pivotal roles that women play.

Apart from proverbs, there are other Shona idioms, similes and metaphors that depict the importance of women. Although in their literal sense these expressions make special reference to mothers, they apply to all women. In a traditional set up, every woman is a mother. This stems from the caregiving and nurturing qualities in women. There are common expressions in the Ndau culture such as:

- *Hapana akakosha saamai* (no one is as important as a mother). This echoes the facts raised above, emphasizing that women are the pillars of the home.

- *Kushinga samai* (as brave as a mother). This is because mothers can risk or sacrifice their lives for the sake of their children because of their love and care for them.

Kunaka moyo saamai (as good hearted as a mother). This stems from the backdrop that a mother's love and care for her children is unconditional. Even when the child messes up, the mother does not withhold her love and care for him/her.

These are some of the traits that are found in women. Hence, women are vital and by virtue of these traits, they gain respect in society. An analysis of the above demonstrates how the Shona culture respects and reveres women (despite being patriarchal in nature). In fighting SGBV among the Ndau people of Chimanimani, there is need for continual celebration of such positive status of women from a cultural perspective. This can be of significant importance in challenging SGBV given how the Ndau are culture bound.

Mhiko nezviera-era (taboos and avoidances) in fighting SGBV

Mhiko nezviera-era are Shona avoidance rules that govern human behaviour in a Shona traditional cultural setup. Dodo (2012) contends that taboos are societal beliefs that are strongly adhered by the Africans. Taboos regulate human life and control behaviour. In the same vein, Masaka and Chemhuru note that, "taboos provide moral sanctions that help in shaping a person's '*unhu*'" (Masaka and Chemhuru, 2011:135). Taboos prevent bad habits and enhance social order. Hence, taboos can be taken as valuable indigenous cultural resources that can be utilized in fighting against SGBV. By ensuring proper behaviour, taboos can be appropriated to come up with a gender violent free society.

Tatira (2014) argues that not all Shona beliefs are useful to the present society. However, he acknowledges that there are some beliefs and values that continue to be helpful. These beliefs and values can still be appropriated in contemporary Shona society to address societal problems. These cultural beliefs have a profound influence in the lives of the Shona, for that reason, beliefs (taboos) command authority. Shona cultural beliefs derive their authority from the supernatural realm and this makes them effective in controlling human behaviour. For instance, there is a strong belief that breaching the taboos triggers spiritual punishment (Tatira 2014:106). Hence, the Shona people strive to live by the traditional prescriptions to avoid angering the spirits.

As noted by Masaka and Chemhuru (2011), there are taboos that encourage good behaviour, some promote good health while others preserve the environment. It is these indigenous Ndau cultural beliefs that encourage good behaviour in terms of relating with women that this chapter seeks to explore. The Ndau of Chimanimani have such taboos that protect women, a use of these could be of great significance in mitigating against SGBV. The Shona people have a unique way of transmitting social values (Tatira 2014:146). They therefore become key in instilling good values. They prohibit a behaviour and give reasons for such prohibition. There are a number of taboos that can be used to prohibit SGBV. These include:

Ukachaya mai unotanda botso (if you beat up your mother, you will become a ritual beggar). An analysis of this taboo demonstrates how Shona beliefs revere mothers and protect women from physical violence. Dodo and others submit that if one assaults his/her mother, they will face serious misfortune (Dodo et al 2012). It is believed that maternal spirits are more ruthless than the maternal spirits when grieved. There is a common saying that *mudzimu wamai unouraya asi wababa unorwadza chete* (the mother's ancestral spirits can punish by killing the offender but the father's only torments) (Tatira 2014). Of interest to note is that there are no taboos relating to one's father. In an interview with Mbuya Ndiadzo, she explained that: "*baba havana ngozi asi mai ngekuti mutorwa*" (ill-treating one's father does not attract avenging spirits but ill-treating one's mother does because the mother is regarded as a stranger) (Mbuya Ndiadzo, interview, 2019). Tatira's observation of the absence of taboos that relate to beating or disrespecting the father is that probably fathers, (because of patriarchal privileges and dominance) can employ other strategies to discipline the child (Tatira 2000). From this analysis, one can conclude that the Shona culture always instils values to protect the vulnerable section of society. This is clear from the proverbs, riddles and taboos that protect the marginalised in society, for instance, persons living with disabilities and the elderly are protected by social values such as these.

Apart from the taboos that protect women as indicated above, some taboos protect women as wives. For example, according to Tatira (2014), the Shona believe that if one beats up his wife, it attracts *ngozi* (avenging spirits). Mbuya Musoni, further intimated that, "*Patsika dzedu kuchaya mukadzi hakutendedzwi, zvinokonzera ngozi.*" (In our culture, we believe that wife battering attracts avenging spirits). If such cultural beliefs are harnessed and utilised, they could go a long way in fighting the problem of physical violence against women. On the same note, Sekuru Sikochi pointed out that:

259

Madzimambo haatendedzi zvekuti mukadzi achaiwe. Mwamuna akachaya mukadzi, nyaya ikaenda dzimbabwe, unotongerwa kuti uripe. Dzimwe nguwa unonzi uripe mwombe dzimwe nguwa mbudzi nekuti indaa yaanonga atanga neadzimu ekumusha kwake (Chiefs do not permit wife battering. If the husband is reported to the chief's court for beating up his wife, normally, he will be asked to pay a fine to compensate the wife. The fine can be a cow or a goat because wife battering is regarded as a crime against her ancestral spirits).

Dodo also echoes the same sentiments, noting that the Shona uphold the belief that if a man beats up his wife, it will result in one being afflicted by the ancestral spirits of the wife's clan and he may never be able to marry again. As a corrective measure, the husband will be required to pay huge sums of cattle to the wife's family. This is informed by the entrenched belief that this kind of crime is not a violation of the state rules, but a disruption of the community's spiritual harmony (Dodo 2012).

The Ndau also have incest related taboos. If appropriated in the context of SGBV, these taboos can protect women and girls from sexual violence. Incest can be defined as a sexual relationship between relatives. Manyonganise and Museka (2010) explain how incest results in child sexual abuse whereby the main victims of incestuous child abuse are girls because of the gender inequalities within the Shona society. The media, both electronic and print is also awash with news alluding to the same. For instance, the Sunday Mail of 5 July 2020 had the following headline, *Disturbing spike in fathers abusing children.* According to this news item, this was because of lockdown restrictions which the government put in place to curtail the spread of Covid-19 (the novel coronavirus). Although this was referring to Zimbabwe in general, the same is also obtaining in Chimanimani. However, the situation in Chimanimani is further compounded by the fact that the lockdown restrictions came at a time when the community was already reeling under the aftermath of the Cyclone Idai disaster. By the time this chapter was written (March 2021), quite a number of families in Chimanimani were still living in temporary shelters (one roomed tents) which were provided to them by the humanitarian agencies such as UNICEF because their homes were swept away by the Cyclone Idai floods in March 2019. Such living conditions expose young women and girls to the vulnerability of SGBV, including incestuous relationships.

Be that as it may, it has to be borne in mind that Shona social values are against incest and it is strictly forbidden. The Shona condemn *makunakuna* (incest) as a repugnant action which attracts severe punishment from the ancestors. Taboos associated with incest demonstrate how the Shona indigenous values abhor SGBV by forbidding incest in which case the girl child is the most vulnerable. The Shona culture naturally protects the girl child. The above is the general perception of incest taboos in Shona societies. On the same note, the Ndau generally confirmed that incestuous relationships are rare, given how they anger the ancestors who can punish the living by causing calamities such as drought. Having discussed how social values such as proverbs, metaphors and taboos can be useful tools in fighting against SGBV, the ensuing section focusses on Shona beliefs that can be utilised in mitigating against SGBV. The section presents reconstructed Shona cultural beliefs that are positive to women in the face of SGBV.

c) Reconstructed Shona Cultural beliefs

As demonstrated above, there are Shona cultural practices that are harmful to women in the light of SGBV. Wife inheritance, appeasing avenging spirits, *chimutsamapfihwa* and *kuzvarira* marriages are some of the most harmful cultural practices that promote SGBV and pose a challenge in the era of HIV and AIDS. However, the contemporary Shona culture is making efforts to deconstruct harmful cultural behaviour and to reconstruct positive cultural values.

i) *Sarapavana* (caretaker/guardian overseer) concept

"Culture is dynamic and adaptive, cultural customs, beliefs and practices are not static but they change over time" (Williams and Happer, 2015:41). As society progresses, new cultures dominate. Although the concept of *sarapavana* has always been in existence, it has become more profound in the contemporary society. The *sarapavana* concept seeks to replace harmful practices such as *kugara nhaka* (wife inheritance). The *sarapavana* is a caretaker or an overseer who cares for the wife and children of the deceased. The traditional Shona culture does not allow room for social orphans. Thus, upon the death of biological parents, a social parent is appointed to take care of them. The rationale behind this is to ensure that the children have a helper or a guardian (Chiweshe 2015). The practice should be celebrated as positive and redemptive in light of SGBV. Women have been abused sexually through widow inheritance and *chigadzamapfihwa* as discussed earlier in the chapter. However, the caretaker practice has gained traction and it has liberated women given that the

261

caretaker (*sarapavana*) does not have sexual rights. In light of the foregoing, it can be argued that the Shona culture has some aspects that are gender sensitive and liberative to women, these practices play a formidable role in protecting women from SGBV. Thus, a utilization of these positive cultural practices is instrumental in addressing the challenge of SGBV from a cultural perspective.

ii) *Kuzvarira* (Credit/Arranged marriages)

As has been explained above, this is a form of marriage where the poor father gives a young or unborn girl in marriage to a rich man in exchange for food, a clear demonstration of violence against the girl child. While the idea of borrowing food is noble, it is the repayment method which is problematic in the context of SGBV that is, marrying off an innocent young girl without her consent. Research however, revealed that there are some Shona cultural practices which can be appropriated in this respect. The Shona have what they call *Kandiro enda, kandiro dzoka* (if you borrow a plate full, you pay back a plate full). This means a debtor can only pay back what he/she borrowed has borrowed from the creditor. For example, if you borrow money, you pay back with money, if you borrow a cow, you pay back with a cow. If this cultural rule is applied in the case of credit marriages, it therefore, means the poor girl's father would have to pay back the rich man in form of food, instead of marrying off his daughter. Normally, this food would be in form of maize. As Mbuya Ndiadzo put it:

> *Mazuwa ano anhu aakuti akakwereta magwere esadza ngenzara, haacaharipi ngekuroodza mwanasikana. Unotozopetudzawo maagwere* (These days, if a person borrows maize to cook *sadza* (thick corn meal porridge) because of starvation, he no longer pays by marrying off his daughter. Instead, he pays back in form of maize) (Mbuya Ndiadzo, interview: 2019).

Clearly, an appropriation of such positive cultural aspects of the Shona culture would go a long way in fighting against SGBV.

iii) *Ngozi* (Restitution)

As noted by Shoko and Chiwara (2015), *mushonga wengozi kuripa* (the best solution in dealing with an avenging spirit is through restitution). It is a social reality among the Shona that whenever someone committed a crime which invokes the *ngozi* spirit, there will be need for compensation. For that reason, the *kuripa ngozi* practice should be continued as it is a deterrent to would-be murderers. The problem however, arises when ways of paying restitution violate women's rights and freedom. Instead of continuing with the harmful cultural practice whereby restitution for the *ngozi* spirit entails paying large sums of cattle and a virgin girl, it would be helpful to embrace the alternative forms of restitution within the Ndau culture, methods that do not entail using the girl child as part of the compensation paid. As indicated above, Sekuru Sikochi highlighted that, *"Pakuripa ngozi, pakasaiswa mwanasikana panoiswa mombe, mhou nemwana wayo kuti zvimiririre mwanasikana"* (When compensating avenging spirits, if a virgin girl is not provided, a cow and its calf can be given to stand in for the virgin girl) (Sekuru Sikochi, interview: 2020). Adopting this method would be an important adjustment which preserves the noble practice of paying compensation to the aggrieved spirit whilst protecting women from being used as sacrificial lambs. In so doing, the Ndau of Chimanimani will be maintaining their cultural practice of *kuripa ngozi* in a more gender sensitive manner. Deconstructing cultural aspects which are toxic and which expose women to violence is celebrated as a positive move towards fighting against SGBV. The fight against SGBV does not call for total loss of a people's culture, but a deconstruction of harmful elements.

Conclusion

This chapter has laid bare the fact that although the Ndau culture of Chimanimani community has beliefs and practices which are harmful in light of SGBV, it must be appreciated that the Ndau culture is not always bad news to women. It has also foregrounded the fact that regardless of its patriarchal nature, the culture, if well analysed, can be harnessed and embraced and it can make great strides in curbing SGBV. It is our contention that through the use of indigenous cultural resources such as taboos, proverbs and idioms, the challenge of SGBV can be addressed. Indigenous cultural resources should play a pivotal role in dealing with violence against women given how laws and policies that were put in place have failed to yield meaningful results. Hence, we conclude by reiterating that sexual and gender based violence must be fought from within, i.e., making use of African resources to solve African problems arising in an African setup.

References

Arnfred, S. (2001). "Simone de Beauvoir in Africa: Woman = the Second Sex? Issues of African Feminist Thought," in *JENDA - A Journal of Culture and African Women's Studies* 2: 1.

Bhasin, K. (1993). *What is Patriarchy?* Gender and Environment, New Delhi: University of Delhi.

Bourdillon, M.F.C. (1987). *The Shona Peoples: an ethnography of the contemporary Shona with reference to their religion.* Gweru: Mambo Press.

Chitakure, J. (2016). *Shona Women in Zimbabwe-A Purchased People?* Wipf and Stock

Chitando, E. (2015). "Do not tell the person carrying you that s/he stinks: reflections in *ubuntu* and masculinities in the context of sexual and Gender Based Violence and HIV," E. Mouton *et al* eds. *Living with Dignity: African Perspectives on Gender Equality*, Cape Town: SUN MEDIA.

Chiweshe, K. (2015). "Reproducing patriarchy on resettled land" C. Archambault, *etal* eds. *Global Trends in Land Tenure Reforms: Gender Impacts.* London: Routledge.

Dodo, O. (2021). "The socio-recreational dispute resolution values of native alcoholic beers in Chikomba District," *African Journal of Social Sciences.* Vol.2 (2) 415-423.

Domestic Violence Act [Chapter 5:16] 2007.

Dube, Musa. (2002). "Postcoloniality, Feminist Spaces, and Religion." In Donaldson, L. E and Pui-lan, K. eds. *Postcolonialism, Feminism, and Religious Discourse,* New York, London: Routledge.

Gelfand, M. (1973). *The Genuine Shona: Survival of African Culture.* Gweru: Mambo Press.

Gwandure, C. (2012). "Sexual desire and expression among girls in traditional Shona context" *Anthropologist,* 14 (5) 415- 423.

Jewkes, R. (2002). "Intimate partner violence: causes and prevention." *The Lancet,* Vol. 395 (1) 1423-1429.

Katembo, A. (2015). "Reducing cases of Gender Based Violence in Mashonaland Central Province: Zimbabwe," Unpublished MA dissertation. .

Klinken, V.K. (2013). *Transforming Masculinities in African Christianity: Gender Controversies in times of AIDS,* London: Ashgate Publishing Ltd.

Lewis, D. (2008). "Discursive Challenges for African Feminisms." *QUEST: An African Journal of Philosophy / Revue Africaine de Philosophie* 20, 77-96.

Mananzan, M.J. and Oduyoye, M.A., *et.al.* (Eds.) (1996). *Women Resisting Violence: Spirituality for Life.* Maryknoll, New York: Orbis Books

Manyonganise, M. and Museka, J. (2010). "Incestuous Child Sexual Abuse in Shona Society: Implications on the educational achievements of the girl child," *Zimbabwe Journal of Educational Research* Vol. 22(2) 226-241.

Mapuranga T.P. (2013). "Tozeza Baba: gender based violence in Oliver Mtukudzi's Music." *Journal of Music Research.* 9(1) 58-70.

Mapuranga, T.P. (2010). "A Phenomenological Investigation into the effects of Traditional beliefs and practices on women and HIV and AIDS, with specific reference to Chipinge District, Zimbabwe." PhD Thesis. University of Zimbabwe.

Masaka, D. and Chemhuru, M. (2011). "Moral Dimensions of Shona Taboos (Zviera)." *Journal of Sustainable Development in Africa.*13 (3): 132-148.

Matsa, W. (2012). "Who is dependent, 3rd or 1st World, Women or Men? Salient features of Dependency and Interdependency," *Journal of Sustainable Development in Africa.* 14(2) 202-215.

Mbiti, J. S. (1990). *African Religions and Philosophy.* Oxford: Heinemann Educational Publishers.

Mohanty, C. T. (1991). "Under Western Eyes: Feminist Scholarship and Colonial Discourses". In *Third World Women and the Politics of Feminism*, (ed) Mohanty, Chandra Talpade, Ann Russo, and Lourdes Torres. Indianapolis: Indiana University Press.

Mutsvairo, S. *etal* 1996. *Introduction to Shona Culture.* Eiffel Flats: Juta Zimbabwe Pvt Ltd.

Njoroge N. (2006). "Let's Celebrate the Power of Naming" in Phiri I.A and Nadar S (eds) *Women, Religion and Health: Essays in Honour of Mercy Amba Ewudziwa Oduyoye,* Orbis Books: Maryknoll, New York, pp59-74

Nkutu, A. (2010). The 3rd African Feminist Forum Conference Report, 2010 http://awdflibrary.org:8080/xmlui/handle/123456789/82 (Accessed 15 February 2021)

Nyoni, C. (2008). "Socio-cultural factors and practices that impede upon behavioural change of Zimbabwe Women in the era of

HIV and AIDS," Unpublished PhD thesis, KwaZulu Natal: South Africa.

Oduyoye, M.A. and Kanyoro, Musimbi R. A, (1992). (Eds.) *The Will to Arise: Women, Tradition, and the Church in Africa*. Maryknoll, New York: Orbis Books.

Oduyoye, M.A., (1994). 'Feminist theology in an African perspective', in R. Gibellini (ed.), *Paths of African theology*, pp. 166–181, SCM Press, London.

Oduyoye, M.A. (1995). *Daughters of Anowa: African Women and Patriarchy*, New York: Orbis Books.

Phiri, I.A. and Nadar, S. (2006) "What's in a Name? - Forging A Theological Framework for African Women's Theologies," *Journal of Constructive Theology*, 12 (2), 5-24

Shoko, T. and Chiwara, A. (2015). "Mukondombera: HIV/AIDS and Shona Traditional Religion in Zimbabwe" *Journal for the study of Religion in Africa and its Diaspora*, 1(1) 5-17.

Skinner, S. and Ruether, R. (2006). *Encyclopedia of women in religion in North America: Women in North America*. Bloomington: Indiana University Press.

Smith, P. (2001). *Cultural Theory: An Introduction*. New York: John Wiley and Sons.

Taringa, B. (2014). "Implication of the portrayal of women in Shona proverbs for gender sensitive teaching and learning in Chishona" *ZJER*, Vol 26 (3) 395-408.

Tatira, L. (2014). "Shona belief systems: finding relevancy for a new generation." *Journal of Pan African Studies*. Vol. 6(8) 106-118.

Walby, S. (1989). "Forms and Degrees of Patriarchy," S. Jackson ed. *Women's Studies: A reader*. New York: Harvester Wheatsheaf.

Wangulu, E.F. (2011). *Traditional Leaders on the Frontline: Addressing Harmful Cultural Practices to Reduce Gender based Violence and HIV in Southern Africa*. Pretoria: SAFAIDS.

Williams, L.S. and Happer, P.D. (2015). *Understanding Medical Surgical Nursing*, Philadelphia. F.A. Davis.

Zvingowanisei, S. (2018). "Religion and Spirituality: A comparative analysis of marriage in Islam and African Traditional Religion in Zimbabwe" in M. Maddahi (ed) *Spirituality and Religion in the Contemporary World*. Qom: Al-Mustafa International Publication and Translation Centre.

Chapter 14

Bemba *Imbusa* as African Indigenous Knowledge Framework for Life-Giving Marriage

Mutale Mulenga Kaunda

Abstract

This chapter critically engages with the indigenous Bemba premarital teaching *imbusa* for young brides. *Imbusa* are teachings that every young Bemba bride has to go through before marriage. It prepares them for agency in marriage. This chapter demonstrates how Bemba women of Zambia learn, negotiate, and resist certain oppressive views of women. At the centre of this teaching is *banacimbusa* and the young brides. The centrality of *banacimbusa* is highlighted and what kind of teachings are necessary for the marital agency of Bemba women. The study is framed within Nnaemeka's (2003) feminist postcolonial concept of Nego-feminism.

Keywords: Bemba, Imbusa, AIKs, marriage

Introduction

This chapter[4] explores the importance of *imbusa*[5] teaching among the Bemba people and its indigenous preparation of Bemba women for their agency in marriage. Anthropologists[6] and missionaries have been the pioneers on the research regarding *imbusa*, however indigenous Zambians[7] have taken up the research and are *Imbusa* is an African indigenous knowledge instruction which demonstrates

---

[4] This chapter is part of my Master's thesis "A Search for Life-giving Marriage: The *Imbusa* Initiation Rite as a Space for Constructing Wellbeing among Married Bemba Women of Zambia". Master's Thesis University of KwaZulu-Natal, Pietermaritzburg.

[5] *Imbusa* is a Bemba premarital teaching for women. It is taught through songs, proverbs, dance using sacred emblems/visual aids handed down to Bemba brides before the wedding.

[6] For instance, Audrey Richards from the 1930s to 1980s, Thera Rasing around 1090s and 2000s, Naomi Haynes around 2000s.

[7] Christine Mushibwe, Mutale Mulenga Kaunda, Jonathan Kangwa, Lilian Cheelo Siwila, Sylvia Mukuka, Kapambwe Mulenga to mention just a few.

Bemba women's agency in marital issues. Mercy Amba Oduyoye (1995b:11, see also Tamale 2005:9) succinctly maintains that in Africa, ritual practice is intricately linked to practically every aspect of life: marriage, birth, puberty, death, mourning, politics, war, social roles, religion, kinship structures, identity construction and so on. The connection between ritual and the status of women in marriage is one of the more controversial issues which have been discussed by African women theologians (Oduyoye 1995b:134). This chapter explores the various ways in which the *imbusa* marriage ritual can be analysed both as an oppressive and empowering resource. The high regard and perception of marriage as sacred in Africa is what necessitates performance of rituals in which matrilineal Bemba women were perceived as *cibinda wa ng'anda* (head/owner of the house) in pre-colonial Bemba society (Chammah Kaunda 2012:6 see also Kaunda and Kaunda 2016); this is why it was and still is important for women to be instructed by their elder matrikin regarding their life as married women between two weeks to two months before the wedding, (six months in the pre-colonial and colonial era).

Imbusa among the Bemba people is clearly understood to signify one of the rituals that have persisted and is resilient through centuries as a tradition of marriage initiation as Kaunda (2016) and Sylvia Mukuka (2018) have explained. At the core of this elaborate socio-cultural institution is *banacimbusa* (marriage instructors, tutors or bearers of traditional marital teachings). *Banacimbusa's* role is to mentor young women *muntambi ne fishalano* (time-honoured indigenous social values) "in a wide range of sexual matters, including pre-menarche practices, marriage preparation, erotic instruction and reproduction" (Tamale 2005:9). In a sense, the young woman receives instructions on how to relate and live with her in-laws, her sexual agency in marriage and how to relate to her husband among many other teachings. Without receiving *imbusa* instructions, a bride is seen as unfit to handle marriage. The teachings revolve around issues of sexual intercourse in which the woman is taught how to satisfy her husband and get satisfaction from the sexual act. The *imbusa* rite is a strong tool used in the construction of female identities among the Bemba. This chapter is based on interviews with ten Zambian married women who at the time of the interview were living and working in Pietermaritzburg South Africa using convenience sampling.[8] Due to the fact that as a researcher I did not know many Zambian married women who have gone through *imbusa* ritual living in Pietermaritzburg and that most of the ones I was introduced to were very busy women, convenience sampling was inevitable. Convenience sampling selects participants out of their availability with no previous rationale (Durrheim 1999:50). Thus, I was introduced to a number of married Zambian women to whom I verbally presented my research interest; some showed interest and others were not so eager because the teachings are a secret not to be shared with the non-initiated and writing about them would be sharing this rich wisdom with those who may not have received the teaching. Others felt that as a result of becoming Christians, *imbusa* was pagan and they did not wish to engage with pagan issues.

A Brief Overview of *Imbusa*

Imbusa ritual is also known as *ukuombela ng'anda* (ritual performance for a viable home) which follows after *ukucindila icisungu* (dancing for the wonder of initial menstruation) recognized by Bemba people of Zambia (Kaunda 2016: 5; See also Mukuka 2018: 149). Being a matrilineal people, Bemba women owned property, land and so on, this meant that at marriage, a man was the one who moved to his wife's village. In contemporary times, marriage is neo-local as both wife and husband make their homes in a neutral place: neither wife's nor husband's family land. Bemba people practiced matrilocal or uxorilocal marriages prior to the industrialization and the migration from rural to urban areas.

Central to *imbusa* is *banacimbusa* and the bride. *Banacimbusa* is a married woman who received *imbusa* teachings before marriage and has a marriage that is exemplary in her community and has the ability to pass on these teachings as well. After being taught and being married *banacimbusa* continue to mentor the young woman and when they notice the ability to engage and especially teach others, that mentorship is turned into invitations to go and teach, thereby preparing the woman to become *nacimbusa*. Usually, the bride's mother selects a woman she sees capable of instructing her daughter in marital matters (Kaunda 2016: 179). And when the selected woman has done a diligent work, other mothers in the community take note and continue to advise others to have their children

---

[8] This is part of my unpublished Master of Theology thesis in Gender and Religion from the University of KwaZulu-Natal.

instructed by that *nacimbusa*. Some *banacimbusa* are well known that some mothers travel six hours to ask for their assistance. There is no committee that appoints *banacimbusa* to take up positions. The *imbusa* teaching process has three phases, Victor Turner has noted that ritual usually has three phases; separation, liminal and reintegration. In *imbusa* teaching first seclusion where the bride is taught either in her bedroom between 2 weeks to 2 months or in *banacimbusa*'s or paternal aunt's house. Second the liminal phase which is the state of being in between or betwixt; a bride is married and not yet married in this case the teachings qualify her for marriage. Third reintegration back into society, the bride gets back into the community as a married woman. In this period of instructions, a lot is taught, from caring for in-laws, caring for the home, caring for the spouse, keeping marital secrets to marital sex. The sex topic takes up a large portion of the teaching because sex is an important aspect of Bemba marriage. Elsewhere I have explained that

> ...sex is considered a significant element of the cultural fabric among the Bemba, sex education is a life-long learning process which begins in early childhood and continues through life. As early as eight years, girls are encouraged to play with their genitals to get familiar with all their body parts and to facilitate sexual intercourse at a later age. They are taught how to make contractions with their vagina as well as how to elongate their labia minora in groups- giving them a sense of kinship... (Mutale M. Kaunda and Chammah J. Kaunda, 2016: 160).

Imbusa is taught using schematic or naturalistic forms of paintings. Mushibwe (2009: 114), writing on the Tumbuka people of Zambia, affirms that the Bemba speaking people of the Northern part of Zambia use schematic forms of drawings during the initiation ceremonies. The common drawings of pictures and models called the *imbusa*, an artistic array of a variety of symbols, models and drawings using the three colours red, black and white, can never be understood unless *banacimbusa* or *uwaombelwa* (a woman who has gone through the teaching) explains them. Victor Turner (1969:7) rightly affirms that "it is one thing to observe people performing the stylized gesture and singing the cryptic songs of ritual performance and quite another to reach an adequate understanding of what the movements and words mean to them". *Imbusa* teachings undergird the status of married Bemba women. The teaching constitutes secrecy of one's marriage. As a married woman who got *imbusa* instructions, there is need to keep marital issues secret. *Banacimbusa* instruct women to be diligent in keeping marital secrets because only untaught women will share their marital issues. The danger of keeping secrets is that women never discuss the abuse that they may encounter in their marriages. These secrets are well guarded by all women who have gone through *imbusa* (Mushibwe 2009:133-134). Mushibwe feels that this is what ensures the reproduction of the women's own suppression and reinforcement of male superiority. Lillian Siwila (2011:18,) agrees with Mushibwe that:

> The teaching on secrecy in marriage is so intense that some of the proverbial songs sung for the bride during the wedding are to tell her to keep secrets in her marriage. As much as this helps to keep the integrity of the community and the marriage, this teaching has also contributed to the silencing of women even when there is abuse in the family.

Due to the way *imbusa* is conducted, that is, the young brides are to learn in silence without asking *banacimbusa* questions, if a bride asks questions she would be seen as being presumptuous: some of these instructions are replicated in various homes where the wife is silent and the husband is the decision maker. Some women negotiate and navigate these teachings for their wellbeing while others take these teachings on silence entirely regardless of the effect it may have on them.

Negotiating *Imbusa* for Agency

This chapter uses the theory of nego-feminism coined by a Nigerian woman in the diaspora, Obiomma Nnaemeka (2003: 360-361) as "the feminism of negotiation; not ego feminism". I locate nego-feminism as a postcolonial and decolonial theory used in this study to understand the *imbusa* ritual as an indigenous Bemba marriage teaching. Indigenous tradition does not happen in a vacuum, it is made in everyday negotiations, in this case for instance it can be used by Bemba women to empower each other for cultural transformation. Before encountering various cultures and religions, Bemba women were perceived as *cibinda wa ng'anda* (head of the home), *kabumba wa mapepo* (creator and priest of prayers), and *nacimbusa wa chisunga* (guardian of tradition) (Hinfelaar 1994: 12; see also Kaunda 2010; Rasing 2001; Kaunda and Kaunda 2016: 165). These three positions were influential community offices for Bemba women. Encountering various cultures and religions such as Christianity modified how the *imbusa* was taught, the Catholic priests insisted on being part of *imbusa*[9] so that they can teach women Christian marriages and compile literature for the priests that would come later. This changed how *imbusa* is taught, for instance, much of the teaching now tend to have major focus on sex teachings and wives submitting to their husband more than the agency of women in marriage and society; in short it took on the form of a Christian patriarchal teaching. This chapter is not arguing for a reclamation of Bemba cultural past that has been change rather as Njoki Wane (2013: 94) argues, "perhaps more than anything else, reclamation is about rediscovering the central tenants of our Indigenous cultures and applying them to our present context." The practice and teaching of *imbusa* in contemporary Zambia reflects what Sabelo Ndlovu-Gatsheni (2013a: 3) says: "the structural, systemic, cultural, discursive, and epistemological pattern of domination that has engulfed Africans since the Conquest". Therefore, the question is not whether cultural transformation occurs, but rather, the kind of transformation that occurs.

Obiomma Nnaemeka (2003) argues that African women negotiate culture in everything they do; motherhood, marriage and family. Men have had a greater advantage in many aspects of life and often, women have been left out, however, women have a way of navigating culture that brings them at equal terms with men. This chapter uses Nego-feminism as a lens to examine the ways in which *imbusa* as indigenous knowledge can be used as a resource of agency for Bemba married women. This is important because it demonstrates how *banacimbusa* can become more aware of gender issues that they need to engage with in their premarital teachings. Nego- feminism as a theory is based on the premise that women do not just passively appropriate patriarchal cultural demands but are constantly negotiating and navigating culture. Nnaemeka (2003: 362) succinctly explains that in order to reconcile theory and engagement, there is a need to clear the ground in order to "dwell/duel not only on what theory is but, more importantly, on what theory does, can and cannot do, and should and should not do". Nego-feminism in this chapter is engaged in order to show the importance of *banacimbusa's* role as central to the *imbusa* teaching to explicitly engage *imbusa* in ways that offer life-giving marriages for Bemba women.

---

[9] No men- including Bemba men were and still are not allowed in this teaching space, but the white Catholic priests insisted until they were allowed. The priests insisted on teaching certain aspects in order for *imbusa* to take on a Christian perspective.

All the interviewed women clearly stated that the *imbusa* initiation rite is a very important space for Zambian culture; their dilemma is that only women are the recipients of the teachings. What is taught to a woman between two weeks to two months is summarized in an hour for the man. It is as though *banacimbusa*'s intention is to report to the groom that the bride has been given marital instructions. *Imbusa* initiation rite is a method for premarital teaching and counselling of women for viable marriages. It is not only brides who benefit, rather also works as a marriage enrichment program where every woman who has undergone the ritual has an opportunity to refresh themselves. Therefore, it cannot be over-emphasised that the *imbusa* space has to be more open to include the current issues regarding violence against women which often times is committed by intimate lovers such as husbands or boyfriends. In this chapter, I propose a basis and structure (framework) of *imbusa* teachings for life-giving marriage in order to demonstrate the viability of life-giving marriages.

This is not in any way exhaustive. And, because *banacimbusa* are central to *imbusa* initiation rite and the crucial subject of *imbusa* teachings is sexy, I propose to focus on the three critical components of *imbusa*: first, I propose an African feminist b*anacimbusa* because I want to glean from within African- Bemba culture for those realities that promote women's wellbeing and agency. Second, since *imbusa* is a form of teaching, there is a need for African feminist *imbusa* pedagogy. Third is the need for a holistic approach to sex instruction, since much of the *imbusa* teaching floats around marital sex. This *imbusa* sex instruction has often focused on women pleasing their husbands. The proposal here is to demonstrate that married women need as much sexual satisfaction as their husbands.

The Need for African Feminist *Banacimbusa*

The proposal for feminist *banacimbusa* who are aware of gender inequalities, in the context of gender justice, is made with a view to building a life-giving marriage. A life-giving marriage is one in which decision making is mutual for both husband and wife embraces respect, dignity and justice for the couple. A just-marriage cannot be conceptualised without acknowledging the role of *banacimbusa* among the Bemba people of Zambia. *Banacimbusa* are crucial to the *imbusa* initiation rites and the formation of women's marital identity, it is therefore vital that their role in the feasibility of a just marriage (life-

273

giving marriage) is articulated here. The question is what kind of *banacimbusa* are needed for envisioning a life-giving and affirming marriage? I propose an African feminist *banacimbusa*.

African feminist *banacimbusa* are women who are aware and concerned with women's dignity within a marriage and women's status in society. For this to happen, *banacimbusa* need to undergo a process of transformation, a deliberate consciousness-raising and internalization of theories from African feminist understanding. Currently *banacimbusa* do not intentionally include gender inequality issues in their *imbusa* teachings. Unfortunately, brides are not allowed to ask questions during the teaching, they are given an opportunity to ask questions once or twice during the 2 weeks to 2 months' ritual. However, due to the way the teachings are given the brides ask questions that would please banacimbusa often times. I define feminist *banacimbusa* as Bemba woman marriage instructors who decisively, intentionally and consciously works to dismantle patriarchy and hierarchical structures in marriage and society in order to foster gender equality, to awaken women to oppression and social gender imbalance, and to empower women to stand up for their rights by exposing them to resources necessary for envisioning equality in marriage (Robertson 1994:11). Three ways in which this can achieved can be identified as follows:

Firstly, there is a need for progressive *banacimbusa*. Since *banacimbusa* are central to *imbusa* teachings, there is a need that they keep up with gender empowerment discussions. There have not been changes in the content between the interviewed women that received their teachings in 1982 and those who received them in 2011. Two of the interviewed women observed that there is a need for the teachings to be made more modern than they currently are. Another participant said she thinks that "we are in an environment that is trying to empower women, more and more women are very independent, some teachings are more of the opposite of what they [independent women] are trying to do". She further expressed the need for *imbusa* to be shaped in a way that would modernize it, "shape better women in marriage", because as it is currently taught, "it belittles women, makes them feel like they are someone else in their workplace or friend's home, and someone else in their home where they feel belittled". *Imbusa* in the precolonial times was taught to women because women held important positions in community and they needed agency and knowledge to lead. This teaching undergirded woman's agency and solidarity with one another in homes and in public spheres. Another participant L stated that it was in the Christian teachings that some of the things that were taught *in imbusa* were re-taught in the modern way. Yet, *imbusa* should be taught not just in a modern way but it needs to carry a feminist orientation. It should be influenced by contemporary calls for social justice and gender equality. *Imbusa* should be concerned with the equal distribution of power that would pay attention not only to gender, but to all forms of oppression and exploitation of women in society. This can be achieved by *banacimbusa* with a feminist perspective and vision of social justice with an agenda for a socio-cultural, economic, political and religious transformation for equality and realization of human rights for the entire community. This means that *banacimbusa* with a feminist perspective will need to articulate *imbusa* teachings in a contextualized manner to reflect the culture and socio-political context, and at the same time reflect the global call for gender justice and human rights for all.

Secondly, this point stems from the first, there is a need for *banacimbusa* to be schooled and educated in the issues that are under current discussion among African women and even some male scholars who are passionate about gender equality. If Zambian women will be helped to go into a life-giving marriage which translates into public spheres of work and career, *banacimbusa* as central actors in the *imbusa* rite need to be aware of recent issues that African women are raising. Mercy Oduyoye (1995:10) clarifies that the people involved in the ritual practices (*banacimbusa* and initiates in this case) are the ones who can take note and evaluate the usefulness and necessary changes for the ritual or rite. In fact, it is true that culture is not static, it is constantly transforming itself as it encounters various cultures. Chammah Kaunda (2012:140), similarly discussing theological education for gender justice, stresses the need for a relevant, fruitful and life-affirming education. It is important that in order to prepare women for a life-affirming marriage, *banacimbusa* be educated on such issues that are relevant to women's lives. If and when *banacimbusa* are schooled in issues such as gender based violence, they would teach the young brides on how to speak out against violence or any form of abuse in marriage and other spaces they find themselves in. With the education on relevant issues concerning women, *banacimbusa* can also put ideas together and write a book for the purpose of feminist *imbusa* initiation rites.

Thirdly, the need for a booklet containing common content of *imbusa* teachings would be vital for coherence because one out of the ten interviewed women explained that "you know I just finished my secretarial studies that time so they used to tell me 'at least these days you girls have been to school so you can ask your husband for sex, but before we never used to'". The rest of the interviewed women said they were taught never to ask for sex from their husbands because it is not honourable for women to ask for sex. The above participant emphasized that it depends on the people who are teaching, and these are *banacimbusa*. This means that although the teachings are still as they were in the distant past, there are some *banacimbusa* who will teach an uneducated woman not to ask for sex from her husband while they would teach an educated woman that she can ask because she is educated. Imbusa as a space for solidarity among Bemba women has to transcend certain things such as inequality. Women need to be taught to use their agency, educated or not. If *banacimbusa* in Zambia take an initiative and write a booklet on such teachings with a feminist orientation, it would be very helpful in reaching and achieving life-giving marriage for Zambian women. This booklet should affirm cultural practices such as drama, clapping, singing, dancing etc., together with suggestions emerging from African women scholars. *Banacimbusa* need to formulate and write the booklet to help even the up-coming *banacimbusa* on how to go about the initiation rite. The only written accounts of *imbusa* were written by white male priests and some white female and male anthropologists to communicate what the ritual is about. Few Bemba and other Zambian scholars have started writing on this important topic.

An African Feminist *Imbusa* Pedagogy

From interviews with ten Zambian women living in Pietermaritzburg, it can be argued that *imbusa* initiation rite is a banking system (See Freire 1969) method of teaching. A young woman or bride is not allowed to have eye contact with anyone and is not allowed ask questions during the teaching. This is important to understand because among the Bemba people eye contact demonstrates audacity and impudence. One participant observes that, "...reading between the lines, my husband is perfect; this is what they were not saying but which I could hear. And as a girl who had been to university there were times I would say 'what about him?' But of course, I didn't ask them because culturally it is wrong to challenge elders". This shows that there is a need to develop feminist

276

imbusa pedagogy because the brides have questions that are never asked and their concerns are therefore never clarified. For a long time, *imbusa* has utilized a banking approach where *banacimbusa* have been constantly perceived as handing down knowledge to the bride. This form of teaching has been condemned as domesticating and not emancipating (Freire 1969). Knowledge must be perceived as a shared commodity rather than handed down. Life-giving knowledge is dialogical; such that both *banacimbusa* and the bride should think and dialogue together. The *imbusa* itself must become a liberative[10] environment for women by suggesting a new way to be initiated into *imbusa*. It can become a safe space of conscientizing one another in an interconnected web of relationships in critical solidarity with women who care about each other's wellbeing in a life-affirming marriage.

One goal of the liberative feminist *imbusa* pedagogy should be to learn to respect each other rather than create fear and intimidation in young women during the teaching process. It should be a safe environment where the young women can express their fears and hopes, with an understanding that there is a listening mentor. Unfortunately, even asking questions is taken as disobedience and is seen as arrogance. Rachael Nyagondwe-Fiedler (2005:57) explains how the initiates' heads are bowed as they enter the house for initiation in Malawi Christianised *chinamwali* among the Chewa/Nyanja initiation. Similar to *imbusa*, this bowing down is a sign of respect. This is the same for the Zambian women going through the initiation; they have to slightly bow their heads, avoid eye contact and not ask questions, rather just listen to *banacimbusa*'s instructions and obey. This is why the *imbusa* initiation rite should be used as a dialogical space, allowing the initiates to ask questions and suggest things if possible during the teachings. By so doing, the young bride is alerted to know that even in her home, she can ask questions where she does not understand and that her input in the home is valuable and necessary. Thus, *imbusa* teaching should be done in a participatory and equality centred approach in which there is sharing of power. The aim should be to develop independence in the young woman. In this way, *imbusa* pedagogy will be concerned with gender justice, overcoming domination and dependency of women on men as women find their own voices in the process of *imbusa*.

---

[10] Asking questions or being given a chance to ask questions is a step that shows that the space is liberative and allows voices to be heard.

A Holistic Approach to Sexuality

Isabel Phiri and Sarojini Nadar (2009:13) have proposed that "an African feminist ethics of sexuality is needed in order to promote safe practices in the context of HIV". My aim in this section is to propose a framework for such ethics in the Zambian context. A holistic approach to sexuality in imbusa must affirm the non-dualistic African world-view of reality, especially because in contemporary imbusa women are taught to focus on satisfying their husbands while their sexual satisfaction is rarely referred to overtly and explicitly. There is no dichotomy between religion and secular, spirituality and material, man and woman, husband and wife, mind and body, emotion and intellect and so on. Scholars have observed that these dualisms hold the foundation that sustains patriarchy in society (Harrison 1985:149). By overcoming them, patriarchy will fundamentally collapse and give way to mutual respect and valuing of one another. Sex in marriage is one of, if not 'the crucial topic' in *imbusa* initiation rites that is taught extensively. All the ten interviewed women are in agreement that sex is the most taught during the rite; however, the whole teaching is only for women. As a "big glue and indicator" as one participant explained, sex in marriage should be for the benefit of the husband, while the wife's duty seem to be that of performing and exciting (waist movements that bring pleasure to) the man. Beverley Harrison (1985:149-50) has argued that:

> The moral norm for sexual communication in a feminist ethic is a radical mutuality- the simultaneous acknowledgement of vulnerability to and need of another, the recognition of one's own power to give and receive pleasure and to call forth another's power of relation and to express one's own. The sexual ethic of patriarchy – our present operative ethic- has ownership as its formative value. We are to possess total right of access to and control of another's body – space and the fruits of another's body, if the other is female. A norm of control prevails, which is why so-called marital fidelity really means only sexual exclusivity for the female spouse.

Following the trend of this argument, I propose three principles for gender justice regarding marital sex. These are in no way exhaustive rather they are the benchmark for *banacimbusa* and the teachings they give.

First, women should be taught a radical mutual responsibility when engaging in sex. Harrison calls for radical mutuality as a feminist ethic for sexual communication. The radical nature of this ethic demands that both the wife and the husband are satisfied when it comes to sex in marriage without the wife being the satisfier and the husband being the satisfied. Margaret Farley (200:217) quoting Karen Lebacqz, notes that sex can be harmful even in marriage because "eros, the desire for another, the passion that accompanies the wish for sexual expression, makes one vulnerable...capable of being wounded". This is the more reason why women in Zambia should be taught mutual responsibility and agreement concerning sex in marriage. Marcy Oduyoye (2006:22) cogently observes "the question of sexuality cannot avoid the relationship of men and women in marriage". She further notes that it has been believed that a woman is to be a "monotheist" while a husband can freely worship other women's bodies as a "polytheist" in marriage. I argue therefore that if Zambian people will reach a place of gender just sex, proper sexual relations must not be differently defined between the wife and husband (Oduyoye 2006:22). In short, husband and wife should not have different understandings of sexual relations. The wife and husband should have equal access to each other's bodies. One of the interviewed women lamented that,

> ... if they [banacimbusa] modified it to something more modern, what is happening, women know what they want, just to try and bring a balance to it, it would shape better women in marriage. But now because it's a conflict of what a person is, it's kind of like you are somebody else in your work environment, your friend's environment but when you are at home, you feel like you are completely nothing, when you are supposed to feel the same in all spheres of life. So now if the most intimate action... act that you have between you and your husband makes you feel belittled, the whole household you are in, you literally feel you can't make any impact in the house.

This means according to this comment that the *imbusa* space is fitting; however, the teachings need to be tweaked and catch up with current happenings in the world. This is where it is also important that men are taught how to treat and sexually satisfy their wives. Sex must be a mutual pleasure "in the context of genuine openness and intimacy" (Harrison 1985:87). *Imbusa* teaching regarding marital sex currently upholds patriarchy and reinforces husband control and domination of his wife.

Second, in relation to the point above, women should own power, have agency to give and receive sexual intimacy. *Banacimbusa* instruct women to be active and perform sexual activity for their spouse fulfilment, importantly is that a married woman should never say no to her husband's sexual advances. This is almost equal to not consenting. If women are taught not to refuse their husbands sex, it is not clear at what point they are to say no because according to the interviews, except for menstruation, a woman must give her husband sex at all costs. This means that while men own their bodies, women do not. This is to say that there is a need for both husband and wife to mutually participate in the sexual act without one feeling forced or as a giver of pleasure only. This mutual responsibility and participation when it comes to sex gives women dignity as well. Nyambura Jane Njoroge (2002:41) affirms that when attention is not paid to women as intrinsic beings, the destruction of their God-given identity and human dignity is imminent.

Third, sex is perceived as the reason for longevity in marriage and that it is up to women to make the marriage work. Thus, in *imbusa*, a woman is taught that after each sexual encounter with her husband, she should clean his penis and thank him. A participant explained:

> ...after you've finished (the sexual act) then you must kneel down and (claps her hands) zikomo (thank you). You thank him because he has desired you and that's an honourable thing, if he can desire you. And they said to me if he desires you every day, it's an honourable thing, if he desires you once every week you must start to get worried, so already what they were saying to me is that this sex is a big glue and a big indicator of how your husband loves you or how your husband wants you, if he doesn't want you, you must look at it as a red light, what is it that is going on? What is happening? That was very important.

However, the interviewed women expressed discomfort with this teaching. The subliminal message is that sex is for longevity of marriage for a woman, not for a man, because if as a married woman her husband does not desire her and she is unable to ask for sex then there is inequality. Thus, sexual entitlement, equality and mutual access to their bodies as wife and husband, is significant for a life-affirming marriage. During the interview, one participant explained that the actions of her mother during the *imbusa* rite – she was cooking and doing many things for *banacimbusa*- indicated to her that her mother wanted her to take the teachings very seriously. This is her explanation,

...so already the way am going to start my married life as a young woman is based on what I can see and what I cannot see what was said and what was not said. For me what they were not saying, I could see it also, they never literally said if 'you don't perform well you will be brought back and the lobola money will be sent back it will be a shame in the family," but I could hear it. And it said to me that I don't want to be the one who brings shame on the family so whatever it takes am going to make this work. So, you get into marriage with that mindset that I've got to make this work and if it shows any signs of failure the first person you question is yourself. In fact, reading between the lines, my husband is perfect, this is what they were not saying but which I could hear.

This shows that marital sex according to the *imbusa* teachings is important for women to preserve their marriages. Thus, it is important that women be made aware that their sexual needs are as important as the husband's and that they do not have to live in a marriage being fearful of not satisfying the husband- which is tantamount to divorce or being sent back to be re-taught hence bringing shame on the family and *banacimbusa*. This also means that *imbusa* should consider and include both the wife and husband in its teachings.

Conclusion

This chapter has proposed a framework for a life-giving *imbusa* teaching that can lead to a life- affirming marriage. The focus was on the *banacimbusa* as central actors in the *imbusa* initiation rite. Second, it proposed an alternative in the *imbusa* pedagogy from a banking approach to a feminist liberative approach. Finally, I have made some suggestions for an African feminist holistic sexual ethic. Sex is one aspect which is crucial to the *imbusa* teachings. Within these two frameworks I have explained the need for mutual responsibility and participation in the marriage, and not allowing one to be more important to the marriage than the other.

References

Farley, Margaret (2008). *Just Love: A Framework for Christian Sexual Ethic.* New York: Continuum.

Freire, Paulo. 1996. *Pedagogy of the Oppressed*. Harmondsworth: Penguin Books.

Harrison, Beverley W. (1985). Making the Connections: Essays in Feminist Social Ethics, edited by Carol S. Robb. Boston: Beacon Press.

Kaunda, Chammah J. (2012). "Reclaiming the Feminine Image of God in *Lesa*: Implications for Bemba Christian Women at the Evangel Assembly of God Church in the post-Missionary Era," *Journal of Constructive Theology*, 16/1, 5-29.

Kaunda, Mutale Mulenga and Kaunda Chammah, Judex. (2016). "*Infunkutu*- the Bemba Sexual Dance as Women's Sexual Agency," *Journal of Theology for Southern Africa* 155 (July 2016 Special Issue) pages159-175.

Kaunda Mutale Mulenga. (2016). Negotiated Feminism? "A Study of Married Bemba Women Appropriating the *Imbusa* Pre-Marital 'Curriculum' at Home and Workplace". Unpublished PhD. Diss., University of KwaZulu-Natal, Pietermaritzburg.

Mukuka kasapatu-, Sylvia. (2018). A Quest for Embracing Indigenous Knowledge Systems in the United Church of Zambia: Pastoral Care and the Imbusa. Unpublished PhD. Diss., University of KwaZulu-Natal, Pietermaritzburg.

Durrheim, Kevin (1999). "Research Design", pages 33-59 in *Research in practice: Applied Methods for the Social Sciences*, edited by Terre-Blanche, Martin, Kevin Durrheim and Desmond Painter. Cape Town: University of Cape Town Press.

Ndlovu-Gatsheni, Sabelo. (2013a). Coloniality of Power in Postcolonial Africa: Myths of Decolonization. Dakar: CODESRIA.

Njoroge, Nyambura (1997). "The Missing Voice: African Women Doing Theology." *Journal of Theology for Southern Africa*, 99 (November), 77-83.

Nnaemeka Obioma (2003). "Nego Feminism: Theorizing, Practicing, and Pruning Africa's Way," *Signs: Journal of Women in Culture and Society*, Vol. 29 no. 21: 357 - 384.

Nyagondwe-Fiedler, Racheal. (2005). *Coming of Age: A Christianized Initiation among Women in Southern Malawi*. Zomba: Kachere Series.

Oduyoye, Mercy A. (1995a). *Daughters of Anowa: African Women and Patriarchy*. Maryknoll: Orbis Books.

Oduyoye, Mercy A. (2006). "Women and Ritual in Africa", pages 9-24. *In The Will to Arise: Women, Tradition and the Church in Africa*, edited by Oduyoye, Mercy and Kanyoro, Musimbi. Pietermaritzburg: Cluster Publications.

Phiri Isabel and Sarojini Nadar. (2006). "What's in a Name? - Forging A Theological Framework for African Women's Theologies," *Journal of Constructive Theology*, 12/2, 5-24.

Phiri Isabel and Sarojini Nadar. (2009). "'Going Through the Fire with Eyes Wide Open': African Women's Perspective on Indigenous Knowledge, Patriarchy and Sexuality". *Journal for the Study of Religion*, 22 (2): 2-22.

Robertson, Lyn. (1994). "Feminist Teacher Education: Applying Feminist Pedagogies to the Preparation of New Teachers," *Teachers Feminist Teacher*, 8/1 (Spring/Summer), 11-15.

Tamale, Sylvia. (2005). "Eroticism, Sensuality and "Women's Secrets" among the Baganda: A critical Analysis," 936,http://agi.ac.za/sites/agi.ac.za/files/fa_5_feature_article_1.pdf [Accessed 10/09/12].

Tsoka, Chiloane. (2012). "Cultural Observations facing Women Managers: A South African Perspective," Gender & Behaviour, Vol. 10, No. 2: 4949-4973

Turner, V. W. (1969). The Ritual Process: Structure and Anti-structure. Ithaca, N.Y.: Cornell University Press.

Wane, Njoki. (2013). "[Re-]Claiming my Indigenous knowledge: Challenges, resistance, and opportunities," Decolonization: Indigeneity, *Education & Society*, Vol. 2, No. 1: 93-107.

Chapter 15

Sexuality and AmaXhosa Women's Agency: South African Indigenous Women's Agency in Sexual Matters

Munyaradzi Mawere & *Andile Mayekiso*

Abstract

This chapter is an attempt to reflect on sexuality and South African indigenous women's agency in sexual matters. Drawing from notes from research – ethnographic life histories and narratives of the AmaXhosa [young] women gathered during fieldwork in Gugulethu of South Africa's Western Cape suburb, we sought to investigate whether indigenous young South African women really consciously exercise their agency in sexual relationship matters, and if so how they manoeuvre and challenge the perceived 'men's power' and patriarchal inclinations to the extent that they engage in multiple sexual encounters just as men do or even more than what men do.

Keywords: Sexuality, women, culture, Western Cape, South Africa.

Introduction

Jewkes and Morrell (2012: 1) argued in their paper that "gender inequalities give men considerable relational power over young women, particularly in circumstances of poverty and where sex is materially rewarded". Importantly though, for the purpose of our discussion in this chapter is their view that, "young women are often described as victims of men, but this inadequately explains women's observed sexual agency" (ibid).

Drawing from notes from research – ethnographic life history narratives gathered by the authors from indigenous South African young women in Gugulethu of Western Cape Province of South Africa, we sought to investigate whether these women consciously exercise their agency in sexual relationship matters. Gugulethu is dominated by the Xhosa-speaking people (*pl*: AmaXhosa). The narratives demonstrated that women, like their male counterparts, have agency, to decide when and how they exercise this agency in these sexual relationships. The challenge these women face when engaged in multiple sexual relations, unlike men who participate in similar multiple sexual relations, is deleterious societal labelling which stigmatises and portrays women as *izifebe* (morally loose), whereas men, on the other hand, are celebrated through appraisal naming such as *udlalani* (a playboy) accompanied by positive connotations. Such men are celebrated and portrayed as desirable, including by women.

The question that comes to the fore, however, is: Why women involved in similar sexual relationships normally receive pejorative labelling while their male counterparts are celebrated? In view of this and other such questions, this chapter is an attempt to validate whether young indigenous AmaXhosa and South African women in general *really* enjoy the same agency in sexual matters as their male counterparts.

Statement of research design

This chapter was developed from the authors' studies in Gugulethu – one of the residential locations in South Africa's Western Cape Province– which started late in 2008 as part of the Western Cape sites for the multi-country study for Prevention of Mother to Child (HIV) Transmission (PMTCT[11]) Effectiveness in Africa: Research and Linkages to Care (PEARL) conducted by the Infectious Diseases Epidemiology Unity (IDEU) in the School of Public Health at the University of Cape Town (UCT). The study deployed a qualitative ethnographic research approach, particularly participant-observation for data collection. Participant observation is the process that enables researchers to learn about the activities of the people under study in the natural setting through observing and participating in those activities (Mawere, 2014). Participant observation offers such intimate first-hand experience or what Geertz (1983: 6) calls "thick descriptions" – finest details possible – in all their dealings. Observations were supplemented by structured and semi-structured in-depth interviews with other community elders including traditional healers, church leaders, political activists, and a wide range of community elders, mostly women. All the interviews were conducted in isiXhosa, the language conversant with both the participants and the second author. Of the participants, the two isiZulu and seSotho-speaking men speak fluent isiXhosa; they have fully assimilated into the AmaXhosa community. All eight female

---

[11] PMTCT stands for Prevention of Mother to Child (HIV) Transmission

participants were Xhosas and their ages ranged from between 18 and 41. The 41 year old woman is the only one considered 'married', as all others were either staying with their boyfriends or visiting regularly – at least four times a week. Besides, the first author conducted focus group discussions with both men and women to provide a platform to share their experiences and beliefs, to tease out issues raised during one-on-one sessions, reflect and challenge each other's opinions on fathering and relationships in general. All the interviews were recorded after gaining permission from the participants. The use of a tape recorder was explained to the participants before each session and they gave permission. All sound files were then transcribed and translated by the authors.

Gugulethu, though is a multi-racial location and with hot spot areas to be avoided at all cost, is largely dominated by the Xhosa-speaking people (*pl*: AmaXhosa). The PEARL study collected clinical data to determine PMTCT drug coverage in Gugulethu but also added a community survey of households with children less than two years of age. The authors fully participated in their activities as far as they invited him and insofar as these excluded criminal activities. As such, being a participant observer was very useful because it provided critical moments to obtain more insights on how young women organise their sexual life in their attempts to exert their agency as humans in relationships. The authors soon established good connection with Sizwe's family in Gugulethu, and the community at large was helpful in alerting the first author of possible danger. For instance, where gang fighting would likely to be involved, they would send them text messages and that helped a lot.[12] Once the researcher-participants' relationships were much stronger, it became easier to not only talk about sexual matters but also sleep over, observe, and accompany women visiting different men for a sleep over.

Even though the sample on which this discussion is based on is relatively small and born of prior research with a specific subset of participants, nevertheless, the patterns observed here are very similar to those reported in large surveys. Studies (Richter *et al*, 2010; Posel & Rudwick, 2013) have been reporting for some time now that marriage rates continue to drop among indigenous people of South

---

[12] During the Infants Project, both female field work assistants from Gugulethu were mugged. All recording tapes, bags, note pads, mobile phones, jewellery including a wedding ring were taken from them. We reported the incident to the police, but we never heard from them and we never recovered any of the items. So, when I started my field work I was very aware of the dangers I was exposed to.

Africa and there is no indication of them improving in these current economic times[13]. Similarly, in this study marriage rate is very low; while all the men are fathers, only two of the twelve participants who form the core sample of men for this study regarded their relationships as marriage[14], which means about 83% of the men are unmarried fathers.

Findings

In general, indigenous people in Africa are known for their hospitality, kindness and respect. As part of these attributes, they often find ways and names to refer to certain things in their daily lives as part of their respect. For instance, elders among the Xhosa speakers avoid the usage of the following terms: *ukulalana, ukwabelana ngesondo or ngocantsi, ukutyana, ukuzumana, ukututsana,* (which all refer to the act of sexual intercourse). For elders, these terms should only be used, if at all, in enclosed and private spaces. To refer to the sexual performance, AmaXhosa (plural) would rather say something like *ukutsiba iziko* (literally meaning to jump the fireplace but in this context, referring to the act of performing sexual intercourse). Among the AmaXhosa at least, once one marries as a man, older men[15] in the community would encourage the newly married man to jump the fireplace at night so that he can grow (impregnate his wife) his own family. Generally, elders would despise sexually starving a woman especially within marriage. When writing about sex, even if only imaginative, one must borrow from the locals' terminology, their ways of talking and performing this act, sex. The following are some of the [literal] terms used by both men and women during conversations surrounding sexual matters – *ukuheva* (to have); *ukuphana* (you give, I give); *ukumenza* (do someone sexually); *ukututsana* (to test each other); *ukuyihloma* (to shove it in a tight place); *ukuyifaka* (to put it in); *ukutyiwa* (eating someone); *ukuzumana* (sudden sex); *ukutshinana* (slang for having sex); *ukuzekana* (to take each other); *ukukhwelana* (to be on top of each other). Undoubtedly, some

---

[13] This is not to say marriages among Africans have ceased because there is a compelling argument that marriages are being initiated but because of their processual nature, are not completed within the lifetime of a partnership.

[14] Ta Pat's living arrangement with Neliswa is problematic as she believes that as long as he has not paid for *lobola*, their living together is cohabitation.

[15] It is highly unlikely to be your own biological father, and this is again due to respect than anything else. Black Africans avoid the subject on sex with their own children

of these terms are considered impolite and inappropriate to use especially with elders around as they describe sex as rough and animalistic. But this is the language young people in the studied community employ in their daily conversations either to fantasise, lure a potential sex partner or just as a way of fitting in. To fit in in these conversations means having more than one sexual partner.

One body of literature in which the question of sexual identity and multiple relationships is addressed is that on concurrency as it emerged during the HIV pandemic[16] (see Legarde *et al.* 2001), particularly showing how these relationships contribute to the rapid spread of the pandemic in Africa. These studies dismiss the view that HIV is "for poor people" and is spread because of poverty. The question then is, if poverty, as these studies show, is not the driving force as normally believed in public discourse, how can we account for differences in infections among South Africans? One way of doing this is to look closely at the ways that sexual behaviours are understood locally. To do so, we examine practices of *udlalani* (a 'player') and *isifebe* (a loose woman) but also refer to some of the terms highlighted above. Based on our findings, we argue that among other factors, the social significance of *udlalani* enables men to achieve 'womanising' as a form of social status; ownership of a *hokkie* (shelter – shack) and a bed is another form of enticing women. We, however, add that women, especially African women, who are often seen as lacking agency when it comes to sexual negotiation, are not always mere victims of men's sexual misconduct or culture, but have some form of agency except of course in specific cases such as rape.

During fieldwork, it was observed that terms such as "wheelbarrows, spare wheels and armpit lovers" are popular in the townships among youths to describe their sexual partners or secret lovers. What the literature calls 'concurrency' is explained by men and women in Gugulethu as simple desire, rather than a transactional relationship as is so often suggested in the HIV literature (Fuller, 2003; Hunter, 2010). Of course, 'womanising' and its link to performative masculine identity-making is not a new or ethnically specific phenomenon. Participants described these sexual games as *siyatyana nje ukuzonwabisa* ("sex for fun") and is embraced by both men and women in the Gugulethu community. It is worth noting though that our participants not only perform these sexual games for social

---

16 While none of the men in my study admitted to knowing their HIV-status, I do know the status of some of their girlfriends and children because of earlier research for the Infants' Project, from which my study derives.

289

status, but the reality is that as they put it: *"imnandi isex"* (sex is good) and it gives them pleasure and comfort. Hence, some girls are referred to as *imnandi laweyi* than other girls because in bed they perform better than others. 'Better' is evaluated in terms of their taste and wildness. The cases below are selected because they depict everyday life for these participants but also offer a wonderful opportunity to confirm that women exercise their agency in sexual matters as they are in control of sexual relationships:

Both acts of "play" for *udlalani* (womaniser) and *isifebe* (a loose woman [17]) have serious implications for children born out of these casual sexual encounters as illustrated below. Early in 2012, Mabhanti became involved in one of these games with a woman in her early twenties. The young woman already had two boyfriends at the time and both of whom knew about each other. In such cases men might believe that they are actually 'playing' this woman while the opposite is also true. In early March, she fell pregnant. She was not certain who the father was. In a conversation with her, she revealed she was just having a good time with Mabhanti but also wanted to show her boyfriends that as an unmarried woman she can do whatever she wants with her body. The men refused paternity testing due to its high cost. Ultimately, a solution was reached; an elderly woman would perform *ukufaniswa kosana* (a Xhosa indigenous way of evaluating and identifying the baby's father) once born to ascertain the real father. This woman was in complete control of her 'relationships' with all these men. She decided whom she would sleep with and when and all men had to play by her rules or risk being dumped.

Unfortunately, despite being considered "a spare wheel" or "armpit lover" *(umakhwapheni)*, Mabhanti, was excited about the pregnancy and the thought that he had fathered a second child, unveiled himself, telling his friends that he was the father. He did not, however, initiate any "damages payments," but started to intervene in the woman's lifestyle. He ordered her to stop using drugs during pregnancy saying, *"I do not want to have a mentally disturbed child because of you smoking drugs."* He told me *"I also told her that as soon as she gives birth I will take that thing [she is carrying] and give it to umamomncinci (my aunt) because I cannot allow my child to grow up kwavula zibhuqe (a loose family)" (Interview, 31 Jan 12).* Ironically, he did not modify his own

---

[17] *Isifebe* is different to *umakhwapheni* (armpits lover). The latter is a secret lover. *Umakhwapheni* is more than a sexual partner; there might be gifts exchanges and expectations for other favours.

behaviour, including drug-use to try to set an example. This is a typical patriarchal behaviour. What started as a sexual game for pleasure was now a serious issue.

His attempt to control this woman's lifestyle only led to them fighting. To show that this woman was in control of her decisions and life in general, she refused to stop using drugs demanding that Mabhanti should also stop. As expected he refused, saying that his smoking did not affect the baby she was carrying. Within a month of their public arguments, she told him that he was not the father of the baby. Both her other boyfriends started claiming paternity. One of the men had an interest in this pregnancy. In his mid-forties, he had not fathered a child, so he refused to be side-lined. By the time the baby was born, Mabhanti had "moved on with his life". He had a new girlfriend and two other occasional sexual partners. He lost interest in the child even though he still contemplated the possibility that he might be the father. He said he could not waste his time clinging to one woman because *"there are many fishes in the sea; I have found the biggest one now"* (Field notes, 10 Nov 12). Further, it was her decision not to use any of the suggested pregnancy prevention measures. In our conversations she never asked her sex partners to use condoms and none of them wanted to use it.

There are a few issues to digest from this story. Firstly, it is common for two men to date a woman simultaneously or for a woman to date more than one man at the same time. Secondly, the issue of proving paternity is critical. The use of elders to determine or identify the "real" father is a long standing African way of determining child's paternity in situations where there is uncertainty. Let us return to Mabhanti's 'armpit lover' and her child. It seems that a decision in the best interests of the child was made by the elders, and this was not contested.

We frequently heard stories about mothers making a deliberate decision to allow a capable man to support the child's well-being, only later to be told that he is not the 'real' father. Considering the expenses involved in raising a child, there is a probability that the young lover and the elders colluded to let the older man support the child "for now". This suggests that even when fathering is understood as a social act of care rather than a biological act of generation, the status of the father is not certain; things can change any time in the future. Player too entertained many sexual partners. One memorable day, Player started offloading his recent encounter with one of his sexual partners. He allowed the first author to record their conversation:

P: *Hey Ta Ager ndimphindile futhi lamntana. Imandi laweyi and nayo iyazifela ngam ndiyayibona nje (Hey Ta Ager I did that girl again. She is so nice in bed and I can see she also enjoys me).*

A: *Tell me more. What happened?*

P: *She didn't want to go to her boyfriend last night. She is naughty... she realised that my girlfriend is not here and came back. Yonela just disappeared; I don't know where she was last night. Maybe she has a new boyfriend you can never know with these girls. So laweyi (that girl) came here and we were just smoking with the guys. Enye yezizibhanxa zam (one of my stupid friends) brought a bottle of Jack Daniels and we drank it. After 11:00pm I asked them to leave because I wanted to sleep and they all left. Leweyi just pretended to be leaving with them but a few minutes later she knocked on my door and told me that she wanted to sleep here. Rhaa! Ta Ager andinomyeka ezizele kum (Dam! Ta Ager I could not let her go, she is the one who came to me) I gave her what she wanted. I was also honey; you know these drugs we use go down there (pointing to his private part).*

A: *Did Yonela not come back that night?*

P: *Even if she had come back we were not going to open that door. She would have either gone back to where she was or had to knock in the main house but I know my mother would not have opened for her... lamntu wayesendodeni mani Ta Ager (She was with a man Ta Ager I know that)*

A: *Did you guys use a condom?*

P: *Ta Ager uzawube ufuna icondom umntu elapha wena? (Ta Ager would you be searching for condoms when a girl is here?). Hayi Ta Aija sudlal'apha. (No Ta Ager don't play here) (Field notes, 18 August 2012).*

In an earlier conversation with Yonela, she told the first author that,

I have three children and their father's family is helping me to provide for these two because my mother (a schoolteacher) is taking care of my first daughter but when I meet a man maybe we were smoking together or having a drink sometimes I realise that it is too late to go home so I sleep over and sex just happens. We don't have to be in a relationship, he is giving me a place to sleep and his girlfriend is not there so why not? There are plenty girls out there for men to fish so if he avails himself to me why not... because I know my boyfriend is doing the same thing (Interview, 12 May 2012).

Player, like other men in the research group, does not seem to have managed the transition from boyhood to manhood despite his initiation. His girlfriend is fully aware that as a man Player will sleep with girls as he wishes and so is she. Instead of fighting with him, Yonela quietly but not secretively, does the same. Player is fully aware that when she does not come home at night she must be with another man.

Similarly, Nonzaliseko (27) is involved in sexual encounters with a number of men who fulfil her sexual needs. A mother of two (a girl who is 6 and a boy who is 9) from different men, owns a *hokkie* with a makeshift three quota bed. The bed base is made of beer crates which is quite common in informal houses around Cape Town. At one stage, we counted about four sexual partners living around Gugulethu and two other men in Eastern Cape (EC) who were all actively involved with her. The men in EC were both taxi drivers who frequent Cape Town as long distance taxi drivers. The men knew they needed to make arrangements in advance to visit especially when planning to sleep over. Communication was very important to avoid fights. She explained that:

> *Men can be silly when they know you depend - only dating him - on them, you don't have another man… you visit him and find another girl sleeping, mind you its nighttime. I don't want to find myself in such a situation. I don't have a problem with the number of men I have as long they respect my house and my children) (Interview, 10 Oct 2012).*

Nonzaliseko works as a packer at Shoprite and on weekends she sells beer and meat in her house. She is also receiving child support grant for her two children. Financially, she is doing fine but she does ask her partners to help with money for transport and saloon. It was never a concern for Nonzaliseko that by sleeping with several men she might be deemed 'damaged', a terminology normally used by elders to discourage women from sleeping with many men.

The last case we selected is that of Zoleka (33), Siyabulela's sister. She is the mother of a 10-year-old boy, Lukhanyo. In an interview with the first author, she revealed the circumstances that led to her pregnancy, thus:

> *I don't like being stuck with one man because I like having fun, to go out and drink. Drinking, smoking and sex make me forget about my problems. If I have one man who always expect me to be at his place when he comes back from work… wow yhu hayi (no) not for me. I told you my story about how I had my son… I only seduced that boy and he fell for me. He is good looking but I did not want to have a long term affair with him. All I wanted was to have a beautiful child from a*

handsome man and that's what I got.[18] We slept and that was it for me. He wanted more but I told him to leave me alone and never visit me at home. It is all about having fun Andile especially when you are drunk because I went to a party there in Khayelitsha and that's where I met that guy. I don't want him and his family near my child and he knows that…That time I was a lesbian but Nomonde (Zoleka's mother) kept pressurising me to have a child. She was so desperate to have a grandchild from me. I think she thought maybe I was barren so I just did what I did to satisfy her but now I am in love with my son. Andiyifuni lakaka yendoda (I don't want that rubbish of a man) near my son (Interview, 3 Dec 2012).

This story is a further illustration to show not just what this 'game' means from a female perspective but also a demonstration of how South African women can and do exercise their agency on sexual matters. She allowed herself to fall pregnant for what she described as "social reasons" and not because she was ready to be a parent or desirous of a child. Her mother wanted a grandchild from her in part to avoid her daughter being labelled in the community as *idlolo/akazali* (barren) or lesbian. Zoleka was able to exercise her agency to silence her mother but also towards this man.

However, being *udlalani* rests on performing a particular masculine identity. It produces status in a context in which there are limited opportunities for such. For a woman to be labelled as *isifebe* or *unontyintyi*[19] is an embarrassment not only to her image but to her children and family as well. Such a girlfriend degrades her boyfriend's social status in his community; he is looked down by associating himself with *ikati* (a cat). A typical example in this study is Sizwe. He gets frustrated whenever Minazana disappears to her boyfriends' nearby. Minazana is very clear in exercising her agency in their relationship with Sizwe. She is quick to remind Sizwe together with his family that they did not pay lobola for her therefore cannot control her lifestyle. In our conversation one afternoon he seemed helpless, telling me that,

It has been two weeks now we have not seen her here (at home) but people see her in that street. I know she is there and everyone here (at home) knows that she is with that guy. She is embarrassing me to my family and friends now… the worse thing ndiyayazi lekaka yentwana (I know this rubbish of a person). If it was not for my

---

[18] Her pregnancy was well-planned. Before attending the party she says she went to see a doctor and confirmation that she was ready for conception.

[19] Female alcoholic. The term *nontyintyi* does not apply to men. An alcoholic man is called *inxila* in Xhosa and *isidakwa* in Zulu

children I would chase her away I cannot live with someone like this. How can you marry someone like that? (Field notes, 14 Oct 2012).

Here, Sizwe acknowledges Ayanda as his. On this occasion, it gave him pride being a father of more than one child, just like it must have felt for his own father to have as many children as he had. Minazana's actions are embarrassing for him but she complains that he does not satisfy her needs.

In a context in which young men's access to valued roles and statuses is limited, certain performances of masculinity take precedence. Silberschmidt's (2001:657) work in Kenya also reveals that socio-economic changes in the rural and urban areas has increasingly systematically disempowered men resulting in men's lack of social value, self-esteem and economic value. Because young men are disempowered, they often find alternative ways to cope with their frustration and alienation from the mainstream social life. Often, they resort to doing drugs, violence over women and sex. Silberschmidt's findings are resonate with ours in Gugulethu where almost every man who participated in our study confessed having multiple casual sex with different women. Sizwe is the only exception. He is afraid to approach women (not least in case they learn that he is not initiated); hence his girlfriend calls him *isishumane* (a man who is scared of females). The irony is that he is "faithful" and conforms to the ideals of marriage even though not in one.

Conclusion

This chapter has examined agency of indigenous young AmaXhosa women in a South African place known as Gugulethu in Western Cape Province. Our study found out that African women, depending on their contexts or socio-cultural environments, unlike what other studies have revealed, do have agency except in few cases where they are raped. It is apparent that in an environment such as Gugulethu, both young men and women, are trying to find their way in a situation that has given up on them. In turn, the young women are claiming back their position in society as full human beings by challenging patriarchal tendencies where it is seen as acceptable for a men to have many sexual partners but the same society dehumanise women who live a similar lifestyle. Young women in this study insist that it is their own choice and decisions to engage in multiple sexual relationships thereby confirming that women have the same freedom and agency as that which men have about their bodies.

295

References

Fuller, N. (2003). *Work and Masculinity among Peruvian Urban Men: The role of men and boys in achieving gender equality*, International Labour Organization (ILO).

Geertz, C. (1983). 'From the native's point of view': On the nature of anthropological understanding, in: his *Local knowledge: Further Essays in Interpretive Anthropology*, New York.

Hunter, M. (2005) Cultural politics and masculinities: Multiple-partners in historical perspective in KwaZulu-Natal. *Culture, Health & Sexuality*, 7(4): 389-403.

Jewkes, R, & Morrell, R. (2012). Sexuality and the limits of agency among South African teenage women: Theorising femininities and their connections to HIV risk practices. *Social Science Medicine* 74 (11): 1729-1737.

Legarde, E., Auvert, B., Carael, M., Laourou, M., Ferry, B., Akam, E., Sukwa, T., Morison, L., Maury, B., Chege, J., N'Doye, I., & Buve, A. (2001). The study group on heterogeneity of HIV Epidemics in African Cities. Concurrent Sexual Partnerships and HIV prevalence in five urban communities of sub-Saharan Africa. *AIDS*, 15, Pp. 877-884.

Mawere, M. (2014) Forest Insects, Personhood and the Environment: *Harurwa* and Conservation in South-eastern Zimbabwe. *PhD Thesis*. University of Cape Town, South Africa.

Posel, D., & Rudwick, S. (2013). Marriage and ilobolo (bridewealth) in contemporary Zulu society. African Studies Review.

Richter, L., Chikovore, J. & Makusha, T. (2010). The status of fatherhood and fathering in South Africa. *Childhood Education*, 86, Pp. 360-365.

Silberschmidt, M. (2001). Disempowerment of men in rural and urban East Africa: Implications for male identity and sexual behaviour. *World Development*, 29(4): 657-   671.

Chapter 16

"*Ndiyindoda* (I'm a man)": Public Secrets, Harm and Pain in Xhosa Male Circumcision

Andile Mayekiso & Munyaradzi Mawere

Abstract

Male circumcision (*ukwaluka* in Xhosa), though is always associated with excruciating pain, is an old age practice among the Nguni people of South Africa, especially the Xhosa men due to its health and cultural significance. The production of a man in Nguni societies (Xhosa included) requires the ability to withstand severe continuous pain inflicted through *umdlanga* (assegai) and *ukubopha* (the wrapping). One's ability to publicly display *ukunyamezela* (to endure and overcome pain) not only is a sign of bravery, but also accords a man an adored social status and some modicum of respect, making him *indoda yonkwenene* ("a real man"). For the Xhosa people, the practice of *ukwaluka* was (and in fact remains) a traditional ritual with great cultural and social regard. Traditionally and culturally, a Xhosa male body is expected to go through great pain and be introduced to ancestors by spilling blood of an animal and circumcision to leave an identity mark for communal recognition. In this society, any man who does not go through this culturally approved path is ostracised. He is called by insulting names and constantly reminded of his inferior social status. However, the mark which becomes critical during *ukudodisa* (initiate's interrogation about his manhood journey) on its own is not sufficient. One can still be labelled an *inja* despite having the correct mark on his manhood if his behaviour and actions are deemed unmanly or boyish. In this chapter, we tease out and theorise and the identity of 'real man' in the Xhosa society, particularly how 'real' masculinity is an acquired social status produced through pain and secrecy. The chapter concludes that manhood in the Xhosa society is not only a birthmark but something discoverable, cultivatable, nurturable, and [re-]activatable through time to different degrees of potency depending on one's ability to withstand pain.

Keywords: male circumcision, public secrets, harm, pain, Xhosa, South Africa

Introduction

Contrary to female genital mutilation, male circumcision (MC) is not unique to a specific group of people but rather a universal practice across many cultures. The uniqueness of this ritual is on *why* and *how* it is performed (i.e., traditional versus hospitals) and most significantly is the age at which groups prefer to perform this rite of passage which subsequently result in specific meanings and meaning-making. According to Mogotlane, Ntlangulela & Ogunbanjo (2004:57), this ritual is considered by many (Nasrallah, 1985; Williams & Kapila, 1993; Ozdemir; 1997) to be the oldest of all the [human] surgical procedures as evidenced by drawings of cave dwellers from the Paleolithic age and the ancient Egyptian tomb of Ankh-Mahor in 2400 B.C respectively, which depict circumcised men and some Egyptian mummies who were found to have been circumcised. Peltzer *et al* (2007:658) also report that MC was and "...is common in most of West Africa". With regard to the practice of male circumcision in Africa, Peltzer *et al* further suggest that:

> Male circumcision seems not to be traditionally practised in some areas such as central-eastern Cote d'Ivoire, central Ghana, and southwest Burkina Faso (28% among the Lobi in southwest Burkina Faso; while the national prevalence is 90%). Many countries in Central and Eastern Africa have at least 50% male circumcision among their adult population: the prevalence varies from approximately 2 and 5% in Burundi and Rwanda to 70% in Tanzania, 84% in Kenya and 93% in Somalia. In southern Africa, the MC prevalence is the lowest: around 15% in several countries (Namibia, Swaziland, Zambia, Zimbabwe) although higher in others (Malawi 21%, Botswana 25%, South Africa 35%, Lesotho 48%, Mozambique 60%, Angola 66% and Madagascar 80%) (*ibid*).

It is clear from these figures therefore that, in Africa male circumcision is not as widespread as one would imagine for various reasons. One set of explanation for this is that it might have been "...stopped by European missionaries and colonial administrators. In Zululand and Swaziland, for instance, male circumcision was abandoned during wars in the early 19th century, presumably because of the difficulty of holding the circumcision 'schools' during the continual fighting" (UNAIDS, 2007 in Peltzer *et al*, 2007:658). Among the Venda people in South Africa, Dionisio and Viviani (2013:210) also argue that anthropologists such as Grant (1905),

Wheelwright (1905), Junod (1927), Harries (1929) and Hammond Tooke (1974) agree that male circumcision is not a traditional Venda practice. West and Morris (1982) believe that among Venda people, MC possibly '...started at the beginning of the last century, probably by imitation, as it was dangerous for an uncircumcised man to travel through the neighbouring Sotho territory: he was likely to be caught and detained by force and MC was performed on him".

In South Africa, Xhosa-speakers are among those ethnic groups who still perform this ritual preferably in a traditional manner. According to Ngxamingxa (1971), the earliest available records by missionaries suggest that the practice among Xhosas dates as far back as 1886. If done the traditional way, it is performed by a traditional surgeon (known as *ingcibi* in Xhosa) (who could also be a traditional healer) ideally to boys aged between 18 and 25. We should highlight though that, the age at which this ritual is performed varied as there was no set rule but rather an expectation that boys in their twenties should go for it. It is only in recent years with the involvement of government that there are specifics in terms of age categories, a point we will return to later in this chapter.

The focus in this chapter is on the significance of pain as shared by participants in this study. We are interested in theorising the socio-political implications for individuals when *abakhwetha* (initiates) fail to overcome the amount of pain inflicted on them during the whole period circumcision ritual is carried out. At an individual level, the failure to conquer this pain would render such individuals *amakhwenkwe* ('boys') despite their age and going through part of the passage rite such as having their foreskins removed the traditional way and having gone through this rite of passage with its deep "secrets" in terms of sacred terminology that initiates learn and the value of seclusion in building a Xhosa man associated with the practice. By and large, the Xhosa circumcision is considered a secret thus, it is necessary for one to reflect on these secrets and other such rituals associated with the practice in view of the recent events surrounding the release of the films called *Inxeba* as well as *Umthunzi Wentaba*.

Inxeba, Umthunzi Wentaba and "Public Secrets"

According to Manderson *et al* (2015:184), "a secret is something that goes beyond that which is shown and told". How then does a secret becomes public – a public secret? Writing about public secrets,

Taussig (1999:1) argued that "when the human body, a nation's flag, money, or a public statue is *defaced*, a strange surplus of negative energy is likely to be aroused from within the defaced thing itself". Some (Mookherjee 2006; Simmel 1906 in Manderson *et al*, 2015:184) have argued that "various cultural institutions and structures - kinship systems, initiates, age and gender, secret societies, and guilds - sustain the idea of private information and secret knowledge even when such secrets are public knowledge". Public secrets in this case becomes that information that is revealed only to a specific group of people like initiates such that it continues to be a secret to many – the public. Such information is private only to the designated group such that people may be killed when they decide to reveal secrets even where these might fall under the category of "public secrets", be it at government or community level.

The above remarks about secrets summarise what we have witnessed recently in South Africa about the movie, *inxeba* – the wound. The film is about a close relationship between two men in the context of the Xhosa initiation ritual known as *ulwaluko* (traditional male initiation). The main character, Xolani, a factory worker, joins the men of his community at the beginning of the annual initiation ceremony in the mountains of Eastern Cape Province (Mabasa, 2018). Xolani has been asked to act as *ikhankatha* (the initiate's guardian) but soon realises that this role will provide him with the opportunity to re-establish his sexual and romantic relationship with Vija, another character in the movie. When Xolani is assigned the role of *ikhankatha* for Kwanda, a young man from Johannesburg, he quickly realizes that Kwanda is also gay, and Kwanda soon recognises the nature of the relationship between Vija and Xolani. Tensions due to jealousy soon rise between the three men. Sexual relationships between men might be recognised and constitutionally accepted by the current South African government, but it is a practice that is largely frown upon by many in the countryside especially elders. In the countryside, similar to most townships in Cape Town such as Gugulethu and Khayelitsha, such relationships are usually maintained in secret due to violent acts or even rape against those individuals who are gay (or lesbian in the case of women) as a way of 'teaching them a lesson'.

The public's reaction to the movie, *inxeba*, led to the movie being classified as pornographic in nature leading to its subsequent banning. The film was accused of cultural insensitivity because people believed that it portrayed secretive initiation rituals even though at the time of the outcry many might not have even seen the full movie. Interestingly, some have questioned this reaction towards the movie citing, for instance, Nelson Mandela's *Long Walk to Freedom*, which did not receive similar criticism, leading to accusations that complaints about the film are instead motivated by homophobia (Adriaan, 2018). A day after the film's release in South Africa, cinemas in the Eastern Cape Province were forced to cancel screenings of the film and offer refunds because of protests, intimidation and vandalism that occurred at the time. Nu Metro Cinemas subsequently cancelled screenings countrywide, while Ster-Kinekor continued to show it outside of the Eastern Cape. The film's producers filed complaints with the Human Rights Commission and the Commission for Gender Equality over threats and violence (Mabasa, 2018) emanated from the film screening. There were reports that crew and cast members received death threats and as such were forced to go into hiding. The big question that has circulated in the media is: "Is it not acceptable for gay Xhosa men to show respect, appreciation and willingness to uphold their culture rather than going to hospitals [for circumcision] or even ignore this ritual?"

It seems the type of media through which "a secret" is revealed can or does determine how the audience will receive and react to its 'unveiling'. For example, the article by Ntozini and Ngqangeni (2016), *Gay Xhosa men's experiences of ulwaluko (traditional male initiation)* speaks directly to the same narrative covered by *inxeba* but it did not receive the same attention and scrutiny. One would also imagine a different response if this was conveyed as storytelling via radio stations, for instance. Nevertheless, it is important to remind the reader that the practice of *ukwaluka*[20] (male initiation/ circumcision) is considered a secret by its people as seen in recent marches, with some submitting that we should not be writing, publishing or debating it in public because it is a sensitive aspect of some people's culture.

---

[20] Some terms referring to this process are used interchangeably and sometimes it is not clear what people are actually referring to until further explanation is given. For example, the term *ukwaluka* (initiation), *wolusiwe* or *udlangiwe* (he has been circumcised/initiated) may refer to the act of foreskin cutting but also means the initiation procedure has happened. As Vivian (2008:13) warns, the term "initiation" (the Xhosa term – *ukwaluka*) is ambiguous because "it also refers to the induction of a healer, which, of course, does not involve circumcision per se." In her work she prefers the term circumcision to refer to *ukwaluka* to avoid this confusion and overlap. We follow her usage.

However, the reality is that in recent years, the ritual among Xhosas has been clouded by negativity; initiates dying or 'losing their penises' due to infections, improper cutting, bad treatment by *amakhankatha* and many other factors as shown below and the matter is already stimulating conversations in all sorts of media platforms, including Facebook and Twitter. The most contentious of the latter was a very graphic and controversial television programme called *Umthunzi Wentaba* (Shadow of the Mountain) shown on South African Broadcasting Corporation (SABC) in 2007. Due to public outcry and opposition "to the graphic portrayal of circumcision" from the Congress of Traditional Leaders of South Africa, the National Heritage Council and ANC chief whip Mathole Motshega, the SABC had to cancel its viewing until an edited version was approved later (2010-12-05, page 1. http://www.citypress.co.za). In other words, there is a history of censoring films about initiation and circumcision, and while the ostensible reasons for doing so have to do with ideas about what is appropriate (or inappropriate) to show (e.g., circumcision), part of what underlies the anxiety has to do with the place of the unseen, unshareable in the making of codes of masculinity and femininity. The media and involvement of the national Department of Health (DoH), in particular, have publicised "the secrets". The DoH's intervention is mainly, at least that is what we are made to believe, to "protect" the lives of innocent young boys who either die during rites of passage or have their penises removed (Mgqolozana, 2009). When we write about this ritual we are therefore engaging in a public discourse which at least the first author of this chapter is very familiar with as a Xhosa man. At personal level, he neither supports its publicity nor condone the loss of innocent lives of the young men.

It seems the challenge associated with this ritual is lack of accountability, assertiveness and general lack of leadership from elders who are supposed to be the custodians protecting its nobility and integrity. Their failure to step-up and protect its integrity has inevitably prompted even women, as mothers of these young boys who become victims, to no longer affording to take a back seat about what happens "in the bush", making this a 'public secret' of some sort. We would like to offer an ideal-type account interspersed with observations from the first author's personal experience and those of my research participants in Cape Town.

Heald (1982:15) argued that "when a ritual has this much significance for a people, it is important to enquire into what values are being affirmed and why a single ritual complexity is so charged". This is even more so with the Xhosa circumcision judging by an overwhelming outcry to *inxeba*. Undoubtedly, the movie is quite similar to *Umthunzi Wentaba* in terms of its portrayal of the graphic images of this ritual. As the title indicates, the film aims to reveal what many still consider to be a secret. The movie does not prepare one for what is about to happen but goes straight to the point when young boys sit before *ingcibi* with his briefcase full of blades/knives[21] displayed in their faces. Attempts to stop cinemas from showing this movie have proved futile because copies of the movie are already available on the streets of Johannesburg and elsewhere sold only for R10. So, the battle is lost already. In a society that is battling to deal with social abnormalities such as rape against women and children, the so-called corrective rape or punishment of gays and lesbians, including still deaths of initiates, this kind of reaction to cultural practices remains questionable.

The State: Xhosa Circumcision - a Public Health Issue?

In their study, Dionisio and Viviani (2013:215) reported that their participants "...were convinced that MC enhances sexual pleasure and that women prefer circumcised men, mainly so they can be sexually satisfied. MC, therefore, is regarded as a procedure through which a boy acquires social status, enhances his opportunities for sexual relations (as he can be chosen by women), together with his sexual and reproductive capacities". Furthermore, Peltzer *et al* (2007:659) observe that:

> male circumcision in most of Africa is a holistic concept with multiple and interconnected dimensions – religious, spiritual, social, biomedical, aesthetic and cultural. The traditional male rite precedes marriage, typically entails physical brutality, seclusion, testing, esoteric knowledge, death and rebirth imagery, name changes, dance, masked costumes, and dietary and sexual taboos.

Across all spheres, there is an agreement that MC has huge health benefits for individuals such that no attempts or even suggestions were made to stop the practice. In recent years, the significance of MC prompted government in South Africa to get involved. Government, in consultation with traditional leaders, agreed that

---

[21] Because what is shown in the movie is not the traditional *umdlanga*.

there should be a policy guiding the manner this ritual is conducted. According to Vincent (n.d: 11),

> The Eastern Cape's circumcision legislation sets the legal age for circumcision at 18 but boys of 16 and older may be circumcised with the permission of their parents or guardians. This is in line with the new Children's Act (Act No. 38 of 2005) which was signed into law in June 2006. The Children's Act (Chapter 2, Section 12 (8) prohibits circumcision of male children under the age of 16 except when performed for religious purposes or for medical reasons. The Act also stipulates that male children older than 16 may be circumcised only with their consent and after proper counselling.

However, even with the state intervention, the ritual has continued to be marked by scandals and deaths of young initiates till this day. Vincent (2008:434) reported that "in 2006, there were 19 deaths of initiates in the Eastern Cape reported by October alone. A further 63 Eastern Cape initiates underwent penile amputations and a total of 562 were hospitalised". More so, during winter circumcision period in 2018, 19 young initiates lost their lives (Ngcukana, 22 July 2018). All this happened under the watch of the provincial health department. This therefore seem to be enough justification for "outsiders" to show interest on this ritual.

It is important also to note that there are areas in Eastern Cape where male circumcision ritual was allegedly not practiced but due to peer pressure at institutions of higher learning, young boys go back to their fathers to demand this ritual to avoid discrimination in urban cities. This is allegedly the major reason for high dates rates, amputations and 'failed manhood' in those areas that have no history of practising *ukwaluka*. For things to go smoothly, one needs a responsible *khankatha* and a well-managed support structure. In the case of the first author, he was assisted by his brother who, even though there was an appointed man as his *ikhankatha*, was always there to make sure he was well looked after[22].

As alluded to earlier, AmaZulu have not practiced *ukwaluka* since Shaka's time, although some might now be doing it privately through the health institutions because the national department of health is

---

[22] The more I wanted water without *ithuthu* (wood ash), the less sleep I had because I needed to change my *isichwe* quite often than normal. On the eighth day, the day of *ukosisa* (slaughtering of a sheep to allow me to go outside, search for *izichwe* and eat any food) I was almost healed. It took me five more days afterwards to heal properly and stop the wrapping completely.

encouraging all men in South Africa to get circumcised for health reasons. Circumcision has been shown to reduce HIV infection. An initial short-term randomised controlled study on male circumcision led by the Agence nationale de recherche sur le sida (ANRS) at Orange Farm in South Africa revealed a reduction of 60-75% in the risk of female to male transmission of HIV-1 in circumcised men (Auvert *et al.*, 2005 in Peltzer *et al*, 2007). It was such findings that prompted the Zulu King, Goodwill Zwelithini, to also support male circumcision for his kingdom. In an interview with CNN in 2010 (1 July, page 1), King Zwelithini stated thus: "I don't want to lose any of my Zulu people. As I've revived this circumcision, I'm showing my love to my people. Let's hold our hands together. But you young ones, accept – listen to your king's call" (Gwala, 2010:1). Another aspect of this ritual especially among Xhosa speakers is a growing tension between initiates who perform this ritual in urban settings versus those who do it in rural areas.

Rural-urban circumcision war

Mfecane (2016: 204) remarked that "uncircumcised Xhosa speaking males are generally referred to as boys, *amakhwenkwe*, irrespective of their age or social status. They are not allowed to marry or perform rituals. (Similarly), medically circumcised men are equally viewed as being inferior to traditionally circumcised men and are given negative labels" (see also Peltzer and Kanta 2009; Mavundla *et al.* 2010). Another category that we feel has not received the sort of attention it deserves is the ever-growing tension between Xhosa initiates who perform this ritual in rural settings versus those who undergo it in urban environment which is generally associated with lack of culture. While initiation remains central to masculine identity-making, not all men are initiated and, particularly in urban areas, there are great debates over the place and value of this aspect of identity-formation, and the rural-urban contrasts that shape it.

Ten of our male participants were born and raised in Cape Town, leaving only two men born in the countryside; Ta Pat (44) and Sizwe (35). All the men in our study were initiated except Sizwe because, as is common practice in Nguni kinship systems, he self-identifies as Zulu though his mother identifies herself as Xhosa. The use of *ukwaluka* (circumcision) as a cultural practice and marker of male social status through the inscription of male bodies produces tensions among initiated men at different levels (Ngwane 2001;

Mgqolozana 2009). Connell (2005) draws our attention to the fact that even in one cultural setting there are different versions of what it means to be a man. This is evident among the initiated amaXhosa men (or Xhosa men) who interact with Sizwe, a Zulu man born to a Xhosa woman and Zulu father. *Amadoda welokishi or onolokishi* ("Township men") with whom we worked are accommodative, in their approach, to men like Sizwe, someone who has not gone through circumcision, whereas *onolali* or *amadoda asezilalini* (rural or countryside men) do not compromise on 'man' versus 'boy' differences. Firstly, in our study, these tensions emanate between those who perform the ritual in the countryside through *ingcibi* (a traditional surgeon), and those initiates within the same group but for different reasons, as alluded to by Thando Mgqolozana (2009), finish their circumcision in hospitals and not in the 'countryside bush'. This has serious implications for the future of such young men in the community. The second category of these conflicts is between *onolali* (rural or countryside men) and *onolokishi* (township men). Both these terms carry derogatory meanings. *Unolali* (singular) is associated with darkness, backwardness and those thought of to be in need of civilisation, whereas *unolokishi* (singular) is seen as someone who is modern, 'current' and 'up-to-date'. *Unolali* regard *unolokishi* as lacking traditional ways of life and therefore useless to communal life. Such men are often labelled as 'lost' sheep in need of a shepherd. Countryside men see themselves as superior, as representing 'real Xhosa men' because they *stick* to *traditions* whereas *onolokishi* are viewed as 'lesser men' and inferior. The last group of men who are regarded as boys despite them also having the [circumcision] mark[23] engraved on their bodies are those who perform their initiation in hospitals, often referred to as *amakhwenkwe* (boys), *amadoda kanesi* (Nurse's men). It draws our attention to the generational conflicts between models and modes of masculinity that differentiate between 'urban' and 'rural' modes of life. Also interesting is the fact that during traditional ceremonies, these men exclude a man like Sizwe when it is time to either eat the food or drink traditional beer.

---

[23] Again *ukudodisa* (man's initiation interrogation) is used to establish whether a man has stitches on his penis or he healed through the use of *isichwe*. Hospital stitches are easily identified and once found out one can even be beaten up for being accused of taking chances with real men.

Ndiyindoda, Pain and Shame

Mfecane (2016:204) writes about constructions of masculinity among the Xhosa people of South Africa. Although acknowledging that a lot has been written about this ritual, he is very critical about the lack of theorising the notion of *ulwaluko*. He argues that "South African research on men and masculinities has been characterised by academic dependence on the West to provide theories of masculinity upon which research questions and empirical research are based" (2016:205). Generally, literature on Xhosa initiation and masculine identity-making is surprisingly quiet on the value of pain in the making of a man except for studies by Makhubu, (2012), Mgqolozana (2009), Ntozini & Ngqangweni (2016). We argue in this chapter that, based on the first author's personal experience and contemporary debates among isiXhosa speaking people who participated in this study, the ability to withstand pain is an essential indelible marker in the making and production of men in Nguni society. Signs indicating that one is unable to handle pain have serious implications for one's future social standing. It is clear from the comments below that, pain is an important marker in one's ability to endure hardships in the [countryside] bush but also in life. In a group discussion (19 July 2012), men shared their experiences:

Vuyo (35): *Gents ziyabuya kulakaka, ubuyazi nje xakuzobetha u-6 late okanye ekuseni ukuba kufuneka ubeyindoda, uqine* (Guys it's tough in that shit, you knew before 6pm or in the morning that you will need to be a man, be strong).

Mabhanti (29): *Bekusithi xasekusinyiwa phaya ndizisole ukuba bendisiyaphi* (when the going gets tough I used to regret going there). *Ivele iqaqambe leweyi zimnke inqgondo* (this thing would be so painful to a point where you lose your mind).

Ta Pat (44): *So nawe wenze lento yalapha yokutshintsha kabini ngemini?* (So, you also did this thing of changing twice per day?)

Vuyo: *Yhaa may Ta senzanjalo, kanti nina aniyitshintshi le-wayi?* (Yes, my big brother that's what we did, don't you guys change this thing that side?)

Ta Pat: *Kuthi ngu-waya waya... bobona budoda obo mfowethu, not le-wayi yenu apha! Ngamasimba la enziwapha maan ndiyazibona ezintwana zifaka ezi-weyi zasemahozi. Hayi mfowethu ayibobudoda kum obo mna ndanyiswa zintlungu 24/7.* (To us it's all day long... that is real manhood my brother, not this thing of yours here! What is done here is bushtit man, I see these

307

boys applying those things from hospital. No, my brother that is not manhood to me. I suffered with pains 24/7).

Shayela (24): *Kwezantsuku ndandisela ku-grand but ngobabusuku ndasela nditshaya neganja but nothing, zangendinxile tu because ndandicinga ngaleweyi yosikwa. But yintlonti lena yacingwa ngamakhehla bafowethu* (days before I was drinking... it was all awesome but that night I drank and smoke dagga, but nothing happened, I didn't get drunk at all because I was thinking about this thing of cutting. But this thing of our grandparents is naughty).

Ta Pat: *Kunzima for mna uthetha ngalento nani ngoba nina nifaka izinto anifani nathi, thina sinyiswa sisicwe imini nobusuku so andiboninto ndinoyithetha nani ngokoluka...* (it is difficult for me to talk about this issue with you because you use things to minimise pain. For us, we suffer with that leaf day and night so I don't see anything that I can discuss with you about circumcision) (Group Discussion, 19 July 2012).

The conversation soon became an attack on and undermining of other men by Ta Pat. Other group members could not really challenge or argue with him also because of the large age gap between Ta Pat and the others. In fact, Xhosa codes of respect for elders intervened in what might otherwise have become a heated conversation. Knowing that men have killed each other before on this topic, the first author (who carried out interviews) decided to introduce another topic for discussion. He felt it might be better to continue this conversation with individuals rather than in a group setting.

AM: What do you remember most about your circumcision Ta Pat?
Ta Pat: *Kumnandi esuthwini xaseluphilile, but asoze ndizilibale ezantlungu. Usaluka wam kwaqalwa ngaye wakhala xa imdlanga langcibi kuba yayinguye ususothu... ithe isithi makathi — ndiyindoda!! Zange liphume ilizwi... ithe ifika kum ndabe sendizixelele ukuba asoze ndikhala. Yabona xa kutshintshwa isichwe funeka ulunge ngoba lamadoda ajonge inyawu zakho ukuba zenzani. Once bakubone zishukuma bayazixelela ukuba uyoyika and lonto bazayothetha ngayo esiXhoseni. Uyabona lento ingakwenza woyike nabantu... ubanexhala xakufika indoda ngoba izawuthi khulula ibone, lonto ithi uzawufaka isichwe esitsha* (it's a lovely experience in the bush once you heal, but I will never forget those pains. My initiate friend was circumcised first, and he cried when the surgeon cut him... he had to go first as the owner of the hut... by the time the surgeon asked him to say, I am a man!! His voice disappeared... when the surgeon came to me, I already told myself that I will not cry. You see when they change that leaf, you need to be ready for it because other men will be watching your feet's movement. Once they see that

your feet is moving/shaking, they tell themselves that you are scared and they will spread that rumour in the village. You see this thing can make you even fear other people... you become scared when a man arrive because he will say strip I want to see, that means you must put a new leaf) (Interview, 15 August 2012).

The first author also asked Player the same question earlier:

AM: Player what do you remember most about your circumcision?

Player: *Hey my man yilamini yokuqala because ndafika ndalala phaya but uvuka kwam kwakuligazi nje nasebhayini lam. Athi lamabhuteri kukusela utywala lento yandiphisa kakhulu. Inoba ndizoyijonge leweyi kwisuku lesibini because ndandiyoyika. Iyaqaqamba lashiti yathiphela lo-8 days ndabe ndibhityile nam* (Hey my man it is that first day because when I arrived there I fell asleep but when I woke up there was blood all over even on my blanket. Other men said to me it's because I drank too much alcohol that is why I bled that much. I think I only looked at my wound on my second day because I was scared. That shit is painful, by the end of that 8 days I was thin) (Interview, 6 August 2012).

The saying '*indoda ayikhali*' (a man does not cry) is a way of discouraging men from expressing their feelings through crying. When Ta Pat's friend cried, it immediately gave other men something to gossip about in the village but also raised doubts about his ability to withstand what was about to come. In the countryside, no anaesthetics are allowed throughout the process and should one be seen/heard making noise, he will be labelled as *usisi* (a sisi), *umfazi*[24] (a married woman), indicating that one is not strong enough or 'not man enough' (*sisifede*). In the contrary, for one to be considered *indoda yenene* ('a real man'), one has to overcome this brutal but rewarding process.

Makhubu (2012:505) state that "The body is a primary site from which violence can be articulated". She further (ibid) argues that in Xhosa male circumcision, it is imperative that pain be experienced consciously in the process of constructing masculine identity. A man

---

[24] The belief that women are weak and cannot withstand pain is misleading. It shows men's arrogance and lack of understanding the pain women going through for instance when giving birth but also the emotional pain many African women endure in marriages. As alluded to earlier in chapter 1, my mother lost her baby because she was not given time to care for her. Her mother-in-law hated my mother because she wanted my father to marry another woman but my mother *wanyamezela* (she persevered). What is needed from us men is to understand why someone would go through such pain when her parents are still alive and could have easily provided for her.

is thus defined, in this context, by his capacity to endure pain. Ta Pat's friend regardless of how he handled the process afterwards, that cry will always be attached to him as a sign of weakness. The common denominator of strength, virility, endurance and resistance in this case is socially performed pain.

Because of fear and valorisation of pain, some boys do not see what happens to them during initiation (*ukudlangwa* – the cutting stage) as they would rather be 'dead' due to alcohol overdose. As Shayela indicated above that he tried to overdose himself with alcohol and dagga but due to fear of the unknown he could not get drunk. I have also observed and assisted many boys taken to the bush in wheelbarrows because they have consumed alcohol and other drugs so that they do not see *ukudlangwa*. As such, Mayatula and Mavundla (1997:18) report in their study that alcohol use prior to, and after the procedure in attempt to ease pain, has been implicated in excessive bleeding sometimes leading to death.

As soon as *ingcibi* finishes, the initiate must pronounce the words after the surgeon *Ndiyindado!* (I am a man!)[25] as can be seen and heard from the movie, *inxeba*. This is a critical moment in testing one's ability to withstand pain and still show a brave face to other men because, due to the pain just been experienced, one's voice is likely to be shaky. The worst thing that can happen is to cry. Crying is regarded as a sign of weakness and fearfulness, and it immediately raises eyebrows about the initiate's ability to withstand pain going forward because the pain due to the cutting off of the foreskin is nothing compared to the pain that will follow until one is fully healed. The pain inflicted on the initiate differentiates men who undertake this journey in rural settings from those who circumcise in urban areas. To men initiated in the villages, men who are initiated in urban areas are considered "not men enough" because they do not experience the amount and intensity of the pain we go through there.

---

[25] The drunken ones never get to say this and one will always be reminded of this day by his friends and other men especially in conflict situations. In our village my brothers and I stand in good position even from the elders because we never touched alcohol, a sign of a strong man with big heart, even though we had plenty of it available to us. In my case there were 19 bottles of brandy excluding beer cases and *umqombothi*. It must be said that while there can be bad treatment and lack of care of initiates in seclusion, their intoxication and body shock to a complete new way of life plays a part in them landing in hospital. Because of the pain some do not tend to their wound until it is too late and these are the ones who are quick to blame others when things go wrong. One has to be mentally and physically ready for *ukwaluka* because it is not child's play.

310

This explains some of the controversy around the state's suggestion that circumcision be undertaken in hospitals.

Isichwe (singular) that Ta Pat spoke about above sticks on the wound and it must be removed and a new one placed every 10 to 15 minutes 24 hours a day[26]). The wrapping and undoing of the wound is called *ukutyama*. Failing to remove *isichwe* (foreskin) as often as possible makes the wound wet, hence delaying the healing process. The removal of *isichwe* is similar to spilling spirit to an open wound; it feels like fire. Those initiated in urban contexts generally do not go through this process. For them, these changes (wrapping and unwrapping) happens twice a day, very early in the morning and again early evening[27].

Silverman (2004: 421) state that *ukwaluka* involves 'physical brutality, seclusion, testing, esoteric knowledge, death and rebirth imagery, name changes, dance, masked costumes, and dietary and sexual taboos.' A well-known Xhosa author, Peter Mtuze (2004:41) sees *ukwaluka* as a "…gateway to manhood in the same way that baptism is the gateway to Christianity" (2004:41). It is true that there are slight differences on how the practice of *ukwaluka* is performed in different areas as shown by the testimonies of this study.[28] Furthermore, Vincent (2008:14) writes that the stripping of the boys' clothing (blankets) "…symbolically [marks] the break with boyhood and the entry into a transitionary phase en route manhood." Basing on the first author's informed first-hand experience and our deep metaphysical and epistemological reflections as authors, our analysis and interpretation of the stripping of the boys differ. Here, we propose a materialist argument; that the stripping of youths is to enable water to be thrown at them so as to enable the *ingcibi* to grasp their foreskins. To be considered a real man among the Xhosas one must avoid anything to do with hospitals. Those who go there first for the foreskin removal are considered *amadoda wephepha* (paper men) or *amadoda kaNesi* (Nurse's men).

---

[26] Sleeping is considered a luxury; you hardly get a chance to take a nap.

[27] Some are known to make use of betadine ointment which makes them less men in social standing to us because it neutralises the pain one experiences.

[28] For example, Wilson (1952:200) states that after the foreskin is removed, the initiate's father would give it to him to swallow. I have heard such stories many times especially when I was still a boy but consider this an insult that humiliates and undermines "other" people's culture. What happens to the foreskin is kept secret to discourage witchcraft.

Conclusion

Culturally, a Xhosa male body must go through much pain and be introduced to ancestors by spilling blood of an animal and circumcision to leave an identity mark for communal recognition. However, the mark which becomes critical during *ukudodisa* (initiate's interrogation about his manhood journey) on its own is not sufficient. One can still be labelled as *inja* despite having the correct mark on his manhood if his behaviour and actions are deemed unmanly or boyish[29]. Similarly, we have theoretically compared this with Mehta (2000:79), in his paper on Indian Muslim male circumcision, which shows how Muslim male bodies are "...constituted through the ritual of circumcision, called *khatna*". His work also shows how pain from circumcision is central to the making of men and a shared sense of male community, thus "each male must bear this pain and witness it in another" (Mehta, 2000:80). The production of a man in Nguni societies requires the ability to withstand excruciating continuous pain inflicted through *umdlanga*[30] (assegai) and *ukubopha* (the wrapping). One's ability to publicly display *ukunyamezela* (to endure and overcome pain) not only is a sign of bravery, but also gives a man adored social status and respect, making him *indoda yonkwenene* ("a real man"). In this chapter, we have teased out the identity of 'real man' in the Xhosa society, particularly how 'real' masculinity is an acquired social status produced through pain and secrecy. In this society, any man who does not go through this culturally approved path is ostracised. He is called by insulting names and constantly reminded of his inferior social status. We have, however, demonstrated that the use of *ukwaluka* (circumcision) as a cultural practice and marker of male social status through the inscription of male bodies produces tensions among initiated men at

---

[29] An interesting observation is that even though a new man runs to the river with boys and other men chasing him to wipe off his white ochre but once he comes home he should not run even if the rain is pouring down on him. I watched with keen interest a new man who had gone to fetch his newly found girlfriend from another village when the rain was pouring with lightening. His girlfriend run to a nearby house and found shelter between the houses but he continued to walk home. She later followed him. For a new man to be seen running he would be labelled as acting like a boy, meaning he did not leave behind his boyhood acts. As a man you are expected to walk slowly with dignity.

[30] *Umdlanga*[30] hold a different meaning to the Xhosa people than the everyday use of the term *ukusikwa* (to cut – usually by a knife). *Umdlanga* is usually kept with traditional herbs so that evil spirits could not affect it when it is time for usage.

312

different levels. It draws our attention to the generational conflicts between older and young more schooled men and between models of masculinity that differentiate between 'urban' and 'rural' modes of life.

References

Adriaan, R. (19 February 2018). "Inxeba shows how far African storytelling still has to go". *The Citizen*. Retrieved 20 October 2018.

City Press. (2010). Graphic circumcision drama returns to SABC. (Published: 2010-12-05, 12:56). http://www.citypress.co.za

Dionisio, E., & Viviani, F. (2013). Male circumcision among the Venda of Limpopo (South Africa). In Denniston, GC., *et al. (eds.), Genital Cutting: Protecting Children from Medical, Cultural, and Religious Infringements*, DOI: 10.1007/978-94-007-64071_14.

Grant, W. (1905). *Magato and his tribe*. J. Royal Anthropological Institute 4:267.

Gwala, X. (2010). *Zulu king promotes circumcision to fight HIV/AIDS*. Available: http://edition.cnn.com/2010/WORLD/africa/07/01/circumcision.south.africaaids

Hammond-Tooke, W. D. (1974). *The Bantu-speaking peoples of southern Africa*. London and Boston: Routledge and Kegan P. Publ.

Harries, C. L. (1929). *The Laws and customs of the BaPedi and cognate tribes of the Transvaal*. Johannesburg, Hortors Limited.

Heald, S. (1982). The making of men: the relevance of vernacular psychology to the interpretation of a Gisu ritual. *Africa*. Vol. 52(1).

Junod, H. A. (1927). *The life of a South African tribe*. MacMillan, London.

Mabasa, N. (9 February 2018). *Inxeba:* Wounding the Pride and Prejudice of Xhosa men? *Daily Maverick*. https://www.dailymaverick.co.za/article/2018-02-09-inxebawounding-thepride-and-prejudice-of-xhosa-men/. Retrieved 22 October 2018.

Makhubu, N. (2012). Violence and the cultural logics of pain: representations of sexuality in the work of Nicholas Hlobo and Zanele Muholi. *Critical Arts*, Vol. 26(4).

Manderson, L., Davis, M., Colwell, C., & Ahlin, T. (2015). On Secrecy, Disclosure, the Public, and the Private in Anthropology. *Current Anthropology*, Vol. 56, Supplement 12.

Mavundla, TR., Netswera, F. G., Toth, F., Bottoman, B., & Tenge. S. (2010). How Boys Become Dogs: Stigmatization and Marginalization of Uninitiated Xhosa Males in East London, South Africa. *Qualitative Health Research*, 20 (7): 931- 941.

Mayatula, V., & Mavundla, T. (1997). 'A review on male circumcision procedures among South African blacks'. *Curationis*, September, 16-20.

Mayekiso, A. (2017). *'Ukuba yindoda kwelixesha'* ('To be a man in these times'): Fatherhood, marginality and forms of life among young men in Gugulethu, Cape Town. Unpublished PhD thesis. Cape Town: University of Cape Town.

Mehta, D. (2000). *Circumcision, body, masculinity: the ritual wound and collective violence.* In Veena, D. Kleinman, A, Ramphele, M, & Reynolds, P. 2000. *Violence and Subjectivity.* University of California Press: London.

Mfecane, S. (2016). *"Ndiyindoda"* (I am a man): theorising Xhosa Masculinity. *Anthropology Southern Africa*, 39(3): 204-214, DOI: 10.1080/23323256.2016.1208535.

Mgqolozana, T. (2009). *A man who is not a man.* University of KwaZulu-Natal Press.

Mogotlane, SM., Ntlangulela, JT. and Oganbanjo, BJ. 2004. Mortality and morbidity among traditionally circumcised Xhosa boys in the Eastern Cape Province of South Africa. *Curationis*, 27(2): 57-62.

Mookherjee, N. (2006). Remembering to forget: public secrecy and memory of sexual   violence in the Bangladesh war of 1971. *Journal of the Royal Anthropological Institute*, 12(2): 433-450.

Mtuze, P. (2004). Introduction to Xhosa culture. Alice: Lovedale Press.

Nasrallah, P. F. (1985). Circumcision. Pros and cons. Primary Care. 12(4): 593-605.

Ngcukana, L. (22 July 2018). "Time to question initiate deaths". *City Press.* Retrieved 10th November 2018. https://www.news24.com/SouthAfrica/News/time-to-questioninitiate-deaths-20180721.

Ngwane, Z. (2001). 'Real men reawaken their fathers' homesteads, the educated leave them in ruins': the politics of domestic reproduction in post-apartheid rural South Africa. *Journal of Religion in Africa,* 31 (4): 402-426.

Ngxamingxa, A. N. (1971). The function of circumcision among the Xhosa-speaking tribes in historical perspective. *Man: anthropological essays presented to O.F.Raum.* Cape Town, South Africa. C. Struik Publishing. 183-204.

Ntozini, A., & Ngqangweni, H. (2016). Gay Xhosa men's experiences of *ulwaluko* (traditional male initiation). *Culture, Health and Sexuality.* 18(11): 1309-1318. http://dx.doi.org/10.1080/13691058.2016.1182213.

Ozdemir, E. (1997). Significantly increased complication risks with mass circumcision. *British Journal of Urology.* Vol. (80), 136-139.

Pauw, H. C. (1994). *The Xhosa.* Port Elizabeth: Institute for Planning Research, University of Port Elizabeth.

Peltzer, K., Niang, C. I., Muula, AS., Bowa, K., Okeke, L., Boiro, H., & Chimbwete, C. (2007). Editorial review: Male circumcision, gender and HIV prevention in sub-Saharan Africa: a (social science) research agenda. SAHARA-J: *Journal of Social Aspects of HIV/AIDS,* 4: (3): 658-667, DOI: 10.1080/17290376.2007.9724889.

Silverman, EK. 2004. Anthropology and Circumcision. *Annual Review of Anthropology 33,* 419-45.

Simmel, G. (1906). The sociology of secrecy and of secret societies. *American Journal of Sociology,* 11(4): 441-498.

Taussig, M. T. (1999). *Defacement: Public secrecy and the labour of the negative.* Stanford, CA: Stanford University Press.

Vincent, L. (2007). 'Boys will be boys': traditional Xhosa male circumcision, HIV and sexual socialisation in contemporary South Africa. *Culture, Health & Sexuality,* 10(5): 431-446.

Vincent, L. (2008). *Male circumcision policy, practices and services in the Eastern Cape Province of South Africa: Case Study,* WHO/UNAIDS.

Vivian, L.M.N. (2008). *Psychiatric disorder in Xhosa-speaking men following circumcision.* Unpublished PhD thesis. Cape Town: University of Cape Town.

West M, & Morris J. (1982). *Abantu: An introduction to the black people of South Africa.* C Struik Publications, Cape Town, 89-198.

Wheelwright C. A. (1905). Native circumcision lodges in the Zoutpansberg District. *J. Roy Anthropological Institute* 4:252.

Williams, N. & Kapila, L. (1993). Complications of circumcision. *British journal of Surgery.* 80 (10): 1231-1236.

Wilson, MH. 1952. *Social Structure*. Pietermaritzburg: Shuter and Shooter.

Interviews
Group Discussion, 19 July 2012. In Gugulethu.
Player: Interview, 6 August 2012. In Gugulethu.
Ta Pat, Interview, 15 August 2012. In Gugulethu.

Chapter 17

Indigenous Knowledge Systems for Sustainable Cattle Disease Management in Masvingo District, Zimbabwe

Daniel Gamira

Abstract

The purpose of this study was to explore the use of Indigenous Knowledge Systems (IKS) by rural farmers to manage outbreak of cattle diseases in Masvingo District of Masvingo province. The objectives of the study were to examine the use of indigenous knowledge systems to manage young animals for breeding purposes and management of breeding periods, analyse common cattle diseases in the Zimuto study area of Masvingo District, examine ethnoveterinary medicinal plants used by farmers to treat cattle diseases and to identify common plant parts extracted to cure cattle diseases Zimbabwe. Bandura's Social Learning Theory (SLT) was used to lens this qualitative study, which embraced a descriptive case study design. Fifteen (15) farmers with more than 25 years of farming experience were purposively selected to participate in the study. Data was generated through semi-structured and unstructured interviews. Findings reveal that farmers applied IKS to service heifers at 24-36 months, wean calves between 6-8 months, dehorn at 70 kilograms, castrated steers between 8-12 months, practiced rotational grazing to control diseases, dipped animals using tree leaves, shrubs and herbs. Common diseases revealed were black leg, foot and mouth disease, lumpy skin, read water and heart water. Common ethnoveterinary trees were *muvheva, murumanyama, musiringa, mubvumakuvau, muroodze, durura* and *danadare*. The study further highlighted that farmers can apply Bandura's Social Learning Theory to pass on ethnoveterinary knowledge from generation to generation, manage and control disease outbreaks.

Keywords: Indigenous Knowledge Systems, Ethnoveterinary medicine; rural farmers; cattle management; Social Learning Theory

Introduction

Zimbabwe has favourable climatic conditions for cattle rearing, particularly in Natural Regions 3, 4, 5 and 6. These regions are characterised by favourable temperatures from 25- 32 Celsius, ideal for cattle, large tracks of grazing land and favourable rainfall. Masvingo Province which falls in natural region 5 is no exception. Conditions such as rainfall and temperature are deemed suitable for vast cattle rearing. Masvingo Province is home to 1 000 000 cattle (Nyathi, 2008). However, such suitable conditions can come with lots of cattle disease causing organisms such as bacteria, virus, fungi and protozoa. There has been continuous and serious cattle disease outbreaks in Masvingo District from 2010-2020, and these have been attributed to a number of factors such as lack of regular dipping and uncontrolled cattle movement from area to area. The has resulted in depleted herds that has affected the farmer's ability to sell off his animals when the need arises It is against that backdrop that the chapter attempts to evaluate the applications of Indigenous Knowledge Systems in Zimuto area of Masvingo District as an alternative to manage cattle diseases apart from Western approaches.

Indigenous knowledge application and use has been marginalized by colonial governments in Zimbabwe and Africa in general. Therefore, the knowledge has been relegated to represent superstition, despite its abundance and farmers' capability of passing it from generation to generation. European settlers who colonized the African continent in the 19th century sought to destroy, denigrate or marginalize IKS and replace them with Western views and approaches which were in line with their goals of imperialism (Mapira and Mazambara, 2013; Muyambo, 2019). According to Muyambo (2018), IKSs in Africa are known by various names, as people's science, ethno-science, folk ecology, village science and local knowledge. This characterization of IKS was further confirmed by Matsika (2012, p. 209-210), who defined "IKS as the traditional and local knowledge that exists and developed through experiences of local community in process of managing the conditions or context that challenge the people's everyday life." In the context of livestock disease management, IKS is called ethnoveterinary medicine (EVM). EVM is a scientific term for traditional animal health care that encompasses the knowledge, skills, methods, practices and beliefs about animal care found among community members (Marandure, 2016). According to Misra and Kumar (2004), EVM is the

318

community based local or indigenous knowledge and methods for caring for, healing and managing livestock. The above resonates well with the definition by Yigezu, Haile and Ayen (2014), who considered ethnoveterinary medicine as the application of veterinary folk knowledge, theory and practice to treat ailments of livestock. This realization and practice came against a backdrop that treatment by contemporary veterinary medicine has in many countries gone out of reach by ordinary farmers, often due to high costs and non-coverage (Eguale et al., 2011; Iqbal et al., 2005; Yigezu, Haile and Ayen, 2014). Therefore, EVM provides valuable alternatives to and complements Western style veterinary medicine which has become inaccessible due to high costs synthetic drugs.

Objectives of the study

The objectives of the study were to examine indigenous knowledge systems used for cattle management systems, examine common cattle diseases in Zimuto area and assess common ethnoveterinary medicinal plants commonly used by farmers to treat cattle disease and to identify plant parts extracted to treat cattle ailments

Literature Review

Livestock production is an integral part of the agricultural systems in many parts of developing countries (Wanzala et al., 2005). This is so because livestock serves diverse functions and roles, including the provision of food, income, employment and draught power, the dung is used as fuel and fertilizer (FAO, 2011; Picamarra et al., 2011). That livestock production attracts lots of ailments to poor rural communities who can hardly afford to buy western drugs and have to resort to IKS. According to MAO (2012) livestock diseases negatively affect income and farming activities of the rural poor which in turn has implications on the livelihoods of the farmers. A lot of studies on ethnoveterinary medicine points to the fact that cattle diseases can be treated successful using different forms of indigenous knowledge systems in Zimbabwe and in Africa. In support of such practices The World Health Organization (WHO) during the Alma-Ata proclamation in 1978 declared the important roles of ethno-botanical products in veterinary and human medicines and further declared them considerably safe. In 1996, the American

Veterinary Medicine Association officially stated that botanical products are safely used in complement of National Intervention Program in livestock diseases Yigezu, Haile and Ayen, 2014). Therefore, the use of ethno-botanical products finds support globally.

Cattle are affected by diseases that affect their efficiency and contribution to rural livelihoods. Therefore, medicinal plants are used and are important for rural communities for the treatment of livestock and cattle diseases. Many indigenous veterinary beliefs and practices persist in a wide majority of livestock raisers, particularly in the developing countries (Iqbal et al., 2005). Such medicinal plants have been used since human evolution. The use of ethnoveterinary traditional knowledge has been reported worldwide in such countries as India (Sri and Vakrama, 2010), Nigeria (Musa et al., 2008), South Africa (Toyang et al., 2007), Zimbabwe (Matekaire and Bwakura, 2004 and Pakistan (Hussain et al., 2008; Khan et al., 2010) to cure numerous livestock diseases, cattle diseases and their control, remedies, clinical practices of treatment and prevention, management, feeding and breeding strategies.

Many scholars have reported on the use of indigenous knowledge to treat cattle diseases. A study by Kidane et al. (2014) reported on 46 ethnoveterinary plant species from 28 families that are used to livestock diseases where leaves and succulents are commonly used to treat Black leg. A related study by Yigezu, Haile and Ayen (2014) reported a total of 74 plant species of ethnoveterinary medicinal plants identified for treating 22 different livestock ailments mainly against Black leg. A study by Regassa (2004) revealed that about 80-90% of livestock population in Ethiopia is believed to rely on traditional medicine for the treatment and control of diseases. Several studies reported on use of traditional veterinary practices in Ethiopia. Giday and Ameni (2003) reported on 83 medicinal plant species used for the treatment of 37 types of livestock ailments. Sori et al., (2004) identified 77 different plants used by Bosana pastoralists to treat and prevent a wide range of livestock diseases. In addition, Yineger et al (2007) reported on 74 veterinary medicinal plant species that were distributed among 64 genera and 37 families were used to treat animal diseases. Yirga et al. (2012a) and Yirga et al (2012b) found 22 plant species for treating 18 different livestock ailments. Gebrezgabiher et al (2013) documented 29 medicinal plant species belonging to 23 various families. Achyranthes aspera L. (10.4%) Calpurinia aurea (Ait) Benth (9.6%), Nicotiana tabacum (9.6%) and Malva parviflora

L. (7%) were the most frequently reported plant species. Herbs were the most widely used for the treatment of various ailments constituting the largest percentage (60%) followed by trees and shrubs with 24.3 and 15.7%, respectively. Shilema et al 2013 reported 14 medicinal plants and also identified seven species used to repel tsetse flies. Studies have shown that 95% of cattle diseases are of tick origin. From above studies, it is clear that most medicinal plants are used to treat diseases such black leg, heartwater, redwater, anthrax and internal parasites such as liver-fluke, roundworms and hookworms which are similar to ailments that affects the Zimbabwean national herd

Social Learning Theory (SLT)

Indigenous knowledge systems (IKSs) are learnt, practiced and passed on orally from generation to generation. Young farmers and pastoralists learn IKSs through observation, imitation and modelling therefore the use and application of Social Learning Theory (SLT). This is true of Matsika (2012) who defined IKS as the traditional and local knowledge that exists and is developed through experiences of local community in the process of managing the conditions or context (cattle disease outbreaks) that challenge the people's everyday life.

Social learning theory is increasingly cited as an essential component of sustainable natural resource management and the promotion of desirable behavioural change among farmers (Muro and Jeffrey, 2008). This theory is based on the idea that we learn from our interactions with others in a social context. Separately, by observing the behaviours of others, people develop similar behaviours. After observing the behaviour of others, people assimilate and imitate that behaviour, especially if their observational experiences are positive ones or include rewards related to the observed behaviour. According to Bandura, imitation involves the actual reproduction of observed motor activities (Bandura, 1977).

SLT has become perhaps the most influential theory of learning and development. It is rooted in many of the basic concepts of traditional learning theory including Indigenous Knowledge Systems (IKS). This theory has often been called a bridge between behaviourist learning theories and cognitive learning theories because it encompasses attention, memory, and motivation. (Muro and Jeffrey, 2008). However, on this regards, Bandura believes that direct reinforcement could not account for all types of learning. For that reason, in his theory he added a social element, arguing that people can learn new information and behaviours by watching other people. Studies by Matekaire and Bwakura (2004), Masimba et al. (2011) and Yigezu, Haile and Ayen (2014) reiterated that the knowledge of ethnoveterinary practices was mostly passed down generations orally which solely depends on the collective memories of just a few practitioners within communities. Their study revealed the sources of EVM knowledge as grandparents and parents (61.5%), friends (20.5%), neighbours (12.5%), and others (6.5). According to the elements of this theory, there are three general principles for learning from each other.

General principles of SLT

The principles of social learning are assumed to operate in the same way throughout life. Observational learning may take place at any age. Insofar as exposure to new influential, powerful models who control resources may occur at life stage, new learning through the modelling process is always possible. (Newman B.M. & P.R, 2007).
SLT posits that people learn from one another, via:
- *Observation;*
- *Imitation; and*
- *Modelling*

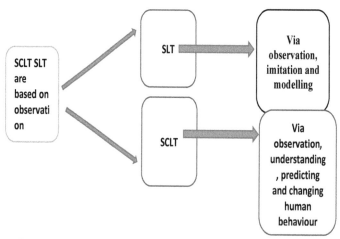

Figure 1: Process of SLT and SCLT based on observation

322

Methodology

This section of the study looks at research approach, paradigm and design and population and sampling and data collection method.

The methodological structure of the study, its location and research approach, nature of study and methods of data generation are depicted in Figure 2 below. Thereafter, each methodological choice is explained.

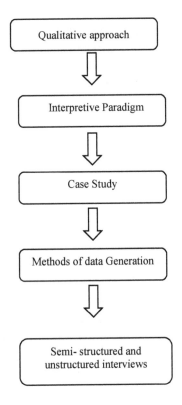

Figure 2: Representation of instruments and methods used in the study

Approach

Qualitative research methodology was used in this study as it sought a large amount of in-depth data from a small number of participants (Veal, 2005). A qualitative study involves getting answers or views from participants of the study who are farmers in the study area (Creswell, 2013). According to Johnson (2010) qualitative research is a type of inquiry that uses different techniques in data collection, for example face to face interviews, with the purpose of carrying out a realistic analysis of the data generated based on the notion that reality is socially constructed. It entails getting answers from the people themselves, about what they think of as reality, see as reality, feel as reality, and define as reality; the answers come in the people's own words, hence the term qualitative (Creswell, 2012: 2013). The main characteristic of qualitative research, according to Creswell (2012), is that it seeks to explore a central problem and develop a detailed understanding of the central phenomenon from the perspective of the participants (in this study, farmers from Zimuto area). Thus, the role of the researcher is to provide a description of human experience as it is experienced by the participants (Creswell, 2012). By using a qualitative approach, the researcher was able to obtain a rich and in-depth understanding of how farmers use indigenous knowledge systems to manage cattle diseases.

Research paradigm

Every scientific inquiry is inevitably framed within a paradigm, regardless of whether the researcher is conscious of this or not (Hammersley, 2012). A research paradigm defines and influences the research process and outcomes in several ways, such as decisions to be made regarding the nature of the phenomenon explored, theoretical framing, literature, methods or research design (Hammersley, 2012; Hussein, 2015). A paradigm positions the philosophical thinking on what the researcher views as reality (ontological) and how the study should proceed (epistemological) and informs the treatment of the expected results in knowledge generation, which can ultimately improve human welfare (Žukauskas, Vveinhardt and Andriukaitienė, 2018). Scholars define a paradigm differently, but many embrace the idea that a paradigm is a fundamental belief system or worldview that informs and guides the researcher (Barker, 2003; Descombe, 2010; Creswell, 2012; Walliman, 2011; Neuman, 2000). In this regard, Hamersley (2012, p. 2) sums up a research paradigm as a "set of philosophical assumptions about phenomenon to be studied (ontology), about how they can be understood (epistemology), and the purpose and product of research".

The current study on IKS and sustainable cattle disease management falls within the Interpretivist- Paradigm (IP). In the interpretivist paradigm, reality can only be interpreted through the meaning that participants give to their world, which can only be discovered through language. Interpretivism is associated with symbolic interaction, analytic induction and grounded theory (Schwadt, 2007). People construct meaning out of their experiences as evidenced by social learning theory. Through the application of IKS people develop knowledge of cattle diseases in their communities be able to manage livestock ailments. Reality in this context comes from smallholder farmers who were the participants and data were generated through individual or face to face interviews. Hammersley (2012, p.57) asserts that the Interpretivist Paradigm (IP) emerged out of the realisation by social scientists that "people unlike atoms, chemicals or even non-humans forms of life interpret or give meaning and value to their environment and themselves, the centrality of the human being as the primary research instrument or source of views is important". In this study, the interpretation and application of ethnoveterinary knowledge by farmers is the basis of the research.

Case Study Design

A case study is the study of a case within its real-life contemporary context or setting (Yin, 2009; Shuttleworth, 2008; Cohen, Manion & Morrison, 2007). A case study is defined by Creswell (2012) as "an in-depth exploration of a bound system which could be an activity, event, process or individuals" (p. 462). In describing the underlying philosophies of case study research, Njie and Asimiran (2014) suggest that case study research is often grounded by the time during which data is generated or intended to be generated, the phenomenon and its context. The study took place from 2018-2020 to study how farmers in Zimuto area apply indigenous knowledge to manage cattle disease outbreaks.

Denzin and Lincoln (2005), Yin (2009) and Vos, Strydom, Fouche and Delport (2011) believe that case study research is not a method, but a choice of what is to be studied; a strategy of inquiry, a methodology or a comprehensive research strategy. The hallmark of the case study approach, according to Lapan, Quartaroli and Reimer (2011) and Cohen, Manion and Morrison (2013), is that the methodology provides thick descriptions of participants' lived experiences of, or thoughts about, and feelings for, a situation, using multiple data generation sources such as semi-structured interviews, field visits and observations This ensures that the issue is explored through a variety of lenses, which allows for multiple facets of the phenomenon to be revealed and understood (Baxter and Jack, 2008). Thus, using multiple data generation sources allows the researcher to converge the data in order to gain a deep insight into the case. Baxter and Jack (2008) further contend that the strength of the case study approach lies in its being concerned with rich and explicit descriptions of events relevant to the case; its focus being on individual actors or groups of actors, seeking deep understanding of their views. The other strength is that the researcher is involved in the case, because the case study may be linked to the researcher on a personal or professional level. In this instance, the researcher is a small-scale cattle farmer.

Description of the study area

The study was located in Zimuto area of Masvingo District of Masvingo Province in Zimbabwe as shown on the map. In terms of geographical location, the town is in a dry arid province most suited for cattle ranching. This is the home province of the Karanga people of Zimbabwe, who survive mostly by rearing cattle, with a few crops for subsistence purposes.

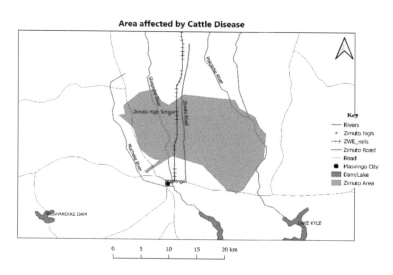

Map 1: Showing study area affected by cattle diseases

Sampling

In this study, convenience and purposive sampling techniques were employed.

Convenience sampling
Sampling is considered here to be convenient because the study was conducted where the researcher is a practising farmer in the area under study. According to Etikan, Musa and Alkassim (2016), convenient or accidental sampling is when members of the target population meet certain practical criteria such as accessibility, geographical proximity, availability at a given time or willingness to participate at any given time. Darnyei (2007, cited in Farrokhi & Mahmoudi-Hamudbad, 2012) is of the view that the only criteria for convenience sampling is convenience to the researcher. This resonates well with the view of Bless, Higson-Smith and Sithole (2006, p. 172) who says that "samples so chosen are convenient for researchers in terms of time and money" In this case, the researcher had easy access to most farmers in the area.

Methods of data collection

Semi-structured and unstructured interviews
Male participating farmers were purposively selected on the following criteria, they had to be farmers of long term communal or smallholder experience, were of age +45 years of age, owns cattle as part of their farming experiences.

The qualitative study employed semi-structured and unstructured interviews with 15 smallholder farmers of more than 40 years of farming experience in Zimuto area. The predominantly male participants were conveniently selected to be participants and coded Participant 1-15 (P). The idea was to obtain rich information from the farmers about ethnoveterinary practices on cattle diseases. An interview is a personal investigation where the interviewer collects information personally from sources (smallholder farmers in Zimuto area). The researcher was on the spot and had to meet participants to collect data (Kothari and Garg, 2014). The semi-structured and unstructured interviews allowed the use of a set of predetermined questions of highly standardised techniques of recording. Among many its advantages, the method yields more information that is a greater depth, allows the researcher to overcome resistance from the interviewee, allows for more flexibility because it offers opportunities to restructure questions depending on responses. The interviewer can possibly collect supplementary information about the respondents' personal characteristics and environment which if often of great value in interpreting result.

Results and Discussion

The objectives of the study are given below and underpin any discussion that are being discussed. Responses are therefore being discussed under emerging themes:-
1. Examine indigenous knowledge systems used for cattle breeding system
2. Examine common cattle diseases in Zimuto area and
3. Assess common indigenous/ethnoveterinary medicinal plants commonly used by farmers to treat cattle disease.

Therefore, discussion of results will be based on research objectives.

Respondents' Gender

All respondents were males 100%. This is so because the care of livestock (cattle) in Zimbabwe and many parts of the world is largely a male domain from youth into old age (Moritz, Ewing and Garabed, 2013). This was supported by Kidane, Maesen, Andel and Asfaw (2014) who argues that knowledge of ethnoveterinary plants are predominantly held by males than females.

Results
Objective:-Examine indigenous knowledge systems used in selecting and management of breeding animals

The study discusses results obtained with respect to objective given above as themes. The study established the following indigenous knowledge practices (themes) on cattle management that could ensure good, parasite and disease resistant animals.

Theme 1: Management of breeding animals (heifer, cows)

The study established that Indigenous knowledge systems were used to manage different types of animals, more important the female animal (cows, heifers). The basis was that a healthy cow would conceive well and the management through IKS would then ensure a strong young animal that would resist diseases and parasites. Diskin and Kenny (2016) found that the lifetime productivity of the beef-rate which are all a function of nutrition therefore cows and heifers should be maintained on a steady plane of nutrition as practiced by indigenous farmers in the study area. Greenwood et al. (2009a in Greenwood, Clayton and Bell, 2017) argues that severe, prolonged undernutrition of pregnant ruminants, especially during late gestation, can permanently retard body and wool growth of their offspring.

Theme 2: Servicing of heifers

Management practices included serving heifers at the correct age of 30 or 36 months, served to the right bull that belonged to the village selected on certain qualities. In North America, a majority of Bos taurus heifers (breeds such as Angus, Hereford, Simmental, and Charolais) are expected to calve for the first time at 22 to 24 months of age (at which time they are referred to as primiparous cows) (Day and Nogueira, 2013). Age at puberty in beef heifers can influence economic efficiency of beef production through effects on both age at first calving (2 vs. 3+ years of age) and the time of conception of heifers in their initial breeding season (Day and Nogueira, 2013).

Bulled heifers were kept separately and denied access to the village bull again until calving. Indigenous cattle herding was assigned to an elderly herd man who would ensure strict compliance to proper breeding management. There was need to properly manage cows so that they would conceive well, herders needed to observe heat periods and utilize the period well by ensuring that the cow on heat meets the bull on time observing servicing for three times. For a female animal, there was need to ensure that animals get well grazing before breeding season. The indigenous practices ensured that all cows should not be used for draught power. This was done to ensure conception and good growth of the foetus. This is supported by the below excerpt:

In-calf animals should be given separate grazing so that will produce strong calves which will later on resist parasites and disease outbreaks (P5, P7, P8- Interview);
In-calf animals should be given separate grazing so that will produce strong calves which will later on resist parasites and disease outbreaks (P5, P7, P8- Interview);
Avoid housing calves in muddy kraals because this would encourage kidney diseases leading to small and sicky animals (P10- Interview).

Once heifers or cows calve no milking could be allowed to ensure enough milk access to the calf for 2 months.

Theme 3: Weaning age

Good management practices included early weaning at 6-8 months. Studies by Chimonyo et al., (2000) revealed that majority of household in communal areas practiced early weaning of 6-8 months which is beneficial as it prevents loss of weight of the cow and improved conception. This result resonates well studies by Day and Nogueira (2013) who also revealed that most beef heifers are weaned from their dams at 6 to 8 months of age in the USA, and it has been clearly demonstrated that plane of nutrition from weaning to the onset of the breeding season can impact age at puberty.

Theme 4: Dehorning

Indigenous knowledge systems practiced dehorning of young animals which had attained an estimated 70 kilograms body weight. Dehorned animals grew faster and stronger because feed was distributed evenly to all parts of the body. IKS used a hot wood to remove growing horns and animals were expected to recover as soon as they were dehorned as supported by this excerpt:

> *As soon as the calves started growing, dehorning would be done very early, the idea was to distribute meat growth very early through the whole body thereby ensuring good and strong animals that would resist parasites and diseases later in life (P15-Interview).*

However, in case of dehorned animals developing wounds IKS used a number of medicines and mixtures such as salt was used on wounds. A study by Zhou and Chinamasa (2020) found a medium sized shrub found in Makonde District in Zimbabwe, *Muvengahonye (cathiumhuillense)* is used to treat cattle wounds associated with dehorning or broken horn. The shrub's tender leaves and twigs are crushed, mixed with salt and soda. The mixture's juice is squeezed out and dropped on the open wound.

Theme 5: Castration

Castration is an accepted and important animal husbandry procedure in old time and even today. Castration of very young animals is apparently less stressful than castration of older animals Capucille, Poore and Rogers (2002). Reasons for castration are to reduce aggressive animal behaviour, improve carcass quality and control of unwanted matings.

Indigenous practices used open knife method of castration and use of wood ashes to treat the wood. Studies by Capucille, Poore and

Rogers (2002) argues that operators may use any type of clean, sharpened blade or an instrument specifically designed for scrotal incisions, such as a Newberry castrating knife. Methods described include incising over each testis separately, transecting and removing the ventral third to half of the scrotum, or incising the ventral half of the scrotum through its lateral aspects (i.e., using a Newberry castration knife). The common goal with each method is to establish an opening large enough to allow drainage and prevent fluid accumulation.

Theme 5: Rotational grazing

Rotational grazing is a common practice in cattle rearing with twofold aims, to control ticks and to give grass enough time to recover. Tick borne diseases (TBD) remain a global animal threat. Herding of cattle is the most common method of cattle rearing in Zimbabwe. Cattle are herded during the day and penned at night. In cases where there is limited grazing land, all the cattle from the entire village may be considered as a single interbreeding flock with no attempts of controlling mating. Herds from different households of the same village, however, may graze separately where there are vast tracts of grazing land.

IKS practiced rotational grazing of pastures by restricting cattle movement from disease infested areas to safe places, restrictions on cattle movement from one area to another, use of maize stalks to prevent black leg. The following excerpts support these practices:

> At the same time avoid grazing animals in marshy areas to minimize chances of foot rot, make use of dry areas (P2-Interview);
> Once there was a suspected outbreak of diseases people would move their animals from local kraals (matanga) to madhanga (safe, new kraals/ new grazing places) to avoid parasites diseases (P7-Interview).

The change of cattle location for one or 2 months was based on managing disease outbreak. Studies by Ndebele et al., (2007) encouraged local leaders with IKS to formulate by –laws governing movement of livestock during the dry season.

Theme 6: Dipping of cattle

Rotational grazing is a common practice in cattle rearing with twofold aims, to control ticks and to give grass enough time to recover. Tick borne diseases (TBD) remain to be a global animal threat (Ybañez, Mingala, & Ybañez, 2018). Many scholars reported

331

on the impact of ticks on cattle production, Sungirai, Moyo, De Clercq, and Madder, (2016) found cowdriosis, mastitis, anaplasmosis, body damage and babesiosis as TBDs, Meneghi, Stachurski, and Adakal, H. (2016) reported on trapanosomiasis and rift valley fever while Boucher, Moutroifi, Peba, Ali, Moindjie, Ruget, and Cardinale, (2020) revealed that many TBD as East Coast Fever, anaplasmosis, babeosis, heartwater and cowdry. These findings are further resonates well with Perveen, Muzaffar, and Al-Deeb, (2021) who found 55 tick species causing theilerosis, babesiosis and anaplasmosis in Middle East and North Africa (MENA). The above studies are confirmed by Kernif, Leulmi, Raoult, and Parola, (2016) who argues that ticks are considered the second most common vectors of pathogens after mosquitoes where over 900 tick species worldwide which are capable of transmitting a wider range of pathogens.

IKS practiced dipping of cattle using herbs, tree leaves and shrubs mixed and administered topically, administration of worm remedies using local available resources from trees, shrubs and herbs obtained from habitats. The following excerpt supported this practice:

Indigenous knowledge systems practiced breeding of Mashona type of cattle, an animal that has a thick skin that is capable of resisting tick infestation. The proliferation of ticks came with the exotic breeds that used to frequent dipping and encouraged tick breeding and tick infestation (P2-Interview).

Studies by Nyahangare, Mvumi and Mutibvu (2015) reported on over 51 plant species were reportedly effective against cattle ticks and other livestock parasites. The most frequently mentioned plants were in descending order, *Cissus quadrangularis* (30.1%), *Lippia javanica* (19.6%), *Psydrax livida* (14.9%) and *Aloe* species (14.9%). Most of the plant materials were prepared by crushing and soaking in water and spraying the extract on animals. Ethno-veterinary medicine (EVM) provides alternatives for controlling both internal and external parasites in livestock production systems that are environmentally friendly, relatively cheap and not prone to development of resistant parasitic strains. According to a survey conducted in Gutu District, Zimbabwe by Masimba, Mbiriri, Kashangura, and Mutibvu (2011) found that households relied on conventional medicines alone in treating poultry diseases. Ninety five percent of the households used traditional medicines only whilst the rest employed a combination of traditional and conventional remedies Marandure (2016).

Objective 2: To examine common cattle diseases in the study area

Theme 1: Diseases, Black leg, foot and mouth, lumpy skin, gall sickness, redwater and heartwater in the study area

The study found common diseases affecting cattle included black leg, foot and mouth disease, lumpy skin, gall sickness, redwater, heartwater and anthrax which resonated well with findings from studies by Ndebele et al (2007) who revealed common diseases in Gwayi area such as heartwater, gall sickness, blackleg, , contagious abortion, tuberculosis and lumpy skin. The study established that Indigenous knowledge systems were used to manage different types of cattle animals, more important the cow. The basis was that a healthy cow would conceive well and the management through IKS would then ensure a strong young animal that would resist diseases and parasites. Management practices included early weaning 6-8 months, rotational grazing of pastures, control of cattle movement from disease infested areas to safe places, restrictions on cattle movement from one area to another, use of maize stalks to prevent black leg, regular dipping of once a week using herbs, tree leaves and shrubs mixed and administered topically, administration of worm remedies using local available resources from trees, shrubs and herbs obtained from habitats.

Objective 3: Assess common indigenous/ethnoveterinary medicinal plants commonly used by farmers to treat cattle disease

The study found complementary practices to use of trees, shrubs and herbs used by indigenous cattle farmers as follows:

Wood ash is used to kill ticks in kraals
Soaked duty bags against black leg
Coarse salt against foot and mouth disease
Chi'ai + salt against heartwater
Salt alone used against internal parasites
River reeds (Raffel fauna) the leaf or stem pierced on the eye lid to cure eye cataract.

This meant that trees, shrubs, and herbs were not used in isolation, each practice complemented each other. The below is a list of trees commonly used through IKS:

Table 1 List Trees and parts used to cure cattle diseases

Tree Name	Part used as ethnomedicine	Parasite/ Disease
Muvheva/ Musungwe	Leaves/ bark/Roots Leaves/ Bark/	Goitre Internal parasites
Murumanyama (wingpod)	Roots leaves	Foot and Mouth disease
Musiringa (Persian lilao) Muroodze	leaves leaves	Heartwater Gall sickness
Mubvumakuvu (mukwa)	Leaves/ Bark/Roots	Dosing, Goitre, Bottle jaw
Durura	Leaves/Bark/ Roots leaves	Kill ticks in kraals Induced lactation- removal of blocked teat
Dandare	Leaves	
Muvengahonye (horse wood)	Leaves	
Mutamba (monkey orange)	fruits leaves	spraying tail region/eyelids Internal parasites Internal parasites
Murunjurunju (wingpod)		
Damba		
Gavakava (Agave)		

Source: Compiled by Author, 2020.

The study report of 12 ethnoveterinary plants that are used against common diseases in the study area. These medicinal plants are commonly available for everyone to use. Common plant parts are leaves, fruits, bark and roots that are crushed and mixed with water administered mostly topical, oral and nasal. Many scholars reported on lots and lots of ethnoveterinary medicinal plants in Africa, Europe, Middle East and in Zimbabwe pointing to plant parts that are commonly used in each case.

Muhammad, et al. (2014) found a total of 24 medicinal plant species used as ethnoveterinary belonging to 22 genera and 19 families. Studies by Khana (2009) in Pakistan reported of 35 plant species for treatment of various diseases of cattle. Studies have described that leaves and fruits of Azadirachta Indica has anti-parasitic and ant- coccidal potential significantly validated in animals (Tipu et al. (2006). Tabutu et al. (2003) further reported that plant infusion is used to treat East Coast fever and mastitis. Therefore, local people are highly dependent on local knowledge for herbal remedy to treat various ailments (Nigam and Sharma, 2010). Further studies by Raveesha and Sudhama (2015) conducted through open ended questionnaire, frequent field visits and interviews found a total of 52 medicinal plants to treat anthrax, foot-and-mouth disease, bloat conjunctivitis, dysentery, fractures, snake bites and rot tail. A recent study by Mulualem et al (2017) using semi-structured interview, field observations reported that 90% of livestock population is dependent on traditional medicine for primary health care services, with most coming from plants. An interview study by Rutter et al (2012) reported on 56 distributed in 49 genera and 35 families indicated to have 23 different medicinal uses, with leaves constituting 46%, , bark 15%, roots and fruits 10%.

Furthermore, an individual interview, group interview, guided field walks and observations by Botha, Van der Merwe and Swan (2001) reported 45 plant species representing 24 families to cure retained livestock placenta, diarrhoea, gall sickness, fractures, eye inflammation, general ailments, fertility enhancement, general gastrointestinal problems, heartwater, internal parasites, coughing, redwater and reduction in tick burden. A related study by Moreki, Tshireletso and Okoli (2012) to identify and document plants and practices for retained placenta in cattle using Rapid Rural Appraisal , identified 13 plant species used for treatment of retained placenta with most plant parts coming from barks (57, 14%), roots (40,48%) and bulbs (11,90%). In most rural areas where modern medicine is inaccessible to farmers, ethnoveterinary medicine (EVM) is often used to treat a number of cattle ailments. A study by Bussman (2006) reported that for smallholder farmers in Kenya, conventional veterinary drugs have become very expensive and therefore, unaffordable and causing them to seek low cost. The study reported of 40 plant species in 26 families which were useful in traditional management of various cattle ailments. A study with elderly persons, cattle owners, traditional healers and housewives in Polsara Block, Ganyan district, Orissa, India reported 24 plant species belonging to 20 families. Frequently used plant parts were leaves 33.33%, oils 29.17% and rhozomes 25.0%. The low cost and almost no side effects of these preparations made them adaptable by the local community. This view is supported by McGraw and Eloff (2008) who reported that livestock keepers in many developing countries with restricted access to orthodox veterinary health care services commonly use traditional remedies to treat their animals when diseases are encountered. The use of herbal remedies to treat animals was widespread among smallholder farmers in the Eastern Cape largely because of low cost, convenience and ease to administer (Masika et al. 2000).

Conclusion

Based on study objectives as stated above the results that management through IKS found that heifers are serviced at between 24-30 months of age, calves are weaned between 6-8 months of age, dehorning of weaners at 70 kilograms body weight, castration of steers between 8-12 months, rotational grazing was mainly done to control cattle diseases and dipping was aimed at controlling common tick borne diseases. IKS used a number of herbs, shrubs and tree parts to dip animals. Common cattle diseases were black leg, foot and mouth, lumpy skin, redwater and heartwater. Common tree species found to be effective against above diseases are musungwe, murumanyama, (wingpod) musiringa (Persian lilao), mubvamakuvu (mukwa), muroodze, durura, mutamba, muvengahonye (horse wood) and many others listed on Table 1. The study recommends that further studies be carried out on more shrubs, herbs and trees that can be used against cattle diseases in other regions of Zimbabwe, farmers be trained to use IKS to attend to cattle disease outbreaks, carry out regular dipping to control tick population and to sustainable manage common ethnoveterinary shrubs, herbs and trees.

References

Aberdeen, T. (2013). Yin, RK (2009). Case study research: Design and methods. Thousand Oaks, CA: Sage. The Canadian Journal of Action Research, 14(1), 69-71.

Bandura, A. (1977). Self-efficacy: toward a unifying theory of behavioural change. *Psychological review, 84*(2), 191.

Baxter, P., & Jack, S. (2008). Qualitative case study methodology: Study design and implementation for novice researchers. The qualitative report, 13(4), 544-559.

Bertram, C., & Christiansen, I. (2014). Understanding research. An introduction to reading research. Pretoria: Van Schaik Publishers.

Bless, C., Higson-Smith, C., & Sithole, S. L. (2006). Fundamentals of Social Research Methods: An African Perspective (ch. 2). South Africa: Juta & Company Ltd.

Boucher, F., Moutroifi, Y., Peba, B., Ali, M., Moindjie, Y., Ruget, A. S., & Cardinale, E. (2020). Tick-borne diseases in the Union of the Comoros are a hindrance to livestock development: Circulation and associated risk factors. *Ticks and tick-borne diseases*, *11*(1), 101283.

Capucille, D. J., Poore, M. H., & Rogers, G. M. (2002). Castration in cattle: techniques and animal welfare issues. *Compendium*, *24*(9), 66-73.

Cohen, L. M., & Manion, L. Morrison (2011). Research Methods in Education. London: Routledge Falmer.

Cohen, L., Manion, L., & Morrison, K. (2007). Observation. Research methods in education, 6, 396-412.

Cohen, L., Manion, L., & Morrison, K. (2013). Validity and reliability. In Research methods in education (pp. 203-240). Routledge.

Creswell, J. W. (2013). Steps in conducting a scholarly mixed methods study.

David A. Kolb. (1984). Experiential Learning: Experience as the Source of Learning and Development. Prentice Hall.

Day, M. L., & Nogueira, G. P. (2013). Management of age at puberty in beef heifers to optimize efficiency of beef production. *Animal Frontiers*, *3*(4), 6-11.

De Meneghi, D., Stachurski, F., & Adakal, H. (2016). Experiences in tick control by acaricide in the traditional cattle sector in Zambia and Burkina Faso: Possible environmental and public health implications. *Frontiers*.

De Vos, A. S., Delport, C. S. L., Fouché, C. B., & Strydom, H. (2011). *Research at grass roots: A primer for the social science and human professions*. Van Schaik Publishers.

Descombe, M. (2010). Ground rules for social research: Guidelines for good practice, vol. 2.

Diskin, M. G., & Kenny, D. A. (2016). Managing the reproductive performance of beef cows. *Theriogenology*, *86*(1), 379-387.

Eguale, T., Tadesse, D., & Giday, M. (2011). In vitro anthelmintic activity of crude extracts of five medicinal plants against egg-hatching and larval development of Haemonchus contortus. Journal of Ethnopharmacology, 137(1), 108-113.

Eguale, T., Tadesse, D., Giday, M., 2011. In vitro anthelmintic activity of crude extracts of five medicinal plants against egg-hatching and larval development of Haemonchus contortus. J. Ethnopharmacol. 137, 108–113.

Etikan, I., Musa, S. A., & Alkassim, R. S. (2016). Comparison of convenience sampling and purposive sampling. *American Journal of Theoretical and Applied Statistics*, 5(1): 1-4.

FAO, 2011. World Livestock 2011. Livestock in Food Security, p.115.

Gebrezgabiher, G., Kalayou, S., Sahle, S., 2013. An ethno-veterinary survey of medicinal plants in woredas of Tigray region, Northern Ethiopia. Int. J. Biodivers. Conserv. 5 (2), 89–97.

Giday M and Ameni G (2003). An Ethnobotanical Survey of Plants of Veterinary Importance in Two Woredas of Sothern Tigray, Northern Ethiopia. SINET: Ethiop. J. Sci., 26 (2): 123136.

Greenwood, P., Clayton, E., & Bell, A. (2017). Developmental programming and beef production. *Animal Frontiers*, 7(3), 38-47.

Hammersley, M. (2012). Methodological paradigms in educational research. British Educational Research Association.

Husain, S. Z., Malik, R. N., Javaid, M., & Bibi, S. A. D. I. A. (2008). Ethnobotanical properties and uses of medicinal plants of Morgah biodiversity park, Rawalpindi. *Pak J Bot*, 40(5), 1897-1911.

Iqbal, Z., Lateef, M., Jabbar, A., Gilani, A.H., 2010. In vivo anthelmintic activit Azadirachta indica A. Juss. seeds against gastrointestinal nematodes of sheep. Veterinary Parasitology 168, 342–345.

Kebede, A., Ayalew, S., Mesfin, A., & Mulualem, G. (2017). An ethnoveterinary study of medicinal plants used for the management of livestock ailments in selected kebeles of Dire Dawa Administration, Eastern Ethiopia. *Journal of Plant Sciences*, 5(1), 34-42.

Kernif, T., Leulmi, H., Raoult, D., & Parola, P. (2016). Emerging tick-borne bacterial pathogens. *Emerging Infections 10*, 295-310.

Khan, M.N., Sajid, M.S., Khan, M.K., Iqbal, Z., Hussain, A., 2010. Gastrointestinal helminthiasis: prevalence and associated determinants in domestic ruminants of district TobaTek Singh, Punjab, Pakistan. Parasitology Research 107, 787–794.

Kidane, B., Van Der Maesen, L. J. G., van Andel, T., & Asfaw, Z. (2014). Ethnoveterinary medicinal plants used by the Maale and Ari ethnic communities in southern Ethiopia. *Journal of Ethnopharmacology*, 153(1), 274-282.

Kothari, C., & Garg, G. (2014). Research Methodology: Methods and Strategy. New Age International.

Lapan, S. D., Quartaroli, M. T., & Riemer, F. J. (2011). *Qualitative Research*, 74.

Lincoln, N. K. D. Y. S. (2005). *The Sage handbook of qualitative research*. Sage.

Mapira, J., & Mazambara, P. (2013). Indigenous knowledge systems and their implications for sustainable development in Zimbabwe. *Journal of Sustainable Development in Africa, 15*(5), 90-106.

Marandure, T. (2016). Concepts and key issues of ethnoveterinary medicine in Africa: A review of its application in Zimbabwe. *African Journal of Agricultural Research, 11*(20), 1836-1841.

Masimba, E. S., D. T. Mbiriri, M. T. Kashangura, and T. Mutibvu. "Indigenous practices for the control and treatment of ailments in Zimbabwe's village poultry." *Livest Res Rural Dev* 23, no. 12 (2011): 2-9.

Matekaire, T., Bwakura, T.M., 2004. Ethnoveterinary medicine: a potential alternative to Orthodox Animal Health Delivery in Zimbabwe International. J. Appl. Res. Vet. Med. 2 (4), 269–273.

Matsika, Chrispen, 2012. *Traditional African Education: Its Significance to Current Education Practices with Special Reference to Zimbabwe*, Mambo Press, Gweru

McCorkle, C. M. (1986). An introduction to ethnoveterinary research and development. *Journal of ethnobiology, 6*(1), 129-149.

McCorkle, C.M., 1986. An introduction to ethnoveterinary research and development. *Journal of Ethnobiology* 6, 129–149.

McGraw LJ, Eloff JN (2008). Ethnoveterinary use of southern African plants and scientific evaluation of their medicinal properties. *J. Ethnopharmacol.*, 119(3): 559– 574

Misra, K. K., & Kumar, K. A. (2004). Ethno-veterinary practices among the Konda Reddi of East Godavari district of Andhra Pradesh. *Studies of Tribes and Tribals, 2* (1), 37-44.

Misra, K. K., & Kumar, K. A. (2004). Ethno-veterinary practices among the Konda Reddi of East Godavari district of Andhra Pradesh. *Studies of Tribes and Tribals, 2*(1), 37-44.

Moreki, J. C., Tshireletso, K., & Okoli, I. C. (2012). Potential use of ethnoveterinary medicine for retained placenta in cattle in Mogonono, Botswana. *Journal of Animal Production Advances, 2*(6), 303-309.

Moritz, M., Ewing, D., & Garabed, R. (2013). On not knowing zoonotic diseases: Pastoralists' ethnoveterinary knowledge in the far north region of Cameroon. *Human organization, 72*(1), 1-11.

Muro, M., & Jeffrey, P. (2008). A critical review of the theory and application of social learning in participatory natural resource management processes. *Journal of environmental planning and management, 51*(3), 325-344.*n public health, 4,* 239.

Musa, U., Abdu, P.A., Dafwang, I.I., Katsayal, U.A., Edache, J.A., Karsin, P.D., 2008. Ethnoveterinary remedies used for the management of Newcastle disease in some selected local government areas of Plateau State Nigeria. Nigerian Journal of Pharmaceutical Sciences 7, 126–130.

Muyambo, C. (2019). *The impact of corporate entrepreneurship culture on the quality of interventions by market systems development organisations. a case of AgroBiz* (Doctoral dissertation).

Muyambo, T. (2018). *Indigenous knowledge systems of the Ndau people of Manicaland Province in Zimbabwe: a case study of Bota Reshupa* (Doctoral dissertation).

Ndebele, J. J., Muchenje, V., Mapiye, C., Chimonyo, M., Musemwa, L., & Ndlovu, T. (2007). Cattle breeding management practices in the Gwayi smallholder farming area of South-Western Zimbabwe. *Livestock Research for Rural Development, 19*(11).

Neuman, W. L. (2000). The meanings of methodology. *Social research methods, 60,* 87.

Newman, B. M., & Newman, P. R. (2007). Theories of human development: Lawrence Erlbaum.

Nigam, G., Sharma, N.K., 2010. Ethnoveterinary plant of Jhansi District, Uttar Pradesh. Indian Journal of Traditional Knowledge 9, 664–667.

Njie, B., & Asimiran, S. (2014). Case study as a choice in qualitative methodology. *Journal of Research & Method in Education, 4*(3), 35-40.

Njoroge, G. N., & Bussmann, R. W. (2006). Herbal usage and informant consensus in ethnoveterinary management of cattle diseases among the Kikuyus (Central Kenya). *Journal of ethnopharmacology, 108*(3), 332-339.

Nyathi, N. (2008). Context of the goat sector in Zimbabwe. *Enhancing income and livelihoods through improved farmers' practices on goat production and marketing. Edited by van Rooyen and Homann. International Crop Research Institute for Semi Arid Tropics (ICRISAT),* 7-10.

Perveen, N., Muzaffar, S. B., & Al-Deeb, M. A. (2021). Ticks and Tick-Borne Diseases of Livestock in the Middle East and North Africa: A Review. *Insects, 12*(1), 83.

Pica-Ciamarra, U., Tasciotti, L., Otte, J., Alberto, Z.., 2011. Livestock assets, livestock income and rural households. Cross-country evidence from household surveys, Joint Paper of the World Bank. FAO, AU p. 18.

Regassa, F., 2004. The role of traditional medicinal in animal health care in Ethiopia. In: Urga, et al. (Eds.), Traditional Medicine in Ethiopia, Ethiopian Health and National Research Institutes, Addis Ababa, Ethiopia, pp. 53–66.

Sadia Bibi (2008) Ethnobotanical Properties and Uses of Medicinal Plants of Morgah Biodiversity Park, Rawalpindi,Pak., J. Bot.,40(5):1897-1911.

Shilema, A., Zerom, K., Mussa, A., 2013. Ethnoveterinary practices against animal trypanosomosis in Amaro district, Southern Ethiopia. Int. J. Med. Plants Res. 2 (7), 238–241.

Shuttleworth, M. (2008). Qualitative and quantitative research design. *Ann Arbor, MI.*

Sori T., Bekana M., Adugna G and Kelbessa (2004). Medicinal plants in the ethnoveterinary practices of Borana pastoralists, Southern Ethiopia. Int J Appl Res Vet Med, 2: 220–225.

Sungirai, M., Moyo, D. Z., De Clercq, P., & Madder, M. (2016). Communal farmers' perceptions of tick-borne diseases affecting cattle and investigation of tick control methods practiced in Zimbabwe. *Ticks and tick-borne diseases, 7*(1), 1-9.

Tabuti, J.R.S., Dhillion, S.S., Lye, K.A., 2003. Ethnoveterinary medicines for cattle (Bos indicus) in Bulamogi county, Uganda: plant species and mode of use. J. Ethnopharmacol., 88, pp. 279–286.

Tabuti, J.R.S., Dhillion, S.S., Lye, K.A., 2003. Ethnoveterinary medicines for cattle (Bos indicus) in Bulamogi County, Uganda: plant species and mode of use. J. Ethnopharmacol., 88, pp. 279–286.

Tipu, M. A., Akhtar, M. S., Anjum, M. I., & Raja, M. L. (2006). New dimension of medicinal plants as animal feed. *Pakistan Veterinary Journal, 26*(3), 144-148.

Toyang, N.J., Wanyama, J., Nuwanyakpa, M., Django, S., 2007. Ethnoveterinary medicine. A practical approach to the treatment of cattle diseases in subSaharan Africa. Agrodok 44, 88.

Van der Merwe, D., Swan, G.E., Botha, C.J., 2001. Use of ethnoveterinary medicinal plants in cattle by Setswana-speaking people in the Madikwe area of the North West Province of South Africa. Journal of the South African Veterinary Association 72, 189–196.

Veal, A. (2005). Creative methodologies in participatory research. *Researching children's experience: Approaches and methods,* 253-272.

Walliman, N. (2011). *Your research project: Designing and planning your work.* Sage Publications.

Wanzala, W., Zessin, K. H., Kyule, N. M., Baumann, M. P. O., Mathia, E., & Hassanali, A. (2005). Ethnoveterinary medicine: a critical review of its evolution, perception, understanding and the way forward.

Ward, H.G.1989. African Development Reconsidered: New Perspectives from the Continent, Phelps-Stokes Institute Publications, New York.

Ybañez, A. P., Mingala, C. N., & Ybañez, R. H. D. (2018). Historical review and insights on the livestock tick-borne disease research of a developing country: The Philippine scenario. *Parasitology international, 67*(2), 262-266.

Yigezu, Y., Haile, D. B., & Ayen, W. Y. (2014). Ethnoveterinary medicines in four districts of Jimma zone, Ethiopia: cross sectional survey for plant species and mode of use. *BMC veterinary research, 10*(1), 76.

Yineger H., Kelbessa E., Bekele T., Lulekal E (2007). Ethnoveterinary medicinal plants at Bale Mountains National Park, Ethiopia, Journal of Ethnopharmacology, 112: 55–70.

Yirga G (2010b). Ethnobotanical Study of Medicinal Plants in and Around Alamata, Southern Tigray, Northern Ethiopia, Current Res J. Bio. Sci., 2 (5): 338-344.

Yirga, G, Teferi, M, Gidey, G, Zerabruk, S., 2012b. An ethnoveterinary survey of medicinal plants used to treat livestock diseases in Seharti-Samre district. North. Ethiop. African J. Plant Sci. 6 (3), 113–119.

Yirga, G., 2010. Assessment of indigenous knowledge of medicinal plants in Central zone of Tigray, Northern Ethiopia. Afr. J. Plant Sci. 4, 006–011.

Yirga, G., Teferi, M., Brhane, G., Amare, S., 2012a. Plants used in ethnoveterinary practices in Medebay-Zana district, northern Ethiopia. J. Med. Plants Res. 6, 433–438.

Zabbar A, Akhtar MS, Muhammad G, Lateef M (2005). Possible role of ethnoveterinary medicine in poverty reduction in Pakistan: Use of botanical anthelmintics as an example. J. Agri. Social Sci., 2: 187195.

Chapter 18

Indigenous Food Intake: An alternative for Mitigating Food Insecurity and Refined Foods Related Diseases?

Annastacia Mawere (nee Mbindi) & Munyaradzi Mawere

Abstract

Since the dawn of colonialism, Africa and Zimbabwe in particular has suffered dislocations, misrepresentations, and castigation of its values and ways of life, including indigenous foods. To date, global food production and discourses on food intake remain dominated by the Global North. Worse still, concerted effort has been made by [former] colonial government(s) to instil brainwashed thinking, colonial education curriculum, colonial legal systems, foreign economic models and policies, and self-denial in indigenous Africans. Sadly, the dislocation, misrepresentations and castigation of African values and ways of life, including feeding habits, have been carried over from colonial Africa into the so-called "independent" (or post-colonial) Africa, of which Zimbabwe is not an exception. This chapter examines the role of indigenous food as an alternative for mitigating food insecurity and refined foods related diseases in an African place – Masvingo Province of Zimbabwe. For purposes of this study, qualitative data were collected through both formal and informal interviews, focus group discussions, direct field observations, and participatory observations. Based on the findings that indigenous foods are valuable in many ways, we argue that there is need to recognize the efficacy of indigenous food in Zimbabwe given its nutritional value, possibility to mitigate food insecurity and the fact that food can serve as both a cultural and religious expression of any given people. Our argument thus concurs with Nzewi (2007) and Mawere's (2011) argument that contemporary Africans must strive to rescue, resuscitate and advance African original intellectual legacy or challenge the onslaught of externally manipulated forces of mental and cultural dissociation now rampaging Africa, aimed at obliterating the African original intellect and lore of life.

Keywords: Indigenous Food, Intake, Impact, Perceptions, Zimbabwe

Introduction

African indigenous foods are as old as human history on the African soil. Because no one can survive without food, food is a physiological necessity for human nourishment. As Sibanda (2019) observed, the production and consumption of food are common processes amongst all human beings in order to attain a flourishing life. Even the so-called 'primitive' and 'underdeveloped' societies have their own means of [food] production and at least consume food for nourishment.

Interestingly, this realisation calls for the need to recognize the value of all foods, indigenous foods included that give nourishment and nutrients to humanity. In any case, food is embedded in the cultural system, the cultivation, the preparation and its consumption, which all contribute significantly towards the formulation of a people's identity claims. It is a cultural manifestation and an identity mark of any people. Sibanda (2019) concurs with Nhemachena (2017) that matters of health are defined in terms of the connection between food and the social, cultural, biological, community and spiritual harmony. As noted by Nyathi (2017), food is part of human identity as its significance goes beyond nutrition. This is corroborated by Nhemachena (2017) who argues that food comes with religious, political, social, cultural, economic, gender and epistemic baggage that frame what we eat and how we eat. Fajans (1998) also agrees when he argues that what we eat, how we eat, when we eat and with whom we eat varies across groups, spatial and temporal dimensions, but deploys an overarching influence on identity and human flourishing. In African indigenous culture, for example, food is used to show love, acceptance and humanity (what is generally understood as an expression of *[h]unhu/ ubuntu*). In line with this understanding, Puoane *et. al* (2006) note that food is associated with happiness; if there is no food in the house people become frustrated and unhappy. Puoane *et al*, go on to note that "if you visit someone's house and not given food you feel that you are not welcomed".

We should hasten to mention that the focus of this chapter is not food in general, but indigenous food, particularly perceptions of the Shona people of Masvingo Province of Zimbabwe on indigenous food intake. Indigenous foods are defined in this study as edible foods – vegetables, fruits, drinks, legumes and cereals – that are indigenous/native to a region and its people, and are linked to the people's culture and heritage. There are changes in food culture and

346

dietary habits occasioned by globalisation, westernisation and changes in food production practices through time. When westernisation hit up Africa, commercial farming was introduced and forests were cleared to make way for cash crop farming. According to Robson (1976), these clearing and cultivating activities modified the existing ecosystems and eliminated some wild indigenous food trees as well as some wild [uncultivated] food crops, which were part of the traditional food systems. The trend towards commercial farming and the attendant destruction and erosion of ecosystem diversity negatively affected and contributed to the dramatic decline in the cultivation and availability of indigenous foods. This decline and supplanting of indigenous food resources from regional and national food systems coincided with the emergence of food shortages (or food insecurity), which inversely promoted the production of Genetically Modified Organisms (GMOs). It is assumed that increased urbanisation and large movements of populations to urban centres with reduced access to indigenous foods exacerbated the decline of traditional foods intake (or at least the agentic 'power' of indigenous foods consumers) while increasing the intake of refined foods, including GMOs. The agency of indigenous people was affected in a way. At this level, this discourse on indigenous foods intake reminds us that every race has agency, but that agency is not a birthmark or a permanence. It is something discoverable, cultivatable, nurturable, and [re-]activatable (see also, Nyamnjoh, 2020) through time to different degrees of potency.

In view of [African] indigenous foods intake, what has remained least understood, however, is the impact of [indigenous] people's abandonment of indigenous food in favour of refined foods – foods that have been processed and stripped of their nutritional values such as fibre, vitamins and minerals. Thus, to date, there is dearth of literature on the impact of westernisation on [African] indigenous food intake, and on whether indigenous foods can possibly contribute food security and a health society, especially with reference to Zimbabwe. It is this gap that has prompted us to interrogate the perceptions of locals, in a Zimbabwean place known as Masvingo Province, on the contribution of indigenous foods to food security and the establishment of a health society.

Indigenous food in practice and perspective

This section grapples with the conceptualisation of indigenous food and teases out reasons for going (or not going) for indigenous foods by locals.

The expression "indigenous food" (also known as traditional food) can only be fully unpacked if we understand the terms "indigenous" and "food" separately. The term 'indigenous' can be understood with other names such as 'local' or 'traditional' (Lanzano 2013). Hoppers (2002) makes an essential contribution towards the conceptualisation of IKSs by, first and foremost, attempting to define the word 'indigenous'. For her the word indigenous refers '... to the root, something natural or innate (to) ...' (2002:8). Similarly, for Mawere (2014a: 4), the term 'indigenous' literally mean original, first, native to a place or aboriginal people to an area.

On the other hand, food is anything that people or animals eat or drink or that plants absorb in order to sustain life and growth. Food is the main source of energy and of nutrition for animals, and is usually of animal or plant origin. More importantly, food include both liquid drinks and solid substances that are consumed for purposes of sustaining life.

Having unpacked "indigenous" and "food" separately, it is important to note that indigenous food is the diet consisting largely of the foods one's centuries-old ancestors ate and drank for their health and well-being (Puonne *et al.* 2006). It is the opposite of refined food, which is food that has been chemically altered (*Ibid*). In this study, indigenous foods are defined as edible foods – vegetables, drinks, fruits, nuts and grains/cereals – that are native to a region and its people, and are linked to people's culture and heritage.

Many people have become conscious of the importance for eating health food. It is generally believed that the large chunk of nutrients for a health body comes from indigenous foods. Nevertheless, there is a challenge for many Africans who are seeking ways of using indigenous foods available to them to achieve good health, especially given that some scholars like Corola (1999) question the health status of African traditional foods. However, Kuznesof *et al* (1997) reported that African indigenous foods are very healthy and one can achieve good health by eating [African] indigenous foods and by controlling how much you eat, including fruits and vegetables in the diet and eating lighter meals for supper. In another study, Cordian *et al* (2005) note that in a study that was conducted over a 20 year period in 187 countries across the world, home to 89% of the world population, it was observed that diets from the sub-Saharan Africa are healthier compared to diets from other parts of the world. This is because African foods are more natural, richer in dietary fibre (which helps to prevent heart diseases, fight cancerous substances) and are generally lower in added sugar, fat and sodium.

In Masvingo Province, some of the traditional foods that have been consumed for centuries now include *amarunthus hybridus* (palmer's pigweed/ *mowa* in Shona), *bidens pilosa* (blackjack/mutsine in Shona), *cucurbita pepo* (pumpkin leaves/*boora* in Shona), *derere* (okra), *howa* (mushroom), *dakataka* (peanut butter stew) and traditional fruits such as *tsubvu* (vitex payos), *matamba* (monkey oranges), among many others. Based on our fieldwork, below we provide a list of [some] common African indigenous foods in Masvingo whose nutritional values and health benefits can be summarised as below:

Table 1: Selected African Indigenous Foods, Nutritional Values and Health benefits

Indigenous foods	Nutritional value	Health benefits
Amarunthus hybridus (palmer's pigweed/ mowa in Shona)	**Anti-cancer nutrients, fibre, folic acid, vitamin C & K.**	• Prevents the onset of diabetes • Lower cases of cancer
*Vigna unguiculata (*cowpeas leaves/*Munyemba*)	Proteins, calories, minerals, vitamins, fibre/roughage, folic acid (as in the case of cowpea) (see also, Goncalves *et al,* 2016)	• Prevents the onset of diabetes • Lower cases of insomnia (as in the case of cowpea leaves (see also, Goncalves *et al,* 2016) • Beneficial effects against atherosclerosis, brain dysfunction, stroke, cardiovascular diseases (CVD), and cancer.

Cucurbita pepo (pumpkin leaves/*muboora* in Shona)	Fiber/roughage, minerals, Vitamin (A & C), water, carbohydrates, fat and protein	• Improves skin health and helps to defend against infections. • Lower cases of heart disease • Helps to control blood pressure • Lowers symptoms of asthma, flu, and colds • Improves body abilities to fight infections • Normalize menstrual periods in women.
Blackjack (bidens pilosa/ mutsine in Shona)	Fibre, antioxidants and sterols	• Alleviate several health conditions including sexually transmitted diseases, malaria, and urinary tract infections. • Reduced risk of heart disease, cholesterol abnormalities, diabetes, high blood pressure
Hibiscus esculentus (okra / derere)	Antioxidants (known as polyphenols), protein, folate, dietary fibre, fat, magnesium, carbohydrates, vitamin A, B6 and C.	• Vitamin C is a water-soluble nutrient that contributes to your overall immune function, while vitamin K1 is a fat-soluble vitamin that's

		known for its role in blood clotting. Polyphenols may improve heart health by lowering your risk of blood clots and oxidative damage (Tressera-Rimbau *et al* 2017).
Cleome gynandra *(spider leaf/ Nyevhe* in Shona)	Iron, calcium, magnesium, proteins and fibre.	• Improve eyesight • Can be used to treat scurvy • Known to improve production of milk for breastfeeding mothers • Good for weight loss • Improves digestions • Improves overall body performance and provides energy • Creates a healthy skin and hair • Lower body cholesterol • Reduces chances of getting cancer (see Kenya Fruits Exporters, 2020).

Indigenous 'African' fruits e.g., marula (Sclerocarya birrea), mauyu (baobab fruit/adansonia digitata), tsvubvu (vitex payos/chocolate berry), matamba (Strychnos spinosa/monkey oranges)	Fiber/roughage, carbohydrate, Vitamin, minerals (e.g., zinc, potassium, sodium, magnesium)	<ul><li>Beneficial effects against atherosclerosis, brain dysfunction, stroke, cardiovascular diseases (CVD), and cancer.</li><li>Good for blood pressure healthy blood pressure, controlled blood sugar, optimum heart health, and to fight cancer</li><li>Good for cardiovascular diseases CVDs</li></ul>
Millets (e.g., pearl millet, Finger millet, proso millet, and foxtail millet)	Vitamin (A, K B2,3,5,6,9), protein, fat, carbohydrate, minerals (Calcium, magnesium, iron, zinc, potassium, phosphorous, sodium)	<ul><li>Reduces risk factors for CVDs</li></ul>
Sorghum bicolor (mapfunde/Sorghum)	Polyphenols, fibre, and antioxidants	<ul><li>Good for heart diseases, fighting cancer and diabetes</li></ul>

Source: Compiled by Authors, 2020

Methodological concerns and theoretical keystones

This study, which was carried out in Masvingo Province of Zimbabwe, deployed a qualitative ethnographic research approach, particularly focus group discussions (FGDs), formal and informal interviews, and participant observation as well as documentary analysis to gather relevant information on perceptions of different interlocutors on the contribution of indigenous food to food security and the nurturing of a health society. The study was carried out continuously for the period stretching between December 2018 and

January 2020. Masvingo Province was purposively selected for two major reasons that it was convenient to both authors and because the province remains a cultural beacon of Zimbabwe, with traditional dishes still being served in many restaurants in the province, including the famous Great Zimbabwe Monuments' Hotel. As Bourdillon (1976) aptly captures, traditionally, the basic food of the Shona people (the largest ethnic group in Masvingo and Zimbabwe in general) is *sadza* (stiff porridge) made from ground maize or millet, and their main crop is maize or millet grown on fields of a few acres. They also grow rapoko and sorghum as well as a range of vegetables to provide relish to eat with thick porridge. Sour milk and meat from domestic and wild animals are also eaten as relish. The diet may be supplemented by various wild fruits, seeds, and edible insects. Wild fruit trees are traditionally protected for the food they provide such that in Masvingo, there are still large, protected forests such as the famous Norumedzo Jiri (see also, Mawere, 2014b). Below is the map of the studied area – Masvingo Province – including its seven districts:

Figure 1: The Map of Zimbabwe showing Masvingo Province and its seven districts

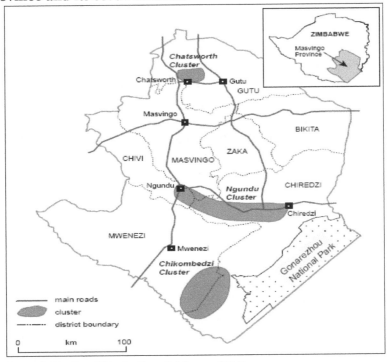

Source: Bikita Rural District Council (Mawere, 2014).

353

Ethnographic research approach such as FGDs, interviews and participant observation were deemed most appropriate to gather data for this study because it provides what Geertz (1983:6) and Nyamnjoh (2020: 2) have respectively called "thick descriptions" and "thick and thin descriptions" –thoroughly detailed information about the studied subject. Participant observation, for example, is excellent for providing such data. Marshall and Rossman (2009) describe observation as the systematic description of events, behaviours, and artefacts in the social setting chosen for study. Observations enable the researcher to describe existing situations using the five senses, providing a written photograph of the situation under study. Participant observation is therefore the process that enable researchers to learn about the activities of the people under study in the natural setting through observing and participating in those activities.

In terms of theoretical analysis, this study was guided by the Afrocentric theory, which was formulated and popularised by Molefi Kete Asante and Ama Mazama though had been used by earlier scholars such as Kwame Nkrumah. According to Sibanda (2019) Afrocentricity is a response to Eurocentricity and the related cultural bias, racism and pejorative Western scholarship on Africa, Africans and their cultural heritage, both at home and abroad. As Asante (2009: 1; see also Asante, 1998) himself describes, "Afrocentricity is a paradigm based on the idea that African people should re-assert a sense of agency in order to achieve sanity; a *constructural* adjustment to black disorientation, decenteredness, and lack of agency". In other words, the Afrocentric theory (or Afro-centrism/Afrocentric theory) is a theory that calls for African phenomena, activities and way of life to be looked at and be given meaning from the standpoint and world view of Africans themselves. This is to say, Afro-centrism argues that using colonial and western perspectives in order to understand African realities always results in distortions, misinterpretations and misrepresentations.

In view of this study, it is therefore prudent that the indigenous foods intake in Zimbabwe be interrogated and interpreted by the [indigenous] Zimbabweans (in this case, the Shona people of Masvingo Province) themselves as they tap their knowledge and experiences into solving daily challenges confronting them. This is in tandem with Sibanda's (2019) argument that, Afrocentric theory seeks to promote the agency of African people in prioritising an African frame of reference and holistic lifestyle. This theory is applicable to the current study since the indigenous foods are placed at the periphery where people think that eating indigenous foods is old fashioned and eating Western foods is highly prestigious. Using this theory as its theoretical bases, this chapter argues that traditional foods intake can help to ease the tapestry of food insecurity and the burden casted by diseases linked to consumption of foreign and [artificially] refined foods.

Reflections on perceptions of the 'locals' on indigenous food intake

In the recent years, food insecurity in Zimbabwe as elsewhere has increasingly become a real menace. Worse still, there has been an upsurge in the number of people suffering from cancer, diabetes and obesity. As World Data Atlas (2016), for instance, reports thus, "in 2016, female obesity prevalence for Zimbabwe was 25. 3 %. Female obesity prevalence of Zimbabwe increased from 7 % in 1975 to 25. 3 % in 2016 and is growing at an average of annual rate of 2.28% since 1997". The question that comes to mind is: 'Why food insecurity and diseases like cancer, diabetes and obesity have become a major risk in Zimbabwe these years?" Drawing from these submissions, the overarching question for this study is: Can indigenous food intake be an alternative for mitigating food insecurity and promoting a health society? In order to answer this overarching question, the study seeks to address the following sub-questions:

i). What are the causes of food insecurity and increasing outbreak of diseases such as cancer, diabetes and obesity in Masvingo Province?

ii). Which African indigenous food stuffs are normally consumed by the people of Masvingo Province?

iii). What are the perceptions of people on African traditional foods in Masvingo?

iv). What is to be done in order to rescue [African] traditional foods from extinction as a result of westernisation in Masvingo Province?

In view of the first question, it was revealed that with the advent of colonialism in Zimbabwe, the country has adopted heterogeneity in its culture, rituals, lifestyle and food. Mawere (2014c) captures this aptly when he argues that in colonial Zimbabwe, as elsewhere on the African continent, African culture, indigenous knowledge, traditional medicine, African traditional foods and all other things with the tug 'African' were despised and relegated to the periphery if not totally obliterated. Nyathi (2017) concurs with Kuznesof *et al* (1997) who observed that African Indigenous foods are referred to as 'poor people's foods' by some people who are mentally colonised such that it can be argued, the negative attitude towards indigenous foods is founded in the historical colonial food consumption habits of African consumers contrary to the local socio-cultural and food source references of the past. Since Zimbabwe was a British colony, its people have followed some English customs including food and diet. Siamonga (2016) noted that the majority of people no longer eat traditional foods as they have adapted to European food and as a result some taboos associated with Zimbabwe traditional food and customs have diminished. This is corroborated by Robson (1976) who notes that with increasing urbanisation, the trend in dietary simplification continues as more and more women find employment outside the home, have less time for the preparation of family meals and so go for high energy and low nutritional value foods. Similarly, Kuznesof *et. al* (1997) reported that indigenous foods are perceived to be "old fashioned foods". It is believed that Africans used to consume specific indigenous foods because they had the knowledge, skills and time to prepare such products as finger millet (*mhunga* in Shona), sorghum (*mapfunde* in Shona) and rapoko (*rukweza* in Shona) (*Ibid*). This is to say that because of westernisation, the younger generation has more diverse food purchasing and consumption patterns, that is, a preference for novelty and food convenience. One of the participants in her late 70s, Mbuya Tariro (not her real name) concurred when she said:

Kare isu taitswa mapfunde, mhunga nerukweza tokuya tobika sadza nemiriwo yedu yechivanhu kusanganisira derere, mufushwa, musine nemimwewo. Zvino imi vana vanhasi inongova iyoyo yekuti hatina nguva yekugadzira nekubika chikafu chechembere chinononoka kuibva uye tine mari yekutenga twunonaka, asi ndizvo zvokupedzai/Long ago, we used to pound and grind sorghum, finger millet and rapoko and prepare it with traditional relish like okra, dried vegetables, blackjack and others. You, young generation now always say "we no longer have time to prepare old fashioned foods, and now have money to buy taste food, but this is what is killing you".

Similar submissions were given in view of the increasing outbreak of diseases such as cancer, diabetes and obesity. Another participant who was a former graduate at Great Zimbabwe University, John, had this to say:

Kubva zvangotanga utongi hwevadzvinyiriri vemadokero muAfrica, zvinhu zvedu zvose kusanganisira zvekudya nekumwa zvakatanga kutarisirwa pasi, kunyange zvazvo tsvakurudzo zhinji dzava kutaridza kuti chikafu chechivanhu chine hutano uye chinobatsira kudzivirira zvirwere zvakaita segomarara, shuga nekukura muviri/Since the dawn of colonialism in Africa, all systems were understood to be African (including African Traditional Foods) were treated with contempt. Researches these days however point to the health benefits of traditional foods, including fighting diseases like cancer, diabetes and obesity.

This buttressed earlier studies by scholars like Nhemachena, Mawere and Vladmir (2009), among others who generally argue that traditional foods are healthier than refined foods, which in most cases result in heart-related diseases, diabetes, cancer and obesity. In fact, scientific research attribute most of these diseases to be caused by consuming fatty foods processed food with high starch content, sweet foods as well as Genetically Modified Organisms (GMOs). As argued by Mawere and Nhemachena (2017), westernisation (through Genetically Modified Organisms GMOs) divorced Africans from their traditional foods and this caused a plethora of diseases such as diabetes and obesity. They further argue that GMOs can result in genetic and hormonal imbalances and can adversely alter the genetic constitution and identity of humans. Similarly, Vladmir (2009) argued that a more western diet in some emerging countries could have a more detrimental effect on global health and hunger than population growth. Cordain *et al* (2005) concur with Vladmir (2009) that western diet has health implications. They asserted that in the United States, chronic illnesses and health problems either wholly or partially attributable to diet represent by far the most serious threat to public health. They further reveal that sixty-five (65%) of adults aged 20 in the US are either overweight or obese, and the estimated number of deaths ascribable to obesity is 280184 per year, while more than 64 million Americans have one or more types of cardiovascular diseases (CVD) which represents the leading cause of mortality (38.5% of all deaths) in the United States of America. The same study reports that cancer is the second leading cause of death (25% of all deaths) in the US and an estimated one-third of all cancer death is due to nutritional factors including obesity. While such literature focuses exclusively on the USA, what remains clear is that refined foods are detrimental to health and Africa and Zimbabwe in particular should take a leaf from such studies to also assess the extent to which the chronic diseases which have wreaked havoc in Masvingo and Zimbabwe in general are a result of diet and nutritional factors.

Later studies such as those by Batis *et al* (2011) have revealed that traditional African diet may reduce colony cancer, the second leading cause of cancer death in countries like USA, and which affects a greater proportion of African-Americans than rural Africans, indicating that diet plays an important role in disease prevention. In order to investigate how traditional diets affect risk factors for colon cancer, researchers assigned 20 middle aged African Americans to a traditional African heritage diet (averaging 55g fibre daily and 16% calories from fat, with foods like mangos, bean soup and fish) and 20 middle rural South Africans to typical American diet (averaging 12g fibre daily and 52% calories from fat, with food like pancakes, burgers, fries and meatloaf). The study reveals that in only two weeks' time, the African-Americans had reduced the inflammation of their colons, improved their resistance to cancer and increased the diversity of their healthy gut bacteria. On the other hand, the rural Africans on American diet fared worse, producing more bile acid (a risk factor for colon cancer), while decreasing their diversity of healthy gut bacteria. These results indicated that an African traditional diet can help promote a healthy digestive tract (potentially reducing colon cancer risk), and that rapid improvements can come with a change to healthier foods.

In response to questions 2 and 3, it was reiterated that traditionally, people in Masvingo depended on stiff porridge (*sadza*) made from mealie-meal from millet, sorghum and rapoko as their staple food. The consumption of these foods along with other indigenous foods has dramatically diminished in Zimbabwe in favour of refined foods, even though it is scientifically proven that these foods are beneficial, heath-wise. No wonder why scholars like Sibanda (2019) has argued that due to westernisation food can be a blinding fetish. He noted that 'Coca-colisation' and 'McDonaldisation' have effects on the food industry which causes many problems in today's world. Likewise, Mawere and Nhemachena (2017) argued that Genetically Modified Food threatens ethics, morals and human rights, in so far as it erodes the genetic constitution of humans which is the foundation of human identity, human ethics, society, culture, morality and law. They argue that the use of GMOs is to deny Africans legitimate ownership of their resources. It was propounded by Nhemachena (*Ibid*) that scientific reports have indicated that GMOs cause infertility, impotence, cancer and other diseases, particularly for impoverished people in Africa who are prone to buy the cheap GMOs. Nyathi (2017) asserted that the condition or state of the food that we eat transfers to consumers. We become what we eat. This applies to the various characteristics of food. It could be its chemical makeup. For Nyathi, consuming GMO food makes us GMO. People may be turned to GMOs because of hunger and poverty. This was confirmed by one participant, Mai Tindo, who is a cross-border trader. Mai Tindo thus said:

*Vanhu vazhinji muno nenyaya yenhamo nezhara tiri kudya maGMOs nyange tichizviziva kuti anokuvadza. Ini pandinoenda kunohodha kuSouth Africa, ndinotongotengawo machicken cuts nemapotatoes emaGMOs iwayo nokuti anenge akachipa uye kuno haanetsi kutengesa/*Because of hunger and poverty, many of us here feed on GMOs even though we are aware of their detrimental effects to our healthy. Personally, when I go to South Africa for trading, I normally buy GMO chicken cuts and potatoes because they are cheaper and here on our market, they sell faster.

The revelation by Mai Tindo really calls for the need to conscientise people of the effects of consuming GMOs and refined foods, which in fact are chemically altered. Instead, people should be encouraged to consume traditional foods, which are natural and not chemically altered. According to Dayakar *et al* (2016), the regular consumption of traditional foods such as sorghum and millet has been reported to be associated with a myriad of health benefits. It is important to consume the grains of their seed coat. Millets are responsible for the prevention and reduction of oxidative stress, having anti-cancer, anti-diabetic and anti- hypertensive properties and are also important in the prevention of high blood pressure and high cholesterol levels. It is also recommended for blood pressure conditions, liver disorders, asthma and heart diseases. Again, Arya (2014) recommended the intake of millet to lactating mothers with inadequate milk production as this help to boost their milk production.

Specifically responding to question iii, it was reiterated that food is an expression of culture, hence the need to promote traditional foods intake. Sekuru Mandiva of Zaka, for instance, had this to say:

*Aaah, ko handiti chikafu chedu ndicho chivanhu chedu here? Chivanhu chinowanikwa muchikafu, ndiko saka tichifanira kukoshesa chikafu chedu chechibarirwe. Tikasachikoshesa tatotadza kukoshesawo chivanhu chedu/*Aaah, don't you know that our food is our culture? Culture is embedded in food. This is why it is important to respect our traditional foods. If we fail to respect our traditional foods, we will have failed to respect our culture.

This reverberates with Nyathi's (2017), argument that food goes beyond nutrition since food is also a cultural expression. It is also in synch with Leach's (1976) earlier pronouncement that food is culture. For him, the human species has always placed strong importance on cultural identity. Being able to identify someone as belonging to one group or another was an issue of safety and security. Food became a way of quickly identifying people. Besides, for Leach, food is a way to connect to our heritage and to our own cultural identity. Thus, food is a way to identity: who you are, where you come from and the history of your people. By the same token, Murcott (1982) observes that elaboration of the cultural significance of food and eating focuses on social values, meanings and beliefs rather than on dietary requirements and nutritional values. He appreciated that African people's food choice is neither random nor haphazard, but exhibit patterns and regularities. Further, eating habits are not solely a matter of the satisfaction of physiological and psychological needs, nor merely a result of individual preference. Food has also been seen as a cultural affair, people eat in a socially organised fashion. Thus, food can be seem to convey a range of cultural meanings not only in terms of occasion but also social status, ethnicity and wealth.

Responding to the concerns of the last question, one participant from a focus group discussion in Gutu (one of the provinces in Masvingo) had this to say:

*Kudya kwedu kwechivanhu kunofanira kuremekedzwa nokuti kwaiita kuti vakuru vedu vekare vararame nguva yakareba. Zvakare kwaiita kuti vararame vasina zvirwere zvatekeshera mazuva ano segomarara neshuga/*Our indigenous food should be respected because it is this food which enabled our forefathers to live longer. It also enabled them to live free of diseases such as cancer and diabetes which are common today.

This submission was interesting in that it buttressed earlier studies by scholars like Nzewi (2007) and Mawere (2011), among others. Mawere (2011), as with Nzewi (2007), for example, argue that contemporary Africans must strive to rescue, resuscitate and advance African original intellectual legacy or at least challenge the onslaught of externally manipulated forces of mental and cultural dissociation now rampaging Africa, aimed at obliterating the African original intellect and lore of life. The call by these scholars has been premised on the realisation that the question of indigenous foods intake, as that of indigenous knowledge systems (IKSs), is fundamentally important though often overlooked, as it relates to identity, culture and human flourishing in African societies.

Conclusion

This chapter has argued that indigenous foods intake can be an alternative for mitigating food insecurity and health problems and diseases associated with refined foods in Zimbabwe as elsewhere. Grounding the arguments was the assertion that nations like Zimbabwe can mitigate the effects of food insecurity and menaces of "modern" diseases such as cancer, diabetes, obesity and others. Using the [African] indigenous foods example, we have illustrated and advanced the possibility of achieving a hunger free and "modern" disease free Zimbabwe. Instructive to our interest in indigenous foods, we noted that prior to the introduction of western foods, traditional foods used to be dominant to millions of people in Zimbabwean rural areas, as in other such African places. However, the advent of colonialism marked a significant turning point in the history of indigenous foods intake. The western culture, including feeding habits, had a huge impact on the continent and culture of Africa. We admit that the impact of westernisation on indigenous foods intake has been neither dominantly positive nor negative, but what remains crystal clear is that western imperialism has led to the abandonment or at least underestimation of the health benefits of indigenous foods. Indigenous foods intake discourse reminds us that every race has agency, but that agency is not a birthmark or a permanence. Instead, agency is something in the process of becoming – discoverable, cultivatable, nurturable, and [re-]activatable – through time to different degrees of potency, such that as Molefi Kete Asante believes, "it is not enough to know; one must act *(or re-activate his/her agency)* to humanise the world". We therefore conclude that the re-activation of our agency to humanise the world through consumption of natural health foods such as the larger chunk of [African] traditional foods in order to mitigate food insecurity and promote a health society is not only worthwhile but more urgent now than ever.

References

Arya, J. (2014). *Food is Your Best Medicine,* Arya Publishers, Pune: India.

Asante, K. M. (2009). *Afrocentricity,* South African City Press Column.

Asante, K. M. (1998). *The Afrocentric Idea,* Temple University Press: Philadelphia.

Batis, L. *et al.* (2011). The Role of Traditional Diets in a Healthy lifestyle, *The Journal of Nutrition,* 141(10): 1898-906.

Bourdillon, M. F. C. (1976). *The Shona people, revised edition: An ethnography of the contemporary Shona with special reference to their Religion,* Mambo Press: Gweru.

Cordain, L.; Eaton, S. B.; Sebastian, A.; Mann, N. (2005). Origins and evolution of the western diet: Health Implications for the 21st Century. *The American Journal of Clinical Nutrition,* Vol 81, issue 2, 2005.

Corola, L. (Ed). (1999). *Changing Food Habits: Case Studies from Africa, South America and Europe,* Harwood Academic Publishers: Australia.

Dayakar, R. B. *et al.* (2016). *Millets value chain for nutritional security: A replicable success model from India,* CABI: India.

Fajans, J. (1988). The Transformative Value of Food: A Review Essay, *Food and foodways* 3(1-2):143-166.

Geertz, C. (1983). 'From the native's point of view': On the nature of anthropological understanding, in: his *Local knowledge: Further Essays in Interpretive Anthropology,* New York, 3-16.

Gonçalves, Alexandre; Goufo, Piebiep; Barros, Ana; Domínguez-Perles, Raúl; Trindade, Henrique; Rosa, Eduardo A. S.; Ferreira, Luis; Rodrigues, Miguel (2016). Cowpea (Vigna unguiculata L. Walp), a renewed multipurpose crop for a more sustainable agrifood system: nutritional advantages and constraints, *Journal of the Science of Food and Agriculture* 96 (9): 2941–2951. doi:10.1002/jsfa.7644.

Hoppers, C. & Odora, A. (2002). Indigenous Knowledge and the Integration of Knowledge Systems. In Hoppers, C. & A. Odora (eds.): *Indigenous Knowledge and the Integration of Knowledge Systems:*

Towards a Philosophy of Articulation. Claremont: New Africa Books (Pty) Ltd.

Kenya Fruits Exporters, (2020). "Health Benefits of Eating African Indigenous Vegetables", Nairobi: Kenya.

Kuznesof, S, Tregear, A., Moxey, A. (1997). Region foods: A Consumer Perspective, *British Food Journal* 99 (6):199-206.

Lanzano, C. (2013). What Kind of Knowledge is Indigenous Knowledge? Critical insights from a Case Study in Burkina Faso, *Transcience* 4 (2): 3-18.

Leach, E. R. (1976). *Culture and Communication,* Cambridge University: Cambridge

Mail & Guardian, (19 Sept 2016). "Indigenous African foods: Five forgotten super-foods", Pretoria: South Africa.

Marshall, C. & Rossman, G. B. (2009). *Designing Qualitative Research.* London: Sage.

Mawere, M. (2011). *African Belief and Knowledge Systems: A critical Perspective,* Bamenda: Langaa.

Mawere, M. (2014a). *Culture, Indigenous Knowledge and Development in Africa: Reviving Interconnecting for Sustainable Development,* Langaa Research & Publishing CIG: Bamenda.

Mawere, M. (2014b). *Environmental conservation through Ubuntu and other emerging perspectives,* Bamenda, Langaa.

Mawere, M. (2014c). Forest Insects, Personhood and the Environment: Harurwa (Edible stinkbug) and Conservation in South-eastern Zimbabwe, *PhD Thesis,* University of Cape Town: South Africa.

Mawere, M. and Nhemachena, A. (2017). Human Culling and Super- colonialism? Human Rights Issues of Doling Out Genetically Modified Food in African Mawere, M. and Nhemachena, A. (eds). *GMOs, Consumerism and the Global Politics of Biotechnology: Rethinking Food, Bodies and Identities in Africa's 21ˢᵗ Century,* Bamenda, Langaa.

Murcott, A. (1982). *The cultural significance of food and eating,* Cambridge University: Cambridge.

Nhemachena, A. (2017). Food, Health and Science in Africa: Locating GMOs Debates in the Shifting Global Epistemological Terrains in Mawere, M and Nhemachena, A (eds). *GMOs, Consumerism and the Global Politics of Biotechnology: Rethinking Food, Bodies and Identities in Africa's 21ˢᵗ Century,* Bamenda, Langaa.

Nyamnjoh, F. (2020). "A post-covid-19 fantasy on incompleteness and conviviality." In: "Post-Covid fantasies," Catherine

Besteman, Heath Cabot, and Barak Kalir, editors, American Ethnological Society website, 27 July 2020, [https://americanethnologist.org/features/pandemic-diaries/post-covid-fantacies/a-post-covid-19-fantasy-on-incompleteness-and-conviviality].

Nyathi, P. (2017). *Beyond Nutrition: Food as a Cultural Expression*, Amagugu Publishers: Bulawayo.

Nzewi, M. (2007). A contemporary study of musical arts informed by African indigenous knowledge system: Illuminations, reflections and explorations (Vol. 4). Pretoria: Ciimda.

Puoane, T., Matwa, P., Bradley, H. & Hughes, G. (2006). Socio-Cultural Factors Influencing food consumption pattern in the Black African Population in an urban township in South Africa, *Human ecology*, 14 (14): 89-93.

Robson, J.R.K. (1976). Changing food habits in developing countries, *Ecological Food Nutrition*, vol 4, 251-256.

Siamonga, E. (2016). *Western influence on taboos associated with Zimbabwean food*, The Patriot, Harare.

Sibanda, F. (2019). Promoting Human Flourishing through Rastafari Foodways in Africa in Christian Green, M. (Ed) *Law, Religion and Human Flourishing in Africa*, Africa Sun Media, Stellenbosch: South Africa.

Tressera-Rimbau, A., Arranz, S., Eder, M., and Vallverdú-Queralt, A. (2017). Dietary Polyphenols in the Prevention of Stroke, Oxidative Medicine Cellular Longevity, https://doi.org/10.1155/2017/7467962.

Vladmir, P. (2009). *Global food crisis: The challenge of changing diets*, Pragon House: Minnesota.

World Data Atlas (2016). "Zimbabwe - Female obesity prevalence as a share of female ages 18+", Khoema Enterprise Data Solutions: Khoema.

Chapter 19

Rethinking Indigenous Knowledge Systems in Systematic Problem-Solving and Decision-Making: A Case of Shona Indigenous Families

Fortune Sibanda & Bernard Pindukai Humbe

Abstract

The world-over, conflicts are inevitable in society. Africans have particular ways of conceptualizing conflict contrary to the Western conception of conflict resolution which mainly depends on the Roman-Dutch judiciary court system. In Africa, conflicts are as natural as peace. Conflicts are sometimes regarded as struggles over values and claims to scarce status, power and resources in which conflicting parties seek to neutralize, injure or eliminate their rivals. This chapter seeks to rethink African Indigenous Knowledge Systems (AIKSs) in systematic problem-solving and decision-making patterns in Shona indigenous families. The research posits that indigenous conflict resolution techniques, encompassing pacifism, mediation, adjudication, reconciliation, and negotiation as well as cross-examination that are employed by the Shona people, offer great prospects for peaceful co-existence and harmonious relationships in indigenous families. By using a *Sankofa* theoretical framework and the phenomenological and sociological approaches to describe and analyse data collected through observation, interviews with knowledgeable family revered figures and researchers' personal experiences, the study concludes that Shona indigenous ways of dispute resolution provide an opportunity to interact with the parties concerned and promote consensus-building, social bridge reconstructions and enactment of order in the society.

Keywords: Conflict resolution; AIKS; pacifism; mediation; adjudication; reconciliation; negotiation

Introduction

Globally, conflicts are inevitable in society. In Africa, conflicts are as natural as peace. Africans have particular ways of conceptualizing conflict contrary to the Western conception of conflict resolution which mainly depends on the Roman-Dutch judiciary court system

(Ajayi & Buhari 2014). Conflicts are sometimes regarded as struggles over values and claims to scarce status, power and resources in which conflicting parties seek to neutralize, injure or eliminate their rivals (Onigun & Albert 2001). According to Ajayi and Buhari (2014:138), conflict resolution in traditional African societies provides an opportunity to interact with the parties concerned and "it promotes consensus-building, social bridge reconstructions and enactment of order in the society". This suggests that African societies fall back on their social capital anchored on African culture and indigenous ways of knowing and experiencing the world contained in myths, songs, proverbs and folktales, among other avenues, in order to resolve conflicts. This is intangible heritage. Unfortunately, some of these African Indigenous Knowledge Systems (AIKS) have been debased by Western cultural imperialism, which diluted the African spiritual and cultural values (Mawere 2014:26), including those that encompass problem-solving and decision-making in indigenous Shona families.

This chapter seeks to rethink African Indigenous Knowledge Systems in systematic problem-solving and decision-making patterns in Shona indigenous families. The research posits that African indigenous conflict resolution techniques, encompassing pacifism, mediation, adjudication, reconciliation, and negotiation as well as cross-examination that are employed by the Shona people, offer great prospects for peaceful co-existence and harmonious relationships in indigenous families. This implies that there is great potential in utilising values of conflict resolution drawn from African Indigenous Ways of Knowing (AIWK). As such, the abandonment of African cultural values in preference of Western-styled litigation systems may not necessarily bear positive outcome, given that the success of Western culture was dependent on technological superiority rather than rational superiority (Mawere 2014:34). Western technological superiority created a centre-periphery dichotomy that placed African values at the margins in contradistinction to Western ones (Sibanda 2011). Apparently, AIKS in systematic problem-solving and decision-making that are made without consensus-building could be detrimental to social stability and tranquillity in families.

This chapter employed the phenomenological and sociological approaches to describe and analyse data. From the phenomenological approach, *epoche* (bracketing), descriptive accuracy and *eidetic* intuition, which focus on the meaning of phenomena (Cox 1996), were the most useful elements for the study. Through the sociological

366

approach, the element of collective consciousness characterised by social support, social networking that results in defining in-group and out-group social identities. The sociology of religion also reinforces social norms such as rites of passages like marriage customs and the regulation of sexual behaviour in society (Bourdillon 1990). In this way, the two approaches are used in a complimentary manner in the study. The data were collected through participant observation, interviews with twenty knowledgeable revered figures that were both purposively and conveniently sampled and researchers' personal experiences. The interviewees consisted of twelve adult males and eight adult females who participated in the study on the basis of a voluntary informed consent. Before further interrogating these issues of problem-solving and decision-making in Shona traditional families, we turn to the theoretical framework that informed the study.

Theoretical Framework

This qualitative research utilised the Sankofa perspective as a theoretical framework. Sankofa by its nature, is going back into history or to tradition in order to reclaim what is positive of the past and move forward with it. According to Slater (2019:1), the word "Sankofa" is an African term that originated from the Adinkra ethnic group of the Akan people in Ghana who speak Twi language. The breakdown of the word presents "*san*", which means to return; "*ko*", which means to go; and "*fa*", which means to fetch or to seek. Therefore, when translated, the word "Sankofa" means, "Go back and get it"; or "Go back and take it" (Slater 2019:1). The word itself is represented symbolically and visually by a mythic bird sometimes depicted as flying forward whilst looking back with an egg in its mouth, which represents the future. Literally, this implies that 'it is not taboo to fetch what is at risk of being left behind" (Ibid: 2). This is applicable to AIKS in systematic problem-solving and decision-making in Shona indigenous families.

Essentially, Sankofa is used in mapping out the future, correcting mistakes of the past and learning from experience. The motive behind all this is to assemble the best from the past in order to attain the full potential of society. As Slater (2019:2) further asseverates, "whatever we have lost, forgotten, sacrificed or been deprived of, can be reclaimed, revived, preserved and perpetuated". In the context of this study, the Sankofa tradition can be employed as a method for unearthing the wisdom from African religious belief systems, creeds, codes of behaviour, rituals, spirituality and tradition (Slater 2019) as applied to AIKSs in systematic problem-solving and decision-making in Shona indigenous families. It also emerges that Sankofa is consciousness of the past used for the present purposes. Being aware of the socio-cultural environment and its deep-seated values enables the contemporary individual to find his/her ways into the way of life in his community (Grayson 2000). Through AIKSs in systematic problem-solving and decision-making, it is assumed that the individual would have reached a period of self-discovery and cultural awakening, when s/he can make a conscious effort to re-discover his/her heritage, as well as evaluating its innovative and creative potentials. Consistent with decoloniality which aims at "setting afoot a new humanity free from racial hierarchization and asymmetrical power relations in place" in the postcolony (Ndlovu-Gatsheni 2015:488), Sankofa enables communities to retrieve the ornaments of the past as a method for building a creative tradition for the future in which AIKS in systematic problem-solving and decision-making patterns are endemic.

The Shona People's Understanding of Conflict

Although there are many variations in African family life, certain features pertain to all of them. The most prevalent variant of the African family is the nuclear family. Besides the nuclear family, the extended family is also key among the Shona people and is hinged upon *ukama* (relationality/kinship) (Gelfand 1981). Hence, the African family is a large closely knit community of blood relatives consisting of the life and destiny of each of its members. In short, kinship constitutes the paramount social reality for all African peoples (Paris 1995:77). Like any other ethnic groups in Africa, the Shona people have a deep-seated loyalty to their kith and kin. They condemn any kind of violence among relatives and place great stress on harmony and tranquillity (Gelfand 1992:11). Within the Shona society, collateral relatives enjoy a high status and great affection. They regard the respect extended to members of the same lineage as something that makes for additional solidarity and strength. A person is judged by his/her manners and the respect he/she accords to another person. Clearly, in a society like that of the Shona who are accustomed to live so close to each other in a village, it is imperative for the code of behaviour to be carefully practised by all without exception. Every person should be humble (*kuzvininipisa*), not to be proud (*kuzvikudza*) or aggressive (*kuita ushungu*) (Gelfand 1992). This suggests that no matter one's age and family position, no-one is allowed to create the feeling that s/he is superior for any other reason other than that of his/her slot in the social hierarchy. Every person deserves to be accorded respect by virtue of being a human being.

Given the above set-up, the Shona people have an understanding of problems and how to manage them. According to Pokras (1989), problems of all sorts have three common components: first, problems brew an undesirable situation in a family. Secondly, a desired situation. Sometimes there is a drive to better the undesirable situation. Thirdly, obstacles between undesirable and desirable situation. These are things that stand in the way between the current situation and the family's goal of addressing it. This component of a problem requires the most work, and it is the part where decision making occurs (Pokras 1989; Huitt 1992).

The major sources of problems/conflicts are land, chieftaincy, personal relationship issues, family property, honour, death, infidelity, matrimonial fall-outs, witchcraft, paternity and impregnation of the girl children. In resolving these kinds of conflicts, the principles of equity and justice, which are entrenched in African customs and traditions, are upheld. The problems are dealt with by a Shona family court (*dare*) whose membership is mixed in terms of gender and age. Although the functions of this social institution may vary, the underlying purpose in dealing with a crime or a problem is to maintain peace, alliances, justice, bestow honour and sanction family members for deviant behaviour. Among the Shona people, crime is an act that offends the strong and definite dispositions of the collective family consciousness, and so is considered harmful to the ancestral spirits. Usually, the problem solvers and decision makers, among others, in a family court, include sacred practitioners such as nephew (*muzukuru*), father (*baba*), mother (*mai*), grandfather (*sekuru*), grandmother (*mbuya*), aunt (*tete/babakadzi*), village head (*sabhuku*), headman (*sadunhu*) and Chief (*Ishe/mambo*). Notably, this set of religious functionaries goes beyond the immediate and extended blood family members to encompass some of the communal elders. In some exceptional cases of conflict resolution, the expertise of a *n'anga* (traditional healer) is utilised in Shona communities. In the interest of space, the next few paragraphs explore three selected sacred practitioners involved in conflict

369

resolution in Shona indigenous families, namely, *baba, tete* and *muzukuru*.

In Shona families, the most senior member of the nuclear family, who is normally the father figure (*baba*), has a special role to play in AIKS problem-solving and decision-making. *Baba* is held in high regard and treated with infinite religious respect and prowess. From his religious position, sitting on the ancestral chair and maintaining a nexus between his family members and the ancestral spirits, he plays an instrumental role in the resolution of family conflicts as a custodian of all family cultural traditions and practices. This is particularly so because he is considered to be an embodiment of the beliefs, hopes, fears and aspirations of his family members. Thus, his judicial functions include reconciling human and spiritual forces. In patrilineal society, a father's brother is usually thought of as a kind of father and receives the respect due to the status of a father.

Next is *tete*. The office occupied by *tete* shows the paternal role which women (for instance, the father's sisters) may assume in a Shona family. It is not natural for Shona people to distance girl children, including the married ones, from their parents' family. What is expected of them is to continue assuming their reciprocal social responsibilities with family members back home. Failure to do so could jeopardize their status both in paternal and marital families. The 'aunting' role she performs in her natal family earns her the title *zitete remhuri* (family aunt). The expression connotes familial belonging, which is the primary social reality for all Shona people. Participants outlined the following roles to be performed by *zitete remhuri* in managing family problems: guiding and counselling and administering of rituals in Shona rites of passage such as marriage. In some instances, aunting can be a mediating agency in managing dialectical tensions in family relationships (parental, sibling, spouse, or significant other). About four forms of response to dialectic tensions have been put forward by Baxter (1993) in Sotirin & Ellingson (2005), namely, prioritizing, neutralizing, transcending, and reframing. The third person is *muzukuru* who happens to be a child of a family *tete*. A *muzukuru* can perform a mediatory role in the management of problems or he/she can serve as a *samarinda* (custodian of a deceased uncle's family).

When an issue is to be solved, the venue where the issue is to be resolved is very important. In religious terms, the venue reminds one of sacred and profane space (Eliade 1959). There is exterior venue (outside space) and interior venue (inside space). For the interior venue could include a kitchen. A kitchen is the ideal place for settling some family disputes this sacred space is regarded as the abode of family spirits (*vadzimu*). In the kitchen there is a sitting pattern followed by those who are attending the family court session. Men sit on *Chigaravakwati* (a sitting bench in the kitchen). The sitting arrangement has it that the elderly member of the family occupies the first sitting position right from the door. The Ndau people, a Shona-related ethnic group, calls this is position at the door *mungxho*, which is reserved for the most senior male member of the family. This sitting pattern is very convenient when the traditional protocol of communication *(murandu)* is being implemented. *Kurandudzana*, which derives from *murandu* is a formal pattern of communication done between family members, starting from the youngest adult member ascending to the most senior member. The same protocol is observed by women who would be sitting to discuss the issue. With this communication pattern in place, the Shona usually use group problem solving skills. All the family members constituting the *dare* sit in a circular pattern, which naturally shapes them into a Community of Inquiry (COI) that would contribute on an equal footing to debates. The Shona proverb which says *maonera pamwe chuma chemuzukuru* (the bride-price of a niece calls for a communal participation), is evoked where a communal approach to problem-solving is adopted. Along the same lines, we can also find proverbs such as *chara chimwe hachitswanyi inda* (one finger cannot squash a louse) and *rume rimwe harikombi churu* (one man cannot surround an ant-hill), as informative AIKS in systematic problem-solving and decision-making in Shona indigenous families.

Patterns of AIKSs in Systematic Problem-Solving and Decision-Making in Shona Indigenous Families

The study gathered through the participants that AIKS is critical in problem solving and decision-making in Shona indigenous families and the two correlate. One elderly man concisely said, "In a Shona family set up, members cannot solve a problem without making a decision". From the fieldwork we carried out in Buhera District, we noted that generally there are several problem-solving steps followed by Shona indigenous families. They use a group solving technique that depends on consensus among family members. The problem-solving process involves thoughts, discussions, actions, and decisions

371

that occur from the first consideration of a problematic situation to the decision goal.

The process starts from identification of the problem. The family elders make sure that if a problem is to be solved successfully, they have to establish the source and nature of the problem. When an issue is brought before a family court, normally the petitioner does not have to rely on assumptions. In determining the nature of the problem both symptoms and causes are important to consider. Among others, the following are the questions which are asked the complainant in an endeavour to gain a clearer understanding of the problem or situation: What is the problem which made you call for this meeting? How did you come to know that the problem exists? Is this a problem in itself or a symptom of a deeper, underlying problem? Who/what is involved? Why is it an urgent matter? What have the effects been so far? What have you done to try and address this problem? (https://opentextbc.ca/workinginfoodserviceindustry/chapter/effective-problem-solving-and-decision-making/).

In a family court session that we attended pertaining to a girl who was impregnated by her sister's husband, responding to questions from a family nephew (*muzukuru*), a mother told the family court that she had observed physical changes on their daughter who had been vomiting regularly. Using AIKS, she noticed this when they had gone to work on the fields. Having an enlarged naval and vomiting made her to suspect that it was a symptom of pregnancy for her daughter. This was the tip of the ice-berg. So, she asked the family court to interrogate their daughter on whether she was pregnant or not. In Shona society, the mother of the child is not deemed as the owner of the child such that she refers the responsibility of establishing the truth of the matter to the owners, that is, paternal family members. Since the matter was beyond the control of the mother, other revered members of the family were engaged. The consultation process encompassed *muzukuru*, *tete* and finally *baba*. This was the Input phase of AIKS in systematic problem-solving and decision-making in which a problem was perceived and an attempt was made to understand the situation or problem.

The second stage was when the family court analysed the problem, taking cognisance of the family's understanding of the issue at hand. Through observation during this particular family problem, the girl at the centre of the discussion remained silent, despite the fact that she was given an opportunity to respond in order to give her side of the story. This is important in systematic problem-solving and decision-making so as to avoid complaints that the family court sessions are unfair. As researchers we wondered why it was like that. We were informed that it was part of a cultural attribute in which the gender dynamics were at play. In other words, the girl-child could not readily respond in matters where she is at fault and silence symbolised submission and guilty conscience, which are a form of pacifism in AIKS. In this particular case, meaning was conveyed through the context surrounding verbal communication, which also affected group communication. In fact, basing on African Indigenous Ways of Knowledge (AIWK), there is a communication style in which much of the meaning in an interaction is conveyed through nonverbal cues and silence. The court and daughter avoided making reference to sex directly. Through the Indigenous Knowledge Systems, members at the family court understood the sex discourse meaning even if the message was indirect. The family court agreed that a possible alternative was to assign the *tete* to cross-examine her niece for proper information on the prevailing problem. *Tete* took the girl outside the main family court gathering. This is where the creative side of problem-solving really comes in. The Shona explain this through proverbs such as *Chidembo hachivhirwi paruzhinji* (A civet cat cannot be skinned in public). Such an aside interrogation in problem-solving is also a face-saving strategy that is common among the Shona people as evidenced by the aunt's action in taking the girl away from the court environment for some further interrogations. It was not an easy task since the girl could not readily divulge the details surrounding the pregnancy. Tapping from AIKS, *tete* employed persuasion by spending more time searching for answers which eventually paid off. We also learnt that gender stereotypes sometimes influence the roles that people play within a group in the context of AIKS in systematic problem-solving. For example, the stereotype that women are more nurturing than men led the court members to expect that the *tete* would play the double role of being a supporter of the girl and or being a harmonizer within the family court.

The third step was to gather information or facts relevant to solving the problem or making a decision. From the aunt's feedback, the sister's husband who was a *Mukwasha* to the family in question, was responsible for the pregnancy. The girl informed *tete* that the two were in love following *babamukuru's* (sister's husband) proposal that he wanted to take her as a second wife with the hope of fathering a boy child. The family court had to be tactful in weighing the possible

373

options to adopt in solving this problem. In fact, it was imperative to come up with a decision to have this problem solved. In this case, decision-making was a selection process where one or other possible solutions were chosen to reach a desired goal. Basically, there were two positions adopted by the family court: first was that the impregnated girl had to elope to her man (*kutizira/ kutiza mukumbo*). The second option was that the girl had to stay at home. After the two positions were generated, the family court assessed each of them to see how effective they might be in addressing the problem. They considered the following factors:

- Impact on the marriage of girl's elder sister;
- Effect on family and community relations;
- The religious legality of the marriage;
- Moral standing of the girl's family questioned for the pregnancy;
- Whether the pregnancy was a result of consented action or rape;
- Whether the present case could be used to set a precedent before the family court.

This was a Processing phase in which alternatives were generated and evaluated and a solution to the problem was figured out. However, the basic problem-solving process remains the same even if the problems identified differ.

The next stage was that of decision-making. The origin and urgency of the problem were some of the situational factors that influenced decision-making. The family elders decided that it was unacceptable for the girl to stay at home with her pregnancy. The subsequent step was implementation of the decision. But among the Shona people, certain elements of the solution may need to be delegated out to various people inside and outside the family court. The aunt was assigned to accompany her niece to her husband the very day the court session was convened. This was a marriage arrangement known as *kutizira* (elopement) In this case, a family court member was assigned to implement a particular part of the solution based on their role in the decision-making and also because it connects to their area of expertise. This was the Output phase which included planning for and implementing the solution.

The final step was evaluation of the outcome of the decision made and implemented by the girl's family. The Shona people are aware that whenever a decision has been implemented, it is vital to evaluate the results. The outcomes of the decision to make their daughter elope had some contestable consequences. One possible outcome was that the girl would be accepted by her sister's husband as a second wife. This meant that arrangements to pay *roora* (bride-wealth) had to be organised. They needed a *munyayi* (a go-between in marriage) to facilitate the process. The other possible outcome would be that the elopement would brew tensions in her sister's marriage. Her elder sister would have serious conflicts with her younger sister that she had come to destroy her marriage. She would also accuse her husband of infidelity, for he had cheated on her with her younger sister. Jealousy and competition between the two sisters would become the characteristic feature of the polygamous marriage. This last stage is also known as a Review phase in which the solution is evaluated and modifications are made, if necessary. The outcomes helped in generating valuable information about the decision-making process, the appropriateness of the decision, and the implementation process itself. This information became useful in improving the family's response the next time a similar decision is to be made.

Rethinking Family as a Neglected Resource for Problem-Solving: Critical Reflections

Shona indigenous families are never a homogeneous phenomenon such that even the use of AIKS in systematic problem-solving and decision-making are bound to differ. It is clear that the family remains an important social unit in systematic problem-solving and decision-making. Within a typical Shona indigenous family, problem-solving and decision-making are a result of collective effort. What is key is consensus. The main players of consensus building are family revered figures such as *baba*, *tete* and *muzukuru*. In this study, these three proved to be pillars of AIKS in systematic problem-solving and decision-making through using the techniques of mediation, adjudication, reconciliation, and negotiation as well as cross-examination that offered great prospects for peaceful co-existence and harmonious relationships in the Shona indigenous family in question. This is in contrast to modern trends where their roles are sometimes neglected in family affairs and their contributions are sometimes not solicited. Whereas the nuclear family and civil courts are in vogue in most contemporary families pertaining to problem-solving and decision-making, this study has shown that the extended family can adequately manage domestic problems encountered in Shona indigenous families. The use of the extended family ensures the nurturing of indigenous values and claims for the protection of family dignity and accountability of all the stakeholders involved on the basis of AIKS in systematic problem-solving and decision-making.

In line with the above, AIKS expressed in songs is of paramount importance in value orientation and value-grounding to build and sustain the community's interests (Muwati 2018:xiii) towards systematic problem-solving and decision-making in Shona families. Singing as far back as 1993, the late Zimbabwean Sungura music star, Leonard Dembo, referred to the importance of having many children in families in the album *Mazano* (Ideas) and through lyrics of the song, *Mazano*. Of particular interest to this study is Dembo's reference to the different roles played by children along gender lines. For instance, he sang, thus: "*Dai mwamupa vanakomana vakawanda rudzi rwake rudikidiki…Mozomupa vanasikana vakawanda, madzitete anopa mazano*" (May you bless him with a lot of boy children because his lineage is very small… May you also bless him with a lot girl children, aunts who are advisers of the family). The lyrics from Dembo's song are a mirror of the pillars of a typical Shona indigenous family anchored in AIKS, which are in tandem with the principles of the Sankofa tradition that draws from the past in order to inform the present and the future.

On one hand, and from a patriarchal perspective, *Mukwasha* (sister's husband) impregnated his wife's young sister (*muramu*) as part of his desire to have boy children since he had none with his wife. Essentially, the need for a boy child is often exaggerated within families where the birth of a boy is highly celebrated as an assurance for the expansion of a lineage (*dzinza*). On the other hand, Dembo's song teaches that the girl child is equally important since they will become *madzitete anopa mazano* (aunts that give ideas and advice) in their paternal families. With reference to this study, Dembo's narrative shows that *zitete remhuri* (the aunt of the family) is central in family networks in AIKS in systematic problem-solving and decision-making. They are essentially, revered family members of much significance. Given that aunts are paradigmatically female, a focus on the 'aunting' relationship also attended to processes of gendering and gendered identities and drew attention to the pernicious sexism that continues to colour conceptions of familial roles and kinship relations (Sotirin and Ellingson 2005). Findings of this study confirm that enactments of extended kin relationships like aunting are guided by "kinscripts," which designate within a particular network, who is obligated or entitled to perform certain types of tasks (kin-work), when such tasks should be done (kin-time), and how the process of assigning kin-work should be handled (kin-scription) (see Stack & Burton, 1998 in Sotirin and Ellingson 2005). This explains why the aunt is called a 'female father' (*babakadzi*) among the Shona people. The title and role the aunt plays shows why Shona people intimate that women are treated with respect and honour.

Conclusion

This chapter has demonstrated that some Shona indigenous families effectively continue to utilise AIKS in systematic problem-solving and decision-making. They prize consensus in problem-solving and decision-making. In this process, family revered figures such as *baba*, *tete* and *muzukuru* are of much significance. In their family roles, these religious functionaries tap from AIKS such as oral art forms like folktales, songs, proverbs, riddles and idioms to embellish their systematic problem-solving and decision-making patterns. The use of family courts to resolve disputes on the basis of AIKS adequately serve the needs of the people and defies the over-dependence on western courts. The study concludes that Shona indigenous ways of dispute resolution provide an opportunity to interact with the parties concerned and promotes consensus-building, social bridge reconstructions and enactment of order if utilised in this 21st century Zimbabwe.

References

Ajayi, A.T. & Buhari, L.O. (2014) "Methods of Conflict Resolution in African Traditional Society", *African Research Review*, Vol. 8 (2), pp. 138-157.

Bourdillon, M.F.C. (1990) *Religion and Society: A Text for Africa*, Gweru: Mambo Press.

Dembo, L. & Barura Express (1993) *Mazano* (Album), Harare: Record and Tape Promotions.

Eliade, M. (1959) *The Sacred and the Profane: The Nature of Religion*, London: Harcourt Brace.

Gelfand, M. (1992) *The Genuine Shona, Surviving Values of an African Culture*; Gweru: Mambo Press.

Gelfand, M. (1981) *Ukama: Reflections on Shona and Western Culture in Zimbabwe*, Gwelo: Mambo Press.

Grayson, S.M. (2000). *Symbolizing the past: Reading Sankofa, Daughters of the Dust & Eve's Bayou as histories.* Lanham, MD: University Press of America.

Huitt, W. (1992) "Problem Solving and Decision Making: Consideration of Individual

Differences Using the Myers-Briggs Type Indicator," *Journal of Psychological Type, 24*, 33-44.

Available at http://www.edpsycinteractive.org/papers/1992-huitt-mbti-problem-solving.pdf

https://opentextbc.ca/workinginfoodserviceindustry/chapter/effective-problem-solving-and-decision-making/).

Mawere, M. (2014) "Western Hegemony and Conquest of Africa: Imperial Hypocrisy and the Invasion of African Cultures" In M. Mawere & T.R. Mubaya (Eds), *African Cultures, Memory and Space: Living the Past Presence in the Zimbabwean Heritage*, Bamenda: Langaa Research & Publishing.

Muwati, I. (2018) "Introduction: Singing Nation: Music and Politics in the Decade of Crisis" In I. Muwati, T. Charamba & C. Tembo (Eds) *Singing Nation and Politics: Music and the Decade of Crisis in Zimbabwe 2000-2010*, Gweru: Midlands State University Press.

Ndlovu-Gatsheni, S.J. (2015) "Decoloniality as the Future of Future", *History Compass*, Vol. 13(10), 485-496.

Onigu, O. & Albert, I.O. (Eds.) (2001) *Community Conflicts in Nigeria, Management, Resolution and transformation.* Ibadan, Nigeria: Spectrum Books Limited.

Paris, P.J. (1995) *The Spirituality of African Peoples: The Search for A Common Moral Discourse*, Minneapolis: Fortress Press.

Pokras, S.(1989) *Systematic Problem-Solving and Decision-Making.* California & London: Kogan Page.

Sibanda, F. (2011) *African Blitzkgrieg: Phenomenological Reflections on Shona Beliefs on Lightning*, Saarbrucken, LAP Lambert Academic Publishing GmbH & Co. KG

Slater, J. (2019) "Sankofa - the Need to turn back to move forward: Addressing Reconstruction Challenges that face Africa and South Africa Today", *Studia Historia Ecclesiasticae*, Vol. 45(1).

Sotirin, P. J., & Ellingson, L. L. (2014). The "Other" Women in Family Life: Recognizing the Significance of

Aunt/Niece/Nephew Communication. In K. Floyd & M. Morman (Eds), *Widening the Family Circle: New Research on Family Communication*, California: Thousand Oaks, (pp.51–68).

Chapter 20

The Role of the Institution of *Sahwira* in Resolving Conflicts at Household and Community Level: Case Study of Domboshava People

Moses Chundu

Abstract

The chapter investigates the role of the institution of *sahwira* in conflict management and peace-making and also whether the role is still prevalent in Zimbabwe. The study made use of a case study of Domboshava, a rural community north of Harare metro province. Key informant interviews and focus group discussions involving the traditional leaders and elders in Domboshava revealed that the practice is still alive. The study revealed that although the institution is still prevalent in Domboshava, the functionalities have been somewhat diluted by modern day institutions in the likes of funeral parlours, churches, modern legal systems and counselling services. For a peri-urban community, the effects of urbanisation are now being felt with a good proportion of the citizens being foreign to the community, hence not having friends at the level of family *sahwira*. There is scope for the government of Zimbabwe to deliberately seek to revive this critical institution by officially recognising local community grievance redress mechanism and mainstreaming the institution of *sahwira* in the current peace building and conflict management frameworks.

Keywords: Conflict management, indigenous knowledge system, peace building, family, rural Zimbabwe.

Introduction

Conflict has escalated as a challenge in modern communities starting at household level all the way to geo-politics. This has manifested in rising incidences of domestic violence, divorces, suicides, murders, underdevelopment and wars among tribes and nations. In Zimbabwe there has been a rising trend in domestic violence evidenced by the rising number of cases reported to the police, the number of counselling sessions in churches and incidences of domestic violence reported on social media (Makomo & Chisaka, 2020). Conflict has always been an inevitable societal reality but communities always had localised ways of dealing with the same embedded in their cultures. The advent of modernism and globalisation has tended to disenfranchise Indigenous Knowledge (IK) owing largely to hegemonic scientism. Scholars have, however, demonstrated that there is much to learn from indigenous and community-based approaches to the 21st century existential challenges that confront humanity (Berkes & Shaw, 2012; Thornton & Manasfi., 2010; Berkes & Shaw, 2012; Thornton & Manasfi., 2010).

One of the institutions that was integral to managing and resolving conflicts in Zimbabwe is 'Sahwira[31]' who is more of a covenant family friendship. The nature of the relationship confers certain rights and responsibilities which come with immunity on the part of the *sahwira*. The immunity inherent in the office allows the *sahwira* to play an intermediatory role in face of conflicts given the space and ability to speak the truth in love. The social standing of *sahwira* was such that they were acceptable in their local contexts.

The study sought to explore whether the institution of *sahwira* is still prevalent in Zimbabwe. It also sought to establish the extent to which the institution is still relevant and explore the modern developments that might have rendered the institution weak. The null hypothesis is that the institution of *sahwira* has been neglected in favour of modern-day burial and counselling facilities with those families still practising it experiencing less violent conflicts. There is, therefore, scope to raise awareness and encourage citizens to embrace this ancient old institution and ensure that every individual/family has a functional *sahwira* as provided for in the Zimbabwean Shona culture. The result will help raise awareness and adoption of effective indigenous knowledge that had been discarded in favour of Western practices.

Literature Review

Ndlovu-Gatsheni (2015) argues that, whilst Africans can easily give a date of when they were colonised and when colonisation ended, it is difficult for them to understand the depth of colonialism in their psyches and, hence on their cultures and way of life. This is so because, colonialism is not just an episode but it is viewed by

---

[31] The term sahwira (family-recognized best friend) refers to a close friend with whom you can share the deepest details of your life. Some have called sahwira the sibling one chooses to have.

Ngugi waThiong'o as a practise of power and a reconstitution of society as well as a production of knowledge and subjectivity (Lovesey, 2014). The disfranchisement of the institution of *sahwira* is in the context of dismemberment as developed by Ngugi (Wa Thiong'o, 1992) in his book, *Decolonising the Mind: The Politics of Language in African Literature,* which highlights the depth of colonialism, coloniality and alienation in Africa. The concept captures not only physical fragmentation but also epistemological colonisation/colonisation of the mind, as well as the 'cultural decapitation' that resulted in deep forms of alienation among Africans (Ndlovu-Gatsheni, 2015). The cultural decapitation resulted in Africans dropping some of the most tried and tested cultural institutions and practices that had worked for centuries in favour of the 'modern' western ideologies and concepts. It is in this context of coloniality and dismemberment that the institution of *sahwira* has been endangered. The study, therefore, sought to establish to what extent this institution is still intact and whether there is still scope to leverage it for managing conflict.

The role of the institution of *sahwira* in conflict resolution and peacebuilding is rooted in the social movement theories by (Conway, 2004) which view social movements as producing knowledge about current realities, alternatives and means of changing it. (Wallace, 2010) argue that this movements-based knowledge is similar to grassroots community-based peacebuilding. Similarly, (Leung et al., 2002) argue against Western mainstream conflict theories as being adequate to describe conflict behaviours in East Asian cultures. They went on to develop and justify their own indigenous theories of conflict management in East Asia.

Africans had their own original peace-making strategies of the African people and communities, which they used historically to ensure peace prevailed in their communities. Whether the existing literature speaks of principles, methods, approaches, and mechanisms of conflict resolution in Africa or of conflict resolution traditions and management tools in Africa, they are essentially implying the African peace-making wisdom. This wisdom has evolved within African societies rather than being the product of external importations. Progressively, international actors are compelled by reason to no longer suppress Indigenous wisdom and forms but support the programs to mainstream them (Genger, 2020). Whilst critics argue that there can be no homogenous African Indigenous peace-making approaches because of the disparities of space and time or of the historical experiences of the people and their communities, there is enough evidence that these approaches work at the community level. Proponents have gone further to state that the Indigenous peace-making wisdom of Africans has a lot to offer to the world in this age of globalization and paradigm shift through its key overriding ideology of humanism (Genger, 2020).

In support of the efficacy of indigenous peace-making initiatives, Genger (2020) outlined the following key elements of African Indigenous peace-making wisdom and its approaches as presented by HamdesaTuso (2011).

- African Indigenous peace-making approaches are by nature methodologically dialogic and interactive, and not argumentative and adversarial.
- Encourages active participation and facilitation where it is open to every member of the conflict community: the conflict parties, their family relations, witnesses, as well as the members and elders of the community which promotes ownership.
- Use Epistemological Forms (stories, riddles, myths, moral and spiritual values, folk-tales, parables, lessons from nature, and metaphors) to facilitate the dialogic process, determine the truth, and arrive at the fundamental goal of restorative justice.
- Have embedded Control Principles such as spiritual beliefs, oath-taking, swearing, divine and ancestral curses and blessings, ostracisation and exile, as well as the invocation of the oracle to determine truth, inculcate discipline, and thwart behaviours that escalate conflict.
- Ideologically, African cultural ideas and beliefs form the foundation for the peace-making procedure, and they include the following: truth-telling, respect, social responsibility, open or collective participation, communalism, and egalitarianism.
- The Fundamental Goals of African Indigenous peace-making approaches being structured to achieve the restoration of broken feelings and relationship, preservation of communal harmony and individual welfare, and holistic healing of the conflict parties and community.

- There are also preconditions or procedures that enhance the success of Indigenous peace-making, namely narrative, remorse, apology, forgiveness, acceptance of affordable compensation, and reconciliation.
- Rituals are also used to seal the goals of Indigenous peace-making. These rituals include handshakes, shared meals, breaking spears and arrows, singing and dancing, festivals, and the consumption of certain herbs.

Methodology

The study makes use of in depth-interviews and storytelling with traditional and community elders. A qualitative approach is applied through the use of detailed key informant interviews and focus group discussion to collect IK from the target community of Domboshava. The research also adopted a case study design where Domboshava peri-urban communal area was purposively selected for convenience of data collection in face of covid-19 induced travel restrictions. The study focused on key informants such as senior citizens and traditional leaders in the two villages of Zimbiru and Mungate. Qualitative data were collected through 17 key informant interviews and eight focus group discussions sampled using convenience sampling procedures. Besides the two village heads being considered as key informants, the rest of the informants were picked at the two major commercial centres being Zimbiru and Mungate business centres. The focus groups meetings covered three youth groups, two elderly women groups and three elderly men groups.

Domboshava is a peri-urban community 27km north of the city of Harare in Ward 4 of Goromonzi District, Mashonaland East Province, Zimbabwe. It still has all the structures of traditional society being in place, notwithstanding the rapid housing developments taking place as citizens take advantage of cheap rural land close to the city. The new residents capitalising on cheap land also meant diversity in cultures allowing for other perspectives from other tribal groups in Zimbabwe. Tribal authority is slowly diminishing as migrants not only assume land rights but also assume, in some instances, tribal roles in land allocation to fellow migrants and to some tribal members (Ingwani, 2019). Thus, the cultural practices are also bound to be diluted, hence being able to collect views beyond the Domboshava people. For instance, whereas the Soko (monkey) totem are the original inhabitants, analysis of the 17 key informants shows that only 12% were of the original totem whilst for the rest of the respondents there was a different totem for each of the remaining respondents across 15 totems. This only show the extent of dilution of the original inhabitants.

Presentation and Discussion of Research Findings

The key informants covered all the key people groups being the youths (23%), those in the 30–40-year age group (30%) and over 40-year-olds (47%). About 53% of the respondents claimed to have lived in the area for a period up to 15 years, 18% having been in Domboshava for periods between 16 and 30 years, whilst 29% confirmed having lived in the community for over 30 years. Thus, notwithstanding the high influx of non-indigenous people, the respondents had lived in the area long enough to understand and be influenced by the traditions of the Domboshava people. Annexure 1 gives the Word Tree which shows a visualisation of findings from what respondents had to say about *sahwira*.

Definition of the Institution of Sahwira

The term *sahwira* is defined differently mainly according to functionality. Table 1 below summarises the three main definitions that emerged from the key informant interviews and from the focus groups. Focus group discussion, FDG03 gave the most balanced definition encompassing the key roles by defining sahwira as *"someone who helps families in difficult times, someone who keeps family secrets and assist during funerals".*

There is a gender dimension to the definition as alluded to by key informant, KI08 who defined sahwira as *"a very close friend who helps during difficult times. Sahwira can be both husband and wife. This helps if the help needed can only be done by a woman".* Thus, it is a role that can be assumed by a couple to allow for the right gender to handle gender sensitive matters in the families concerned. The fact that *sahwira* is an intergenerational friendship also featured as alluded to by key informant, KI13 who said such friendship is *"passed from generation to generation, being the more intimate friends of family most respected".*

Table 1: Definition of Sahwira

Question: What is your understanding of the term sahwira?		
Understanding of the term *sahwira*	Sources who mentioned the same	Percentage of Total
Someone who is close to you, very trustworthy and a confidant you can trust with personal and family information.	KI04, KI05, KI08, KI09, KI11, KI12, KI14, KI15, KI16, FGD01, FGD05, FGD06, FGG07, FGD08	56
A close friend whom you share personal life stories and cares about you in all times, someone who can be with you through thick and thin.	KI03, KI06, KI10, KI13, KI17, FGD02, FGD04,	28
A person who handles family funeral, burying the dead family members and be in charge during traditional processes.	KI01, KI02, KI07, FGD03,	16

Source: Author

Although they used different terms to describe it, the community was generally in agreement on the definition of *sahwira*. In discussions with the Village Heads, it also became apparent that there are two variants of this; one being the traditional version which was more at family level and passed from generation to generation and the other being more personal where it is a friend one chooses for himself/herself and may not outlive his/her generation. It appears the definitions above related more to the later version, partly reflecting the peri-urban nature of the community as the traditional versions seemed more prevalent in the rural communities.

Roles and Responsibilities of Sahwira

Sahwira as a mediator in conflict situations

A *Sahwira* is someone who can play the role of mediator in difficult situations at home involving close family friends like a child or spouse and facilitate reconciliation. Table 2 below gives the views of respondents on the role of *sahwira* in managing conflicts in families and in communities.

Table 2: Role of Sahwira in Managing Conflicts in Families and Communities

Question: Do you think sahwira played a role in managing conflicts in your family? Specify		
Role played by *sahwira* in managing conflicts in families.	Key sources who mentioned the same	Percentage of Total
Sahwira plays a major role in managing conflicts as they act as mediator without being biased between family member(s) and *vanyarikani* (in-laws)	KI01, KI02, KI03, KI05, KI06, KI07, KI11, KI13, KI14, KI15, KI16, FGD01, FGD03, FGD04, FGD05, FGD06, FGD07, FGD08	72
Because of their flexibility and freedom of speech, they can approach and resolve conflicts without offending anyone and they handle family politics.	KI04, KI06, KI07, KI08, KI09. KI10, KI12,	28
They can mediate misunderstandings between community leaders and members without the leadership being offended.	KI02, KI03, KI04, KI05, KI08, KI09, KI10, KI11, KI12, KI15, KI17	44
They have limited roles in families as they are only regarded useful during funerals.	KI16, KI17	8
These days *sahwiras* are the causes of disputes and family politics as they are now greed and untrustworthy.	FGD02,	4

Source: Author

Asked whether they think *sahwiras* played a role in managing conflicts in families, this is what one key informant had to say *"Yes, sahwiras have flexibility of addressing anything in any way they want and they can be heard; in families they play part in managing disputes between family members either of inheritance or just general misunderstanding which might breed hatred"* KI06. Key informant, KI02 had this to say regarding the role of sahwira in promoting peace and resolving conflicts at family level. *"Yes, because they solve disputes amongst our family members. There are times that we have huge disagreement to the extent of hating each other but our sahwira comes and solves that, sharing jokes and losing the tension in the process".*

Respondents also felt that the role of *sahwira*s in conflict management holds even at community level with the majority of respondents feeling that by virtue of *sahwira* managing conflicts at household level, the effects are felt at the community level. As one of the respondents put it *"Yes, mubatanidzwa (unity), health families mean healthy communities"* (KI13). Key informant, KI15 had a slightly different transmission mechanism, arguing that *sahwira*s ensure *"peace and mediation before issues escalate to chiefs"*, hence promoting peace at community level. One of the focus groups had this to say about conflict management roles at community level;

> *Yes because of their freedom of speech they can address anyone without being offended. Sahwira can tell communities leaders where they are doing wrong and can approach dispute communities or families so that they come to an agreement"* (FGD01).

However, in one group, FGD02, it was felt that these days *sahwira*s are the cause of disputes and family politics as they are now greed and untrustworthy.

Sahwira as an undertaker

The *sahwira* has a responsibility of burying members of one's family upon death. The traditional burial rituals involve preparing the body for burial as well as physically laying the body in the grave on the day of burial. Almost eight percent of key informants did not see much role of *sahwira* in conflict management, limiting their role to funerals and funeral related rituals. For instance, key informant, KI07 had this to say about the role of sahwira,

> *This is an individual in charge of family funerals mainly, kurova guva (tombstone unveiling), apprising the ancestors through traditional beer and any other traditional process. Sahwira leads these processes".* Key informant, KI11 concurred on the funeral role saying *"a sahwira is in charge of funerals and burials. Helps in comforting the family during the trying times. Helps financially and support a friend.*

The role at the funeral goes beyond playing undertaker to bringing therapeutic healing to the bereaved by lightening the funeral mood through cracking jokes throughout the funeral. As key informant,

KI08 aptly put it, *"sahwiras help in sickness, cooking, cleaning, feeding and dressing. They help during funerals, He/she oversees the burial and is in charge of the corpse. Manages conflicts at funerals. He/she comforts the bereaved family through jokes and storytelling".* (Bourdillion, 1976) also alluded to this function saying sahwira would make fun of the immediate family members of the deceased to introduce laughter as a way of lightening the grief. Thus, the institution of *sahwira* facilitates healing, reconciliation at the family and community levels also consistent with the findings of Makumbirofa et al. (2019). This role featured significantly during both focus group discussions and key informant interviews. Whilst the pure undertaker roles seem threatened by the emergence of modern funeral parlour services, it is the other funeral related aspects that make *sahwira* an indispensable player during bereavement.

Sahwira as a go between/mediator during marriage negotiations

Sahwiras can also function as negotiators in the traditional marriage negotiations as captured by key informant, KI07 who alluded to one of the *sahwira* roles as *"leading in traditional marriages (roora)".* After serving as a marriage go-between (*munyai*), *sahwira* becomes an inherent part of the conflict management framework for that particular couple alongside auntie-dad's sister (*tete*) and / or uncle-mum's brother (*sekuru*) who also form part of the delegation to the traditional marriage negotiations. Sahwira is *"a mediator in family, siblings and marriages"*, KI13. Beyond the marriage rites, the *sahwira* continues as a pillar of that new marriage with such roles as counsellor and mediator. This role contributed a lot to the low divorce rates that prevailed in the traditional society. It also accounts for the variation in divorce rate between urban and rural communities. However, some respondents especially in focus group discussion, FGD02 were sceptical about the role of *sahwiras* in strengthening marriages when they argued that *"sahwiras of this era now take your weakness as their strength; many broken marriages are because of sahwiras".* These results are in agreement with findings of Chisi (2018) though the later goes a step further to reveal an unpleasant side of *sahwira* in marital matters where *sahwiras* would jokingly embarrass poor sons-in-laws during family functions, again with a degree of immunity.

Sahwira as a whistle blower

If a member of the family has become a nuisance especially involved in witchcraft or destructive rumour mongering and gossiping, Sahwira can expose such acts at a convenient public gathering without recourse. Such actions are meant to bring about repentance by exposing the evil deeds. The thought that a Sahwira could one day expose one in public was enough deterrent by would be peddlers of such lies, hence preventing conflict and promoting peace within the families. However, some respondents felt that the very act of public exposure was a source of conflict in itself, hence was discouraged. This is probably why the role did not feature much in the survey. The role is also rendered ineffective by modern laws in which *sahwira* can actually be sued by anyone who feels exposed, preferring charges of defamation of character as most of the issues lack admissible evidence.

Compensation Framework for *Sahwira*

The roles of a *sahwira* described above are so critical to ensure a peaceful family and community environment to the point of being priceless. They are also invariably risky engagements. The question is what level of compensation made this assignment worthwhile? Apparently, it was more of a voluntary engagement though there were inbuilt mechanism for ad hoc compensation. As Genger (2020) argues, "African Indigenous peace-making is not cost implicating; it is not paid for and has no time boundary. It can be held as many times as needed to arrive at the fundamental goals".

One way of compensating the *sahwira* was to give him/her the freedom of the village where he/she could just grab a chicken or a goat for slaughter without seeking permission to do so. Of course, this was a privilege enjoyed with moderation; it would not happen frequently. In the specific case of the Domboshava people, they cited the following compensation mechanisms depicted in Table 3.

The majority (36%) of respondents attested to the fact that any form of payment to *sahwira* is tokenistic, otherwise there is no payment. For instance, when asked how *sahwira*s were compensated for their roles in society, KI07 had this to say limiting to the compensation after performing funeral rites; "Chirango *(token) - it's a piece or chunk of meat (bandauko) from beast killed for the funeral which was given to a sahwira*". During funerals they could also *"pick item from the deceased's assets or given a token of appreciation"* (KI16). This is consistent with the findings of Bourdillion (1976) who explored the institution of *sahwira* in the 1970s and observed that a *sahwira* was given the status of a special guest during funerals, hence receiving the treatment befitting a special guest with respect to meals and other forms of honour.

Table 3: Compensation of Sahwira

Question: *How are/were sahwiras compensated for their roles in society*		
Methods used to compensate *sahwiras* for their roles in society.	Key sources who mentioned the same	Percentage of Total
They are given money, especially in the modern day.	KI02, KI03, KI04, KI09,	16
They don't demand payment but they can be given a token of appreciation as chicken (*huku*), goat (*mbudzi*) and a special treat on family functions.	KI01, KI05, KI06, KI07, KI08, KI12, KI13, KI15, KI16	36
Being a *sahwira* is a voluntary duty so you are not paid.	KI0, KI11, KI14, KI17	16

Source: Author

The 16% who stated that they are paid cash made reference to it being a modern-day phenomenon not commensurate with the traditional understanding of the concept. However, the compensation doesn't necessarily have to be tied to a specific function but something that comes as a general appreciation of the roles performed from time to time. As key informant, KI08 put it *"sahwira can be given goats and chickens at random times".* Key informant, KI13 concurred on the appreciation of sahwira not necessarily following a specific function performed but being ad hoc and ongoing saying they are given *"Huku (chicken), doro (beer), mbudzi (goats), special treatment on functions as tokens of appreciations".* Thus, *sahwira* appreciation is not limited to funerals only.

Prevalence and Effectiveness of the Sahwira Concept in Modern Society

The study of the Domboshava people revealed that the institution of *sahwira* has been threatened by modern day institutions and practices. On average, 68% of the families still value and utilise this institution. It appears the more urbanised a community is, the more threatened the institution and the more rural and culture-rooted the stronger the institution of *sahwira*.

Asked whether they think *sahwira*s are still needed in this modern generation, this is what some respondents had to say; *"In urban areas no, because sahwiras now have bad intentions, marriages have been broken by sahwiras"* KI08. *"Yes, we do need them because they are very helpful and supportive more than family"* KI10. Despite some conflicting views on the future of this institution, the majority (68%) still felt there is a role for *sahwira* in the modern era. Those who feel otherwise argue that urbanisation has rendered them irrelevant, whilst others cite issues of trust as well as the emergence of funeral parlours which have taken away a central role of managing funerals. See Table 4 below for the details of responses on the future of *sahwira*.

Table 4: Relevance of Sahwira in Modern Society

Question: In your view do you think this institution is still intact?			
Is the institution still intact	Why do you say so	Sources who mentioned the same	Percentage of Total
Yes, but there are now some differences from what it used to be.	*Sahwiras* are no longer trustworthy they take your weakness and destroy you.	FGD01, FGD02, FGD06,	12
No, the roles of *sahwira* were mainly more active on funerals. They have been weakened by the modern systems and urbanisation.	Because of funeral parlour and the presence of *muzukuru* (nephew) the *sahwira* institution lost its value.	FGD03, FGD08 KI05, KI16	16
They are still intact in some areas as they are still involved in traditional rituals and play roles at funerals.	At funeral *sahwiras* are still playing important role as they will be making jokes and oversee the funeral proceedings.	FGD04, FGD05, FGD07, KI01, KI02, KI03, KI04, KI06, KI07, KI09, K10, KI11, KI12, KI17	56

Source: Author

Focus group discussions confirmed the feeling that the institution of *sahwira* is to a larger extent still relevant in the modern era though with diluted roles. There were, however, some reservations of their effectiveness with one focus group, FGD08 actually accusing modern day *sahwiras* of destroying homes. They had this to say *"People are no longer trustworthy. Sahwira has broken marriages, they will use your weakness and secrets against you"* (FGD08). Discussions in FGD01 pointed towards the role of sahwira being still relevant and prevalent in our society by arguing that *"If you go to funerals today you will see that a sahwira is an important institution. Sahwira becomes an immediate family on funerals and he/she controls and oversees the funeral proceedings. Even during conflicts and misunderstanding he/she resolves jokingly"*.

In addition to funeral parlours taking over the roles of *sahwiras*, nephew (*muzukuru*) was also cited as substituting *sahwira*. However, in one of the key informant interviews involving the village head, *muzukuru* was seen as a variant of *sahwira*, hence cannot be seen to be threatening the role of *sahwira*. The ones supporting the continued significance of the role of *sahwira*, whilst acknowledging the advent of modern funeral parlours, argue that other funeral related roles of *sahwira* have remained intact.

Towards Reviving the Institution of Sahwira

There is need to raise awareness through education of the importance of this valuable institution and ensure that the relationships are passed from generation to generation. Where it is not possible because of geography to preserve this institution, there is need to embrace variants of it as long as principles underlying its existence in the first instance are accommodated. These are essentially traditional cures of Africa's modern conflicts and informing the intervention ideal of "collective security" as adopted by the United Nation. Whilst most key informants were unanimous of the importance of *sahwira* and relevance in the modern society, not every respondent managed to proffer possible solutions summarised in Table 5 below.

Table 5: How to Strengthen the Institution of Sahwira

Question: What, in your view, should be done to strengthen this institution?		
Recommendation to strengthen this institution.	Key Sources who mentioned the same	Percentage of Total
Educate the current and future generation especially the youths about the roles and importance of *sahwira*s.	KI01, KI03, KI04, KI05, KI06, KI13, FGD01, FGD02, FGD04, FGD05,	40
To be truthful and honest to each other.	KI07, KI10, FGD3, FGD06, FGD07, FGD08	24
To take *sahwira*s seriously and compensate them every time.	KI02, KI09,	8
None responses	KI08, KI11, KI12, KI14, KI15, KI16, KI17	28

Key informant, KI03 felt *"youths should be educated and know the role and importance of sahwira"*. Key informant, KI13 hinted on the need to review the education curricular by advocating for a *"revamp of education to meet things relevant to us. Disseminate information in our language"*. Focus groups discussion revealed similar interventions to try and save the institution of *sahwira* from extinction. In focus group discussion, FGD01, education as a key strategy to strengthen the institution of *sahwira* was emphasised when the participants agreed that *"communities must educate youths about sahwira, or even to go a step further to school and educate young ones even in countries that have sahwira e.g., South Africa and Zimbabwe"*. These recommendations are consistent with the critical pedagogy theory by Paulo Freire (1972) in his book titled *Pedagogy of the Oppressed* which articulated "a radical theory of education geared to countering dominant and repressive forms of knowledge; institutionally, epistemologically, politically and culturally" (Wallace, 2010, p24).

Conclusion

The study sought to investigate the role of the institution of *sahwira* in conflict management and peace-making and also whether the role is still prevalent in Zimbabwe. The study made use of a case study of the Domboshava people and employed the instruments of key informants and focus groups discussions to get the views of the Domboshava people on the subject. The findings revealed that the *sahwiras* are still prevalent and regarded as still being relevant in modern-day society, especially in their peace-making and conflict resolution roles both at family level and community level. The study, however, revealed that some functions like their key roles during funerals, though still prevalent, have been somewhat diluted by the advent of funeral service organisations. Urbanisation is also viewed as having diluted the relevance of the institution of *sahwira*. To ensure continued existence and relevance of this key institution, it is important that there be a deliberate effort to promote it through educating especially the youths probably through heritage studies. There is scope for further study to understand how this concept if faring in the diaspora and how best to ensure its functionalities are not lost with modernism.

References

Berkes, F., & Shaw, G. B. (2012). Implementing ecosystem-based management: evolution or revolution? *Wiley Online Library*, *13*(4), 465–476. https://doi.org/10.1111/j.1467-2979.2011.00452.x

Bourdillion, M. (1976). Shona Peoples: An Ethnography of the Contemporary Shona, with Special Reference to their Religion. In Bourdillion MFC (Ed.), *cambridge.org*. Mambo Press.

Chisi, J. T. (2018). *Lobola in Zimbabwe: A Pastoral Challenge.*

Conway, J. M. (2004). *Identity, place, knowledge. Social movements contesting globalisation* (Conway Janet M, Ed.). Fernwood.

Genger, P. (2020). Toward Sustainable Security in Africa: Theoretical Debates for the Institutionalization of African Indigenous Peacemaking Approaches. *Peace & Change*, *45*(2), 287–317. https://doi.org/10.1111/pech.12403

Ingwani, E. (2019). Are peri-urban land transactions a disaster in the making? A case of Domboshava, Zimbabwe. *Jamba: Journal of Disaster Risk Studies*, *11*(3). https://doi.org/10.4102/jamba.v11i3.708

Leung, K., Koch, P. T., & Lu, L. (2002). A dualistic model of harmony and its implications for conflict management in Asia. In *Asia Pacific Journal of Management* (Vol. 19, Issues 2–3, pp. 201–220). Springer New York LLC. https://doi.org/10.1023/a:1016287501806

Lovesey, O. (2014). Globalectics: Theory and the Politics of Knowing by Ngũgĩ wa Thiong'o New York: Columbia UP, 2012, 104 pp. *Cambridge Journal of Postcolonial Literary Inquiry, 1*(2), 304–305.

Makomo, A., & Chisaka, B. C. (2020). Factors Underlying the Increase in Domestic Violence Cases in Zimbabwe Despite the Existence of the Anti-Domestic Violence. *Journal of Humanities and Social Sciences Research, 2*(4), 37–47.

Makumbirofa, R., Chikonzo, K., & Chivandikwa, N. (2019). Sahwira and/as endogenous healing and therapy in Shona funerary rituals. In *National Healing, Integration and Reconciliation in Zimbabwe* (pp. 120–130). Routledge. https://doi.org/10.4324/9780429327049-10

Ndlovu-Gatsheni, S. J. (2015). Decoloniality in Africa: A Continuing Search for a New World Order. *Australasian Review of African Studies, 36*(2).

Thornton, T. F., & Manasfi, N. (2010). "Adaptation--genuine and spurious: demystifying adaptation processes in relation to climate change." *Environment and Society, 1*(1), 132–155.

Wa Thiong'o, N. (1992). *Decolonising the mind: The politics of language in African literature.* https://books.google.com/books?hl=en&lr=&id=z60udlv1F_c C&oi=fnd&pg=PP10&dq=Ngugi+waThiong%E2%80%99o+d ecolonising+the+mind&ots=kM7Ss3H34L&sig=0uFg56dN6ns gDiAu8iGylAd1vyo

Wallace, A. (2010). *Grassroots community-based peacebuilding. Critical narratives on peacebuilding and collaboration from the locality of Indigenous and non-Indigenous activists in Canada.* http://hdl.handle.net/10454/4278

Annexure 1: Word Tree (Visualisation of Findings)

Source: Author's compilation from survey data

Chapter 21

African Christian Traditions as Contemporary Sources for African Knowledge Production Systems Impacting Development in Zimbabwe

Nomatter Sande

Abstract

Even in postcolonial contexts, African nations continue to grapple with poverty, health, socio-economic and political challenges. Blame has been on colonialism, and the unsuitability of the Western ideologies to empower Indigenous development favouring African Indigenous Knowledge. Existing literature about African Indigenous Knowledge Systems either discusses Euro-American scientific knowledge's hegemony or the African Indigenous Knowledge Systems' efficaciousness. However, there is not much information about the contemporary African Knowledge Production System. Accordingly, this chapter explores how Zimbabwe's African Christian traditions have metamorphosed to become contemporary African Knowledge Production Systems developing strategic tools to deal with development problems bedevilling Zimbabwe. The study used 'African Spirituality' as an epistemological underpinning and data were gathered using document analysis. The finding of the study is that African Christian traditions in Zimbabwe artistically use divine—spiritual solutions to deal with poverty; protest theology to curb corruptions; divine healings and positive confessions to treat psychological stress as alternative strategies for development. The study concludes that in a postcolonial context, resilient indigenous spirituality and polarised culture, African Christian traditions are contemporary sources for African Knowledge Production System aiding development.

Keywords: Inclusivity, development, African Knowledge Production Systems, African Christian Traditions, Zimbabwe, African Indigenous Knowledge

Introduction

The development struggles bedevilling Zimbabwe, and the rest of sub-Saharan Africa include dealing with issues of like food insecurity, economic meltdown, poverty, climate change, and unstable politics. Current Western scientific Indigenous Knowledge Systems methods to deal with these problems have proved to be compromised, and there is a gap of either revisiting Africa Indigenous Systems or African Indigenous Knowledge production Systems (a detailed definition is given below). Or at least integrate these approaches. African Indigenous Knowledge Systems has been denigrated as unscientific and rudimentary (Nhemachena, 2015). As a point of departure, I argue that contemporary African people subconsciously use their African Indigenous Knowledge Systems but are afraid to accept alternative ways of knowing. As put by "Africans always had their own valid, legitimate and useful knowledge systems and education systems" (Ndlovu-Gatsheni, 2018:1).

In this study, I intentionally take a stance and advance the notion that Indigenous Knowledge Systems are not static but dynamic making it framework for development in Africa. According to Muyambo (2016), there is an urgence to use African Indigenous Knowledge Systems in Africa. The problem is that contemporary Zimbabwe Indigenous Knowledge Productions Systems are not only side-lined but also misunderstood. Therefore, there is a gap to understand how the emergence and prominence of indigenous African Christian traditions are acting as contemporary vehicles for transmitting Indigenous Knowledge Systems and foster development issues in Zimbabwe. Religion, spirituality and spiritual capital are vital elements to consider for community cultural wealth (Yosso, 2005).

In the Zimbabwean context, religious beliefs and rituals permeate the socio-economic, and political paradigms. Accordingly, this chapter explores how indigenous Christian traditions in Zimbabwe have metamorphosed to become contemporary African Knowledge Production Systems disseminating strategic tools for development in Zimbabwe. This chapter is divided into four broad sections—the first section conceptualise the definition of section Indigenous Systems and African Indigenous Knowledge production Systems respectively. Second, section discusses African Spirituality as an epistemological methodology. The development underpinning of Zimbabwe is discussed in the second section as the context of the chapter. In the third section, I discuss how selective African Christian Traditions in Zimbabwe have impacted on development.

Definitions of African Indigenous Systems

The definition of Indigenous Knowledge Systems is contested in scholarship. Notable contributions for the definition discourse comes from (Mawere, 2015; Gudhlanga and Makudze, 2012; Mapara, 2009) among others. Using etymological approach, Mawere (2014) argues that indigenous knowledge is a combination of two words: *indigenous* and *knowledge*. The term *indigenous* means native to a place or area. The word *knowledge* means a personal belief that is somehow justified and with the capacity to influence one's thinking, action and behaviour (Mawere 2014). This definition resonates with Owusu-Ansh and Mji (2013:1) who defined Indigenous Knowledge System as "experiential knowledge based on a worldview and a relational culture". In the same vein, Mawere (2012) propounds that Indigenous Knowledge Systems are local knowledge(s) for a particular culture or society. This assertion is key to this study because it helps to show that Indigenous Knowledge Systems have cultural heritages which are passed from generation to generations. For this study I will conceptualise Indigenous knowledge Systems as a sum total of the knowledge and skills of Zimbabweans which were handed down for generations to adapt to the changing circumstances and environment conditions.

Epistemological Methodology- African Spirituality

Epistemology as a source of knowledge is a universal occurrence leading to either acquiring or understanding human knowledge limits (Ndofirepi and Cross, 2014). Sources of knowledge are complex, including but not limited to "process that relates to social, situational, cultural and institutional dynamics. In their daily lives, people classify cypher, process and assign meaning to their experiences, thereby defining their everyday forms of knowledge" (Ndofirepi and Cross, 2014:293). While I acknowledge that the sources of African Knowledge Production Systems includes cultural hermeneutics, tradition, decoloniality, and African cosmology, but in this study, I used religious epistemology. Religious epistemology is defined as the "study of how these epistemic concepts relate to religious belief and practice (McNabb, 2019:1). Within the religious epistemology, I used African Spirituality in particular as lenses to understand contemporary sources for African Knowledge Production Systems and how they affect development. African Spirituality is holistic permeating the social, economic, and politics of Africans. Indigenous knowledge is the local knowledge – knowledge that is unique to a given culture or society; it helps to understand that Africans are victims of many factors, including colonisation and capitalists. In this study, religious traditions and institutions have a role in motivating people for contentedness and promote human wellbeing.

Similarly, African Spirituality gives psychological freedom which provides people with the reason to live. African Indigenous Knowledge System reaffirm their culture and experience (Muymbo, 2017). It is crucial to respect and value both culture's uniqueness and the indigenous ways of knowing. Almost in the same vein Asante (1990) cited in (Owusu-Ansah and Mji,2013) describes Afrocentricity as a method "that has at its core the understanding of the African identity as rooted, centred and located in the African culture in all aspects- spiritual, social, political and economic" (2013:2).

Thus, to understand how Indigenous Christian traditions in Zimbabwe have metamorphosed to become contemporary African Knowledge Production Systems development strategic tools to deal with development problems bedevilling Zimbabwe, it is vital to focus on African Spirituality. I define indigenous African Christians traditions as churches and ministries which developed in Zimbabwe with less influence of the Western or missionaries' ideologies. Therefore, in this study, Zimbabwe's African Christian traditions are churches that use indigenous cultural paradigms to produce relevant contextual Gospel to meet people's needs. This study argues that African Knowledge Production System produces notions of wholeness and communal living. Knowledge acquisition by the Zimbabweans and the rest of sub-Saharan people is collective and communal hence the need to use African Spirituality.

Nsamenang (2006) explains that African indigenous concepts of intelligence use practical, interpersonal and social domains and these are different from the cognitive academic of the West. I acknowledge that western paradigms of epistemology disenfranchise the African Indigenous knowledge (Ntuli, 2012), but focus on the contemporary African Knowledge Production Systems help to open ways to enhance development at the backdrop that Indigenous knowledge is the local knowledge – knowledge that is unique to a given culture or society. Accordingly, African Knowledge Production Systems are contextual, differing from community to community. While it is correct to say that most of this knowledge has been transferred from one generation to the other through word of mouth and very little, have been documented. However, in terms of African Spirituality, some rituals have remained in the rubric of African Christian traditions informing contemporary African Knowledge Production Systems. According to Sande (2017), there is a religious artefacts coalition between Pentecostals and African Tradition Religion manifesting in demonology, healthy and prosperous life.

The relationship between African Indigenous Religions (AIRs) and Pentecostalism is explained by Muyambo and Sibanda (2018:140) as bedfellows who "extensively use healing, music and dance as a ways of sustaining and celebrating life. However, whilst they are bedfellows, they have remained strangers, rather than partners with good will, in that they have stayed apart and have grey areas that seem irreconcilable".

The interface of Religion and Development in Zimbabwe

The issue of development continues to grow in Zimbabwe and southern Africa. In developing countries, the struggle is to access resources and devise ways that sustain lives. The relationship between religion and development in sub-Saharan African show shift from two separate fields into allies (Chitando, 2020). In Africa, religion is beginning to be considered contributing positively to development. Also, religious actors across the globe were part of Sustainable Development Goals (SDGs). In Zimbabwe, there is still a gap between understanding the interface between religion and development.

Nevertheless, the impact of religion in 'development aspects' like 'politics, social and economics' is noticed. For instance, religions have been a part of achieving independence. A detailed study conducted by Ruzivo (2008) showed that Zimbabwe's diverse denominations and church institutions played a moral influence on political processes. According to Sande and Denga, "pastoral, political voices are alternative critical drivers in reconstructing the Pentecostal political engagement and meaningful development in Zimbabwe" (2019:286).

On the contrary, several Western scientific methods aimed at developing Africa's 'inclusive growth' is an emerging phenomenon with the potential to enhance development in low-income countries like Zimbabwe, sub-Saharan Africa and beyond. There is no unanimous definition of 'inclusive growth'. However, the World Economic Forum conceptualisation of inclusive growth is succinct to this study because it suggests that: "there is no inherent trade-off in economic policy-making between the promotion of social inclusion and that of economic growth and competitiveness; it is possible to be pro-equity and pro-growth at the same time" (World Economic Forum, 2015: vii). Thus, inclusive growth in developing countries is measured with the reductions in inequality and improves people's living standards by dealing with economic, social, and fiscal issues. Be this as it may, I consider inclusive growth to take a broader view by situating the 'inclusive growth' concept within the African Indigenous Knowledge Systems of developing nations. According to Lupton (2017), the inclusive growth agenda focuses on offering a holistic approach to address poverty and inequality.

Selective African Christian Traditions and Development in Zimbabwe

In this study, the African Traditional Religion provides a rich history behind the African Indigenous Knowledge. Further, it helps understand how African Spirituality is evolving or maintained within Zimbabwe's African Christian traditions. The introduction of Christianity by missionary churches was at the backdrop of the African Traditional Religion. Most African Christians traditions have strived to be relevant and embraced African expression of worship. The missionary churches are the mother of African Christian Traditions in Zimbabwe which can be categorised into three broad areas. First, the African Initiated Churches developed which integrated indigenous culture and strived for a liberated African Christianity. The white garment churches, commonly known as the 'Apostolic' churches, are in this category. The association for these churches is called "Union for the Development of Apostolic Churches in Zimbabwe-Africa (UDACIZA) (Matikiti, 2014). Second, is the classic African Pentecostal churches emphasising divine miracles. Third, is the neo-Pentecostal churches manned by self-styled young preachers with artistic prophetic utterances, mighty miracles resulting in mega churches. According to Mujinga (2018), the neo-Pentecostals have unaffiliated category; they attract the middle and the upper-class urban residents and the elite (Togarasei, 2005). Be this as it may be, the questions are how these selective African Christian Traditions in Zimbabwe have impacted development? Based on existing literature about indigenous knowledge system, I discuss factors like politics, economics and social African Christian traditions in Zimbabwe that have metamorphosed to become contemporary African Knowledge Production Systems development strategic tools to deal with development problems bedevilling Zimbabwe.

Politics and contemporary African Knowledge Production Systems for development

Politics is one area impacting development issues. Indigenous knowledge system about politics in Zimbabwe shows that governance structures included kings, chiefs, and headmen, who were regarded as the divine embodiment. In some cases, kings were authoritative figures (Maxwell, 1999), playing the priest, ruler and centre of the community order. Kings were surrounded by and supported by various bodies like the Council of Elders who were responsible for "power check and balances" (Machingura, 2012:177). Indigenous knowledge shows that that power should be regulated because people tend to abuse it (Machingura, 2012).

Post-colonisation

Robert Gabriel Mugabe was the first leader in post-colonial Zimbabwe. However, for the last two decades of his reign "Zimbabwe experienced unprecedented economic decline and international isolation" (Ndakaripa, 2020:363). The new President Emmerson Dambudzo Mnangagwa has lurched from one crisis to another, silencing opposition parties, violence, absence of the rule of law and life has gone worse than was under (former President) Robert Mugabe (Mahere, 2019). Mugabe's royal ideologies were a synthesis of African Indigenous Religion and Christianity producing a *"Mugabology"*—a new religion brand in Zimbabwe (Machingura 2012:13-14). Although the current government incorporated chiefs and headmen, their selection and appointment are politicised (Chigwata, 2016).

The contemporary African Knowledge Production Systems strategic tools for development is embedded within the African Christian traditions. While resembling the Council of Elders who had the responsibility of power checks and balances for the King, African Christian traditions in Zimbabwe raise the government's moral conscience and the ruling party Zimbabwe African National Unity Patriotic Front (ZANU PF). The classic African Pentecostals in Zimbabwe under the Evangelical Fellowship of Zimbabwe (EFZ) participated in writing stern' pastoral letters' to the ZANU PF government condemning their evil deeds of commissions and omissions (Mhetu, 2020). Self -styled prophetic pastors which belong to neo-African Pentecostals like Apostle Talent Farai Chiwenga use 'protest theology' to condemn ZANU PF. Apostle Talent Farai Chiwenga's protest theology use harsh language weaved through Christological message to lambast evil state machinery (Matikiti and Sande, n.d). Another notable preacher is Shingi Munyeza, who uses social media and his business experience to advise how the government can recover and revive Zimbabwe's economy (@ShingiMunyeza, 2018).

A possible explanation for this might be that Zimbabwe's African Christian traditions are acting as a contemporary source of African Knowledge Production Systems for participating in Zimbabwe's democratisation processes. It can be suggested that African Christian churches prophetic voice, protest theology and participation in politics are an essential tool that enhances development in Zimbabwe. There is a case here to argue that a proper African Christian theology involves the interaction between faith, culture and some existential realities. Thus, having theology which pays attention to political imperatives helps to deal with problems affecting Zimbabwe.

Economics and contemporary African Knowledge Production Systems for development

Economics is an essential element of development. Existing literature about indigenous knowledge system shows that African Indigenous Knowledge Production Systems for economic growth was embedded in livestock rearing and farming. Large families and extended families were a resource for manual labour. Ringson and Chereni argued that "children were considered a heritage and a symbol of wealth and security of the society" (2020:101). In the context of modernity and technological development; indigenous approaches dealing with economic development vanished.

Postcolonial Zimbabwe was celebrated for a season for a stable economy in Africa (Potts, 2006). Zimbabwe was branded as a 'Jewel' as well as the 'Breadbasket' of Africa. However, over the decades, the economy has declined. According to Asante (2013), political conflicts between different political and civic groups are the leading cause of economic incomplete. Mlambo (2016) noted that multiple currency systems, cash crises, falling commodity prices, and low confidence in the economy. Matanzima and Saidi (2020:2) argued that "in Zimbabwe, an economic transformation has been highly negative, affecting people's purchasing power and acquisition of basic commodities."

While there are negative connotations that neo-African Pentecostals churches using prophetic ministry to poor people, poverty makes people gullible. In the face of crisis, religious leaders have created what I can call a 'consumeristic faith'. The role of the 'consumeristic faith' is to create 'demand and supply'. Consumeristic faith causes poor people to believe that the solution to poverty is based on positive faith claims. The problem of this created knowledge is that it establishes religious elites. In this way, religious capitalism has become inevitable, whereby the clergy are leading affluent lifestyles because of merchandising the Gospel. Both the Christian leaders and traditional doctors glamorously advertise their spiritual prowess to deal with poverty. Artistically, religious leaders create and teach 'consumeristic faith' which gullible believers keep claiming material benefits, while the leader are the ones with the key to 'supply the demand'. While religious leaders are merchandising the Gospel and cunningly create a consumeristic faith for demand and supply, but on the positive side these religious propagandists and religious business tycoons are providing solutions to poverty through divine means. Therefore, in poverty-stricken contexts and extreme economic stress, religion and spirituality provide strength for coping and surviving mechanisms.

Consequently, this explains that African Christian Traditions are a contemporary African Knowledge Production Systems source to deal with economic decline. Therefore, divine solutions to deal with poverty may create religious propagandist but continually lure suffering people through their charismatic rhetoric. Classic African Pentecostals have a propensity to access the spiritual world. Thus, everything is interpreted from the spiritual world and poverty is regarded as a spiritual force that should be dealt with in that realm. What this means is that to deal with poverty, issues of rituals and myths should be analysed and interpreted within inclusive growth dynamics.

On the downside, uncontrolled religious zealousness creates 'gospel merchandisers'. Without getting embroiled in the hermeneutical issues, African Pentecostals and neo-Pentecostals are accused of commercialising the Gospel. In particular, the neo-

Pentecostals in Zimbabwe artistically make market logistics branding the Gospel in religious artefacts (wristbands, stickers, oils and water) as a trade commodity. To keep the business afloat, it is not surprising that some religious leaders stage-manage miracles, gimmicks and do spectacular performances to lure the wealth of the poor. The central message within the religious landscape in Zimbabwe centre on materialism, emphasising divine blessings and prosperity gospel.

Social and contemporary African Knowledge Production Systems for development

The social element that influences development includes but not limited to culture, traditions, family, tribalism, racism, nepotism, oppression, abuses, ethics and religion. Existing literature about indigenous knowledge system shows that land had a social connotation. Within the practice of *humwe/nhimbe*, communities would come for social engagements and economic production. According to Muyambo "*Nhimbe* as an indigenous knowledge practice is a hub for economic growth for local communities" (2017:177). The land reform issues have produced diverse opinions among Zimbabweans. It triggered unfair land distribution, violence and human rights abuses. Gunda (2018) cited that the land reform problem was that it was carried out based on political expedience rather than promoting the common good. The political gimmicks resulted in those in the echelons of power and comrades benefit from the program (Mujinga, 2018). As discussed above, the church is either getting involved in politics or using protest theology to denounce resources' mismanagement.

Promoting equality is a critical social aspect that enhances development. Indigenous knowledge systems show that the communities were supposed to work together to promote equality. One example is *Zunde raMambo* (King's granary) concept, which stored food for use when supplies are low. However, findings by Ringson showed that "the Zunde raMambo concept from a traditional understanding is no longer in existence. But the idea that has evolved and developed into modern concepts such as NGOs and social welfare programmes" (2020:214). Since Zimbabwe is ravaged with persistent droughts, Muyambo and Marashe (2020) suggests that Zunde raMambo should be prioritised for realising the 2030 Sustainable Goals, 1 (No poverty), 2 (Zero hunger) and 3 (Good health and well-being). To this, the African Pentecostals in

408

Zimbabwe create changing forms of religious beliefs, practices, and emphasis and create new configurations for economics. For instance, giving tithes, working of talents and seeding has the potential to create wealth for believers. However, there is debate that it is the leaders who benefit from these financial activities in church.

The role of families in promoting equality is essential. The family is an important social institution and critical to promote the development of nations. Family, traditions and culture are evolving drastically in Zimbabwe. Indigenous knowledge system shows that indigenous governance relied on family and community resources. Everyone was considered family, brother, mother and sister. Communal working together (*nhimbe/humwe*) signified community-based development mechanisms (Sithole, 2014). The domination and longevity of colonisation, not only eroded Bantu languages but the indigenous cultures and social life were diluted (Mararike, 2014). The prosperity theology which exists within the African Pentecostals and neo-Pentecostals in Zimbabwe is an attempt to promote social equality. The prosperity gospel is aimed at empowering believers and storing wealth in churches. Nonetheless, a comprehensive account for prosperity theology is not intended and beyond this chapter's scope, but the leaders and founders of churches are accumulating wealth being gathered from the suffering believers through the prosperity gospel. Regardless of this negative connotation, the sociological view shows that wealth and success contribute to high social status.

Social justice is another critical aspect which enhances the development of a nation. Within the indigenous knowledge system, dispensing social justice was the duty of kings and chiefs (Machingura, 2012). Currently, the role of kings and chiefs are allegedly taken by the President and his ministers (Ringson, 2020). However, maintaining social justice continue to be challenging in Zimbabwe. To promote social justice, politicians have put initiates to prevent gatherings through the introduction of Public Order Security Act (POSA) and Access to Information Protection Act (AIPA) (Mhandara and Manyeruke, 2013); Supporting ZANU PF would guarantee to benefit from social- welfare and food aid (Chitando, 2011). The church has been lured to support the ruling party and gain some benefits. According to Majome (2016), Zimbabwe's religion and politics are Siamese twins, mostly the political leadership prey for votes. The African Initiated Churches (the apostolic sects) are coerced into supporting politicians by declaring that their leadership is from God. In this case, the church's role in engaging is compromised when it comes to employing a dialogue towards social and political cohesion effectively. However, African Christian traditions can produce contemporary African Knowledge Production Systems for social and political cohesion that promote development in Zimbabwe. Social justice includes sharing resources. Islamic religions encourage adherence to share with the poor.

Paying attention to health issues helps to enhance development in a nation. Indigenous knowledge system shows that the Indigenous Traditional Religion used incantations as 'psychotherapeutic' dimension of wellbeing. In terms of health and wellbeing, African Christian Traditions in Zimbabwe view issues of health and wellbeing as fundamental to their lives (Chirongoma, 2013). Such an approach seems to replace indigenous medicines. Health seeking strategies included consulting soothsayers and traditional healers for a cure (Sande, 2020). Further, the health issue of indigenous people was enhanced by doing hard-chores and eating natural food and wild fruits. The advent of western medicine was through missionary churches. According to Mujinga the African Christian traditions and the mainline missionary churches have been the "base of transformation through education and health" (2018:245). Nevertheless, currently in the absence of stable health care services in Zimbabwe, African classic and neo-Pentecostals are emphasising 'divine healings'. In some extreme cases, the leaders of neo-Pentecostals charges large sums of money for their services. Also, healing is brought by how these African Pentecostal churches encourage their members to confess optimistic about every situation. Positive confession is about using scriptures which gives hope to the believer. Therefore, in the poverty context and extreme economic stress, religion and spirituality provide strength for coping and surviving mechanisms.

Religion is another critical issue when dealing with the social issue that impact development. Zimbabwe's 21st-century religious landscape can be described as a multi-religious with Christianity controlling the significant share of the spiritual market (Mutangi, 2008). Statistically, Pew Research (2012) asserted that in Zimbabwe out of the 12.5 million people, (87.0%) are Christians, (0.9%) Islam, (<0.1%), Buddhism, (<0.1%) Hinduism and (<0.1%) Judaism. Those who belong to other religions are (<0.3%). Without delving in the debate of authenticating Zimbabwe as a 'Christian nation' (Ndoro, 2015), Christianity has become a 'de facto' religion and its rituals taking precedence in many social rites. A number of faith based in Zimbabwe especially mainline especially are making involved in development initiatives. Consequently, there is a focus between the spiritual and material. But as far as addressing the problems bedevilling Zimbabwe African Christian traditions are using Christian ideologies to produce contemporary indigenous knowledge strategies. For instance, Chimuka (2013) argued that neo-African Pentecostals in Zimbabwe have succeeded in dealing with the people's daily life challenges by appealing to the deepest and most profound of human passions creating something the state can never do. If one goes by Chimuka's claim, it becomes clear that religion an essential element in social issues that impact development by motivating them psychologically. Further, based on the description of Zimbabwe's religious landscape described above, African Christian traditions in Zimbabwe slowly are responsible for producing new Indigenous knowledge Production systems in Zimbabwe. This study suggests that paying attention to Indigenous knowledge systems within the Africans' moral and spiritual dispositions to improve inclusive growth and development.

Conclusion

This chapter explored how Zimbabwe's African Christian traditions have metamorphosed to become contemporary African Knowledge Production Systems development offering strategic tools to deal with development problems bedevilling Zimbabwe. Consequently, Zimbabwe's development issues must paying attention to the evolution of citizens' experiential indigenous knowledge and this include religious epistemology. Religious and spiritual experiential knowledge is directly linked to development. Since, Indigenous Knowledge Systems are static it has permeated indigenous African Christian traditions. Using African Indigenous Knowledge Systems, the indigenous Africa Christian traditions are creating new configurations to build economics, challenge corruption and encourage the moral of the people who are in poverty. Therefore, development in Zimbabwe should integrate African Indigenous Knowledge Systems and indigenous African Christian Traditions.

References

Asante, M.K. (1990). *Kemet, Afrocentricity, and Knowledge*. Trenton, NJ: Africa World Press.

Asante, A. (2013). National Economic Collapse and Revival: The Case of Zimbabwe. Degree thesis. *International Business*. https://www.theseus.fi/bitstream/handle/10024/65537/Ashley%20Asante.pdf?sequence=1&isAllowed=y.

Chigwata, T. (2016). The Role of Traditional Leadership in Zimbabwe: Are They Still Relevant. *Journal of Law Democracy and Development*, 7(20), 2-20.

Chimuka, T. (2013). 'Religion and Politics in Zimbabwe: Nascent Foes or Blessed Bed Fellow?' In Ezra Chitando, (ed.): *Prayers and Players: Religion and Politics in Zimbabwe*. Harare: Sapes Books.

Chirongoma, S. (2013). 'Navigating Indigenous Resources That Can Be Utilised in Constructing a Karanga Theology of Health and Wellbeing (Utano): An exploration of health agency in contemporary Zimbabwe'. Doctoral thesis, University of KwaZulu Natal.

Chitando, E. (2020). "The Zimbabwe Council of Churches and Development in Zimbabwe," 1-12. In: Ezra Chitando," *The Zimbabwe Council of Churches and Development in Zimbabwe*, London: Palgrave.

Chitando, E (ed), (2011). Prayers, Politics and Peace: Church's Role in the Zimbabwe's Crisis. OSISA, pp. 43-48.

Delport, C., De Vos, A., Fouche, C. and Strydom, H. (2005). *Research at Grassroots. The Place of Theory and Literature Review in the Qualitative Approach to Research*. Pretoria: Van Schaik.

Gudhlanga, Enna Sukutai and Makaudze, Godwin 2012. Indigenous knowledge systems: Confirming a legacy of civilisation and culture on the African continent. Prime Journal of Social Sciences, ISSN 2315-5051. Vol. 1(4) pp72-77.

Gunda, M, R. (2018). *At The Crossroads: A Call to Christian to Act in Faith for an Alternative Zimbabwe*. Bamberg: University of Bamberg Press.

Lupton, R., Rafferty, A. and Hughes, C. (2016). Inclusive Growth: Opportunities and Challenges for Greater Manchester. Inclusive Growth Analysis Unit, University of Manchester. Lupton, R., & Hughes, C. (2016). Achieving inclusive growth in Greater Manchester: What can be done? Manchester: Inclusive Growth Analysis Unit.

412

Machingura, F. (2012). *The Messianic Feeding Of the Masses: An Analysis of John 6 in the Context of Messianic Leadership in Postcolonial Zimbabwe*. Bamberg: University of Bamberg Press.

Mahere, F. (2019). "Zimbabwe: Is it Worse off than under Former President Mugabe?" BBC News https://www.bbc.co.uk/news/world-africa-49375096.

Majome, M.T. (2016). Religion, Politics and Law. News Day 24 September.

Mapara, J. (2009). Indigenous Knowledge Systems in Zimbabwe, *Juxtaposing Postcolonial Theory in Journal of Pan African Studies*, 3(1), 139-155.

Mhandara, L. & Manyeruke, C. &. H. S. (2013). The Church and Political Transition in Zimbabwe: The Inclusive Government Context. *Journal of Public Administration and Governance*, 3(1), 102-104.

Matanzima, J & Saidi, U. (2020). Religious Rituals and Socio-economic Change: The Impact of the Zimbabwe' Cash Crisis' On the BaTonga Masabe (alien spirits) Ceremony. *African Identities*, DOI: 10.1080/14725843.2020.1811637.

Mararike, C.G. (2014). *Land: An Empowerment Asset for Africa: The Human Factor Experience*. Harare: University of Zimbabwe.

Matikiti, R. (2014). 'The Apostolic Christian Council of Zimbabwe (ACCZ) and Social Transformation'. In: Ezra Chitando, M.R. Gunda & J. Kügler. (eds.): *Multiplying in the Spirit African Initiated Churches in Zimbabwe*. Bamberg: Druckausgabe; University of Bamberg: Press Bamberg.

Matikiti, R., & Sande, N. (n.d). "Apostle Talent Farai Chiwenga and a Theology of Protest in the Midst of Socio-Political and Economic Concerns in the Second Republic of Zimbabwe" (Forthcoming).

Maxwell, D. (1999). *Christians and Chiefs in Zimbabwe: A Social History of the Hwesa People: 1070s-1990s*. London: Edinburgh University Press.

Mawere, M. (2015). 'Indigenous knowledge for disaster management in Africa: Some showcases from Zimbabwe' In Mawere, Munyaradzi and Awuah- Nyamekye, Samuel (eds): *Between rhetoric and reality: The state and the use of indigenous knowledge in post-colonial Africa*. Bamenda: Langaa Research & Publishing CIG.

Mawere, M. (2014). *Culture, Indigenous Knowledge and Development in Africa: Reviving interconnecting for sustainable development.* Bamenda: Langaa Research & Publishing CIG.

Mawere, M. (2012). *The struggle of African Indigenous Knowledge Systems in an age of globalization: A case for children's traditional games in South-Eastern Zimbabwe.* Bamenda: Langaa Research & Publishing CIG.

McNabb, T.D. (2019). *Religious Epistemology: Elements Philosophy of Religion.* Cambridge: University Printing House.

Mhetu, I. (2020). "Under Siege President Mnangagwa.," *New Zimbabwe* https://www.newzimbabwe.com/dump-church-robes-and-join-political-arena-ed-says-to-catholic-priests/.

Mlambo, K. (2016). Addressing Zimbabwe's Current Economic Challenges. RBZ.

Mujinga, M. (2018). 'Religion as a Riding Horse of Politics?' A Critical Evaluation of Political Influence in the Zimbabwean Ecclesiastical Life. Alternation, Volume 23, pp. 244-265. [Accessed 02/01/2021].

Munyeza, S. (2018). Twitter handle @ShingiMunyeza, (Accessed 7 December 2020).

Mutangi, T. (2008). *Religion, Law and Human Rights in Zimbabwe. In African Human Rights Law.* Pretoria: Centre for Human Rights, UP.

Muyambo, T. (2016). Indigenous knowledge systems: An Alternative for mitigating HIV and AIDS in Zimbabwe. *Alternation* 23(2), 289-308.

Muyambo, T. (2017). Indigenous Knowledge Systems: A Haven for Sustainable Economic Growth in Zimbabwe. *Africology: The Journal of Pan African Studies,* 10(3), 172-185.

Muyambo, T. & Sibanda, F. (2018). 'Strange bedfellows or partners with good will? A study of the interface between African Pentecostalism and African Indigenous Religion, Zimbabwe', In Francis Machingura, Lovemore Togarasei & Ezra Chitando, *Pentecostalism and Human Rights in Contemporary Zimbabwe,* Cambridge: Cambridge Scholars Publishing 129-143.

Muyambo and Marashe (2020): Indigenous knowledge systems and development: a case of Zunde raMambo (Isiphala eNkosi) as food security in Zimbabwe. *Indilinga: Journal of Indigenous Knowledge Systems,* 19(2): 1-13.

Ndakaripa, M. (2020). 'Zimbabwe Is Open For Business': Aspects Of Post-Mugabe Economic Diplomacy. *South African Journal of*

International Affairs, 27:3, 363-389, DOI: 10.1080/10220461.2020.1826355.

Ndoro, S. R. (2015). Zimbabwe Is Not a 'Christian Nation'. The Sunday Mail 11 January.

Ndlovu-Gatsheni, S. J. (Ed), (2018). *Epistemic Freedom in Africa: Deprovinvialisation and Decolonisation*. London: Routledge.

Ndofirepi A.P., & Cross, M. (2014). Transforming Epistemologies in The Postcolonial African University? The Challenge of the Politics of Knowledge. *Journal of Education and Learning*, 8(4), 291-298.

Nhemachena, A, (2015). 'Indigenous Knowledge, Conflation and Postcolonial Translations: Lessons from Field Work in Contemporary Rural Zimbabwe' In: Munyaradzi Mawere and Samuel Awuah-Nyamekye, (ed). *Between Rhetoric and Reality: The State and Use of Indigenous Knowledge in Postcolonial Africa*, Bamenda, Langaa RPCIG, 59-106.

Nsamenang, A.B. (2006). 'Human Ontogenesis: An Indigenous African View on Development and Intelligence'. *International Journal of Psychology* 41(4), 293–297.

Ntuli, P.P. (2002). Indigenous Knowledge Systems the African Renaissance. In: Odora Hoppers, C.A. (Ed.), *Indigenous Knowledge and the Integration of Knowledge Systems*. Claremont, Cape Town: New Africa Books, pp. 53–67.

Owusu-Ansah, F.E. & Mji, G. (2013). African indigenous knowledge and research. *African Journal of Disability* 2(1), 1-5.

Pew Research (2012). Global Religious Landscape. Available at. https://www.bc.edu/content/dam/files/centers/jesinst/.../Grim-globalReligion-full.pdf.

Potts, D. (2006). 'Restoring Order'? Operation Murambatsvina and the Urban Crisis in Zimbabwe. *Journal of Southern African Studies*, 32(2), 273–291. https://doi.org/10.1080/03057070600656200.

Ringson, J. & Chereni, A. (2020). Efficacy of the Extended Family System in Supporting Orphans and Vulnerable Children in Zimbabwe: An Indigenous Knowledge Perspective. *African Journal of Social Work*, 10(1), 99-107.

Ringson, J. (2020). The Role of Traditional Leadership in Supporting Orphans and Vulnerable Children in Zimbabwe: African Traditional Leadership Perspective. *Social Work/Maatskaplike Werk*, 56(2):207-219.

Ruzivo, M. (2008). "A Mapping of the Church Groups in Zimbabwe." The Role of the Church in the Struggle for

Democratic Change in Zimbabwe. *Zimbabwe Institute Publications*, 4-14.

Sande, N. (2017). The Impact of the Coalition of Pentecostalism and African Traditional Religion (ATR) Religious Artifacts in Zimbabwe: The Case of United Family International (UFI). *Journal for the Study of Religions of Africa and its Diaspora*, 3 (1), 46–59.

Sande, N., & Denga, B. (2019). "Reconstructing the Nexus of Pentecostalism, Politics and Development in Zimbabwe: Political Voices from the Apostolic Faith Mission (AFM)", In: In: James N. Amanze, Maake Masango, Lilian Siwila, and Ezra Chitando (Eds), *Religion and Development in Southern Africa*, Nairobi: Acton 2,267-286.

Sande, N. (2020). Greening Faith and Herbology in Pentecostalism in Zimbabwe. *Journal of Religion in Africa*, 49, 59-72.

Sithole, P.M. (2014). Community-Based Development: A Study of Nhimbe Practice in Zimbabwe. *Unpublished PhD Thesis*, South Africa, University of the Witwatersrand, South Africa.

Togarasei, L. (2005). Modern Pentecostalism as an Urban Phenomenon: The Case of Family of God Church in Zimbabwe. *Exchange*, 34(4), 349 - 375.

World Economic Forum. (2015). The Inclusive Growth and Development Report 2015.http://www.weforum.org/reports/inclusive-growth-and-development-report-2015.

Yosso, T. J. (2005). Whose culture has capital? A critical race theory discussion of community cultural wealth. *Race Ethnicity and Education* 8(1), 69–91.

Chapter 22

Traditional Music and Knowledge Preservation in Colonial Zimbabwe: Recasting *Chimurenga* Songs as Liberation Heritage & Indigenous Knowledge for Emancipation

Praise Zinhuku & Munyaradzi Mawere

Abstract

Zimbabwe attained its independence in 1980 after an acrimonious, horrendous and excruciating struggle for liberation. Freedom fighters, war collaborators as well as non-combatants amalgamated to fight off an oppressive Rhodesian regime in the 1960s through the 1970s. During this time, chimurenga songs formed an imperative facet of the Zimbabwean liberation struggle, where musicians augmented the struggle for freedom through music. Liberation war songs advanced the struggle for liberty and inspired chivalrous sons and daughters who were fighting in the bush. This chapter explores how chimurenga songs can be tabled as a framework for preserving, memorialising and depicting Zimbabwean liberation war heritage. A case study research design was utilised to carry out the study and data congregated through face to face interviews and archival research. Data analysis was accomplished through thematic coding, permitting the generation of themes from research findings. Research results unearthed that music can be a tool for preserving indigenous knowledge and liberation heritage due to its capacity to evoke memories through activating what can be termed as a 'remembering gaze' in people's minds. On the basis of this finding, the chapter advances the argument that traditional songs are a symbol of national heritage and representation of people's memory as they can be employed to capture 'hard to describe' moments and feelings that occurred in the past.

Keywords: Traditional music, Chimurenga songs, knowledge preservation, heritage, Zimbabwe

Introduction

Zimbabwe attained independence in 1980 after a protracted acrimonious, horrendous and excruciating struggle for liberation.

The road to freedom was mapped through unity of purpose with freedom fighters, war collaborators as well as non-combatants amalgamating to fight off an oppressive Rhodesian regime in the 1960s through the 1970s. During this time, *chimurenga* songs formed an imperative facet of the struggle, with musicians augmenting the struggle for freedom through music. Liberation war songs advanced the struggle for liberty and inspired chivalrous sons and daughters who were fighting in the bush.

This chapter seeks to explore the role played by *chimurenga* songs in preserving, memorialising and representing Zimbabwean liberation war heritage. On this note, the chapter advances the argument that traditional music and *chimurenga* songs in particular can act as a framework for liberation heritage and indigenous knowledge preservation.

Methodological issues and the study area

This study was carried out in Masvingo District in Mavingo Province of Zimbabwe. To gain insights and understanding of traditional music and indigenous knowledge preservation, twenty people were researched with. These were drawn from traditional music experts and heritage preservation specialists in order to analyse and interpret how songs maybe a framework for preserving heritage. This sample was deemed sufficient and appropriate for the major reason that their vast experience and commitment in the music performance and heritage preservation in Zimbabwe was widely appreciated in the whole study area. The sample also included a selection of liberation music produced during the Zimbabwe struggle for independence as a basis for data collection and analysis.

Data was collected through face-to-face interviews, with culture and traditional music experts providing interpretations and detailed explanations. Interview as "a method of data collection that involves researchers asking respondents basically open ended questions" (O'Leary 2004:162), allowed us control over the process while affording us the freedom to express our own opinions as researchers. This is in synch with Borg and Gall (1981), who observed that interviews create a relationship which enables the researcher to solicit more information from the respondents. It costs less than focus groups and it has fewer scheduling constraints (Palmerino, 1999). All responses were tape recorded for further interpretation.

The study also employed documentary analysis and observation as its data collecting methods. Documentary analysis affords the researcher an opportunity to appreciate literature and current trends on the subject being studied, while observation allows immersion in daily life of the subjects under study which results in deepening the understanding of the research problem (also see, Stone 2008). In our case, observation was made on how indigenous dance groups arrange *muchongoyo* performances, songs, instruments, dance pattern and the contexts in which they perform the dance. The observations also assisted in explaining the issue of heritage preservation and dances.

Since ethical issues are likely to arise whenever researching with human subjects, ethical considerations were seriously taken into account. According to Coolican (2004), an ethical consideration is the moral principal (what others call research ethics) that is to be considered when an individual is dealing with research participants. This moral principle stresses that in any research, the researcher should be ethically upright so that the research is trustworthy, dependable and lawful. It is for this reason that Saunder *et al* (2003: 129) describe research ethics as the "appropriateness of the researcher's behaviour in relation to the rights of those who became subjects to work or affected by it". Therefore, consent was first sought from the targeted participants before data collection. These participants were also fully informed of the focus and objective of the study as well as research expectations before participating in the data collection process. Of those who chose to participate in the study, their identity was concealed and information obtained treated with a high degree of confidentiality. Moreover, the researchers stressed that the data collected was principally for educational purposes and not for any personal gain or political advancement. Data collected through documentary analysis, interviews and observation is presented in the ensuing paragraphs.

Liberation war musical arts: A global inquest

Many scholars have studied the role played by war musical arts as evidenced by erudite information amassed about musical war songs in various countries throughout the globe. For instance, an insightful study conducted by Mozara (2015) in former Yugoslavia, sought to ascertain whether music was employed as a tool of reconciliation or a deadly weapon during the conflict. The study provided knowledge on the role played by music during the conflict as well as on how music was used in constructing and reconstructing Yugoslavian identity. The study further uncovered the concept of 'music dichotomy and multifunction' as music was employed both as a weapon during the conflict and as a reconciliatory tool after the conflict.

In the same vein, the Editor, Jardin and fellow scholars carried out an extensive research which surveyed a number of countries such as Russia, German, and Britain among others (Mahiet, 2019). The research mainly focused on exposing the role of music in times of war from the French Revolution to the World War 1. Researchers teased out how the mobilisation of music for political ends was being accomplished by the different European countries engaged as case studies. Some of the researches, for example, traced the history of bag piping in the highlands regiments of the British Army from the middle century to the World War 1. Overall, the amalgamated researches revealed that historically, in Europe as well as the rest of the world, music has always been a useful instrument in war and an efficient motivator for group action (*Ibid*). Contrary to the above presented annotations, this chapter sought to explore how traditional music and in particular *chimurenga* songs can be deployed as a framework for preserving, memorialising and depicting Zimbabwean liberation war heritage.

A review of most African countries revealed that indeed music performed a critical role during the liberation struggle that transpired in those nations. According to Koloko (2012), Zambians launched a struggle for liberation and self-governance from 1953 to 1963 and nationalists employed music to encourage people to support the liberation struggle. Artists like Alfred Mapiki, John Lushi and Bartholomew Bwalya became household names this way as they composed revolutionary songs and enticed people to political gatherings and performed before the leaders take the stage. Thus, music played an important role in resisting, toppling, European colonialism and music remains in the frontline of opposition to evil and subjugation in the region (May, 2007).

Le Roux-Kemp (2014) in a research conducted in South Africa was concerned with explicating the imperative role performed by struggle music referred to as freedom songs played in South Africa during the apartheid era. This research confirmed that music performed a critical part in the struggle for liberation from white dominion and in fact struggle music continues to play an important role in contemporary South Africa. The results were further heightened by this statement which positions that "... there has never been a revolution that did not use songs to give voice to its aspiration or rally the morale of its adherence" (Le Roux-Kemp, 2014: 2).

In a departure from the above presented reviews, this research is unique in the sense that it seeks to demonstrate how traditional music and in particular *chimurenga* songs performance can be used as a framework for preserving liberation war heritage in Zimbabwe.

Protest Music in Southern Africa

Music executes an indispensable role in society as it permeates the social, physical, psychological, economic, religious, cultural and political spheres of society (Flynn 2018; Agawu 2003; Nzewi 2003). Sibanda (2017) confirms that music has the potential to influence people to react in certain ways and in various situations by influencing their emotions. In line with this research, academic chronicles confirm that music executes a critical role politically. For instance, war songs performed an indispensable part throughout the numerous liberation struggles executed in various African countries, especially those in Southern Africa.

According to May (2007), protest music has a long and honourable tradition in Southern Africa. It began in the colonial era in 1897 when the South African song writer Enoch Nkosi composed the classic *Nkosi Sikelelei* Africa (God bless Africa). The song was translated into a rallying cry for the liberation movements in some southern African countries such as Malawi, Zimbabwe and Zambia. In Zimbabwe, *chimurenga* concept as a form of protest music or liberation music originated from the forename of a legendary *Shona* ancestor, *Murenga Sororenzou,* who composed war-songs to embolden his soldiers in pre-colonial Zimbabwe (Andreucci, 2017). Resultantly, in the 1970s, African freedom fighters in bases in Tanzania, Mozambique, and Zambia, and some local Zimbabwean artists yearning for Zimbabwe's independence, derived inspiration from *Murenga's* revolutionary spirit and composed songs in a genus that they called *chimurenga*. *Chimurenga* when translated to English means 'fighting the *Murenga* style' (Kwaramba, 1997). Therefore, the songs that capture the sentiment of war and the longing for freedom became *chimurenga* music and ultimately *chimurenga* songs then refer to melodies that incarnated the temperament of the liberation struggle and craving for sovereignty (Vambe, 2004).

Chimurenga songs are categorised as intangible cultural heritage. Intangible heritage is the legacy of non-physical artefacts that are passed on from past generations and preserved in the present for the benefit of future generations (Mawere 2015; Ngara 2020). Examples of intangible heritage are folklore, [traditional] dance, songs, song lyrics, indigenous knowledge systems, belief systems, norms and values, rites of passages, and traditional ceremonies. It is on this understanding that the 2003 UNESCO Convention describes the term intangible cultural heritage as "the practices, representations, expressions, knowledge, skills—as well as instruments, objects, artefacts and cultural spaces associated therewith—that communities, groups, and in some cases, individuals recognize as part of their cultural heritage (Inawat, 2015). Inexorably, *chimurenga* music as a genus of intangible heritage was an essential aspect of the Zimbabwe liberation struggle were the songs served to encourage the execution of the war and also buoyed the struggle for independence (Chiwome, 1996).

Chiwome further elucidate that, war songs were fundamental to warfare in the African societies. Employing an example of a popular Shona war song, *Bayawabaya* (Kill or get killed), Chiwome argues that war songs 'called people to the battlefront, exhorted fighters and insulted the enemy' (1996: 20). Chiwome also divulged a momentous role performed by *chimurenga* music when he annotated that generally the second *Chimurenga*, created uncertainty and the prospect of death, injury or defeat, thus 'fear was managed by song and dance' (1996: 21). In confirmation, Dwamena (2018:1) expounds that "*chimurenga* songs were central to the century long fight to end the colonial system and Marley's claim that music was the biggest gun because the oppressed cannot afford weapons is more resonant than ever…".

Supporting the same point, Ravengai (1994: 27–39) perceives *chimurenga* songs as popular theatre that was established during the war. He asserts that these songs were sung at *Pungwes*, referring to, 'all night meetings by and peasants to conscientise and rally one another'. As noted by Andreucci (2017:2), "prolific composition of songs of revolution during the 1970s declaring the soil, water, skies, blood, and spirit of Zimbabwe was done to bequeath the country with a legacy of liberation and African independence from the yokes of colonial bondage". He further notes that during the liberation struggle music was produced bereft of instruments, yet the fresh acappella voices pregnant with emotion enunciated the sounds that presaged the revolution.

Chimurenga Music and the Zimbabwe war of liberation

A number of Zimbabwean academics have written substantial and vital information regarding the Zimbabwean liberation war and its music. Chirere and Mhandu (2008) explored how songs from Zimbabwe's war of the liberation documented by Alec Pongweni differ in thrust from the poems transcribed by fellow combatants, Freedom Nyamubaya and Thomas Bvuma. Chirere and Mhandu wondered why the two poets contrast from the singing guerrillas, as the poets cultivate diverse and disparate directions in their comprehension of *Chimurenga* and its corollary. Thus, the results of their study specified that although songs and poetry are generically related, the songs from the war served a single mandate of encouraging the execution of the war, while the poems allowed poets to explore official and unofficial viewpoints of people involved in the *chimurenga*.

Vambe (2004) explored *chimurenga* musical discourses of post-independence Zimbabwe, where he argued that scholars and the general populace have undervalued how multiple meanings can be attached to *chimurenga* songs. He contends that this misconception has encouraged a universally alleged belief that *chimurenga* is a protest genre that is based only on visible and organized forms of struggle by African nationalists in Zimbabwe. However, this parochial understanding of *chimurenga,* according to him, has precluded exploration of the internal contradictions within *chimurenga* as a nexus of various aspects of African cultural nationalism in post-independence Zimbabwe. Resultantly, *chimurenga* protest music, fails to explore its own possibilities as it is capable of protesting the colonial exploitation of Africans as well as criticising the subjugation of women in African society (Ibid).

Also concerned with Zimbabwe liberation war music, Sibanda (2017) in a research entitled *The Impact of Thomas Tafirenyika Mukanya Mapfumo's Music on Zimbabwe's Liberation Struggle,* sought to reconnoitre the impact of music and its power to influence during the liberation struggle. Sibanda was concerned with whether Mapfumo's music during the Zimbabwe liberation struggle had the same influence as the music from other countries during their liberation struggles. The study established that, through music Zimbabwean musicians managed to raise awareness of the holistic nature of the war.

Indisputably, scholars have executed perspicacious researches on liberation war music and heritage centring on different aspects (see for example, Sibanda 2017; Chirere and Mhandu 2008; Andreucci 2017; Vambe 2004; and Chiwome 1996). Nevertheless, a void still exists as nothing much has been researched on how liberation war music can be tabled as a framework for preserving, depicting and memorialising liberation war heritage. Realising this gap, this chapter acknowledges and seeks to redress challenges faced in preserving national liberation war heritage by providing a possibly robust coherent guideline for action. The chapter thus contributes to existing debates on memorialisation and conservation of war songs, liberation war heritage and intangible heritage in general.

Field Perceptions on Traditional Music and Liberation Heritage

Having discussed data on traditional music and liberation heritage literature, the ensuing sections focus mainly on perceptions of the people gathered through interviews and observations during the study.

Songs as a symbol of heritage

Academic analyses and research results unearthed in this study confirm that songs have the propensity to act as a symbol of heritage to any nation despite providing information and history of past events (Matanga, 2015). In support of this proposition, Participant 4 noted that:

> *Nziyo dzechimurenga dzaimiririra uye dzaivewo mucherechedzo wenhoroondo yehondo yokurwira rusununguko muZimbabwe/ Chimurenga* songs were a symbol and representative of the history of the liberation struggle in Zimbabwe.

Underscoring the same point, Participant 6 added that:

> *Nziyo dzehondo zvekarewo imwe yenzira inochengetedza nhoroondo uye nekupa rupawo rwehondo yerusununguko yeZimababwe/ Chimurenga* songs preserved the history and gave identity to the war for the Zimbabwean liberation war.

Inarguably, representatives or symbols of identity are chosen carefully and each depicts distinctive characteristics of a nation. In Zimbabwe, symbols are intrinsic to the Zimbabwean identity and heritage. They help to instil a sense of belonging, pride and patriotism

424

to Zimbabwean people. From an analogous view, Sanga (2011: 189) notes that musical symbols have two functions: "to claim one's identity and to announce one's difference with other identities". Sanga was scrutinising how Tanzanian musicians dissimilarly deploy musical "figures to construct Tanzanian and African identities" (Ibid). Identity is a very important aspect of our heritage, performing an imperative role in conserving our various forms of inheritance, in this case, liberation war heritage.

Moreover, Agawu asserts that, representation or symbolism of music takes three forms: iconographic, metalinguistic and the meta-musical (1992:247). Iconography refers to the use of pictures and visual artefacts of music-making to represent while metalinguistic representation focuses on verbal reports of music making, and documents in archives and libraries as symbolism. Meta-musical form, on the other hand, refers to practical representations in the form of tangible performance. This statement implies that *chimurenga* songs may be deployed as a form of tangible representation through performance. Therefore, the above statement concretises the idea being propositioned in this research, that musical songs in this case *chimurenga* songs can be considered as a symbol of liberation war heritage as they have the power and capability to epitomize.

Brandellero et al (2014) concur that music is undeniably a symbol of national or local heritage just like any other traditional representations such as national and regional insignia, food, drink and sport. They argue that with the growing of consumerism in everyday life, expressions of way of life, orientations and preferences, music and fashion have become effective signifiers of identity, heritage and belonging.

Focusing on memorialisation, Andreucci (2017) asserts that music is responsible for reliving and rebooting the memory bringing to fore forgotten historical legacies. Thus, for him, music reminds us of our past, fundamental values and ethos as there is 'more to the songs than just sound'. Categorically, this research proposes that *chimurenga* songs can also be adopted as a symbol for liberation war heritage in Zimbabwe.

Songs as a depiction and conveyer of heritage
During this research, it was revealed that *Chimurenga* songs performed a critical role of portraying and expressing intangible heritage of the nation Zimbabwe. The songs were used to describe

425

and illustrate moments and feelings that occurred in the past. In support of this vignette, Participant 3 specified that:

Nziyo dzechimurenga dzaifambisa mashoko akakosha ekupa, kuzivisa nekudzidzisa vanhu munguva yehondo. Uye nziyo dzechimurenga dzinobudisa manzwiro nekuratidza zvaiitika nekusanganiwa nevanhu munguva dzehondo/ Chimurenga songs transmitted revolutionary messages to inform, notify and teach people during the liberation struggle. Moreover, *chimurenga* songs conveyed the emotions and experiences of people during the war.

In addition, participants 20, 18, 12 and 1alluded to the same point that *chimurenga* songs transmitted the main cause of the liberation struggle. Participant 1, for example, had this to say:

Nziyo dzechimurenga dzaitakura nekufambisa donzvo nemoto wechimurenga. Saka nekudaro dzine simba rekuchengeta nhoroondo yechimurenga. Tinogona kuva neruzivo rwezvakaitika munhorondo yehondo yechimurenga kubudikidza nenziyo dzechimurenga kunyange tanga tisipo/ Chimurenga songs transmitted the main cause of the liberation war. They have power to preserve the history of *chimurenga* war. We can acquire knowledge of what transpired during the liberation struggle through *chimurenga* songs even though we were not present.

What Participant 1 tells us concurs with Pongweni's (1982) observation that during the Zimbabwe liberation struggle music was an expression of what the Germans entitled *Zeitgeist*. The term "*Zeitgeist*" referred to the entirety of the beliefs, attitudes, strivings, motivations and living forces of the people expressing themselves with given causes and effects in a definite course of events. Philosophically, this statement infers that *chimurenga* songs were indeed a form of *Zeitgeist* as they expressed and embodied the beliefs, dogmas, spirit and emotions of the Zimbabwean liberation struggle. For example, songs like *Muka Muka* (Wake up, Wake up) and *Tumirai vana kuhondo* (Send your children to war) were sung to politicise and educate Zimbabweans about why the war was being fought. The song became the classroom, so to speak just like in South Africa and in Kenya through which the people could access information of what was happening in different parts of the country (Kwaramba, 1997).

In confirmation, Inawat (2015) maintains that music in its original sense was used to convey information and share emotion. This is to say that cultures often use music to describe a moment or feeling that cannot be explained with mere words (Ibid). A case in point is

Chimbetu's song *Ndarangarira musi watisiya gamba*. The song did a splendid but painful task of depicting and portraying the worst scenarios and emotions that materialised during the liberation struggle. The songs narrated the painful circumstances of the war and how liberation war fighters met their fate and perished in the bush far away from their families. The agonizing and inspiring lyric goes as follows:

> **Lead:** *Ndarangarira musi watisiya gamba* (I remember the day a liberation war fighter died)
> **Response:** *Mwana wenyu amai. Amire panguva yakaoma* (Your son mother was facing perilous time)
> *Handikanganwe comrade* (I will not forget comrade)
> **Lead:** *Akashevedzera ndokushevedzera* (He called and he called)
> *Mwana wenyu amai amire panguva yakaoma* (Your son mother was facing perilous time)
> *Shinga comrade* (Be brave comrade)
> **Lead:** *Vana veZimbabwe* (Children of Zimbabwe)
> **Response:** *Zimbabwe iyiyi*
> **Lead:** *Ngatishande pamwe* (Lets work together)
> **Response:** *Zimbabwe iyiyi*
> **Lead:** *Tikurire mhandu* (Lets be victorious against the enemy)
> **Response:** *Zimbabwe iyiyi.*

During the liberation struggle, the meaning of the lyrics of the song *Tora gidi uzvitonge* from *Mbuya nehanda's* prophecy ran deep into the soil and coursed in the blood of every liberation cadre. The inspiring lyrics of the song are:

> **Lead**: *Mbuya nehanda kufa vachitaura shuwa* (Nehanda died saying this)
> **Response**: *Kuti tinotora sei nyika ino* (How were we going to free this country)
> *Soko rimwe ravakatiudza* (There is only one word she told us)
> *Tora gidi uzvitonge* (Take up the gun to achieve freedom)
> **Chorus**
> **Lead**: *Vadzoka kuhondo* (They have come back from the war)
> **Response**: *Shuwa here vakamhanya nemasango* (Oh yes they struggled in the bushes)
> *Vakatora anti air kuti ruzhinji ruzvitonge* (They utilised anti air weapons for all people to be free).

Tora gidi uzvitonge heralded the advent of *chimurenga* war as patriotic individuals were being assembled to join the liberation struggle as the only tactic to attain freedom was through the gun. The message conveyed by the song prompted alacritous individuals to take up arms and fight in the bush. According to Tony Monda, Zimbabwe's *chimurenga* music "extolled the blood and soil values of the liberation struggle, articulating previous bondage, current nationhood, prosperity and freedom: the music is what buoyed the liberation struggle. Sentiments, principles and ambitions are made tactical and tangible by the music and songs of the liberation war" (Andreucci, 2017:3). In agreement, Le Roux-Kemp (2014) annotate that the role of liberation struggle music was to capture the emotions and articulate the conditions of time. Thus, in this study we argue that *chimurenga* songs can be an imperative strategy for preservation of liberation war heritage as they have the ability to convey, depict and store crucial information which can be passed on from one generation to another.

Musiyiwa also noted that *chimurenga* music was and is still a platform that Zimbabweans always resort to whenever they wanted to express their grievances against their leaders and western imperialism (Dwamena, 2018). Memory Chirere & Edwin Mhandu (2008) on the other hand affirm that *chimurenga* songs convey very important liberation heritage information, as these songs line up prominent characters of the liberation struggle like Herbert Chitepo, Josiah Magama Tongongara and Joshua Nkomo. However, the songs also served to ridicule unpopular figures of the war such as Abel Muzorewa, Ndabaningi Sithole, Chirau and others who fell out with the liberation war ideology (Ibid). Another example of a song which conveyed the liberation memories is *Kugarira nyika yavo* (Choosing to free their country). In the song detractive characters during the war were told that the children of Zimbabwe are fighting in the bush not because they like it but to free their country and people out of subjugation. The reverberation of names of the perceived foes of the revolution helped to drum into the fighters' spirit the very names of their misanthropists (Pongweni, 1982:37-40).

Memories are ignited by the sound and songs of Zimbabwe's liberation struggle, reliving the eve of independence on 18 April 18 1980. Moreso, intangible values such as unity, peace, prosperity and socio economic progress is made manifest in the social lubricant of liberation music. *Chimurenga* songs stands to safeguard the memory and legacy of our liberation as an ad hoe examination of the lyrics

428

contained in Zimbabwe's songs (Andreucci, 2017). The songs for liberation convey and depict personal, spiritual and national yearnings as well as articulations of freedom. For example, Green and Jangano's songs *Mbuya Nehanda* is one of the signature tunes articulating the struggle for independence from 1893 to 1980. There are a number of memorable songs of the liberation war that conveyed a wide range of feelings, information and emotions. They include *Zvinoda wakashinga moyo, Hama dzedu dzakapera kufa, Patakatsika* and *Pane Asipo* by the late Simon Chimbetu. These above mentioned songs were described by the late Chingaira as the lubricants of the struggle (Ibid). This is underscored by Vambe (2004) and Andreucci (2017), who *chimurenga* songs were important as they were relevant in the past as well as in the present. Inarguably, *chimurenga* musical memory when revisited ensures the existence of a patriotic populous who are keenly aware of their roots and the welfare and development of the land of their ancestors (Vambe, 2004).

Songs transcribe a nation's indigenous knowledge and heritage

Some indigenous cultures around the world record and pass on important information from one generation to another through various oral means such as poetry, folk songs and cultural visual artefacts besides the use of literary works (Brandellero, Janssen, Cohen and Roberts, 2014). Transcribing is an articulate process which is defined as recording or storing a culture's history. For example, the Ami culture use folk songs to record and transmit vital information to their young ones. This was corroborated by Participants 2, 6, 9, 15 and 13. Participant 2, for example, asserts that:

*Mutsika nemagariro edu nhoroondo yehupenyu hwedu inotambidzwa kune vechidiki kubudikidza nenzira dzakasiyana siyana dzinosanganisisira madetembo, zvivezwa uye nenziyo nemitambo yechinyakare/*In our culture the history of our lives is passed on to the younger generation through the use of various ways such as poems, sculptures, folk music and traditional game songs.

In addition, Participant 13 stated that:

*Mumhanzi yechikare ndeimwe nzira yatinoshandisa kuchengetedza nhorondo yehupenyu hwedu ne tsika nemagaririo edu sevanhu vatema. Nekudaro nziyo dzechimurenga dzakatikoshera sezvo dzichengetedza nhorondo yehondo yerusungunuko madziri patinoimba dzinochengetedza nhoroondo mundangaririo medu nekusingaperi uyewo vana vedu vanozoziva nhororondo iyi/*Traditional music is one of the methods we use to preserve our life history as well as our norms and values as black people. Therefore, *chimurenga* songs are also important for they preserve our history for the struggle for independence in our minds forever and our kids will also know about this history.

A more articulate song is *Mukoma Takanyi* which became known in the late 1970s as *Sendekera Mkoma Takanyi* (Go on, I hear you brother Takanyi). This song is a perfect example of the ideology being brought forward in this research. The song is pregnant with information as it recorded a lot of experiences, emotions and events that occurred during the liberation struggle (Pongweni, 1982: 47). As explained by Pongweni the song deals with many themes which range over a whole panorama of the bitter experiences in the war, before the war, experiences of the masses and of the guerrillas in the field **ibid**. More so in this long song, the soloist chronicles real-life examples of the black man's oppression and segregation by the white system (Andreucci, 2017). Thus, *chimurenga* songs can be a genus for preserving liberation as they are a rich, distinct and simple way of recording treasured past events, memories and experiences.

Songs as an indigenous knowledge and heritage preservation strategy
Exertions to preserve heritage in all its various forms and categories have gained new momentum throughout the world nowadays. Protecting national heritage is economical, as well as historical and also a cultural process (Ekwelem, Okafor, and Ukwoma 2011). As Participants 3, 4 and 19 alluded to, it is also a way of preserving indigenous knowledge for emancipation. Participant 19 explicitly noted this when she said:

> *Nziyo dzechimurenga ndeimwe yenzira yekuchengetedza ruzivo rwedu rwechinyakare inogona kutiunzira pundutso muupenyu hwedu sevanhu veChiShona/* Chimurenga music is one way of preserving our indigenous knowledge for emancipation that can bring sustainable development to us as Africans.

Heritage is based on the aspects of our past that we cherish, want to keep and pass on to future generations and outside world. As rightly observed by Sekler (2001), as long as the heritage remains without falsification and misleading imitations, it will, even in a neglected state, create a sense of continuity that is an essential part of … identity". According to the theory of sustaining and safeguarding heritage, the world has a "shared concern" as heritage in its various forms continue to face possible destruction and extinction such that in the end future generations may not be able to benefit (Slatyer 1983: 138). Resultantly, the United Nations Educational, Scientific and Cultural Organisation (UNESCO, 1989: 138) "adopted a general policy which aims to give the cultural and natural heritage a function in the life of community and to integrate the protection of heritage into comprehensive planning programs".

Moreover, Inawat (2015) affirms that the preservation of heritage is crucial in this case liberation heritage. As defined by the Webster's dictionary, preservation refers to the ability "to keep alive or in existence." Under UNESCO, "preservation" refers to "the safeguarding of and respect for cultural property" during times of peace. Thus, this chapter argues that *chimurenga* songs may perform a critical role in preserving liberation heritage due to its strong capacity to evoke, record and revitalise important memories of a nation's past. To demonstrate the efficacy of *chimurenga* songs as preserver of liberation heritage, this chapter presents a model for preserving liberation heritage through songs which is based on ideas generated from data collected. In addition, ideas propounded by Feather (1996); Inawat (2015) and the UNESCO (1989) recommendations were also incorporated in order to come up with the model for preservation of intangible heritage.

The intangible liberation heritage preservation model presented above seeks to complement efforts by researchers tackling issues on how liberation heritage can be preserved. The first step suggested in this model is acknowledging the existence of intangible liberation heritage, emphasising respect for chimurenga songs and the message they convey and embody in all societal and educational platforms.

The second strategy in preserving intangible war heritage in this proposed model involves the establishment of inventory systems for preserving chimurenga songs. According to Inawat (2015), creating an inventory is effective as it provides additional information such as the identity the geographical and cultural connexions of each song. More so, inventories allows acknowledgement of the origin of intangible heritage and makes each museums responsible for each item.

The intangible liberation heritage preservation model

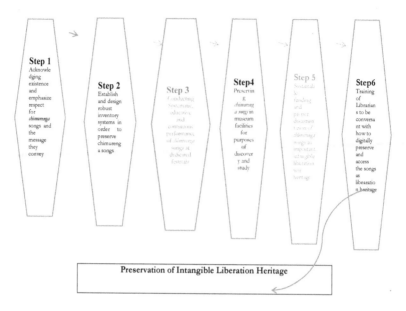

Step 1
Acknowledging existence and emphasize respect for *chimurenga* songs and the message they convey

Step 2
Establish and design robust inventory systems in order to preserve chimurenga songs

Step 3
Conducting Systematic, educative and continuous performance of chimurenga songs at dedicated festivals

Step4
Preserving *chimureng* *a song* in museum facilities for purposes of discovery and study

Step 5
Sustainable funding and proper documentation of chimurenga songs as important intangible liberation war heritage

Step6
Training of Librarians to be conversant with how to digitally preserve and access the songs as liberation heritage

Preservation of Intangible Liberation Heritage

Source: Authors, 2021

Strategy number three consists of conducting systematic, educative and continuous performance of chimurenga songs at dedicated festivals and events. Ebron (2002:23) confirms that representations emerge not only through historic conventions but through performance in this case enactment of chimurenga songs. In support of this strategy, Dwamena (2018) pointed out that in Zimbabwe's liberation war, of the nineteen-sixties and seventies, the military wings of guerrillas based in Mozambique and Zambia would set up choirs to sing chimurenga songs that had recorded the struggle for those to come, thus revolutionaries played these songs at rallies held in urban areas and *pungwes* where guerrillas and peasants would come together and sing in remembrance.

The forth approach for preserving intangible heritage is through maintaining chimurenga songs in museum facilities for purposes of discovery and study to ensure that the war heritage of the nation is preserved. Ogden (1993) affirms that traditionally, libraries and archives preserve heritage collections by providing proper housing, protection from mutilation and theft, library binding, and occasional repair and restoration.

The fifth technique for preserving intangible heritage encompass funding and proper documentation of chimurenga songs as important intangible liberation war heritage Feather (1996) has called attention to the proper handling of library materials by all of those involved as a sort of inexpensive measure by any library or archive.

The final and sixth stratagem for preserving intangible heritage is achieved through mandatory [re-]training of librarians to be conversant with digital preservation and accessing of chimurenga songs as heritage. Digitalisation enables greater access to collections of all types (Hughes, 2004). Mulrenin and Geser (2001) concurs that the conversion into bits and bytes enables access to reach traditional and new audiences by providing admittance to cultural heritage resources in ways unconceivable.

Conclusion

Categorically, the preservation of Zimbabwe's liberation war heritage resources is essential to the sustainable development of the nation. Liberation war heritage preservation facilitates the eminence of cultural continuity of the liberation war history, nurture social cohesion, and creates a context within which to understand and memorialise the past while contemplating the future. This chapter thus sought to explore how chimurenga songs can be tabled as a framework for preserving liberation war heritage, memorialising and depicting Zimbabwean liberation war heritage. It concludes that chimurenga music can be a symbol of national heritage and a tool for preserving intangible liberation heritage.

References

Andreucci, M. (2017) When the land sings: Reliving *chimurenga* music. *The Patriotic Reporter.*

Bennett, A. (2009) Heritage rock: Rock music, representation and heritage discourse. *Poetics*, 37 (5–6): 474–489.

Bourdieu, P. (1991) *Language and symbolic power.* Cambridge, MA: Harvard University Press.

Brandellero, A., Janssen, S., Cohen, S., & Roberts, L. (2014) Popular music heritage, cultural memory and cultural identity. *International Journal of Heritage Studies*, 20 (3): 219-223.

Burgoyne, R. (2003) *From contested to consensual memory: The rock and roll hall of fame and museum*, In: S. Radstone and K. Hodgekins, eds. Frontiers of memory. London: Routledge, 208–220.

Chaney, D. (2002) *Cultural change and everyday life*. Basingstoke: Palgrave.

Cohen, S. (1991) *Rock culture in Liverpool: popular music in the making*. Oxford: Claredon.

Chiwome, E. (1996) *A critical history of Shona poetry*. Harare: University of Zimbabwe Publications.

Convention for the Safeguarding of the Intangible Cultural Heritage, ch. 6 Oct. 18, 2003, http://portal.unesco.org/en/ev.php-

Coolican, H. (2004) *Research Methods & Statistics in Psychology*, in Cooper, C. (ed.) Palgrave Macmillan, New York.

Dwamena, A. (2018) Zimbabwe's powerful music of struggle. *The Patriotic Reporter.*

Ebron, P. (2002) *Performing Africa*. New Jersey: Princeton University Press.

Ekwelem, V. O., Okafor, V. N., and Ukwoma, S. C. (2011) Preservation of cultural heritage: strategic role of the library and information science professionals in South East Nigeria". *Library Philosophy and Practice (e-journal)*. Paper 562.

Feather, J. (1989) Preservation and conservation: A professional issue for the1990s. *New Zealand Libraries* 46 (2&3): 17-25.

Harvey, R. (1996) Preservation in libraries: A reader. *Topics in Library and Information Studies*. Bowke: London.

Koloko, L. (2012) *Zambian Music Legends*. Lulu.com: USA.

Jones, T. (2001). An introduction to digital projects for libraries, museums, &archives (http://images.library.uiuc.edu\resources\introduction.htm.Kwaramba, D. A. (1997) *Popular music and society: The language of chimurenga music: the case of Thomas Mapfumo in Zimbabwe*. Oslo: University of Oslo, pp. 35-36.

Le Roux-Kemp, A. (2014) Struggle music: South African Politics in Song. *Law and Humanities*, 8:247-268.

Madelylan, A. (2019) Coding Qualitative Data: How to Code Qualitative Research (Updated 2020) https://getthematic.com/insights/coding-qualitative-data/.

Mhandu, E. (2008) 'Songs that won the war of liberation and poems that grapple with the war and its aftermath', *Muziki*, 5:2, 271-283, DOI: 10.1080/18125980902798573.

434

May, C. (2007) 'Liberation Music: South Africa, Zimbabwe and Zambia', *Golden Afrique*, 3.

Mozara, Z. (2015) The role of music in conflict: tool of reconciliation or a deadly weapon: case study of war in former Yugoslavia'. *Institute for cultural diplomacy*, Berlin.

Ngara, R. (2020) 'Kayanda musical arts for the installation of Shangwe chiefs: An epistemological, gendered, symbolic, interpretive, community-State model for sustaining [in]tangible heritage in Zimbabwe', *PhD thesis*, University of Pretoria, South Africa.

Ojo-Igbinoba, M. E. (1993) 'The practice of conservation of library materials in Sub-Saharan Africa', Indiana: *Africa Studies Program*, Indiana University.

Pongweni, A. J. C. (1982) *Songs that won the liberation war.* Zimbabwe: The College Press.

"Preservation" Merriam Webster's Collegiate Dictionary, 922 (10th ed. 1994).

Polit, D. F., & Beck, C. T. (2008) *Nursing research: Generating and assessing evidence for nursing practice (8th ed.).* Philadelphia, PA: Wolters Kluwer Health/Lippincott Williams & Wilkins.

Sibanda, S. (2017) The impact of Thomas Tafirenyika Mukanya Mapfumo''s music on Zimbabwe's liberation struggle', *The International Journal of Engineering and Science (IJES),* 6 (9): 42-48.

Smith, M. A. (1987) Care & handling of bound materials. In preservation of library materials. *Conference Library held at the National Library of Austria*, Vienna, April7th-10th, 1986 (ed) merrily Smith, IFLA Publications 40-41 (2): 45-53.

Sanders, P. D. and Browne, L. A. (1998) 'Music self-concept of non-music majors', *Contributions of Music Education*, 25(1): 74–86.

Stephen, V. Flynn & James S. Korcuska (2018) 'Grounded Theory Research Design: An Investigation into Practices and Procedures', *Counseling Outcome Research and Evaluation*, 9:2, 102-116, DOI: 10.1080/21501378.2017.1403849.

Vambe. M. T. (2004) 'Versions and sub-versions: trends in chimurenga musical discourses of post-independence', *Zimbabwe African Study Monographs*, 25(4): 167-193.

Williams, H. (2001) 'Historic cities: The sense of place, sacred and secular.' In Serageldu, I., Shluger, E., & Martin-Brown, J. (Eds). *Historic cities and sacred sites: Cultural roots for urban futures.* Washington DC: The World Ban.

Chapter 23

Dissuading Cultural Atrophy: Promoting Zimbabwean Traditional Dance as Strategy for Reconfiguring National Identity

Praise Zinhuku & Munyaradzi Mawere

Abstract

Addressing challenges imposed by colonialism, westernisation, and globalisation to [national] identity and reconstruction is critical for any postcolonial state like Zimbabwe which, as a matter of fact, has been portentously westernised and suffered from 'cultural schizophrenia' and 'cultural dislocation' (Mawere, 2016) due to the forced 'marriage' between its values and those from the West. National identity is vital for any form of nation building as it revives dogmas of allegiance and *esprit de corps* while instigating national consciousness. [National] identity is a multifarious phenomenon tangled with communal, pecuniary, artistic, macro-culture, historic and geopolitical cohesions. Irrevocably, the question of [national] identity reconfiguration in postcolonial contexts where conceit has been exotically cloaked resulting in the loss of a concrete self-direction, self-esteem and identity consciousness are peremptory. Inarguably, identity encompasses critical cultural ingredients such as linguistic codes, moral values, indigenous knowledge systems, folklore, beliefs and dances, among others. Using an ethnographic approach, this chapter is an attempt to fantasise Zimbabwean traditional dance and position it as a strategy for national identity reconfiguration and restoration. *Muchongoyo* dance, which is one of the Zimbabwean traditional dances, is adopted as a case study, with a view to cast it as an analogue and basis for appreciating how the envisaged agenda can be accomplished.

Keywords: Traditional dance, culture, atrophy, *Muchongoyo*, identity, Zimbabwe

Introduction

Challenges imposed by colonialism, westernisation and globalisation are a threat to national identity, its restoration and reconstruction. National identity is a multifarious phenomenon tangled with communal, pecuniary, artistic, macro-culture, historic and geopolitical cohesions. It is vital for any nation as it revives dogmas of allegiance, esprit de corps and instigate national cognisance. Zimbabwean intellectuals lament that their beloved nation is portentously westernised and suffer from 'cultural schizophrenia' due to the forced marriage between the Zimbabwean values and those from the West. Irrevocably, the question of identity reconfiguration in postcolonial contexts such as those of Zimbabwe, where conceit has been exotically cloaked resulting in the loss of a concrete national identity consciousness and symbols remains peremptory.

The question of identity has been the object of significant scholarly attention and debates (wa Thiongo, 1986; Ranger, 1983; Asante, 1980). Many of these debates centre on understanding the ontological constitution of [national] identity, identifying the nature and features of [African] 'identity' and its historical evolution, in particular, the extent to which it contemporary identity in many African places is the product of colonial 'invention'. While researching on identity, we started thinking reflexively and critically on the practices of different ethnic groups, including their traditional dances in Zimbabwe. What dawned to us was the fact that we are putting so much emphasis on documenting the ontology and features of identity as well as its historical evolution because we are concerned that it is getting lost. What is strikingly lacking though is an emphasis on its reconfiguration and application in real life. The reconfiguration, restoration and application of [national] identity in real life is highly limited and extremely handicapped by the fact that westernisation and colonial legacies have been negatively impacted the lives of the formerly colonised. As such, within Zimbabwean communities, [national] identity is hardly applied for community benefit. The far reaching consequence for this is cultural atrophy. What we should begin questioning ourselves therefore is how cultural atrophy can be averted while promoting the reconfiguration, restoration and application of [national] identity in our daily lives.

Using an ethnographic approach, this chapter is an attempt to fantasise Zimbabwean traditional dance as a strategy for national identity reconfiguration. *Muchongoyo* dance, which is one of the Zimbabwean traditional dances, is adopted as a case study, with a view that it acts as an analogue and basis for appreciating that it represents the various ethnic groups existing in Zimbabwe, and hence; can be collectively roped in as a strategy for national identity restoration and preservation in Zimbabwe. Nonetheless, from an emic approach *muchongoyo* dance was nominated as an analogue and basis for appreciating how the envisaged agenda can be accomplished.

Methodological concerns and theoretical underpinnings

This study adopted a qualitative ethnographic research approach, particularly focus group discussions (FGDs), formal and informal interviews, participant observation, and documentary analysis to gather relevant information on perceptions of different interlocutors on [national] identity and how this can be reconfigured and save as basis for Zimbabweans' national identity. A qualitative research approach was deployed in navigating the field of ethnic dances and national identity reformation so as to provide room for interpretive and descriptive methods to construe and describe how indigenous dances can be deployed to dissuade cultural atrophy (Kumar, 2011) and reconfigure or restore [national] identity. The qualitative method suited the nature of this research as it is most appropriate for studying human behaviour, opinions, themes, motivations and beliefs.

The study was carried out in south-eastern Zimbabwe. Zimbabwe has more than a dozen ethnic groups which practice various [traditional] dances such as *chinyambera, mbakumba, isitshikitsha, muchongoyo, jerusarema/mbende, mbakumba, dinhe*, and *mhande* among many others. However, employing an insider's perspective, the study elected *muchongoyo* dance as a referent and basis for understanding how the connection between indigenous ethnic dances and national identity reformation can be accomplished. *Muchongoyo* was chosen for the major reason that it is one of the most prominent traditional dance in south-eastern Zimbabwe, which is the research area chosen for this study.

Cultural dance experts, selected through purposive sampling, constituted targeted population of the study as they represented the subject of research interest (Goddard and Melville, 1996). Purposive sampling is a participant selection tool widely used in ethnographic studies (Tongco, 2007) where participants should be classified. Ten indigenous dance performers and ten cultural experts who are dance connoisseurs, administrators and advocates in dance education in Zimbabwe were considered for the research study. The chosen sample supplied crucial information to address the research, revealing an insider's perspective concerning the study. It also afforded the researchers an opportunity to get what Geertz (1983:6) and Nyamnjoh (2020: 2) have respectively called "thick descriptions" and "thick and thin descriptions" – thoroughly detailed information about the studied subject.

In terms of theoretical framework, this study is driven by Afrocentricity. The originator and chief propagator of Afrocentricity is Molefi Kete Asante. For Asante (1980), Afrocentricity is a way of life undergirded by a value system and a religious orientation, *Njia*. Asante's vision of Afrocentricity is broad to include every element of human orientation and culture such as art, music, perception, religion, science, history, philosophy, aesthetics, communication, interpersonal relationships, psychology, architecture, politics, geography, language, economics, and fashion (Ibid). It is a paradigm based on the idea that African people should re-assert a sense of agency in order to achieve sanity; a constructural adjustment to black disorientation, decenteredness, and lack of agency" (Asante, 2009: 1; see also, Asante, 1998). Similarly, Sibanda (2019) sees Afrocentricity as a response to Eurocentricity and the related cultural bias, racism and pejorative Western scholarship on Africa, Africans and their cultural heritage, both at home and abroad. This is to say that Afrocentricity calls for African phenomena, beliefs, activities, experiences, and way of life to be looked at and be accorded meaning from the standpoint and worldview of the African people themselves. Afrocentricity, thus, contends that in order to understand African realities, we should not use colonial and western perspectives; otherwise, the end result will be distortions, misinterpretations and misrepresentations. In view of this study, it is therefore important that as Zimbabweans seek to reconfigure, restore and foster [national] identity, the current dialectics of identity are interrogated and interpreted by Afrocentricity. This is in sync with Sibanda's (2019) argument that, Afrocentric theory seeks to promote the agency of African people in prioritising an African frame of reference and holistic lifestyle. The theory is applicable to the current study since African identity is placed at the backseat where people are made to think that associating with the fundamentals of African identity is old fashioned while associating oneself with Western identity is highly prestigious.

Identity and its multiple interpretations

Independence in Zimbabwe was achieved some four decades ago. However, the government is still fronting a gargantuan task of restoring African culture and identity repressed by Europeans during the colonial era. Turino (2000: 31) argues that colonialism created an acute identity crisis that nationalists in post-independent Zimbabwe have to meticulously grapple with. Identity 'crisis' is "the condition of being uncertain of oneself, with regards to character goals, origins, …as a result of disruptive, fast changing conditions" (Fearon 1999:7). For scholars like Ekwuru (1999), if not careful cultural crisis will ultimately result in what he calls "cultural atrophy" – death of a culture. Turino (2000) as with Ekwuru, further highlights that colonialism weakened the Zimbabwean cultural heritage through the introduction of films, television and Western education plunging the nation into cultural dislocation, confusion, and disorientation. As Hobsbawm and Ranger (1983) observed, the invented traditions of African societies distorted the past but became in themselves realities through which a good deal of the colonial encounter was expressed. All this is to say that as a result of colonialism [African] identity was corrupted, distorted and in some cases mangled.

The concept of "identity" is notoriously understood though definable. Peter Weinreich (1986: 14) describes a person's identity as "the totality of one's self-construal, in which one construes oneself in the present and aspires to be in the future". Resultantly, different types of identity such as national identity, ethnic identity and individual identity have been advanced by scholars. Bloom (1990: 52), for instance, looked at national identity as "…that condition in which a mass of people have made the same identification national symbols of the nation…" As a collective phenomenon, national identity can arise as a direct result of the presence of elements from the 'common points' in people's daily lives: national symbols, language, the nation's history, national consciousness, and cultural artefacts (Kelman, 1997). This is to say that national identity, for instance, is a sense of belonging to one state or to one nation as a cohesive whole represented by distinctive traditions, cultures, and languages. Joseph Trimble and Ryan Dickson (2005) delineate ethnic identity as a band or nation of people who share common customs, traditions, and historical experiences. On the other hand, personal identity is understood as self-categories which define the individual as a unique person in terms of their individual differences from other people (Turner, 1992).

Cultural atrophy in this research venture is considered as the wasting away, deterioration or collapse of cultural values, norms, practices, customs and identity due to factors such as globalisation, imperialism, neo-colonialism, acculturation among many other factors (Ekwuru, 1999). For Kariamu Welsh Asante (1996: 13), indigenous dance is the integrated art of movement that is governed by music and controlled by language. In emphasis, Nketia (1979) and Bebey (1975) articulate how "traditional" musicians render indispensable service to the community through directing and harmonising constituents of African communities.

Identity trepidations in contemporary societies: A perspicacious scrutiny

Given the high rate of rural-urban migration as well as geographical relocation of different ethnic groups, preservation, and retention of cultural and national identities remain a major area of study (Ngara, 2015). A research conducted by Smith (2018) in America focused on the Karen people, the largest non-Burman ethnic group in Burma. According to this research, due to violence in Burma, thousands fled into refugee camps and 73,000 Karen resettled in the United States of America. Resultantly, Karen youth in urban areas of the United States began participating in indigenous Karen dance, practicing and performing regularly. Based on such observations, Smith sought to explore the reasons why Karen youth choose to perform their traditional dances in America. Remarkably, results of this research revealed one overriding theme: "If You Don't Know Your Culture, You Don't Know Who You Are" demonstrating that the Karen youths were highly interested in maintaining their social identity with their Karen community and in Karen identity preservation. This study validates that those forced to migrate to a foreign country may face challenges to their sense of identity and belonging when immersed in a society that is unfamiliar to them (*ibid*).

Farleigh (2005) in a research entitled: *Learning to dance while becoming a dancer: Identity construction* as a performing art, presents a new theoretical concept of 'dancer identity'. He investigates the role performed by dancers themselves in distinguishing themselves from others in order to claim a 'dancer's identity' through presenting a self that is unique and unidentifiable. Farleigh's view is corroborated by Bourdieu who argues that "to exist within a social space, to occupy a point or to be an individual within a social space is to differ" (1998: 9). This argument accentuates the importance of distinguishing oneself within a societal setting. Wood (2011) in Brazil and the Caribbean sought to explore the interaction of hybridity and popular culture theories in the representation of national identity in Cuba, Brazil and Puerto Rico through the 20th century. Wood explored cultural products including performance and film literature, and established that hip hop elements of culture which include deejay, emcee, break, and graffiti draw out the intra-American dialogue and foreground the Africanist aesthetic, informing the formation of national identity in the Americas. This research is significant due to its exposure of the manifold routes by which identity and cultural markers travel (*ibid*).

In South Africa, Stinson (2009) explored issues surrounding national identity and nation-building in the post-Apartheid era. He argues that the need to uphold national identity as expressed through traditional practices (such as traditional/indigenous dance) is not only critical but very urgent. In the same quest, Schramm (2000) in a research on *The politics of Dance: Changing Representation of the Nation in Ghana* confirms that indigenous dances play an important role in the formation, recreating, reinventing of and preservation of identity. Schramm (2000) noted with concern that when cultural symbols are taken from a specific context and reincorporated into another context, they take new meanings and also facilitate the construction of new identities. In addition, her research launches a very critical debate by alluding that if indigenous dance performances are to survive and be meaningful in present day, they must be "kept alive not by repetition of the same old traditions… but by artistic imagination which clarifies their aesthetic values and renews their vitality" (Schramm, 2000: 347). As a point of departure from Schramm, our study do not only provide guidelines on how indigenous dance can be a framework for restoring national identity, but also advocates for the conservation of indigenous dance in their authentic form to maintain identity and uniqueness of a particular group of people.

Zinhuku (2013) addresses how community arts groups in Zimbabwe can socially construct and preserve their respective ethnic identities in the face of unprecedented cultural dilution as a result of globalisation. In the same vein, Nombembe (2013) reconnoitred how the Xhosas who migrated to Zimbabwe from South Africa, the Eastern Cape Province arranged music for *umguyo* ritual. Nombembe was curious to investigate whether there are connections and variances between *umguyo*, a boys' circumcision ceremony of the Xhosas in Zimbabwe. The research was determined to reveal how the Xhosas in Zimbabwe managed to retain their identities irrespective of being a small group in this country. From an emic perspective, Nombembe established that music indirectly reveals historical journeys that the Zimbabwean Xhosa people and their music undertook. There is one resemblance between Nombembe's and Zinhuku's research as they did not set out to examine how indigenous dances can be utilised as a framework for sustaining and restoring identities.

Researches on identity and indigenous dances have been executed around the globe focusing on different aspects such as the role of indigenous dances on identity issues and experiences (Zinhuku 2013; Nombembe 2013; Asante 2000 and Wanyama and Shitubi 2012). On the other hand, an academic vacuum is present as no adequate discussion has been tabled on how indigenous dances can be deployed to dissuade cultural atrophy as well as considering their performance as a genus for national identity reformation. Consequently, this study seeks to investigate how indigenous dances can be deployed as a genus for national identity reformation. Subsequently, this work is critical as it seeks to contribute to existing debates on national identity conservation and reformation.

Ethnic dances as national identity

National identity dilemmas throughout Africa are perpetrated by a number of amalgamated clusters of causes such as colonialism, multiculturalism, globalisation, and imperialism, among others (Turino 2000; Stinson 2009). However, Bloom's (1993) theory approaches identity and indigenous dance from an essentialist view thereby emphasising how important identity preservation is as a societal wellbeing of a society. For him, identity provides a sense of organisation in a world full of diverse and unique individuals and community development is also made possible as it produces organised communities through the formation of structures and forms. Consequently, a group identity such as national identity reinforces individual self-perceptions which provide a sense of belonging and it brings a sense of stability and security to individuals who eventually become strong, confident and self-reliant (ibid). In support of the theory of social identity, Tajfel and Turner (1979) affirms that identity is vital to every individual's life, as it is a social construction through which people acquire a sense of belonging.

Contrariwise, the acquisition and maintenance of identity has become vital and problematic (Stinson, 2009). However, many scholars concur that indigenous dances are capable of retaining and reforming national, ethnic and group identities (Johnson 2000; Schramm 2000 and Shauert 2006). Bloom (1990: 37) affirms that it is a natural urge for individuals to promote and defend their sense of identity through practising their ethnic musical, dance and cultural belief practices to support and preserve a sense of identity. We argue that through sustaining the distinctive Zimbabwean ethnic dance performances, national identity can be preserved and restored as ethnic identities form a critical part of national identity formation.

In support of the above sentiments, Merriam (1967) theorised that dance is culture and culture is dance. This statement implies that ethnic cultural dances can be a symbol and representative of a particular group's identity as they embody the culture of a people. In affirmation, we are compelled to theoretically imply that 'dance is identity and identity is dance'. Accordingly, indigenous dances and music performance representing various ethnic groups in any nation become a critical component in (re-)constructing, recreating, reinventing as well as preserving national identity (Schramm, 2000).

In sync with the above line of thinking, the late Steven Chifunyise in an interview with one of the authors of this chapter argued that identity in modern society can only be restored and promoted through practising customs, values, indigenous music and dances to sustain the heritage of any given ethnic group (Interview administered by Zinhuku with Chifunyise, 2013). He also stressed that by maintaining the songs, costumes and dance patterns, dance identifies with the ethnic group and its cultural heritage. For illustration, *muchongoyo* dance which forms the basis of this analysis reflects the identity of the Ndau people through a number of aspects, which are as follows: indigenous costume, songs, musical instruments, and dance pattern.

Muchongoyo indigenous costume

Costumes donned during an ethnic dance performance play a critical role in reflecting and maintaining the identity of a people. As an example, during *muchongoyo* dance, women wear decorated skirts round their waist called *chichakati* or *chikisa*. They also wear a wrapping cloth made from bright Zambia material around their upper torso. They decorate their head, arms, neckline and waist with beads (Sithole, 2013). These costumes are a crucial part of the performance as they assist in elaborating and emphasising their movements. The skirt follows each movement as they sway towards the music each and every small movement is emphasised and given volume.

On the other hand, male dancers wear beautiful skirts made from sheep's skin and vests (see also, Sithole, 2013). Around their arms and legs, they wear *machoba* leggings made from tails of white horses and a head gear made from bird's feathers. Asante (1985) confirms that unlike other traditional dances in Zimbabwe which include *jerusarema, dinhe, chinyambera, mbakumba,* and *muchongoyo* is not a spiritual dance hence the performers are dressed in colourful costumes and headgear. The indigenous costumes are a symbol of identity.

In support of indigenous costumes as a form and symbol of identity, a BBC World News documentary aired on 21 June 2020 displayed the power of indigenous dressing in depicting, showcasing and retaining identity. The documentary was entitled: The Power of Regalia and it featured Pita Taufatofu, a Tonga sportsman. Pita defied Olympic instructions and codes by electing to wear his indigenous costume during the official opening ceremony which attracted a lot of attention from the world. His decision inspired BBC to make a documentary about his decision and how it changed perceptions on indigenous costumes around the world. Furthermore, immediately after the Olympics he was invited to London by Prince Harry for a show and he now commands a huge following on social media in the process popularising and showcasing Tonga culture which had not been known all along (BBC World News, 2020).

Indigenous songs as identity

Songs reveal social, historical, religious, cultural, political and cultural identity of an ethnic group. The manner in which an ethnic group sings is totally unique to their group and one can identify them easily. As a basis for analysis, it is crucial to note that the Ndau people use a singing style that is referred to as *chigure* jumping rapidly from high to low notes. The songs also consist of vocables and characterised by a repetition of one major idea the singer is trying to put across. In addition, in an interview on 19 July 2013, Mukege argued that songs are composed according to the events and issues happening in the community; they mirror what is happening in the society (Interview administered by Zinhuku with Mukege, 2013). In another interview on I9 July (2013), Sithole states that through the songs one can learn of the events that occurred in past; as songs carry the history and identity of a community or nation (Interview administered by Zinhuku with Sithole, 2013). An example of a *muchongoyo* song is Chipinge:

Song Title: Chipinge (performed in *muemeso* section)
Performed by: Airpower Traditional Dance Troupe
Documented by: *Praise Zinhuku*
Date: *20 July 2013*
Place: *Chipinge*
Lead: *Ha yo we waichaye chidhindo mapaso ejoni*
Response: *Chipinge*
Lead: *Ha yo we waichaye chidhindo mapaso ejoni*
Response: *Chipinge Chipinge*

Song interpretation

This song divulges the activities identified with the Ndau ethnic members who had gone to work in South Africa, describing the kind of jobs they engaged in as well as their way of life. Moreover, the lyrics and title of the song also reflect the identity of Ndau people who are located in Chipinge District, Zimbabwe. Songs and dance in Ndau communities in particular draw on themes related to people's life as a repository of their histories, beliefs, values and identity. Resultantly, song and dance become very useful in teaching the younger generation, reflect on the social order and how the 'text' – song content and dance form – relate to the physical environment and man's encounter with a variety of creatures (Ogordoh, 2005). All this points to mean that indigenous dance, as culture in general, is a repository as well as a representation of culture for a particular group of people and therefore should be preserved.

In addition, when Ndau dancers are performing *muchongoyo*, they employ their language, and through their songs one can identify the cultural group from which they belong. In support of the above, the *Cultural Policy of Zimbabwe* (1997) notes that language is the key

447

characteristic of identity and through language people have the power to describe and express their cultural values and norms. As a result, songs become a form or at least a vehicle of identity for the Ndau ethnic group which forms a larger part of the national identity image.

Indigenous instruments and identity

Indigenous musical instruments perform a critical role in preserving ethnic identity of a people. In *muchongoyo* performances, two drums – a big and a small drum –accompany the dance. Sometimes, a third drum known as *gonyana* (friction drum) is sometimes used in *muchongoyo* performance (Interview with Sithole administered by Zinhuku, 2013). The big drum is called a *tangi* and in the Ndau culture, it represented the father while the small is known as *chingomana* (see Figure 1) and represents the mother. The third drum – *gonyana* – which is sometimes used represent the children. These two-sided drums are usually played by two people. There are only two aerophones incorporated in *muchongoyo* performance, the *ferengwana* (whistle) and the *hwamanda* (blowing horn) made from animal tasks especially the horn of an impala. The two idiophones incorporated in *muchongoyo* are the cow bell and *hosho* (shakers).

It is important to note that various ethnic groups in Africa attach great importance to indigenous instruments in dance performance. For example, instruments utilised in *muchongoyo* performance as described above are not for musical purposes only but they also display identity and set them apart from other ethnic groups in Africa (Lidskog, 2016). In agreement, Wolf (2018) asserts that musical instruments are not created for producing music only, but they also function as sacramental objects infused with spiritual connotations, that symbolises cultural identity and beliefs. This is in sync with Barton's (2003) earlier observation that instruments can variably construct both new identities and exhibit existing ones. For instance, traditional musical instruments found in Bapedi society foster, perpetuate and preserve Bapedi cultural identity.

Dance form and structure

Dance form is the invisible elements of a music or dance piece and the way those component parts are united. Therefore, the concept of analysing form in a musical piece facilitates mental capture of the work, provides understanding as well as insights on how to analyse the dance (Esaak, 2013). In an interview with Majeza (2013) which sought to describe form in *muchongoyo*, he clearly stated that *"muchongoyo izita rimwe asi mune zvakawanda zvinobudemo"* meaning *muchongoyo* is one word but the word refers to a number of sections that are found in *muchongoyo* dance.

Muchongoyo comprises of five parts namely, *mungeniso* (introduction), *chibhubhubhu* (development), *muemeso* (salute), *chizingiri* (climax) and finally *mubudiso* (exit). Preserving indigenous dance forms a critical part in maintaining the identity of an ethnic group (Smith, 2018). Moreover, Chen (2015) in a research on ethnic identity and aboriginal ethnic group, found that preserving the form of aboriginal indigenous dances is an important component of culture because it conserves and preserves identity. For instance, the Ndau people as cultural owners of *muchongoyo* dance feel that the whole structure of the dance holds a critical part of their history and identity. Crucial aspects of the dance form must be sustained to avoid distorting the dance form which facilitates the loss of vital pieces of history embodied in that section of the dance (Nketia, 1974).

The nexus between national identity restoration and ethnic dance performances

Indigenous dances embody cultural values, norms and ideals of a community and reflect these through performance (Sklar, 1991; Wulff, 2013). This implies that dances convey cultural knowledge intrinsic to the Zimbabwean identity and heritage, instilling a sense of pride and patriotism in every Zimbabwean's heart (Sanga 2011). From an analogous view, Sanga adds that musical practices have two functions: "to claim one's identity and to announce one's difference with other identities" (p. 189). Consequently, in this chapter we argue that since national identity encompass ethnic identity, ethnic dances that symbolise all the ethnic groups found in Zimbabwe, can be collectively deployed as a basis for national identity restoration through the implementation of varied approaches.

The first approach for identity restoration advanced in this research involves encouraging each and every ethnic group to continuously practice their indigenous music and dance practices to sustain and preserve a sense of shared national identity. In support of the above sentiments, West and Fenstermaker (1995) assert that identity is an on-going interactive accomplishment. This declaration implies that identity cannot be simply put on and then taken for granted by those who claim it. They must continuously display particular qualities which will maintain the validity of that claim. For those who claim a particular identity, it is important to establish a collective form or a sense of group consciousness to show that they are indeed unique and then continually negotiate and reaffirm those boundaries to maintain unique status (Taylor and Whitter, 1992).

Incessant practice of respective indigenous dances by various ethnic groups will contribute to the maintenance, restoration and preservation of national identity. Conspicuously, UNESCO has since declared *jerusarema* dance (also known as *mbende*) as a world heritage and the late Stephen Chifunyise was in the process of petitioning *muchongoyo* dance to be recognised as a world heritage musical practice (Mapira, 2018). This emphasises how imperative indigenous dances are perceived and recognised as basis for preservation of national identity and culture. Thus, the restoration of national identity becomes unfruitful if indigenous dance practitioners fail to perform and execute authentic performances of indigenous dances that give correct representation of ethnic groups.

Retaining authentic instruments, costumes, songs, dance form and structure of all indigenous dances of the different ethnic groups in Zimbabwe, is another strategy for national identity restoration. As observed by Nketia (1982: 6), the challenge however is that "tradition (indigenous dance included) faces the question of authenticity, in particular how one can respond to creative inclinations and remain at the same time true to the norms of the society by maintaining margins of expectations that musical performance generate". No wonder why Agawu (2003: 207) warns that if drumming, dancing, and singing are removed from their original performance contexts (de-contextualised), reduced to musical forms divested of cultural meaning, they lose value in traditional society. Georgiana Gore (1986: 55) weighs in when she argues that:

> Dances are often transposed from one context to another and in the process become secularised. With decontextualisation comes a transformation or even loss of meaning, since such meaning does not reside in the dance movements' alone or accompanying songs and music but rather in the interaction of all elements of performance including the audience's expectations and responses.

She goes on to say that as long as the dance is being performed in the context of a stage, there are changes in both time and certain realities regarding the dance. In other words, performance of traditional dances outside their performance contexts cause dances to transform.

As another strategy to maintain national identity, we propose that regular indigenous dance workshops be carried out to sensitise communities on the importance of indigenous dance performance in preserving identity and the wellbeing of the nation. Workshops intended for indigenous dance practitioners are essential programmes which can be utilised as a strategy to combat challenges affecting the performance of indigenous dances as a form of identity. They will help create a thorough educational experience in a short amount of time, are an appropriate way to impart hands-on skills and provide a way for individuals to pass on ideas and methods to colleagues (Orngreen and Levinsen, 2017). Similarly, Mainwaring, Krasnow and Donna (2010), recommended that workshops enhance the mastery of skills and promote self-esteem, self-efficacy, and positive self-image.

Their research also proposes the need for availing of funds by the government and arts organisations to fund dance performance, research and documentation. Lastly, the research proposes the need to institute 'community policing' by all ethnic groups in Zimbabwe so as to safeguard their indigenous dances performances from uncensored proliferation and distortion to preserve cultural values and identity. Community policing of indigenous dances will involve the designation of cultural dance experts to monitor the execution of indigenous dance performance by community arts groups. This move will assist in making sure that indigenous dances are executed in the correct manner without too much alteration and falsification.

Conclusion

The legacy of colonialism, westernisation and globalisation in general has posed serious challenge to national identity restoration, reconstruction and promotion in postcolonial Zimbabwe. Yet, indigenous dances are important in contemporary society as they embody and transmit the culture of a particular society and preserve individual, group and national identities. Indigenous dances can be deployed as a genus for national identity formation. Using an ethnographic approach, this chapter has fantasised and envisaged Zimbabwean traditional dance as a strategy for national identity reconfiguration. *Muchongoyo* dance, which is one of the Zimbabwean traditional dances, has been adopted as a case study, with a view that it is cast as an analogue and basis for appreciating indigenous culture and identity. Accordingly, we have argued that national identity can be restored through continuous performance of indigenous dances and preserving authentic and original dance patterns, costumes, songs and instruments. We thus conclude that the deployment of *muchongoyo* dance as a basis for identity is a concrete effort to provide a robust framework for reconfiguration, restoration and promotion of national identity.

References

Asante, M. K. (1980). *Afrocentricity: The theory of social change*, Amulefi: Buffalo, NY.

Asante, K. W. (2000). *Zimbabwe Dance, Rhythmic Forces, Ancestral Voices: An Aesthetic Analysis*, Africa World Press: New Jersey.

Asante, K. M. (2009). *Afrocentricity*, South African City Press Column.

Baseline Study on the Cultural sector of Zimbabwe (2009). "Culture Fund Investing in Ideas", *Culture Fund Research Programme*, Sida.

Barz, G. (1997a). "Confronting the Field in and out of the Field: Music, Texts and Experiences in Dialogue", Chapter 3 in Barz and Cooley Eds. *Shadows in the field. New perspectives for fieldwork in ethnomusicology* (Second ed., pp. 3–24). New York: Oxford University Press, pp.45-62.

Barz, G and Cooley, T. J. (Eds). (1997b). *Shadows in the Field: New Perspectives*, Oxford University Press, New York.

BBC World News, (2020). "The power of Regalia", BBC World News Documentary broadcasted on 21/06/20.www.bbc.com.

Bloom, W. (1993). *Personal Identity, National, and International Relations*, Cambridge: Cambridge University Press.

Bloom, W. (1990). Personal, Identity, National Identity and International Relations. Cambridge University Press: Cambridge.

Farleigh, C. (2005). Dancing identity: Metaphysics in motion, *Dance Research* 37 (2): 94-97.

Duri, F. & Gwekwerere, G. (2007). Linking African Traditional Dance among the Ndau of Southeastern Zimbabwe. *Occasional Paper 18*, CASAS.

Ebron, P. (2002). *Performing Africa*, Princeton University Press: New Jersey.

Ekwuru, G. (1999). *The pangs of an African culture in travail*, Owerri: Totan Publishers Ltd.

Esaak, S. (2013). "What is the Definition of Form? [Online]. Available from arthistory.about.com/cs/glossaries/g/f_form.htm. [Accessed on 20 October 2013].

Fearon, J. (1999). "What is Identity (as we now use the word)," Stanford University: Stanford.

Geertz, C. (1983). 'From the native's point of view': On the nature of anthropological understanding, in: *This Local knowledge: Further Essays in Interpretive Anthropology*, New York, 3-16.

Godambe, V. P. (1982). Estimation in survey sampling: robustness and optimality, *Journal of the American Statistical Association*, 77: 393-40.

Gore, G. (1986). "Dance in Nigeria: The Case for a National Company," *The Journal of the Society of Dance Research* 4 (2): 54-64.

Holzhausen, B. (2005). "Traditional Dance in Transformation: Opportunities for Development in Mozambique," *Masters Dissertation*, University of Leeds.

Kelman, H. (1997). *Nationalism, Patriotism and National Identity: Social-Psychological Dimensions*. Chicago: Nelson-Hall Publishers. pp. 171–173.

Kumar, R. (2011). *Research Methodology: A Step by Step Guide for Beginners,* (3rded.), SAGE Publication Ltd, London.

Mapira, N., & Hood, M. M. (2018). Performing Authenticity and Contesting Heritage: The UNESCO-Inscribed Jerusarema/Mbende Dance Of Zimbabwe, *Journal of Asia Pacific Arts* 1 (1): 1-11. https://doi.org/10.31091/lekesan.v1i1.340.

McNamara, C. (1999). *General Guidelines for Conducting Interviews*. Minnesota University: Minnesota.

Nketia, J. H. (1974). *The Music of Africa,* W. W. Norton Company: New York.

Nyamnjoh, F. (2020). "A Post-Covid-19 Fantasy on Incompleteness and Conviviality." In "Post-Covid Fantasies," Catherine Besteman, Heath Cabot, and Barak Kalir, editors, American Ethnological Society website, 27 July 2020, [https://americanethnologist.org/features/pandemic-diaries/post-covid-fantasies/a-post-covid-19-fantasy-on-incompleteness-and-conviviality].

Perman, T. (2010). Dancing in Opposition: Muchongoyo, Emotion and the Politics of Performance in South-eastern Zimbabwe, *Ethnomusicology* 54 (3): 425-451.

Ranger, T. (1983). "The Invention of Tradition in Colonial Africa," In: *The Invention of Tradition,* edited by Eric Hobsbawm and Terence Ranger, 211–262. Cambridge University Press: Cambridge.

Schappi, D. (2005). "Cultural Plurality, National Identity and Consensus in Bhutan", Centre for Comparative and International Studies 5:1-53.

Schramm, K. (2000). The politics of Dance: Changing Representation of the Nation in Ghana, *Africa Spectrum* 35 (3): 339-358.

Shauert, P. (2006-2007). "A Performing National Archive: Power and Preservation in the Ghana Ensemble," *Transactions of the Historical Society of Ghana New Series,* 10:171-181.

Sibanda, F. (2019). "Promoting Human Flourishing through Rastafari Foodways in Africa," In: Christian Green, M. (Ed). *Law, Religion and Human Flourishing in Africa, Africa Sun Media,* Stellenbosch: South Africa.

Sklar, D. (1991). *Five Premises for a Culturally Sensitive Approach to Dance.* New York.

Somerville, P. (2009). Understanding community policing. Policing, *An International Journal of Police Strategies and Management.* 32. 10.1108/1363.

Stone, R. (2008). *A Theory for Ethnomusicology,* New Jersey: Prentice Hall.

Stinson, A. T. (2009). National Identity and Nation-Building in Post- Apartheid South Africa, *Masters Dissertation,* Rhodes University.

The Cultural Policy of Zimbabwe. (2007). [Online]. Available from: http://www.artsinafrica.com/uploads/2011/06/cultural_policy _of_Zimbawe_2007.pdf.[Accesed on 11 July 2020].

Trimble, E. J. & Dickson, R. (2005). "Ethnic Identity", In: *Applied Developmental Science: An Encyclopedia for Research, Politics and Programmes,* Thousand Oaks: Sage.

Tongco D. C. (2007). Purposive Sampling as a Tool for Informant Selection, *Ethnobotany Research & Applications,* 5:147-158.

Turino, T. (2000). *Nationalists, Cosmopolitans, Popular Music in Zimbabwe,* University of Chicago Press: Chicago.

454

Lightning Source UK Ltd.
Milton Keynes UK
UKHW020636180222
398890UK00009B/637